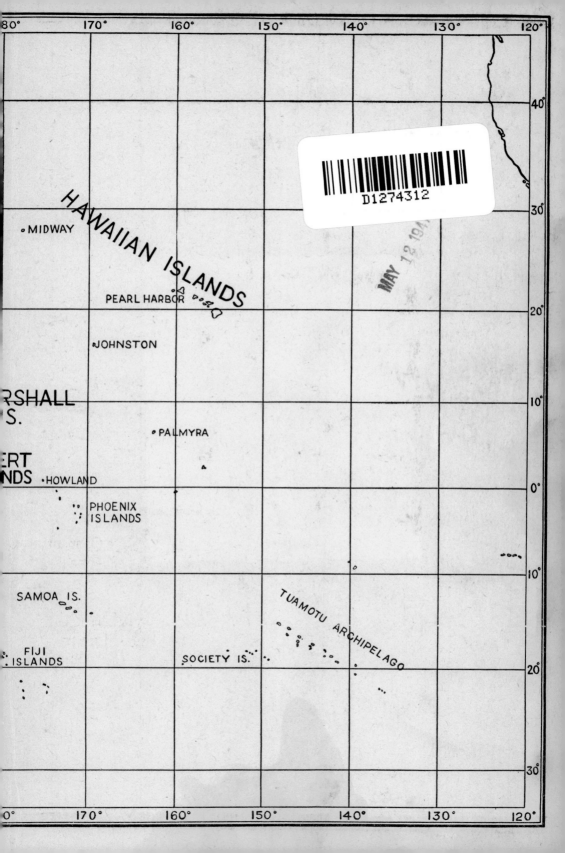

Semper Fidelis

Semper Fidelis

The U. S. Marines in the
Pacific—1942-1945

by

THE MARINE CORPS COMBAT CORRESPONDENTS

edited and arranged by

CAPTAIN PATRICK O'SHEEL, USMCR

and

STAFF SERGEANT GENE COOK, USMCR

WILLIAM SLOANE ASSOCIATES, INC.

Publishers   -   -   -   -   -   -   New York

55669
359
U58

TO THE MARINE DEAD

Introduction

All of the stories in this book were written during the war by Marines who took part in the actual business of beachhead and front line fighting. All of them are true. But they are not merely a collection of combat stories, or tales of heroism designed to enhance the store of Marine legends.

As time passes, the nature of the war in the Pacific is likely to be more difficult to recall than the most incredible experiences in other war theatres. This is so because there was, from beginning to end, less that was familiar or even recognizable to Americans in the jungle and coral islands of the Pacific than anywhere else we fought—to say nothing of the fantastic tricks and tactics of a fanatical enemy.

With this in mind, and drawing from hundreds of stories which originated in countless islands on the way to Japan, we have tried to make a book that reflects the human side of the entire Pacific experience as it will be remembered when the communiques, newspaper stories, and technical accounts are forgotten. In one sense the book aims to fulfill, for the men who served there, the role of guide book to their own memories. The variety of its contents will, it is hoped, give a more rounded record of "how it was in the Pacific" than is available anywhere else at this time.

Thus the combat stories are more than good tales which stand up to our growing perspective on the war; they are selected and arranged to cover the principal types of fighting and areas and campaigns in the movement across the ocean. Particular attention was given to selecting stories which show the variety of types of individual fighters. There are stories of the enemy's strange behaviour and of our own troops in the role of conqueror. The islands and their peoples are described—from the Solomons through the Bismarcks, Gilberts, Marshalls, Samoan group, Marianas, Philippines and Ryukus. Finally there is a section on the special brand of civilization that grew up on the islands after our troops' arrival.

The majority of the work in this book is that of Marine Corps Combat Correspondents. This innovation in U.S. war coverage began when, in the Spring of 1942, Brigadier General Robert L. Denig sent two Marines who had been newsmen to join a combat unit in the Pacific. By war's end, nearly one hundred and seventy-five combat correspondents and a lesser number of public relations officers had been assigned directly to regiments and air wings to live with them in and out of battle. Commanding officers were often cool if not outright hostile to these correspondents, but in spite of censorship and the restrictions imposed by rank—they were enlisted men—their stories trickled back by mail to Marine Corps Headquarters, and editors everywhere published them with no apologies for delays en route. These fighting writers produced principally newspaper accounts—the kind that are in family scrapbooks today. Many of them (not all are represented in this book) won combat decorations, they suffered many casualties, and seven were killed in action. A sizable group became officers.

Unlike civilian war correspondents, the Marine writers were seldom in a position to make immediate headlines—or to patronize officers' clubs. But they enjoyed a compensating advantage because they lived in daily and intimate acquaintance with the men about whom they wrote, whether their regiment was making news on a battered beachhead or resting at some isolated staging base.

In addition there are a few stories by men who went to war with no intention of writing, but were inspired to tell something of their tremendous experience. Also there are noteworthy examples of stories hitherto unpublished for reasons of censorship or the extreme delays on the way to editorial offices 10,000 miles from the islands where they were written.

There is, finally, a small section of this book which is the product of Marine Combat artists and photographers. The conditions under which they worked and fought did not permit a studied approach to the subject. But like everything else in this book, their work was done on the scene, and helps portray the heroism and the hell, the bravado and the boredom, of the war in the Pacific.

P. O'S.

Contents

THE FLYERS' WAR

CASUALTY LIST

THE MEN

THE WORDS THEY SPOKE

THE NATURE OF THE ENEMY

THE ROLE OF THE CONQUEROR

THE ISLANDS AND THEIR PEOPLE

AT HOME ABROAD

Picture Section

1. by Corporal Paul Ellsworth
2. by Sergeant Donald A. Peters
3. by Lieutenant Colonel Donald Dickson
4. by Staff Sergeant John McDermott
5. by Master Technical Sergeant Elmer Wexler
6. by Lieutenant Colonel Donald Dickson
7. by Master Technical Sergeant Elmer Wexler
8. by Lieutenant Colonel Donald Dickson
9. by Private First Class H. Jackson
10. by Staff Sergeant John McDermott
11. by Lieutenant Colonel Donald Dickson
12. by Sergeant William J. Draut
13. by Master Technical Sergeant Elmer Wexler
14. by Master Technical Sergeant Victor Donahue
15. by Sergeant Sherman C. Loudermilk
16. by Sergeant Sherman C. Loudermilk
17. by Lieutenant Colonel Donald Dickson

All photographs by Marine Corps Combat Correspondents

Acknowledgments

"After The Battle" by First Lieutenant Jim G. Lucas first appeared in the *American* Magazine, as did "These Nips Are Nuts" by Technical Sergeant Herman Kogan. "The Battle of the Rocks" by Technical Sergeant Gerald D. Gordon and Technical Sergeant Robert W. Harvey, appeared in *The American Mercury,* November, 1945. "Green Troops On A Blue Beach" by Master Technical Sergeant David Dempsey is reprinted from *The Antioch Review.* The poems, "Song For a Pilot" and "Death" by Captain Richard G. Hubler are from the *Atlantic Monthly* of October, 1944, as is "Letter Home" by Captain Cord Meyer, Jr. "How It Was On Iwo" by Sergeant Francis W. Cockrel, "Above Rabaul" by Second Lieutenant Harold H. Martin, and "Line Company Men" by Master Technical Sergeant Gilbert Bailey, were first published in *Bluebook.*

The following articles appeared in *Collier's*: "Suicide Creek" by Technical Sergeant Asa C. Bordages on May 26, 1945, "Iwo: The Red-Hot Rock" by Master Technical Sergeant Alvin M. Josephy, Jr., Second Lieutenant Cyril P. Zurlinden, Jr., Master Technical Sergeant David Dempsey, Technical Sergeant Dan Levin, and Staff Sergeant Tony Smith, on April 14, 1945, "Close Support Bombing" and "Pangilan's Gift" by First Lieutenant Harold H. Martin, and "Bedside Manner" by Captain Milton Sperling. "The Big Hairy Dogfight" by First Lieutenant Harold H. Martin, is printed by the courtesy of The Ziff-Davis Publishing Company.

The poem "Bloody Ridge" by Major Raymond Henri was published in *Harper's Magazine* as was "Moving The People" by First Lieutenant

Harold H. Martin. "Mobile Hospital" by Technical Sergeant George McMillan is reprinted from *Hygeia,* March, 1945, where it appeared under the title, "All Hands Ready To Save Lives." "Some Japs Surrendered" by Master Technical Sergeant Alvin M. Josephy, Jr., appeared in the August, 1945, issue of *The Infantry Journal.*

"Life On a Bull's-eye" by Captain Patrick O'Sheel, "The Marine" by Staff Sergeant John F. Slocum, and "Mussau Boys" by Technical Sergeant George H. Mattie, are reprinted from the Marine magazine, *Leatherneck.* "They Lived Through Hell" by Master Technical Sergeant Alvin M. Josephy, Jr., "The Gentle Marine" by Technical Sergeant Dan Levin, and "Hizzoner The Mayor of Okinawa" by Technical Sergeant Herman Kogan, appeared in *Liberty* Magazine.

"Master Gunnery Sergeant" by Master Technical Sergeant Alvin M. Josephy, Jr., was printed by *Look,* on December 6, 1945, under the title "My Favorite War Story." "Medicine Hits the Beach" by Master Technical Sergeant Alvin M. Josephy, Jr., is reprinted from *Medical Economics* by special permission, copyright, Medical Economics, Inc., Rutherford, New Jersey.

"The Marine Who Wouldn't Give Up" by Captain Seymour Arnold Gross is reprinted from *Reader's Digest* of January, 1945. "The Battle of Bloody Hill" by Lieutenant Colonel William J. McKennan, the two poems, "Foxholes," and "Everybody Thinks" by Major Raymond Henri, "Epitaph for a Young Marine" by Captain John H. Magruder, "Strange Battle" by Technical Sergeant Dan Levin, and "The Little Chief" by Major Robert Simpson, were all originally printed in *The Saturday Evening Post.*

"Iwo Transport" by Master Technical Sergeant Alvin M. Josephy, Jr., is reprinted from *Sea Power* in which it appeared under the title, "Transport to Iwo." "That Old White Magic" by Master Technical Sergeant David Dempsey (copyright, 1945, by the United Newspapers Magazine Corporation), and "Meeting in Melbourne" by Technical Sergeant Asa C. Bordages (copyright, 1944, by the United Newspapers Magazine Corporation) were first published by *This Week.*

"Peleliu Spa" by Staff Sergeant Walter F. Conway, is reprinted from the *U.S. Navy Magazine,* in which it appeared as "Canteens Empty."

"Midway's Birds" by First Lieutenant Milburn McCarty, and "The Shrine of Tarawa" by Captain Ellis M. Trefethen, which was originally entitled "Tarawa Today," are reprinted through the courtesy of the *New York Times.* "Who Do They Think We Are?" by Technical Sergeant George H. Mattie, is reprinted with the permission of *The New Yorker* (copyright, 1944, The F-R Publishing Corporation), as is "Delegate At Large" by Captain Patrick O'Sheel (copyright, 1945, The F-R Publishing Corporation). And "No Grass Shacks in Kealakaku" by Master Technical Sergeant David Dempsey is also reprinted by special permission of *The New Yorker;* its original title was "Girls Dancing, Trees Resting."

"Guadalcanal" by Captain Herbert L. Merillat is an excerpt from his book, THE ISLAND, published by Houghton-Mifflin Co., and "The Landing" by Private Allen R. Matthews is from a forthcoming book of his to be published by Simon & Schuster.

Semper Fidelis

In Battle

Corregidor Falls

Several hours after our first news of the fall of Bataan, a few survivors came crawling out of the oily water onto the beaches of Corregidor. Some came across the North Channel in small boats which they had somehow managed to find. Others were swimming or clinging desperately to improvised rafts. All were thin, haggard, and unshaven—too exhausted to speak. Three of these poor fellows were found lying half drowned on the rocks near my gun position. Their tiny raft had been swept clear around the end of the island to the side opposite Bataan by the treacherous currents in the channel. We picked them up, carried them up to our kitchen and gave them coffee and food. Then our Navy pharmacist's mate took them in charge for medical attention. They were soon revived enough to talk, but still they were hesitant. A dreadful haunted look was in their darkly circled eyes. One of them whispered, "It's awful to be licked."

As soon as these three survivors were taken care of, I took my field glasses and walked a half mile up to the west end of the island where I could get an unobstructed view across the channel to Bataan. Mariveles was almost hidden in smoke—blazing like an inferno. Occasionally billowing dust and rubble flew high into the air as the flames reached new dumps of ammunition.

Trucks were moving on the road outside Mariveles—Japanese trucks. Our guns opened fire and landed several shells near the tiny moving objects, which scurried like rats for safety. And then the planes were over my head, and I dived for one of the many foxholes dug at intervals near by. There were nine medium bombers overhead, beautiful silver birds droning their way through the angry black puffs of our ack-ack. Then came the mighty "whoosh" of the falling bombs. They landed on top of the cliffs high overhead and sent showers of stones raining down.

The men were nervous and uneasy. One of my sergeants asked me, "Sir, do you think they'll surrender us too?"

"I don't think so," I said.

"We don't wanta quit," he continued. "We'd rather fight it out."

"I guess we all had rather fight it out," I said. "I know I never want to be a Jap prisoner myself."

Before nightfall our fears of being surrendered were allayed when a runner came from battalion headquarters with a copy of General Wainwright's message. That message told us what we wanted to hear: "Corregidor can and will be held." We all took cheer. "Skinny" Wainwright was the apple of our eye that day—and all the time.

But at that very time thirty miles across the bay in Manila a Japanese general was sending messages too—a greasy, well-fed general this, Homma by name, with terrific concentrations of military might at his fingertips to throw against us. And this general's message of the day declared that Corregidor should be taken at any cost. The bloody siege was on.

With remarkable speed, the Japanese rushed hundreds of guns and thousands of men into the Bataan peninsula in preparation for the final assault on Corregidor. In less time than it takes to tell, a hail of shells was raining down on us from guns cleverly concealed behind the hills near Mariveles. The Japs emplaced their guns in the area of our captured field hospitals in Bataan, in the midst of our sick and wounded men whom they had refused to evacuate. They continued to hold groups of our captured men on the roads, near Jap batteries and troop concentrations, so that the guns of Corregidor were helpless. We couldn't fire without killing our own people.

Throughout the month of April, 1942, the terrific bombardment from Bataan continued. Even the appearance of the ground itself was beginning to change. Wooded ravines became stark bare gashes in the ground, every tree splintered and destroyed—not a living thing left. The color of Corregidor changed from green to brown and black, as if seared with flame.

One by one our fixed coast artillery batteries were searched out and destroyed until there was only a handful of guns left. Japanese bombers roared continuously overhead, raining more destruction, and we had no planes to challenge them. We had forgotten what American planes looked like.

The Marines struggled frantically all over the island to keep machine guns and barbed wire emplaced on the beaches, for it seemed sure that a landing was coming. Many of the guns would be destroyed as fast as they could be put in place, particularly in the 1st Battalion area on Monkey Point, at the opposite end of the island from my defense sector.

The water mains were broken by the bombardment, and it was impossible to get water to our troops scattered over the island. Food was getting low. We had been on half rations for months and we were weak, tired, and hungry. We held on in desperation but we knew the end of the story was not far away.

On the night of May 5, I was sitting behind the sandbags in my command post. The guns were loaded and ready; and boxes of yellow hand grenades were opened, conveniently ready for use. The men were extremely nervous, for the bombardment had been particularly heavy during the day. We had been huddled behind the sandbags all day long, cringing, as the shells burst near by, sending showers of stones and hot steel flying over our heads. One man had been seriously hit, and it had been a great risk for the two Navy hospital corpsmen who had come through the shellfire to pick him up in a stretcher. The man died before he reached a doctor's care.

At this particular time a terrific bombardment was falling on Monkey Point, Cavalry Point, and Infantry Point, all situated on the island's narrow tail. We could see myriads of flashes cutting the blackness, and the shells burst, sending great geysers of earth and rubble into the air. Warning orders had already come over the telephone that a landing attack was imminent. Conditions were perfect for a landing in accordance with Japanese doctrine, which calls for night landing assaults. The Japanese could land in the darkness and push their attack by the light of the moon. Most of our searchlights had been knocked out long ago and we had no starshells to illuminate their approaching barges, nor very little else in the way of equipment. It had been that way all through the war.

I sat there watching the telephone, waiting, like a cat watching a mousehole. The men were silent, all straining their eyes into the night, watching the black water and listening.

The telephone rang at last. I jerked the receiver from the hook.

"Enemy marine engines heard approaching Corregidor." That was all.

I crawled out of the gun pit up to the road and walked along, visiting all the gunners, encouraging them and giving final instructions. The men were not nervous now, but grim and determined.

"There will be no withdrawal from your position," I ordered each gun crew. "You will fight your gun where it is."

The Japanese artillery barrage soon shifted from Monkey Point to the central portion of the island. It was obvious that the initial landing would strike the Monkey Point area. I did not expect more than a diversion attack or a feint at our local position.

"Looks like the First Battalion is going to get it out on the point," remarked Corporal Marquez, the squad leader in the gun position.

The 1st Battalion Marines on Monkey Point had been hit hard by artillery. There was little or no protection out on the point from the bursting shells, and many of the guns were already knocked out and the barbed wire flattened.

"Look, look! See the tracers!" shouted Corporal Hagwood suddenly.

The air was full of them over Monkey Point. The landing was being effected.

By this time our communication lines had been cut by the shells, which now were being shifted from the center of the island to our sector. We burrowed down behind the sandbags, wondering how things were going out on Monkey Point and waiting for our turn.

All through the night we watched the battle rage. All we could see were the flashes of the shell bursts and the red streaks of the tracer bullets. Still no barges came our way. Morning brought fresh waves of bombers overhead, and the artillery continued to pound away. We had partially repaired our telephone lines so that I could talk to Major Bradley, our subsector commander. At 11:40 he called.

"I just received orders from battalion headquarters by radio," he said. "Execute Pontiac."

"Aye, aye, sir," I answered.

The code phrase meant, "Destroy your guns and surrender." It was a terrible shock. My expression must have revealed how dazed I was.

Corporal Hagwood, who was standing beside me, asked with great concern, "What's the matter, sir?"

"We just got the order to destroy our guns and surrender," I replied.

I shall never forget the forlorn look on his face, and on the faces of all the men as they learned the news.

Then the telephone rang again. It was Major Bradley, who added more instructions. "Do not destroy any weapons after twelve o'clock noon. Display white flags in plainly visible places promptly at twelve o'clock. That is the time of official surrender."

Feverishly we bent rifle barrels, dismantled machine guns, and threw the pieces into the sea. We crushed field glasses and rolled ammunition boxes over the cliffs into the surf below. We found an old white sheet and tied it up in a tree where it could easily be seen. White flags were appearing on Fort Hughes, Fort Frank, and Fort Drum at the same time.

Some of the men were silently crying. Two Filipino aviation cadets who had been assigned to my machine guns lay beside their broken, twisted gun and sobbed aloud.

"Sir, we have lost our country," one said.

The white flags were up everywhere now. Corregidor had fallen.

But the shells were still showering on the island and the planes were still dropping their bombs. The Japanese were paying no attention to our white flags! Night fell, and the hours of the night were full of horrible suspense. We expected the Japs to close in on us at any minute and wipe us out. All night long they kept up their artillery fire against us until, in the morning, the guns at last were silent. It was May 7. The Japanese planes came zooming low over our positions. We could plainly see the flaming red suns on the wings of the planes, and even the faces of the pilots. They had never dared approach so close before, but now they were proudly vaunting their strength before our weary eyes.

Assembling my Marines, I tried to give them a little encouragement. "We've all done our best," I said. "We've held out longer than anybody ever expected, and what we've done here has probably saved Australia and shortened the war by months or maybe even years. You can hold your heads high when we turn in to the Japs."

A few minutes later we saw Jap soldiers standing high on the edge of the cliff above our heads. They did not come down after us, for the cliff was too steep to descend; but they stayed there watching, fingering their rifles and automatic guns.

We moved the men down the road toward "Bottomside," which was the name applied to the middle area of the island, where the tunnels housing the hospital, the quartermaster supplies, and the general staff were located. We thought that this would probably be the collecting point for prisoners.

A few hundred yards brought us face to face with more Japanese soldiers on the road. They were grim and silent, their torn khaki clothing caked with dirt and grime. They mingled among us, taking away our watches, rings, money, and any other valuables they could lay hands on.

At Bottomside we found thousands of prisoners already collected. The Jap soldiers were mingling with them, still looting. We had a good look at these odd creatures we had hoped to kill. They were not very impressive or terrifying, short and bowlegged in their ill-fitting, baggy breeches, with dirty, ill-wrapped leggings. However, I was impressed by the quick and absolute obedience they were giving to their noncommissioned officer. These were the crack troops who had taken Singapore.

"Ugly little devils, aren't they, lieutenant?" remarked Gunnery

Sergeant William Grant, who had been with us in China before the war.

We were to find out all too soon that their real ugliness was not in their appearance at all, but in their souls.

Finding friends from general headquarters, I asked for full details about the fighting before the surrender. I learned that wave after wave of Japanese had been annihilated, but finally by sheer weight of numbers they had forced a landing and driven toward Bottomside and Malinta Hill, which contained the system of tunnels. The combined Navy and Marine battalion which was in reserve had been committed to the fight, and finally the Japs had been stopped short of Malinta Hill. The situation was actually under control and the Japs had lost very heavily; but General Wainwright, knowing that further landings would be made during the coming night and that we were almost at the end of our food and water supply, decided further bloodshed was useless. Corregidor had held out far longer than anyone, especially the Japanese, had expected.

We slept on the ground at Bottomside that night; next morning they herded us like cattle out toward Monkey Point. Along the road we were sickened at the sight of unburied American bodies strewn everywhere over the blackened, shell-torn ground. The Japs had already cleared away their own dead. Fierce hand-to-hand fighting had gone on here. The bodies were already black and bloated, covered with flies. They were nearly all Marines, for the Marines had borne the brunt of the attack, supported by a naval battalion. I saw one of my good friends lying there by the side of the road. The Japanese would not allow us to bury our dead.

Our destination was a strip of sandy beach where more and more men were crowded into a little barbed-wire enclosure until finally by late afternoon it contained all the captured survivors of Corregidor. The enclosure actually was not more than two hundred yards long and half as wide, yet it was made to absorb seven thousand Americans and five thousand Filipinos.

Everyone suffered severely. The sun was intensely hot and there on the sand there was no shelter. We endured three days without food or water. There was hardly room enough to lie down at night. There were no sanitary arrangements inside the enclosure; and, since the Japs would not allow us to go outside the barbed wire, the ground was covered with human filth. Men were lying in their own excrement, the odor of which was becoming unbearable. It was augmented by the odor of unburied American bodies festering near by; it was days later when the Japs finally allowed us to bury them.

We began to think that the Japanese were going to leave us here indefinitely, until we all were dead. They showed absolutely no concern for our suffering. I had managed to get an occasional mouthful of food from others who, with great forethought, had stuffed their pockets with canned type C ration. One Marine officer drained the radiator of a wrecked truck and shared the dirty water with me and some of the others.

Finally, during the fourth morning, the Japs laid a pipe down from the nearest water supply and fitted it with a single spigot. One spigot for twelve thousand men! We spent the rest of the day standing in line in the blistering sun trying to get a drink. Many were falling unconscious from hunger, thirst, and heat exhaustion. The Japs permitted us to drag the unconscious ones down to the surf to revive them. Some never revived.

The same day they allowed foraging parties to go out in search of food among the stores left on the island. Even so, we were still continuously hungry, for the foraging parties were too weak to carry in enough food on their backs to supply so many men. The Japs made no effort to bring us food in trucks. They did not care to waste their precious, newly captured gasoline for such a purpose.

The Japs sent out weak, staggering parties of Americans to bury the Japanese dead. It was in this way that we were able to estimate the losses they had sustained in storming Corregidor. They must have lost from three to five thousand men killed, counting those who drowned when their barges were sunk by shell fire and never reached the beaches.

Sometimes the Japs would cut off the right arms of their dead, bury these, and burn the bodies. Our burying parties rejoiced at this because it was less work. They even forced our boys to dive into the surf to recover some of the festering Jap bodies from the water.

We had arrived by these few days at the full realization of how much we actually did hate the Japs. They were doing everything in their power to humiliate us and grind us in the dirt. They never missed an opportunity to kick us, slap us, beat us with their rifle butts, or jab us with bayonets. They reduced us to living conditions not fit for animals, in an effort to overcome their own secret sense of their own inferiority and to make us bow down to them as the "superior race." They failed.

We used our shelter halves, blankets, and anything else we could find, to build crude shelters to protect us from the broiling sun. It was stifling hot and all of us were burned red.

On our last night of the terrible three weeks we spent in that pig-pen, the cold rain poured down on us. The rainy season had at last set in.

Fires were being kindled everywhere as the full light of day arrived on this 23rd of May. The men were crowded around each fire attempting to dry out their wet, muddy clothing and blankets. It was like a gigantic assemblage of gypsies.

Excitement was high, for three Japanese transports were lying at anchor off the south dock; and we knew they had come at last to remove us to what we hoped would be better conditions.

On board the ship, Captain Austin Shofner and I found ourselves shoved down in the very bottom hold. No fresh air seemed willing to risk contamination in this foul place. We were bathed in perspiration. Evidently the ship had been used to transport horses, for there were stalls in the hold, fitted with bellybands to hold the horses steady when the ship was under way. The deck was covered with manure.

Next morning we awoke with splitting headaches as a result of the heat and lack of air. We pushed our way through the crowds up to the top of the deck to find the ship just getting under way for Manila. Four hours later, we dropped anchor off Pasay, a suburb of Manila.

"I wonder why they don't unload us at the docks right in the city," I said.

"Oh, that would be too easy," Shof answered. "They would rather make us walk our legs off, and it will be better propaganda if they make us walk all over town for the Filipinos to see."

That was exactly what they intended to do—make a pitiful spectacle of us to impress the Filipinos. Barges took us off the transports and dumped us in waist-deep water a hundred yards from the beach. We waded ashore and were immediately taken in hand by Japanese cavalrymen who were waiting there. They formed us in columns of fours in groups of two or three hundred and started us moving down Dewey Boulevard toward the city. The Jap cavalrymen were clean and well dressed, and the fine horses they were riding must have been captured American horses.

Before long men began to collapse from the heat and the difficulty of the march. The Japanese guards prodded them with their rifle butts and rolled them over to the side of the road, but did not seem to be doing them any serious injury. Probably on this occasion they were trying to give the Filipinos an example of Japanese "benevolence." It is one of their favorite words.

The streets were lined with throngs of Filipino people, who presented almost as pitiful a spectacle as we did. Many of them were openly crying and sometimes they would furtively give us the V-for-Victory sign. They tried to give us water and bits of food as we passed, at the risk of being clubbed by a Jap rifle butt.

"Don't worry, it won't be long," one young Filipino girl called out to me in a low voice as I passed. She was a pretty little creature, so clean and trim in her fresh cotton dress. We had forgotten the music of a woman's voice.

I mustered the best smile I could produce and gave it to her. She answered with the V sign.

Lieutenant Colonel Jack Hawkins

The Battle of Bloody Hill

Save for some narrow patches of coast line and the mountains dominating the interior, the jungle has a firm grip on the island of Guadalcanal. Along the northern shores its hold is somewhat loosened by long fingers of land that mount by precarious steps to the volcanic hills beyond. These ridges dip at intervals into the jungle itself, though some, where the incline is less pronounced, are connected by natural treeless causeways fairly blanketed with grass, often waist high, greenish brown under the rain and in the shadows, dirty straw after days of hot sun.

To the north of one of the chain of hills that form Lunga Ridge—a hill nameless before the battle of September 13, 1942, but thereafter known to the Marines as Bloody Hill—lay Henderson Airfield, a sprawling area chopped out of the coconut groves and tramped into semiflatness by the feet of native slaves and stolid Japanese labor battalions. Winding dirt roads circumnavigated the ridge and led to its crest. Their primary purpose was to provide avenues for moving supplies to defense outposts and to facilitate the movement of some of our artillery.

From an airplane above this ridge, looking toward the sea you could catch occasional glimpses of the crystal-clear Lunga River, which was for many weeks both our laundry and our communal bathtub. To the east lies the Tenaru River. Between those boundaries, as of September, lay the vital area of all we had wrested from the Japs since the beginning of our offensive operations on August 7. This small patch of territory, a few miles each way, was the center of our entire South Pacific strategy—the key that locked the door against assault upon our long supply lines, and that might unlock the portal for our offensive against Japan's island steppingstones northward. It was imperative to our entire long-range plan that it be held. Finally, whoever held Lunga Ridge could dominate the airfield, which the Japs knew as well as we did.

We thought we knew all there was to know about the art of waging war when our division, smartly trained, thoroughly toughened, impressively armed, left American shores for the monotonous passage into the war zone. We were a self-contained army, completely co-ordinated and equipped for precision operations, and we were very tough. But we learned more about war in six weeks getting into Gavutu and Tulagi and Guadalcanal—and staying there—than we ever learned in all the combined years of training under all the most capable military instructors the United States affords.

Few men, you will remember, had come out of the foxholes of Bataan to lend us the advantage of their experience. Our knowledge of Japanese fighting methods—their strategy, their trickery, and their inhuman views of life and death—was hearsay. You cannot learn to fight wars by hearsay. Only by fighting them. The hard way.

By the middle of September we knew a lot about the Jap that was never contained between the covers of a military textbook. We knew that he was well equipped and outfitted for whatever task he was assigned to, with a curiously impressive attention to detail. He didn't go through the jungle in a G string and a singlet, as some people seem to have thought. Instead, he was equipped to meet the rank, clawing, clutching jungle growth with two pairs of trousers—not one —with heavy shirts, gloves, and cloth-covered helmets that made no sound when they brushed against tangled trees and vines. His shoe was a sort of cloven hoof of soft rubber. The Jap's big toe fitted into one compartment and, in his progress through the jungle, he could feel any object beneath his feet, avoiding stones that might roll or twigs that might snap and thus reveal his presence.

We knew Tojo lived well. Not on "a handful of rice a day"—although he could do that, too—but on good canned fish and beef, plenty of canned vegetables, and an unsavory variety of hard candy. In his leisure moments he stank himself up with cheap perfumery, smoked cigarettes from the East Indies, and drank a brand of liquor looted from the Philippines and known as "Old Whisky." His officers regaled themselves with sake.

Meanwhile, Japan's countermoves on Guadalcanal had been prompt and vicious. From the very beginning there was no holding back, no playing for time, no delay to await reinforcements. They hit us with whatever they had handy. And while they were cracking at us from the sea and sky they were reinforcing themselves on land. On one occasion, in fact, they could actually be seen from one of our ridges, engaged in disembarkation operations in broad daylight. They paid for this impertinence with hundreds of lives.

Heartening and discouraging events were crowded in equal mixture into those first five weeks of our occupation. A strong attack was repulsed from over the Tenaru River, and for a day or two we breathed easier. We made thrusts occasionally through the jungle, to find that the Jap had silently faded away. He is a master in the art of disappearing. We went in small expeditions down the coast and arrived to find his supposed concentration withdrawn jungleward. Often we returned empty-handed, but each day brought its lessons, some of them costly. The enemy, meanwhile, was constantly sliding in reinforcements of men and guns, and later of tanks. We needed no superintelligence to tell us that an all-out attack was brewing.

Throughout the week of September 6, the enemy stepped up his counteroffensive. The nightly bombardment, generally from midnight until two o'clock in the morning, grew more intense. The air squadrons made their daily visits in ever-increasing numbers.

An attack was launched on the night of September 12 by Jap infantry, which had landed far to the east of the Tenaru River, according to our belief at the time, and swung in a great arc through the jungle until they had reached a point to the west of Lunga Ridge. It was a combined sea and land attack, with Japanese naval units standing off the coast to the east and lobbing their shells directly over the ridge and into the jungle beyond in the general direction of Colonel Edson's outfit. On the whole, the naval action contributed little more than noise, and the land attack never reached full intensity, leading some of us to believe there had been some miscalculation by the Jap command—that they had intended a full-dress attack that night, but were hampered by failure of some of their contingents to arrive at their base, hence put on only half a show. They did succeed in penetrating our forward lines on the right flank between Lunga Ridge and the river, but no attack came that night on the left flank, where our battalion was holding the slopes of the ridge.

Dawn brought the usual retirement into the jungle by the attacking forces. The night had been but a prelude or rehearsal for the main show.

During the morning came orders for the counterattack. My company was ordered to follow one from another battalion in a joint penetration of the jungle, but our advance was almost instantly halted by concealed Japanese defenses which would have made further effort costly on this narrow front. We withdrew on order—for the moment—circled backward, and went in again, this time with artillery support. We found few snipers in the vicinity, and we succeeded in restoring our former lines.

At 3:30 we had our first meal of the day. The cooks had saved it for us. Since our regular evening meal was scheduled for 4:30, the men went around to the end of the line and began all over again on the second meal. Marines are like that.

The men had had practically no sleep for the past forty-eight hours, so we decided to let them turn in, maintaining a sufficient number on guard. At dusk, or around 6:30 in the evening, there were evidences of a renewal of the conflict. I could hear considerable artillery fire, but the shells were hitting far over the ridge and well forward. Even the thunder of the guns meant nothing just then. I dropped into a doze. I awoke to find a runner from battalion headquarters telling me I was wanted at the command post. I made my way through the dense jungle in the pitch darkness to headquarters and was advised there that the situation up front was threatening and that our company was called for at the ridge.

Word was passed by First Sergeant Marion LeNoir, a young man whose mild manner is a mask for a rugged character and good military toughness, and the men piled out through the rough jungle growth, shook themselves awake, and plodded toward the front.

Most of us realized this was to be the big night. Two days before this action Major James Murray, division adjutant, had said casually to me, "I don't want to worry you, but five thousand Japs are coming over to try to take the field." A few days later the Jap radio said that 4,000 Japs had come over—which was an understatement—and that they had taken Henderson Airfield—which was wishful thinking.

In fighting of this nature, the Marine generally takes any extra weapon he chooses—usually the one at which he is most expert. For heavier weapons we had some 30-caliber Browning light machine guns and some light mortars. The men carried 45-caliber submachine guns. Some of them also had new-type weapons; some relied on the old Springfield, others on the Browning automatic rifle (BAR). We took all the ammunition that could be packed in, plus case upon case of hand grenades. So we went up the slope on the jungle side of the road, loaded down like pack animals.

"I s'pose we get time and half for this, huh, captain," one of the boys said as he went by in the darkness.

Our orders were to stand by along the road until it could be determined where we were most needed. A few minutes later we were ordered across the road into a position along the upper side of the nose of the hill. There we were to tie in with another battalion, which was to hold the right flank. While we were trying to find the other outfit, all hell broke loose. Captain Harry Torgerson, battalion executive officer, and Captain Richard Johnson suddenly found mortar shells dropping too close for comfort and "a jungle full of Japs around them."

On another hill on their right, Captain Justin Duryea's company was being subjected to the special brand of terrorism that is the hallmark of a real Nipponese attack. The sky and jungle were blazing with fireworks and a hellish bedlam of howls. Firecrackers, a cheap imitation of machine-gun fire, exploded in front of, in, and behind their position. Parachute flares that burned brightly for an instant and then bobbed along and went out lighted the scene intermittently. And from the jungle below with the rhythmic accompaniment of the slapping of gun butts, came the chant: "U.S. Marines be dead tomorrow. U.S. Marines be dead tomorrow."

There is purpose behind this bizarre accompaniment of attack. It is designed to mark the pattern of the attack and, second, to terrorize the opponent, to demoralize and confuse him. A third aim is to mask an operation, assault, or sneak attack from another quarter. A fourth is the not unimportant one of arousing the Japs themselves to a fever pitch. Certainly the attack takes on something of the quality of a mad religious rite.

During this strange and horrible movement, other Japanese forces were milling around in the hollow between our hill and the one where Duryea's company was being attacked. There was danger that they might cut off or surround the other companies. They had set out smoke pots and when unholy clouds came rolling in, somebody yelled, "Gas!" It was probably a Jap.

Three thrusts were developing at this time. One had filtered through the jungle on our left, a second had been launched frontally against the hill to the south, and the third was coming from the southwest through the hollow. The last one was momentarily held up just around the corner of the hill, so close that we could hear the Japs jabbering while they organized for assault. They were perhaps seventy-five yards away.

In the uproar, the commanders of the companies on the advanced slopes were ordered to withdraw from their exposed positions to a point where the battalion could be consolidated and a stronger defense set up. In this situation I came upon Major Kenneth Bailey, one of the finest Marine Corps officers in the Solomons—or anywhere else— whose subsequent death was a tragic loss to us. Colonel Edson was on the crest of the ridge and we could not reach him at once. I told the major that my right flank was exposed and that we had no contact with the company with which I was supposed to tie in. All this was happening more rapidly than it can be told. It was obvious that the hill must be held at all cost. Once it was lost, the airfield itself would be gravely imperiled.

After some delay we reorganized the defense of the hill. I moved the company higher up on the slope, spreading them along a few yards from the top. My right flank swung around the nose of the hill and my left extended from the nose down toward the road. At this point, Captain Torgerson took over command of the battalion and, carrying out orders from Colonel Edson to counterattack, moved

Duryea and Johnson's companies forward to a position paralleling our own.

One company took a position on our left flank, from the hill to the road. We had not had time enough to establish any solid defense—no time to dig in, to string barbed wire. We finally got one machine gun in position covering the right flank and had another at the center of our position on the military crest of the hill. A third was set up covering the left flank.

Meanwhile, the chattering Japs had completed their organization for assault. We could mark their coming by the progress of their flares. Above us, at the command post on the plateaulike summit of the hill, Colonel Edson was directing the general operations, and with him was a private named Watson, a cool hand with a positive genius for the work he was called upon to do. Throughout the night he acted as spotter for the artillery placed far to the rear of us. Our guns hurled their shells over us in a ceaseless bombardment of the advancing enemy forces, just where we needed them, right into the laps of the Japs. That night Watson was a private first class. The next day in the field he was made a second lieutenant.

The first assault came vomiting forth from a triangular patch of jungle directly on our left front. There was little rifle fire, but the Japs poured blast after blast of bullets from their Nambus—light machine guns—against our own machine-gun positions. A Nambu is hard to locate because it gives off no appreciable muzzle glare, and it is particularly effective in a night attack. But in fire power there is nothing like our own machine guns. The three we had set up poured it into the oncoming Japs, smashed them back, knocked them over, broke their assault. The guns never jammed. There were screams and bleating, and then comparative silence in the hollow. The firing had lasted perhaps five seconds. It seemed like hours.

The Nambus had located our machine guns and were trying desperately to knock them out. I went over to the right flank to check that gun. The gunners were yelling expressive epithets, of which the Marines have a full vocabulary. We were beginning to lose men, but as fast as one machine-gun crew went down their places were taken by others. Sergeant Keith Perkins, the section leader, was finally handling the gun himself. The action cost him his life—and us a good man.

The attack was almost constant, like a rain that subsides for a moment and then pours the harder. In most of these assaults the Japs never reached our lines. I believe now that they had no definite plan other than the general order to attack, attack, and attack. When one wave was mowed down—and I mean mowed down—another followed it into death. Some of the Jap rushes carried them into our positions and there was ugly hand-to-hand fighting. But not one of our men, to my knowledge, met death that night by a Jap bayonet. Most of our casualties came from the Nambus, mortar shells, or hand grenades.

The Japanese light mortar, carried strapped to the soldier's leg, is a crude, simple weapon. The Japanese hand grenades were of the offensive type, designed to injure and stun the enemy, but lacking the force that would make them dangerous to the Jap soldier, who follows them closely in to come to grips with his stunned opponent. They can be used at short range. Our own pineapples, by contrast, are terrifically destructive, and the man who throws one must be far enough away or it will blast him and his antagonist at the same time. We were thankful for our own grenades. We used them constantly and with deadly effect. We took them out of their cases by hundreds, pulled the pins and rolled them downhill into the noise below. They wrought havoc and a shrill chorus of shrieking arose.

I had established a command post near the center machine gun. Too near, I guess. At any rate, LeNoir and I saw a grenade coming at the same instant. I say "saw" because a Jap grenade often gives a sputter of light from the fuse when it is on the wing. We ducked—the sergeant to the right and I to the left. And I swung neatly into the orbit of another one that I definitely did not see.

As I was rolling downhill I heard somebody yelling, "Don't roll down there!" I thought it was a little funny to be told not to do something I had to do. I don't think I was ever completely unconscious. I remember rolling to the road and—how long after I do not know, although it may have been a matter of seconds—someone's pulling me off the road. It was a private who had been knocked down the hill by the same or another grenade. We struggled to our feet, groggily got our bearings, and felt our way along the fringe of jungle to the collecting station. We met a corpsman from our battalion, who put us in a jeep and bounced us through to safety, barely escaping a hand grenade on the way. I was swabbed with sulfa and given a shot of morphine. The morphine killed the pain, but I lay awake trying to determine the progress of the battle by the sound of the guns. The conflict died at dawn.

First Sergeant LeNoir poked his head into the hospital the next day and grinned at me. "Did I ever thank you for stopping that grenade for me, captain?" he asked. Thereafter he got a tremendous kick out of thanking me almost every time he saw me.

Our casualties had been heavy and some of our best men were gone. But I would say that almost 85 per cent of our casualties were saved for service again. Sulfanilamide is a wonderful thing.

In front of our positions, sprawled in grotesque caricatures of life, were nearly five hundred Japanese bodies. In the jungle, where our guns had blasted and riddled and laced through the thick growth, were many more. All the way back to their base our planes, pursuing them, harrying them, strafing them wherever they could be found, came across remnants of the 5,000. They seemed to have one idea—to get back to where they came from, stopping only to bathe their wounds in the river.

The Japs, or others like them, later came on and on again. They would not give up, short of extermination. A Japanese prisoner said, with crackpot but sinister reasoning, "Make no matter about us dead. More will come. We never stop coming. Soon you all be Japanese."

Lieutenant Colonel William J. McKennan

Bloody Ridge

Who would note such a field! A drop and rise
　　No more than someone laughing might traverse
Without a second breath: hardly a prize
Which gained would gainer's trouble reimburse.
Yet men have crossed ten thousand fields to fall
Debating it. No marked lushness grows
Where blood and bone-dust fertilized the pall
Of green; where friend or foe fell, nothing shows.
This, in the sun, is a hot, sweet field, or pale
In the moon: a field the homesick dreamer might choose,
Unmindful of its sanguinary tale
Remembered only in the cockatoo's
Raucous mimicry of battle cries
And, ghosts of planes, the diving dragonflies.

Major Raymond Henri

Guadalcanal, March 31, 1944

Coast Watchers

In September, 1945, the Marine Corps revealed what Japan had suspected from the beginning of the war—that Allied agents, hidden on Jap-occupied islands, were used as coast watchers to radio information of enemy activity to our troops. These agents were district officers of the British Colonial Service. They remained behind in the Solomons, New Guinea, and New Britain when the Japs moved in, early in 1942. Only one, an Australian stationed near Gasmata, New Britain, was caught. The others evaded the enemy for months, living in caves and native huts, getting information from natives and through their binoculars from the Allied troops farther south.

One of the most spectacular behind-the-lines agents was Martin Clemens, on Guadalcanal. He was commissioned a second lieutenant in the British Army when the British resident commissioner evacuated

Guadalcanal in May, 1942, so that he would not be treated as a civilian spy in case of capture.

Setting up headquarters on a jungle mountain, Clemens radioed to Allied headquarters the information on Jap activities that native police brought him. Once, while swimming in a jungle creek, he was spotted by a Jap plane. Enemy patrols pursued him, led by a Jap agent named Ishimoto, who had posed as a trader in the Solomons. Clemens escaped only by changing his hiding place. Later, after his information concerning Henderson Field and the strength and disposition of Jap troops on the island had aided the Marines in the invasion of Guadalcanal, Clemens had the pleasure of leading a patrol that trapped and killed Ishimoto.

One of Clemens's most trusted natives, Sergeant Major Vouza of the Solomons' police force, was later caught by the Japs while carrying an American flag given him by a Marine. Tied to a tree, he was used as a human dummy for the Japs' bayonets. Then, thinking him dead, the Japs departed. But Vouza regained consciousness, chewed off his thongs, and, with his torn flesh hanging to his body by shreds, stumbled and crawled twenty miles to the American lines. Later he recovered.

Anonymous

And They Send Us Mortar Shells!

The Marine Raiders and Army troopers who captured Enogai and established the northern prong of a steel pincers outflanking the enemy's air base at Munda sprawled on the coral sands of Dragon Peninsula. Before us, less than ten miles away across the Kula Gulf, were the Japanese fortifications on Kolombangara Island. Behind us was a jungle the enemy considered impenetrable.

We were the forces under the command of Colonel Harry B. Liversedge, USMC, of Pine Grove, California—forces including the Marine Raiders of Tulagi and Guadalcanal under the leadership of Lieutenant Colonel Samuel B. Griffith of Frankfort, Kentucky.

Colonel Liversedge that night termed the operation successful. "It was apparent the Japs never imagined that anyone would strike here," he said, "but it was tougher than we expected. Our men held up in great fashion."

We had left Rice Anchorage—a comparatively small group—several hours before dawn of July 5, 1943. We carried three days' rations, the estimate the march would require. Rain and jungle conspired to make this a bad guess. By the time our rations were gone most of our cumbersome gear was gone too—a trail of sodden blankets, shelter halves, mess gear, and field packs littering the jungle.

The element of surprise was figured to be one of our most important weapons. By the morning of July 6 it appeared that it might hold. Like a deadly snake the slithering line of camouflaged men had reached and crossed the Giza Giza River. There was no opposition, except the jungle—not even a Japanese patrol. Hour after hour, throughout the day, the line wound to the southwest. By nightfall the pace began to tell, even on the youngsters. When the order to halt came, we swallowed our emergency rations and fell exhausted to sleep on the wet earth.

We stumbled through swamps all the next day. The communications men, with their heavy radio and telephone gear, were slowed to a crawl. It was raining again. We hadn't bathed or removed our clothes since we started. We just plodded along quietly, dragging one foot after the other, covered with mud and soaked in sweat. That morning we made our first kill. Advance units of Raiders brushed a Jap patrol at Maranusa. We prodded ourselves to renewed alertness, and by midafternoon the machine guns and carbines chattered again. This time it was a fairly sizable force—some 150 Jap troopers and naval landing force men, defending a jungle outpost called Triri. The Raiders swept down on it like hounds after rabbits. By nightfall some 75 Jap bodies were scattered around the little coral ridge. Some of our buddies were dead too, though but a handful compared to the Jap toll. We brought them in to the shattered Japanese command post. Sticks were cut for crosses and the bark shaved off so that they would stand out above the graves against the dark jungle. To the crosses were affixed the identification tags of the dead. The wounded were brought down into the little valley too, carried in improvised stretchers made of ponchos and branches. Mostly their wounds were superficial—wounds of the arms and legs—and the wounded who were conscious watched quietly as Navy corpsmen attended them. But occasionally there was a feeble cry, "Pain! Morphine! Morphine!"

By the morning of July 8 the problem of food became serious. Our command post moved up from Maranusa to Triri. Almost all rations were gone and the men were foraging for Japanese rice and canned fish. Worms got to the rice before we did. By afternoon the Raiders were on the move again, endeavoring to find a passable trail to Enogai, but all trails seemed to lead into impassable swamps. In the later afternoon, the Japs, who had wilted at the first attack, were back again. Rifle fire swept the command post. The Japanese then attempted to counterattack the Raiders established on a small ridge overlooking Triri. Army units held the left flank. Had there been chow there would have been little time to eat that evening.

Up on the slope Marines and the Army units withstood the assault. Night falls quickly in the jungle, and with it the firing ceased. Down in the valley Navy corpsmen and Army medical men worked feverishly, treating the wounded who were spread out on the floor of a thatched shack. That night we held our breath. The hollow was a poor defensive position. But the night passed quietly and by daybreak of July 9 Lieutenant Colonel Griffith's scouts had cut a path through the bush. The unit edged its way out toward Enogai.

The command post was moved to higher ground at Triri better suited for defense. Natives built lean-tos of branches and leaves on a rocky ledge. The wounded were hauled up in litters. Rations were exhausted. Attempts had been made to contact air forces for parachute drops of rations and ammunition, but the heavy jungle growth made communications difficult. The rice that was left was reserved for the wounded.

At noon the word came back from Lieutenant Colonel Griffith: "We are six hundred yards from Enogai. Our advance is continuing." Faces brightened—especially among the wounded—and hopes were further raised later in the afternoon when planes finally located us to drop parachutes with sorely needed ammunition and rations.

The first parachute brought a great wail. It contained a sack of mortar shells and drew cries of "My God! We're starving to death and they send us mortar shells!" But the ammunition was soon followed by cases of K ration and chocolate bars.

By late afternoon there was more good news. Lieutenant Colonel Griffith's men had reached the heights surrounding Enogai, knocked out a lone outpost, ringed the area with machine guns, automatic rifles, riflemen, and mortar crews, and the siege of Enogai was under way. Headquarters moved up in the dark of July 9 with Colonel Liversedge. The Raiders entrenched quietly and awaited an expected mad "Banzai" charge. The night passed quietly.

With dawn of July 10 the Marines opened up on Enogai with a murderous barrage of mortar fire. Shells were lobbed into the Japanese camp, creating panic. Japanese soldiers raced about their camp area as if terror-stricken. Now and then a grenade sailed up at the attackers on the ridge, but the Japs offered little organized resistance. Raiders rushed headlong down the slopes and charged the Jap positions. A sandbagged machine gun, set up as a road block, was swiftly wiped out. The enemy fled in mad confusion down a coral road to the beach. Those not hit plunged into the water, attempting to swim to a small mangrove island offshore. Raider machine guns set on the ridge mowed them down as they floundered in the water. As a Marine machine gunner put it: "It was like shooting ducks!"

Colonel Liversedge, Lieutenant Colonel Griffith, and Captain Clay Boyd of Tucumcari, New Mexico, narrowly escaped death in the assault. The trio walked into the line of fire of a hidden Japanese machine-gun nest, protected by snipers. With bullets screeching over his head, Colonel Liversedge stood quietly surveying the scene until Lieutenant Colonel Griffith shouted, "Down, Harry! Get down!" All three officers escaped injury, but Second Lieutenant Philip A. Oldham, a veteran of Guadalcanal, who had been recently commissioned, was killed as he blasted the nest in the lead of a grenade-throwing squad. His home was in Philadelphia.

It is estimated that 350 Japs were killed in the campaign, including those at Maranusa and Triri. There was another group of shaved-stick crosses on the ridge overlooking Enogai, larger than the small group of graves at Triri, but Marine dead were comparatively few. That night hungry Marines dined on Japanese canned fish, rice, and sake, and sacked Japanese clothing stores to replace their own mud-caked uniforms.

Master Technical Sergeant Murrey Marder

Raiders' Return

After the battle we were a horrible sight. The Seabees and sailors coming ashore, unloading the ships, thought so too. They took one look, trotted to their quarters, opened their sea bags and brought us all their extra clothing. They literally gave us everything—shoes, socks, skivvies and shirts. Inside of two hours every man seemed freshly clothed and I still remember the disconsolate Seabee who wandered by, arms filled with a complete set of clothing, looking in vain for a Raider still in a torn, ragged, wet jungle suit.

Then their cooks took over. They threw the icebox locks overboard. Men by the score wandered aboard ship and were fed until many a cook must have wondered just how he was going to feed his crew next week. Cigarettes, candy, chewing gum appeared. And many a Raider wished to thank many a Navy officer for his taste in cigars.

First Lieutenant Howard E. Biggerstaff

Life on a Bull's-eye

Honest to God, on this island it's like living on a bull's-eye," said Dr. Wimp. He said it as if he were about to cry. His voice was high-pitched with the same fatigue that seemed to be gnawing at his eyes. We passed a number of Marines on the narrow jungle trail and when they greeted him he had barely enough energy to answer their names, pushing the words out in a kind of gasp.

Jesse J. Wimp was a lieutenant in the Navy medical corps, a middle-aged, stocky, energetic man with a booming, infectious laugh. But during our first meeting, on Puruata Island just off Bougainville, he didn't laugh at all. The trail we were traveling that morning led to a bomb crater and to the shrapnel-punctured body of a Marine. The doctor's errand was simply to pronounce the man dead, verify the cause of death, and issue instructions concerning disposal of the remains. Four others had been killed and twenty-one wounded by Jap bombs during the night, and Dr. Wimp and his corpsmen had scrambled about for hours in the evil darkness, straining to hear the moans of the wounded above the ack-ack, working desperately to stop the blood and get the worst cases back to the tiny pillbox "hospital" for plasma transfusions and emergency operations.

It had been like that for five straight nights. Still other nights of terror had gone before; more were to follow. The daylight hours were better, but there were times when enemy Zeros streaked low across the water and strafed the tiny island. Guns hidden on the Bougainville mainland had paid their respects with a few salvos of HE shells.

Puruata Island—the "bull's-eye"—is a geographical trifle, the sort of place cartoonists have in mind when pondering the affairs of castaways. It lies about 1,000 yards off Cape Torokina on Bougainville, where the Marines landed November 1, 1943, and looks for all the world like a handful of jungle that has been plucked from the mainland and cast adrift on the pale green waters of the Coral Sea. The island stretches a mere 700 yards one way and 400 the other, rimmed to seaward by coral reef and on the mainland side by a white sandy beach.

That beach turned out to be one of the most important in all the South Seas. It was the better of the only two beaches in the captured area that were negotiable by the Navy's prime movers, the LSTs. It made Puruata Island the freight yard of the Bougainville offensive— and the favorite target for Japanese bombers.

When General Turnage, commander of the Third Marine Division, referred to the "astonishing success" of the Navy supply system in helping to win the Bougainville campaign, his tribute included the men of Puruata Island. These, in the main, were Marine Pioneers— a unit specially trained in the tasks of unloading ships and establishing supply dumps ashore. From early November to late in January they went about their grueling job with such avidity that they broke all speed records for unloading LSTs, then broke their own record several times. The Navy was grateful. Even at sea the LSTs are a relatively sluggish craft (whence the nickname: "Large Slow Target"). But when beached during an unloading operation, they are a rare invitation to enemy aircraft—like sitting ducks, unable to maneuver for safety. What the Pioneers did on Puruata was as much a victory as any achieved by their comrades fighting in the Bougainville jungle.

It would have been a staggering assignment just to handle the equipment and supplies needed to maintain the combat troops. On top of this, however, came the vast quantities of machines and materiel used to build the three airfields so swiftly created by the Seabees. "And even that's only half of it," said one of the Puruata Marines. "What really hurts is that every damn stick we drag ashore here one day, we spend the next three or four loading back on tank lighters and LCTs to get the stuff over to the mainland. This is just a goddam stopover!"

And so the men of Puruata fought day and night. From dawn till dusk they wrestled chow and ammunition, fuel and guns, trucks and tanks, and steel mat for landing strips. From dusk till dawn they fought for a few hours' sleep between the wails of the air-warning sirens, and tried to ignore the devil's concert of antiaircraft fire and falling bombs. Volunteer gunners rushed to man the machine guns mounted on trucks, and volunteer stretcher bearers rose from the safety of their foxholes to hunt the wounded when the enemy bombs hit home. One night the fuel dump was blasted into an inferno; another night an ammunition pile was ignited. And when these things happened, the men of Puruata, their muscles aching from yesterday's labors and their minds fogged and edgy from the night's ordeal, would give that something extra that wins our battles by risking their lives in salvage work, rolling barrels of oil away from the fire as hoses sprayed over them, manhandling high explosives out of the danger area.

One day when things were quiet, Dr. Wimp was in a talkative mood in his headquarters at the aid station of the Pioneer unit. He had just come back from a beachcombing expedition, his pockets loaded with seashells. He said he was sending them home to Kirksville, Missouri, where his three youngsters would get a kick out of using them to decorate the back-yard fish pool.

"It's been quiet for three days now," he said. "And for three nights, which is a hell of a lot more important. The way things were going, the troops on the front lines actually sympathized with us. It's a fact. I know because I see so many of the battle casualties. They bring them over from the mainland and put them aboard the LSTs going back to rear-base hospitals. They often told me they were just as glad they'd never had to live on Puruata.

"I don't want to see anything like this again. We've had six war neurosis cases and, honest to God, it's amazing we haven't had more. Days like today are what saves us all from going nuts.

"It isn't being afraid so much, although there isn't a Marine on Puruata who won't frankly admit he's been afraid. It's the damn strain when you work like hell all day and maybe get strafed, and then you get bounced around half the night by the bombs and the antiaircraft guns. This island sits out here on the water on a moonlight night just begging for bombs, and every one that comes down sounds like it's going to get right in under the covers with you.

"And when there isn't any moon they come over and drop flares. Jesus, the other night one of them came all the way down and landed in one of our aid stations. It took so long to come down that a couple of Marines claim they got out a book and started to read by the light of it.

"Maybe I see only the worst of it—me and the corpsmen. Incidentally, all my corpsmen have been commended twice by the generals over on the mainland. For instance, it seemed pretty bad the night we used up our last bottle of plasma on the last wounded Marine we brought in. I prayed, honest to God, that the Japs would stay away the rest of the night. They didn't, but they dumped their next load in the water. Thanks to some cross-eyed Jap.

"But what I mean is that nobody else knew at the time about that plasma running out. And we've shot down seven planes between our antiaircraft and the kids who just went out and grabbed a machine gun and started shooting. Hell, it hasn't been one-sided at all, really. Just a nightmare. The Japs never stopped us unloading ships and getting the stuff delivered across the way.

"And you know," Dr. Wimp went on, "you've got to hand it to these crazy Marines. There isn't anything so bad they can't find a wisecrack to fit it. A while ago when we were having our third raid in one night I heard a kid running for his foxhole and yelling: 'Hang onto your false teeth, boys—they may be dropping sandwiches.'

"Honest to God, the only thing I could think about was how good a sandwich would go right about then!"

Captain Patrick O'Sheel

Explosive Eviction

One Marine ordnance officer on Okinawa had a housing problem all his own. Searching a new artillery position for booby traps, he found no mines, but did find one cave, eminently suited, he thought, for his shelter. To discourage other prospective tenants, he put up a sign, "Booby traps. Keep away."

Then he left. Along came Leatherneck Private First Class John E. Coady, of La Crosse, Wisconsin, a demolitions man. He saw the sign and, like all good demolitions men, blew up the cave. The officer is still looking for a good shelter.

Technical Sergeant John Worth

The Beach

Tarawa, the strategic Gilbert Island outpost with its all-important airstrip, saw the bitterest, costliest, most sustained fighting on any front. It cost us the lives of hundreds of United States Marines. (Official reports listed 1,026 Americans killed.) But we wiped out a force of 4,000 Imperial Japanese Marines where we expected to find only 2,000, mostly dead.

Before we started it was great fun. We grinned and chortled. We said, "There won't be a Jap alive when we get ashore."

That was the plan. Naval and air bombardment was to all but destroy the island. The few living Japs were to be so shell-shocked there would be no opposition. I recalled Major Mills's instructions: "We don't intend to neutralize the island. We don't intend to destroy it. We will annihilate it."

As dawn broke, Tarawa was completely enveloped in smoke and flame. Japanese gun emplacements—eight-inchers—continued to reply. Our battleships looked like sullen, defiant bulldogs as they ignored them and continued to pound the shore. At dawn, our planes came in. We could see them disappear into the smoke and flame. We could hear the sputter of their machine guns. We could see the debris raised by their bombs. It was wonderful.

But something suddenly appeared to have gone wrong. We learned that H hour had been delayed 30, then 45 minutes. The pounding continued. There was little doubt there were still living—and fighting —Japs on the island.

Our assault waves were in the water, ready to hit the beach. We were in the second wave, due to hit after the first men reached shore. Without warning, an eight-inch shell hit and exploded ten yards off our side. We dived behind a hatch, laughing at each other as we came out. A second shell hit five yards off, killing a sailor and spraying our deck with shrapnel and salt water. We upped anchor and steamed out of range.

Fifteen minutes later, we climbed into our tank light, sharing it with many other Marines, a truck, and a trailer.

"We have landed against heavy opposition," came the first word from shore. "Casualties severe." It came over our radio as we moved in. We looked grimly at each other.

As we pulled toward the beach, we were met with enemy shellfire. A boat on our starboard side received a direct hit. Five men were killed. We pulled alongside and dragged in the survivors. There was no chance to salvage their equipment. Swiftly we moved out of range. A control boat roared by; a naval officer screamed at us to stay back until we received word it was safe to go in. That was 10:30 a.m.

At 1 p.m. we started in again, moving toward the pier, which appeared undamaged. We were stopped by machine-gun fire.

Corporal Raymond Matjasic, of Cleveland, one of our combat photographers, who had been seated in the cab of the truck, fell to the floor. The truck's windshield was knocked out.

At 3 p.m. we tried again. Shells tore the water on all sides. Two more boats went down, and more Marines died. We backed out again, unable to pick up the survivors. Many of them swam to us and were later moved back to their transports. Many of the wounded drowned.

The sun was punishing. There was no shade. We broke out our rations and nibbled at them. At 5 p.m. the control boat pulled up.

"Do any of you have ammunition?" the naval officer yelled through his megaphone. "We've got to get it ashore at all costs."

"We have a truck," we answered.

"To hell with that," he said, and roared away.

At dusk our battleships and cruisers opened up a terrific antiaircraft barrage. There was only one answer—Japanese planes.

"Prepare to go over the side," a lieutenant said quietly. "They'll strafe us if they get through."

We inflated our lifebelts and waited. They never got through. We were glad. We'd seen two sharks just before dusk.

At midnight the control boat appeared out of the darkness. We were to try again. We inched toward the dock, which was partially wrecked by our own shelling. The hulk of a Japanese merchantman loomed to the right. Two direct hits from our destroyers had put it out of action. On the lookout for snipers, we covered it with our machine guns.

When we reached the dock, snipers in the wrecked ship opened up, but they were firing over our heads. We climbed onto the dock and more snipers fired. We hit the deck. We moved down the dock ten feet. Japs on the beach began throwing mortars our way. We hit the deck again.

Minutes later a second mortar hit directly beneath us. I felt the blast and was sprayed with salt water.

Someone yelled: "Get to the other side! The next one will be right on!"

We were uncertain where to go. The Jap lines were only fifty yards past the end of the pier, and there was no command post. Matjasic and I discarded our typewriters, our packs, and our field glasses and darted to the shore. The last 75 yards of the pier was white coral grit. There was a brilliant moon—at home I would have called it beautiful. We swore at it viciously; we were perfect targets.

Crouched, we sprinted down the pier, silhouetted against the coral. Snipers opened up, and six men fell, screaming in agony. We lay like logs.

"We can't stay here," someone said up the line. "They'll shell hell out of us and we'll all be gone."

"Advance slowly. Five feet between each man. They won't get us all that way."

We started. Three more Marines fell, and we hit the ground. Inch by inch we moved up. Each ten yards cost us the lives of more Marines. Each time I expected to get mine. Finally we were within fifteen yards of the beach. Ahead were shadows.

"Throw away everything, including your camera," I told Matjasic. "We'll come back and get it if we can. We're making a run for it."

A sergeant beside me cracked: "Take your rifle. You'll probably never get to use it, but I might."

I grinned. Ray and I ran for the shadows. It was an anticlimax. Not a shot was fired at us.

On the beach the fire was still hot. We ducked behind the wreckage of a Japanese steam roller, which appeared to be between us and the enemy. I found a shovel and began to dig frantically. Within five minutes we had our first foxhole on Tarawa. It turned out to be the safest spot on the island.

At dawn we found our position precarious. Our own men were on the left of us, the Japs not more than fifty yards on the right. We were in no man's land.

At 6 a.m. a fight began over our foxhole. Scores of bullets nicked off the big steam roller, while we burrowed deeper.

Shortly before noon the Japs were driven back, and we came out of hiding. Our cruisers and destroyers resumed their shelling of the Jap half of the island, knocking out the last remaining big guns. The concussion was terrific, for the shells were landing not more than a hundred yards away. Our planes came in strafing.

I waded and swam through a small bay to reach the opposite shore, but was unable to find anyone. Virtually everyone I knew was reported dead or missing. Far down the beach (not more than fifty yards, but it took me two hours to cover it) I saw a Marine with a camera. Painfully I crawled to him, for my body was one mass of bruises.

He was a stranger.

"Where'd you get it?" I asked.

"From Lucas," he replied.

"Where is Lucas?" I asked.

"Over there," he replied. "Dead."

"I'm Lucas," I told him.

From his description, I decided he meant Sergeant Ernest J. Diet, of Hammond, Louisiana. Later, I found a body I thought was that of our sergeant photographer. I was almost hysterical when Diet showed up twenty-four hours later. He learned finally that the camera belonged to someone else who had found some of my papers. Meanwhile, he had officially reported me killed in action.

I left my foxhole at noon, went a hundred yards, and returned at 6 p.m. It was that tough.

The night was hellish. More men came in, and more were killed on the pier. I slept until 1 a.m., and Matjasic from 1 a.m. until dawn. We had had enough experience with the enemy's infiltration tactics. We had orders to shoot any man who came toward us. During the night we learned that guards on the pier killed a Jap who had sneaked in with a drum of gasoline, intending to set the pier afire. It would have been the end of us, for the pier was loaded with high explosives.

At dawn the enemy sent its first bombers. There were only two of them, and five men were killed.

We awoke to one of the strangest sights in history. We badly needed replacements. Men were being landed five hundred yards from shore in the surf at low tide and were wading in past enemy machine-gun emplacements. Many men fell before they reached shore. In the afternoon Marines were still staggering ashore, carrying the limp forms of buddies between them.

The heaviest fire came from a Jap sniper's nest in the beached enemy merchant ship. Assault waves were held up while our dive bombers went to work on it, dropping high explosives into its hulk. And yet, when the next boats came in, machine-gun fire continued from the blazing ship. We settled the matter by sending men aboard to wipe out the snipers in hand-to-hand combat, and to hold it as an outpost.

Shortly before noon, the Japs opened up on us with mortars. One landed near enough to tear the top off our steam roller, and to deafen me for two days. A Marine who occupied the foxhole next to ours was killed by shrapnel. We dug deeper.

By now, however, the Japs were being forced steadily back. We were able to move about. Snipers continued, but we ignored them. One was killed in a coconut tree fifty feet away.

Still our naval and air poundings continued. On the third day the heaviest fighting took place in a cleared space around the airstrip. One of our tanks lumbered into the clearing. A Jap broke from the bush and tried to throw a grenade in its tracks. He was shot down.

Suddenly there was firing at our rear. Seven Japs had been found in the ruins of a dugout less than ten feet from the command post from which our officers were directing the operations. They were wiped out.

I went with Chief Pharmacist's Mate Roy J. Barnhill, of Salt Lake City, to the front where our men were blasting out a Jap pillbox. The night before, Barnhill had gone back to the Jap lines to pick up six wounded Marines. A Japanese sentry had tossed two hand grenades in their direction. Both were duds.

I returned to the beach to find snipers again sweeping the pier where ammunition was being unloaded. They fired from the wreckage of one of our boats fifty yards away. I ducked into the water on the opposite side, and found five husky military policemen herding a convoy of Japanese prisoners toward the beach in water up to their own waists and up to the Japs' shoulders. Three dead Marines were in the water. The MPs herded the Japs out to a waiting landing barge. As the frightened prisoners climbed aboard, they were subjected to murderous fire from their own snipers. Three were killed.

I got back in time to be in on the battle that broke Japanese resistance on Tarawa. Several hundred Japs were holed up for two days in a bombproof shelter at the end of the airstrip, holding up our advance.

Private First Class Robert Harper, of Houston, Texas, and Sergeant John Rybin, of Laurel, Montana, dashed forward with their flame throwers while automatic riflemen covered them. At the entrance to the bomb shelter, Harper threw his flame on a Jap machine-gun nest, charring three enemy Marines beyond recognition. He poured on more fire. There were screams inside the shelter, and the Marines rushed forward to capture their objective.

Harper returned to our post. "They were all huddled in there scared to death," he said. "I turned on the heat and that was all."

From this point on, our advance was rapid. Following our advancing troops, I came upon one position we had held less than five minutes and counted twenty-seven Japanese who had committed suicide by strapping their feet to the triggers of their rifles, placing the muzzle in their chests and pulling the trigger with a kick.

During the night, the Japs made a final desperate bayonet charge. They killed two of our flame throwers but were repulsed.

And the next morning, November 22, the island was secured. For the first time we were able to sit up without ducking. There were a few desultory sniper shots, but no one noticed them. Staff Sergeant George Stutsman, of Natchez, Mississippi, brought us two cartons of cigarettes and a carton of matches. We got a five-gallon keg of water—a real luxury. It rained briefly, and we stood in the open, soaped, and showered ourselves off.

This was civilization.

First Lieutenant Jim G. Lucas

Suicide Creek

They came to "Suicide Creek." It had no name and it was not on the map, but that is what the Marines called it after they had fought two days in vain to win a crossing. The creek is swift, two or three feet deep, perhaps twenty feet across at the widest, twisting between steep banks. It flows over rocks that make footing difficult, and here and there a tree had fallen into the stream. The banks rise steeply from ten to twenty feet, up to little ridges in the jungle of Cape Gloucester.

The Marines didn't know the creek was a moat before an enemy strong point. They couldn't see that the heavy growth across the creek was salted with pillboxes—machine-gun emplacements armored with dirt and logs, some of them dug several stories deep, all carefully spotted so they could sweep the slope and both banks of the stream with interlacing fire.

Only snipers shot at the Marine scouts who crossed the creek, feeling their way through the thickets. More Marines followed, down into the creek, up the steep bank, on into the jungle. Then they got it. The jungle exploded in their faces. They hit the deck, trying to deploy in the bullet-lashed brush and strike back. Marines died there, firing blindly, cursing because they couldn't see the men who were killing them. Or not saying anything—just dying. The others could only hug the ground as bullets cut the brush just above their heads, like a sweeping blade of fire. They couldn't even help the wounded.

Snipers picked off some of them as they lay there. It's perfect for snipers when machine guns are firing; you can't hear the single pop above the heavier fire. You don't know you're a target until you're hit.

From the American side of Suicide Creek, Marines gave the trapped platoon overhead fire. The idea is to fling such a volume of fire at the enemy's position that he must hug cover and slacken his fire. The overhead fire spread an umbrella of bullets above the pinned-down platoon, enabling them to crawl out and crawl back across the creek, pulling out their wounded.

That's how it went all day as Marine detachments felt for a gap or a soft spot in the enemy's positions along the creek. They would be hit and pull back, and then detachments would push across the creek at other points. They'd be blasted by invisible machine guns, and leave a few more Marines dead in the brush as they fell back across the creek. Then they'd do it all over again.

There was nothing else they could do. There is no other way to fight a jungle battle—not in such terrain, when the enemy is dug in and your orders are to advance. You don't know where the enemy is. His pillboxes are so camouflaged that you can usually find them only when they fire on you. So you push out scouts and small patrols, until they're fired on. Then you push out patrols from different directions until they too draw fire. Thus you locate the enemy. Then you have to take the emplacements, the pillboxes, one by one in desperate little battles.

Private First Class Calvin B. King, of Pen Mar, Pennsylvania, remembers his platoon crossed the creek four times in a single day and four times had to stumble back under enemy fire. And not until the last time did they see a Jap.

"That time we got maybe a hundred and fifty feet into the brush and then we saw them coming at us," he said. "They had slipped around and were coming in from our flank to wipe us out. There were a lot of 'em. I don't know how many. It looked like they was everywhere.

"They didn't make a sound. They were just coming at us through the trees. We were firing, but they kept coming at us. There were too many of them to stop. We had to pull out. Machine guns were shooting at us from everywhere. And all them Japs coming. We'd pull back a little way and stop and fire, and then we'd fall back a little more.

"Somebody was saying, 'Steady . . . Steady there . . .' But I don't know who it was. I just kept firing. You don't think about nothing. You just shoot. Guys were getting hit. We had to pull them along with us. You can't leave a wounded guy for the Japs to get. The things they do to 'em . . ."

There was a private first class from Oakland, California. He was blinded by powder burns. He couldn't know it was only temporary. All he knew was that he was blind in the middle of a battle. He was saying, "I can't see." He was fumbling around, trying to feel his way in the brush. The bullets were cutting all around, but he didn't ask anybody to stop fighting to help him. He just hung onto his rifle, like they tell you to, and tried to crawl out, though he couldn't see where to crawl. Corporal Lawrence E. Oliveria, of Fall River, Massachusetts, grabbed the blind boy by the arm, pulling him along as they withdrew. He'd pause to fire, and the blind Marine would wait beside him, and then Corporal Oliveria would lead him back a little farther. "The boy didn't moan or pray or nothing. He just kept saying, every now and then, 'I can't see.'"

By the time they got back to the creek, the Japanese were close on them, charging now. But the Marines had machine guns at the creek. They piled the Jap dead in the brush and broke the charge.

Another platoon tried crossing the creek at another point. Near the head of the line was "the Swede," a private first class from some place out west. He was a big guy, built like a truck, the last man in the world you'd ever suspect of being sentimental. His big ambition was to send his kid sister through college. It took some doing, but he was doing it on his service pay. The Swede was just stepping into the creek when he got it.

"You could hear the bullet hit him in the stomach," said Platoon Sergeant John M. White. "He just stood there a minute. He said, 'Them dirty bastards!' Then he fell down. He was dead.

"When we got across the creek, the fire was so hot we couldn't do a thing. You couldn't see a single Jap. All you could see was where

· 38 ·

the bullets were hitting around us. And men getting hit. But no matter how bad it got, I never saw one of the boys pass up a wounded man."

Private First Class Charles Conger, of Ventura, California, was one of those hit. A machine gun cut his legs from under him. Nobody saw him. Nobody could have heard him if he'd yelled—the firing was too heavy. He was as alone as a man can be. It was slow, painful, dragging through the brush, crawling head first down the bank, dragging limp legs. He had to pull himself on by inches, then belly down the bank sprayed with bullets as thick as rice thrown at a bride. He tumbled into the creek. The rocks were sharp. He was gasping in the swift water, struggling across against the force of the stream. It was only blind luck that White saw him. White was too far away to help, but he stopped and waved his arms to attract attention, ignoring cover until two Marines who were nearer saw the wounded man in the creek. Those Marines were almost across. Safety lay just ahead. They didn't have to stop. But they went sloshing through the water to the wounded man. They half carried, half dragged him with them.

The battalion tried all day to win a crossing at the creek. In the end, they could only withdraw to the ridge on the American side and dig in for the night. It was getting dusk as one machine-gun platoon finished its gun emplacements. Then the men began digging their foxholes. Most of them were stripped to the waist and they laid aside their weapons as they dug.

That was the moment the enemy chose to charge. They must have slipped across the stream and up the slope and watched the digging. They must have seen that if they could reach those emplacements and get those machine guns, they could swing them and smash the infantry company holding the next section of the line. That is why the Japanese, perhaps fifty of them, did not yell and did not fire a shot. They rushed with bayonets.

Down among his infantrymen, Captain Andrew A. Haldane, of Methuen, Massachusetts, was talking with First Lieutenant Andrew Chisick, of Newark, New Jersey. They heard a Marine yell. They looked up and saw the Japs racing toward the emplacements, and weaponless Marines scattering out of the way. Some had no chance of getting to their weapons. The Japs were hardly thirty yards from the nearest gun and closing fast.

Then more Marines were firing, but it wasn't enough to stop the charge. The nearest Japs were hardly ten feet from the guns. Captain Haldane ran toward the guns, firing as he ran. Lieutenant Chisick ran with him. Others joined the charge, some with bare hands, some with clubs or entrenching tools snatched up from the ground. The Japs reached one gun and swung it to enfilade the line. A Jap was in the gunner's seat. The Marines' charge hit the gun before he could fire a shot. He got a bayonet through the chest. The enemy broke, and the Marines cut them down. More than twenty dead Japs were scattered in the brush by the time it was quiet again.

The Marines were bombed that night. Dive bombers. The enemy set up a heavy fire of tracer bullets to show the bombers where their own lines were and where they should drop their bombs in the dark. Nobody will ever be able to describe a bombing. You can't describe hell. You can only go through it.

The Marines had to take the bombing after a day of battle, without any way of hitting back. The next morning, January 3, they attacked again. The enemy threw mortar shells. Sergeant White saw a shell explode, and ducked down the line to see if anyone was hit. "A kid was sitting there in his foxhole. He didn't have any head. He just had a neck with dog tags on it."

All through that second day, the Marines pushed small units across the creek at different points, still trying to find a soft spot in the Japanese defenses. Each time they were hit. They knocked out some of the machine guns, but each time, in the end, they had to fall back across the creek.

There was a boy firing from behind a log. His face was gray. He stopped firing and looked around. His eyes were dull, without hope. "It don't do any good," he said. His voice was flat. He wasn't speaking to anybody. He was just saying it. "I got three of 'em, but it don't do any good."

Platoon Sergeant Casimir Polakowski—known as Ski—said, "What the hell are you beefing about? You get paid for it, don't you?"

The kid managed a grin. As Ski crawled on down the line, the boy was fighting again, squeezing them off.

A platoon was pinned down in the jungle on their flank. They could neither go forward nor withdraw. They could only lie in the brush, held there by a crisscross net of machine-gun fire, while snipers took pot shots at them. Ski's platoon was ordered to lend a hand. They were bone-tired, but Ski said, "Let's get going," and they got.

Three of them were Denham, Melville, and O'Grady. Private Harry Denham, of Nashville, Tennessee, was called "Pee Wee" because he was so small. They say he went to "some fancy military school." But he didn't ask favors of anybody and he wouldn't back down before the biggest man in the regiment. Just a bantam rooster of a kid who'd take on anything that walked. Private First Class John O'Grady, of Ogdensburg, New York, left the talking for the trio to Denham and Melville. He was a quiet guy who never had much to say to anybody, but he seemed to talk plenty when the three of them were off by themselves. Maybe he told them what he wanted to be after the war. The kids all think about that. It's something to look forward to—and a guy needs something to look forward to. Private First Class John William Melville was called "Pete," but nobody seemed to know why. His home was Lynn, Massachusetts. He was twenty-six, almost an old man. He quit a white-collar job with the General Electric Company in Boston to join the Marine Corps.

Denham, Melville, and O'Grady—and Levy, Jones, and Brown—flung themselves at the enemy's flank so he'd have to break the fire that had the other platoon caught. Men dropped, but they kept going forward, fighting from tree to tree. They pushed the enemy back and held him long enough for the trapped platoon to pull out. That was long enough for the Marines to form a line so they couldn't be rolled up by counterattack.

Another lull then. The jungle was still. First Sergeant Selvitelle asked Ski how it was going. Ski was smoking a cigarette. His voice sounded tired.

"They got Denham, Melville, and O'Grady," he said. They were lying out there in the brush somewhere and he was smoking a cigarette.

The word came to move up. There was firing ahead. Maybe an hour later Ski was behind a tree when he saw a wounded Marine lying in the open. A sniper was shooting at the boy. Ski could see the dirt flung up when the bullets hit. The boy was trying to crawl away, but he couldn't.

Ski ran from cover and pulled him to a tree. The sniper saw him. All the sniper had to do was wait until Ski started to return to his post. Then he shot Ski in the back.

That was about the time Tommy Harvard's platoon crossed Suicide Creek, lugging their heavy machine guns. "Tommy Harvard" was the code name for First Lieutenant Elisha Atkins, who played football at Harvard, belonged to the Dekes and the Owls, and got his B.A. in 1942. "Very quiet and polite as hell" is the way a sergeant described him.

The enemy let First Lieutenant Atkins and about half his men cross the creek before they opened up. Six automatic weapons blasted them at point-blank range. There were at least three machine guns with perfect fields of fire. It happened too quickly for anybody to duck.

Sergeant Wills says, "I saw a man ahead of us and just as I saw he wasn't a Marine they all let fly."

Marines were hit. Somebody was screaming. Corporal John R. Hyland of Greenwich, Connecticut, was frowning as he tried to knock out the nearest machine-gun nest with rifle fire. The screaming man stopped.

Corporal Hyland said, "We ought to get the hell out of here." But he didn't move to go. He kept his place, still shooting at the spot of jungle where he guessed the gunport was, until the order was passed to withdraw.

The machine guns swept the brush just higher than a man lying flat. The trapped Marines rolled down the bank or pushed backward on their bellies until they could tumble into the creek. The screening bush was their only protection against the snipers perched in trees. As they rolled into the stream, they hunkered down as low as they could in the water. Some got down so only their faces showed above the water. All of them pressed against the Japanese bank as bullets slashed through the undergrowth above them, splattering the creek and the American bank beyond.

Two of the Marines had fallen on a big log lying in the creek. One of them was hit in the leg and couldn't move, but he was near enough for Sergeant Wills to pull him into the creek. Other Marines dragged him up against the brush-choked bank; but they couldn't reach the other boy on the log. He lay too far out in the field of fire. He'd caught a full machine-gun burst. He must have had twenty holes in him, but he was still alive. He was hung over the log, partly in the water. He was calling weakly, "Here I am, Wills . . . over here . . ."

They couldn't help him. They could only listen to him.

"Wills . . . I'm here . . . Wills . . ."

There were other wounded in the creek above them. They couldn't help them either. Most of those crouching in the bushes against the bank were wounded, too. The kid on the log was getting weaker. Just listening was harder than anything Sergeant Wills ever had to take.

"He was calling me, and I couldn't help him. All of them were guys we knew, but we couldn't do a thing. We had to lay in the water and listen to them. It was the coldest damn water I ever saw. Their blood kept flowing into our faces."

Their only chance was to creep downstream close against the bank and then make a dash, one by one, for the American shore. A little way down the twisting stream there was a spot where a man would have a chance to make it. Most places, he would have to stop to climb the bank. Only a man who wanted to commit suicide would try that.

It was slow work for the men in the creek, crawling downstream in the racing water, hampered by the thick tangles of vines and brush. Men caught in the vines struggled helplessly.

"Everybody had to cut everybody else loose as we went along," says Private First Class Luther J. Raschke, of Harvard, Illinois.

He found young Tommy Harvard tangled in the vines and cut him loose. "I tried to help him along, but he wouldn't come. He'd been hit three times. A slug had smashed his shoulder. He was losing

· 43 ·

blood pretty fast. But he wouldn't leave. He was trying to see that everybody got out first. He told me, 'Go on, go on!' He wouldn't let anybody stop for him. He said, 'Keep the line moving!' He made us leave him there."

They made their dash; got safely out and reached the line of foxholes to which the battalion had fallen back again after that second day.

But Raschke couldn't forget the wounded officer they'd left in the creek. He said, "I guess everybody else is out."

"Yeah," said Corporal Alexander Caldwell, of Nashville, Tennessee.

"Well . . ."

"Yeah," said Corporal Caldwell.

So they got permission to go back into no man's land to hunt for their platoon leader. Corporal Caldwell took along two more volunteers, for they might have to carry Lieutenant Atkins, if they found him, and they might have to fight their way out. They were Louis J. Sievers, of Johnstown, Pennsylvania, and Joseph V. Brown, of Middletown, New York, both privates first class.

It was getting hard to see when they crawled down to the creek. Raschke stopped. They lay listening, but they could hear nothing except the rushing stream and, now and then, the sound of the Japanese talking. They had to make their choice then. They could go back without the lieutenant. Or they could risk calling. Nobody would blame them if they went back. Nobody would know they hadn't done everything they could do to find him.

Raschke lay on the edge of the stream and he remembers clearer than anything else how close the water was under his nose. The others were in the bush, rifles ready to fire if the enemy discovered him. Not that it would do any good. He'd be dead. For that matter, if the machine guns opened up, they'd all be dead.

"I was scared stiff," Raschke says. "I called as softly as I could, 'Tommy Harvard . . . Tommy Harvard . . .'

"A voice said, 'I'm down here.'

"It sounded weak, but we figured it might be a trap. So I said, 'What's your real name?'"

"The voice said, 'Elisha Atkins.' So we knew it was him. We crawled down and pulled him out. He said, 'God! Am I glad to see you!'"

He was shaking from hours in the chill water, weak from loss of blood, but still calmly Harvard as they carried him to the rear.

During the two days the 3rd Battalion had been fighting vainly to win the crossing of Suicide Creek, the outfit on its left had been trying as stubbornly and as vainly to get across its segment of the stream.

During those two days, Marine Pioneers were toiling to build a corduroy road through the swamp in their rear so that tanks could be moved up to the line. The tanks finally reached the outfit on the 3rd Battalion's left, but they found the banks of the creek too steep for crossing. The gully formed a natural tank trap. So a Marine bull-dozer was called to cut down the banks of the creek and make a fill in the stream so that the tanks could cross against the enemy.

The Japanese saw their danger. They concentrated fire on the bull-dozer. Man after man was shot from the driver's seat—some killed, some wounded. But there was always a Marine to jump in the seat. He had no shield, no protection at all. He sat up in the open like a shooting-gallery target for all the enemy's fire. But the Marine bull-dozer kept on till the fill was made and the tanks were rolling across the creek.

The advance of the tanks made the positions of the enemy opposing the 3rd Battalion untenable. If they tried to hold against the frontal attack of the 3rd Battalion, they would be hit by tanks and infantry from the flank. They'd be a nut in a nutcracker. They had to retreat or be crushed, and they retreated. The crossing of Suicide Creek had been won.

Technical Sergeant Asa C. Bordages

Guadalcanal Encampment

How impatient the grass! The jungle peers through palms,
Awaits the chance to strike our tents with vines,
To cover our roads and paths with mazy roots
And leaves: fantastic systems to lift more wet
Into the soggy air. Like Noah's doves,
Her oily lizards scout, return, but bring
No sign of relief. Meanwhile the grasses thrust
At our rising heels. In the circling hills the clouds
Sulk, conspire with the jungle at bay and the sun
To burn away our vertical orderliness
And our horizontal sterility. Perforce,
Despite all threats, we stay. But when we go,
Try, with your bush, forever to wipe out our traces
Before we forget, forever, there were such places.

Major Raymond Henri

Green Troops on a Blue Beach

Hitting the combat beach was not exactly a new experience to the Marine outfit with which I landed on Saipan. But most of our seasoning had come in a landing that was almost unopposed and, this time, facing the largest body of Jap soldiers Marines had yet encountered was hardly calculated to ease our minds. Generally speaking, there is nothing that can ease the mind of a man in a landing barge except to put him on the beach, safe.

We boated at daybreak, transferring from our transports to an LSD —a formidable-looking ship, the stern of which lowered to decant a holdful of amphibious tractors. Down this ramp we plunged into a sea churlish with the wakes of deploying ships. Our "amtrac" was a command boat and had radio communication with the air observers who hovered over the shimmering white beach and the chalky hills of the island. A young major passed around sticks of chewing gum and warned us to make sure that our cartridge belts were unfastened, in case we were hit and had to swim for it. Our boat would go in with the second wave of the second battalion to land.

A pilot who had bombed Saipan the day before told me later that the soldiers on the island had gone into what appeared to be a sort of ceremonial fit when it became evident that we were going to invade, staging huge war dances, and in general carrying on like an Irish wake that had got out of hand. He said they appeared to relish the idea of the coming battle, which is more than I can say for ourselves. Our bombers tried to accommodate them by starting fires. They promptly danced around these when the planes began to leave.

We nosed out a hundred yards or so from the ship and rendezvoused, waiting for the waves to form. Ahead of us the control boat bobbed just seaward of the reef, bedecked with signal flags that would send us across the line of departure. Idling there, we had a grandstand seat for the show our warships were putting on as a curtain raiser to the landing. We watched the shells bite into the coral sand and shred the palm trees that lined the shore. After an hour the fire was lifted and dive bombers went in for the final strike. They wheeled in formation high over our heads, peeled off, and plummeted savagely down, dropping their bombs a few hundred feet from the ground. As they began their climb the explosions threw bursts of fire, rubble, and a talcum-fine dust into the air. In a few minutes the beach was obscured.

Ahead, the first assault wave—cannon-bearing amphibious tanks —lined up along the line of departure, like nervous horses jockeying for position. At H hour minus 30 the control vessel waved them across the line. They moved in toward the reef and became tiny specks riding deep in the water, their tracks leaving a wake like a stern-wheeler. At H minus 20 the planes stopped bombing and went into a strafing attack. They flew at treetop height and raked the beach, diving at a 45-degree angle from the seaward side and opening fire while still over the water. A friend of mine in one of the first waves told me later that this threw their boat into a dither, as the planes appeared to be firing on them. Empty shell casings were plopping into the water all around them and falling, red hot, into the boat.

Our radioman, his headphones clamped tightly over his ears and the receiver buttoned up inside his poncho, picked up an aerial observer circling jauntily in his small plane. The noise of the amtrac's motor made conversation practically impossible, so his message—that the first wave had landed on schedule—had to be shouted from ear to ear around the boat.

We readied into position. The flag on the control vessel went up and five minutes later the ensign, dressed in oilskins and balancing himself neatly on the deck, waved us over the line. The speed of the tractor plunged us deeper into the sea, cascading a steady spray of water on us; we were thoroughly soaked within five minutes.

Our plane observer had been in the invasion of the Marshalls, where we had overrun our initial objective within a few hours. Now he radioed: "This is not at all like the Marshalls. Not at all." The radioman shouted this into the ear of the Marine next to him, and he in turn passed it on. We looked at each other, and our glances formed a common pool of anxiety. I was conscious of a tightening in my stomach and I knew that if I had been alone I would have been afraid.

Half an hour was to elapse before we hit the beach. Some of the boys tried to read a little paper-bound Navy "expendable." One man was seasick and lowered himself to the deck and vomited.

We were halfway in when word was radioed to land on Blue Beach Two, instead of Blue Beach One, as originally planned. Fire on Blue One was too heavy. We changed our course and headed for Blue Two, about a thousand yards south. In a few minutes our tractor grumbled up onto the reef, lurching tipsily as we crawled over it, giving us the feeling, for that moment, that we were very naked and exposed. We were squatting in the bottom of the tractor and a Marine near me stood up, out of curiosity, and looked over the gunwale. His eye caught a streak of flashing steel not more than three or four feet from his face, and he did a sudden flop on the deck. A moment later this apparition exploded in the water of our stern. He had had the rare, if somewhat unenviable, privilege of actually seeing a shell in transit.

Later, approaching the beach, a few more of us braved our heads over the side. Some of the amtracs had been hit and were flopped over like pancakes on a griddle. There was no small-arms fire in our sector. Except for the beachmaster waving the amtracs inland and a group of wounded awaiting transportation back to the ships, the beach was deserted. There certainly were no Japs. I think most of us would have felt better about it if there had been a few, preferably dead, just to reassure us that they had tried to stop us and hadn't succeeded. Our machine gunner, who had his weapon trained on trees that looked like good nesting places for snipers, turned to me and said, "It gives me the creeps. Like fighting a bunch of ghosts." It gave me the creeps, too, although I didn't tell him.

We advanced inland a few yards, detouring around the trees that had been blown down, and snaked single file along the road to Charon Kanoa. This was a village of white concrete one-story buildings, and ablaze with bougainvillaeas in bloom. For the sake of the record I should like to say that Japanese towns are not made of bamboo and paper—at least not the towns in the Marianas—and from what I could determine they were just a little less strongly put together than Parkchester, and their military fortifications are about as solid as the Croton Dam.

The town had been pretty well messed up by our naval gunfire, yet even the wreckage seemed tidy and intimate, the way the Japanese there had lived. Our tractor rolled down what had been the main street, and it was about all we could do to squeeze through. It obviously had not been constructed with an eye to accommodating amphibious tractors and from what we could discover later even the Japanese had lost their tempers when two trucks tried to pass. We went on to what should have been the town square, but was actually an American baseball diamond. A Buddhist temple stood across the street on one side and the town club was on the other.

Our unit was to pass through Charon Kanoa, mop up any resistance, and join the attack pressing toward the ridge about a mile inland. Before we had gone very far word came back that our forward elements were held up, and we debarked and began to advance on foot.

I remember looking up and seeing a pair of men's drawers impaled on the limb of a tree. There was no sign of its owner, however, or any other living Japanese, and for perhaps half an hour quiet and a caressing sun lay over the town like a soft blanket.

Then a shell crashed thunderously in the wooded area just ahead of us. Another came down. And another. There was no time to dig foxholes, so we flattened ourselves behind trees and in the shelter of buildings that were still standing. Two lieutenants had dived into a small shellhole and were arguing the possibility of the shells' being short rounds from our own warships. Then one crashed very close by. There was an emphatic silence, until one of the lieutenants settled the argument in his familiar Harvard accent. "Definitely hostile," he announced.

A scout and I backed across the road and got into a Japanese stand-up foxhole; together we deepened and widened it and in so doing came across a case of port wine and some papers that had been cached there. We drank a bottle of the wine, which was mild and sweet, and in a short time had passed the remainder out among the command post. We crouched in the foxhole for some time. The shells were falling closer, and more of our men were being hit. Yet there was no panic and very little real fear. Somehow you figured they would never get you. Anyway, the tension was lifted when somebody behind me stood up and said, "Aw, knock it off, Shorty." We laughed for the first time that morning.

At the same time we were sure that our sector had been picked out by the enemy as a special target and when my buddy and I were ordered back to the regimental CP we both felt a sense of relief. We were under the impression that it would be safer. Actually, shells were falling more thickly on that part of the beach than in the town.

A medical aid station next to the CP was overloaded with casualties, and some of us volunteered to dig foxholes for the wounded and help load them on the tractors going back to the ships. One man was brought in with his leg almost blown off between the hip and the knee; the doctor amputated it without removing him from the stretcher. The shell-shock cases began to come in, too—boys who had "cracked up" under very heavy fire at the front and had to be led or carried in. They hid behind trees and cowered at each new shell burst. Some could not remember their names.

We were loading the wounded into tractors later when a private first class stretcher case expressed the desire to relieve himself. A corpsman handed him the helmet of a near-by sergeant, who was also a casualty. The sergeant lay there and watched in horrified fascination as his helmet was subjected to its ultimate indignity. "That I should live to see the day," he groaned, "when a pfc should do that in my helmet."

The shelling went on all night and its pattern became almost predictable; the barrage would last for about fifteen minutes and then let up for half an hour as the batteries were switched to some other target area. These interludes were almost harder to bear than the periods of shelling, creating suspense rather than relief. We went about pretty much as though our lives were charmed, although it was clear from the casualties coming in that a lot of lives weren't. After a while we could estimate where the shells were going to land by the sound of their whistles, and we dived into our foxholes only when the interval between the scream overhead and the "whop!" of the explosion narrowed to a second or less.

Our beachhead was from 300 to 1,000 yards inland along a shore line of two miles. The Japs counterattacked at several points that night. One of these was a large-scale affair supported by tanks. A friend of mine who has seen a tank attack (the only Jap tanks I have ever seen have been going in the other direction, which is a different matter) tells me that even Japanese mechanized warfare retains all the medieval ritualism of the "Field of the Cloth of Gold." After all, the opportunities for chivalry are about as great in a tank as in a suit of armor. The commander in the lead tank unbuttons the turret, stands up, and flourishes his saber over his head. He generally has to stand on tiptoe to be seen. He is answered by a similar flourish from each of his tank drivers, who conclude the gesture with a resounding slap of their sabers across the side of the tank. This, I would say, is a good illustration of the Japanese faith in ritual, as their tanks are admittedly not so good as ours, even when they have been spurred on with a saber.

After what is probably the nearest thing to a ceremonial dance that a tank can participate in, the sabers are then tucked away and the turrets buttoned up. By this time our scouts have usually got the idea that something is about to come off.

I do not know if they went through this rigmarole that night, but it is not unlikely, for they became confused and about half of them went down the wrong road, their drivers giddy, perhaps, from too much warming up. Our antitank guns began picking them off and when the battle was over we had knocked out twenty-eight of them—which was just about all they had. The sabers were considered a prize find.

Day broke over a landscape that reeked of rotting vegetation and gunpowder. Stories began to filter back to the CP from our front lines. There were plenty of heroes, all right, but most of the heroism came from just hanging on. No one had charged a pillbox, or picked up a machine gun to run headlong at the enemy. The American fighting man is much more businesslike, and finds it easier to kill Japs by waiting for them to come to him. A machine gun at night has an attraction for the Jap soldier that is seldom felt by our own boys, and it was not unusual, in the weeks that followed, to find from twenty-five to fifty Japs stacked up on the field of fire of one of our guns. We were told that it was part of their bushido code, and that they had died happy. I hope so, because the machine gunners I knew had not been very happy killing them.

I saw our colonel early that morning, and he told me that we had lost nearly half our men. Then I went back to Charon Kanoa to join my landing team. A few minutes after I arrived, one of our boys looked up and saw a Japanese artillery observer slung in a hammock in a tall tree. He had a transmitter and had been radioing our position to his batteries. A BAR man shot him. "What the hell," he said, "he would have committed hara-kiri if we'd tried to capture him." At the time, we were too indifferent, and tired, to cut him down.

Then someone told me that we had cracked the Jap password, which was "seven lives for the emperor," and meant, in Japanese at least, that each son of Nippon had pledged himself to kill seven of the enemy. As a password, it might come in handy, if you spoke Japanese. I didn't, but I was grateful to know what the odds were on the Jap side of the lines. I made up my mind right there that I wasn't going to be one of the seven, for the emperor, Roosevelt, or anybody else—not if I could help it.

Master Technical Sergeant David Dempsey

After the Battle

The first night after "peace" came to Saipan, we figured it was all over. We didn't even bother to dig in for the night. Sleeping on top was our way of celebrating, although Captain Arthur B. Hanson, an attorney from Bethesda, Maryland, made sure he selected a spot where he said we had a natural defilade.

Even the artillery was silent and, somehow, we missed the whistle of our own shells over our heads and the roar of their exploding in enemy lines. There were still several thousand Japs in what we called "up there," only a mile away, but there was no Jap territory in which we could drop shells. Even the artillery boys were sleeping. Someone complained it was "too damned quiet," but we went to sleep in spite of it.

It was midnight when we were awakened by machine-gun fire. It was Jap, and it was close. We sat up and reached for our rifles. The battle was over, but you couldn't take chances. Our boys were shooting back, and the machine gun went silent.

We waited for the report. It came from a Marine gunnery sergeant along the road. Eight Japs had come down the pike walking upright, bold as brass, machine-gunning as they came. They'd got two of our men before we polished them off. The "gunny" had the light Nambu and there were five dead Japs in the ditch to back up his story. The gunny was plenty sore. But he'd figured they were Marines, and hadn't wanted to open fire till they shot at him. He wondered how many they'd got up the line.

"Hell," we said, "don't they know the battle's over?"

We went back to sleep. We slept until 3 a.m., and Captain Hanson, who always says he's a damned good Washington lawyer but not much of anything else, spotted them first. There were fifteen of them coming over the top of a hill fifty yards away. He challenged, and they hit the deck. We didn't want to be shooting harmless natives, who sometimes wait until dark to surrender, so we put the first burst over their heads. An interpreter began yelling at them, and two of them got up and ran. The interpreter got rifle fire for an answer.

So we opened up with machine guns and canister. The din was terrific, and some of the boys complained they were being cheated out of their first night's sleep in weeks. But when Japs came around looking for trouble, you had to accommodate them. We fired intermittently until dawn, and it was one helluva barrage.

About 5 a.m. we went up on the hill. We counted nine dead Nips, all special troops, who didn't know they'd lost the battle of Saipan. They were armed for bear. All of them carried potato-masher grenades, and enough ammunition to hold off an army. The canister blew their heads off. They were certainly a messy sight.

Down the hill, at six hundred yards, came five badly scared natives, waving the surrender pamphlets we'd dropped the day before. We held our fire, and they came in gratefully to give themselves up.

A minute later, someone opened fire again. A Jap dropped from a tree five hundred yards away. Damned good shooting it was. We found another dead Jap in a cane patch across the road. The outposts got him while we were getting the boys on the hill.

Up and down the road, we counted more than two hundred dead Japs. They hadn't known the battle was over, either, I guess. They tell me we killed more than eleven hundred of them the next day, inside our own lines.

Francis Pierce, of Earlville, Iowa, figured the battle was over, too, and then he spent the night up on Marpi Point. He told me the next morning he wasn't so sure. The Japs had made it hot as hell **for the** boys up there; they'd killed his chief. Pierce was one of six naval hospital corpsmen to start down the cliff after two wounded Marines. He was one of two to come back. And this happened, too, after the battle was over.

The battle might have been over, but we could still count off Marines who died after the flag was raised. Captain Dick Mirrick told me about the death of a Marine captain who'd been just loafing around on a grassy knoll. Eight Japs came up over the rise in squad formation. They hadn't heard, we guess.

And the day after the battle, I met a Jap who definitely wasn't ready to take our word for it. I'd gone up to meet Lieutenant General Saito, who had commanded Jap forces on Saipan. General Saito was as dead as you could ask; he'd blown off the top of his own head with a hand grenade. But down in the ravine we met one of his boys. This character we called Hara-kiri Joe, for obvious reasons. Joe had a hand grenade, and he didn't want us to come too close. He kept asking why we didn't shoot him, and we kept telling him we didn't want to shoot. So Joe started trying to hang himself, all the time keeping us at a distance with a hand grenade, but every time some Marine would cut him down. Joe got tired of that, so the third time he hanged himself he also stuck a rusty scythe in his stomach. We had to carry Joe down the hill to an aid station, but I hear he had his own way. He died that night.

I looked at General Saito, and I thought about the German generals at Cherbourg, who got a nice Channel trip to England, and even free haircuts. I figured Saito could have taken lessons from them. They *knew* when the battle was over.

You can't figure these Japanese. After the battle had been over for three whole days, we were killing almost as many of them a day as we did when we started. Whole areas were still mighty full of them, and we didn't dare wander about too much. I know four Marines who went swimming and wound up by killing fifteen Japs hidden in a cave. The Japs interrupted the swimming party with a shower of grenades. Not much fun in that.

But still, they said the battle was over. We wouldn't know about that. We were only wishing we could get word to the Japs.

First Lieutenant Jim G. Lucas

Routine Mission

The mission was routine. To take an artillery radioman to the battalion at the front and return with the man relieved. It happened every day, rain or shine. A radioman moved with the advance to keep the supporting artillery notified.

Private First Class James C. Kearns, a 23-year-old stocky Marine from Wilkinsburg, Pennsylvania, was the observer going forward. A former schoolteacher, he had hardened into his front-line job during two years of Pacific campaigning. Like the man he was going to relieve, he would spend several days at the front, moving with and ahead of the advance, as liaison between the first lines and the big guns in the rear.

The communiques said coldly that the enemy was retreating. Since the Jap's last vain counterattack in the hills above the Guam beachhead, he had moved back, leaving behind only snipers, stragglers, and harassing units. Tanks and infantrymen of Major General Allen Hal Turnage's Third Marine Division were beating their way after him, plunging through thick underbrush and across red dirt fields. The lines were strung straight across the island, with the Americans shoving the Japanese inevitably into a trap set for them in the island's northern hills.

It was quiet when Private First Class Kearns's jeep set off for the lines. Sporting a new pair of dungarees, he leaned cheerfully on his carbine in the back seat. It was the third time he had set off on such a trip since the campaign began.

The driver, Corporal Wright S. Coulson, of Detroit, Michigan, was bleary-eyed. The big guns had moved forward during the night, and he had had little sleep. He guided the jeep over a bumpy, dusty road and onto an airstrip.

They rolled past a new camp setting up; Marines standing in the open, drinking coffee; a circle of white gauze with a rough sign reading "Nine."

At the far edge of the strip, they paused beside a wrecked Jap plane. Marines were climbing over it, cutting off strips of aluminum for watchbands.

"Where's the front?" Coulson yelled.

A Marine looked up and waved at a fringe of trees. "Way the hell up."

Coulson headed for the trees and came on members of a 37-millimeter gun crew squatting by their gun. They were stirring abandoned Jap powdered milk in their canteen cups.

"I'm looking for the First Battalion command post," Coulson said.

A platoon sergeant stood up and pointed out a new road cut directly into the wall of trees. "They're down that road," he said, "but I don't know how far. I heard they've been moving up all morning."

The jeep started down the new road barely wide enough for it. Dense walls of bamboo, banana, and coconut trees hemmed it in. A lone rifleman was leaning against a fallen log. The jeep pulled up beside him.

"Where's the war?" Kearns called. His laughing voice was like an explosion in the stillness.

The rifleman shrugged. "Might be snipers along this road. Engineers just pushed it through with a bulldozer this morning. They got two Nips trying to interfere. You'll find their bodies up ahead."

"Where's the front?"

"This was it two hours ago. I don't know where it is now."

Again the jeep moved forward. The driver strained for the sound of firing. The air was deathly still. They passed the two dead Japs—twisted ivory-colored bodies lying against the side of the road like wax models. One had a hole in his face. The blood was dry.

The road ran for more than a mile. Near its end, signs of life appeared abruptly. A mortar crew was bivouacked around fresh foxholes in the brush at the road's edge. A bulldozer was noisily flattening out a hump. Finally, the road burst into a clearing. Several hundred dirt-stained Marines were spread over a field, digging shallow foxholes and spreading camouflaged shelter halves.

"First Battalion?" Coulson yelled.

"Five hundred yards up." A Marine waved wearily. "This is the Second."

The driver turned to Kearns. "The Nips are really running," he said.

He bounced up on a hard surface road at right angles to the dirt path over which he had just driven. They were in a valley now. The road ran straight along the depression. Narrow-gauge railway tracks paralleled it on each side. They came on a column of tanks standing along the side of the road. The crews were sprawled on the road, eating C rations.

A man in a crash helmet held up his hand and walked up to the jeep. "Wouldn't go up there."

"Why not?"

"The front's only a hundred and fifty yards ahead." He pointed to where the road twisted into a grove of coconut trees.

"That's where we're trying to go," Coulson explained.

The tankman shook his head anxiously. "They're having some kind of fight up there. It's not healthy."

A jeep suddenly tore down the road toward them and came to a halt. An artillery officer, his face ashen-white, jumped out and ran over to Private Kearns.

"Where are you going?" he asked.

The radioman explained.

The officer shook his head. "First Battalion's up there, all right. But it's pinned down. They ran into a road block. Snipers all around. Looks as if we're a day or two early."

A truckful of artillery surveyors bounced into view and came to a halt behind the officer's jeep.

"We came up to survey," the officer said. He smiled. "No sense out being up there now. Be careful." He went back to his jeep and drove off, the survey truck bouncing after him.

Corporal Coulson and Private First Class Kearns paused uncertainly. They saw a Stinson artillery spotting plane put-put suddenly over a ridge and swoop low above the coconut grove. Straining their ears, they heard the distant cracks of rifles. Two jeeps pulling trailers came up behind and passed them. The trailers were filled with new shoes and dungarees.

"Come on," Kearns said. "If they can go through, so can we."

They huddled low in the jeep and swung out past the tanks. Coulson got up speed, and the jeep bounced crazily across the open valley, heading for the coconut grove.

Suddenly, from the right, a machine gun chattered. The cracks were short and high-pitched. The jeep skidded to a halt. Both men hurtled over the left side. They sat a moment, trying to peer around the jeep and through the brush. Coulson leaned on the fender and lit a cigarette. He watched Kearns squinting toward the field.

"Small-time stuff," the radioman grunted. "The son of a gun won't show himself."

The shooting stopped, and they relaxed.

After a moment, Kearns said casually, "I'm reading a good book about Borneo."

The corporal ignored the remark. A crash sounded in the grove ahead. Then another.

"Mortars," the corporal said.

A jeep, loaded with almost a dozen dust-coated wiremen, careened dizzily toward them from the front. The passengers were crammed against and on top of each other. The machine gun opened up again. The men grinned nervously as they passed. A jeep ambulance followed with two stretcher cases in the back and a man sitting beside them. He had a bloody bandage on his head. He looked back at the road, gritting his teeth and hanging onto the rear railing.

After a moment, Coulson ground out his cigarette. He motioned to the radioman and the two men leaped into the jeep and started off again. The machine gun opened up immediately. They kept low, and the next instant raced into the protection of the coconut grove.

Ahead, a group of Marines on the road stopped them. The grass beneath the trees on both sides was covered with fresh Jap corpses.

The men were breathing heavily. They ignored the sporadic sound of shots fifty yards ahead.

"Ran into two lines of spider pits," explained Corporal Orville G. Einsidel, of Milwaukee, an assistant cook acting as a runner. "The first line let some of us through, then both lines opened fire on us. We hit the deck all around in here. The tanks came up and helped us. Got more than a hundred Japs already."

The jeep moved among the Marines and inched ahead. Tanks were parked on the road and in the grass. A green frame house on stilts stood in the brush at the left. Hospital corpsmen had set up a front-line dressing station before it. The tall grass was matted down by men on stretchers. Several men were clustered around the trailers filled with new shoes and clothing.

Coulson stopped the jeep, and the two men got out.

"I better put on my helmet," Kearns said suddenly. "They might say I was out of uniform." He took off the little green-visored Raider cap he had worn all the way up to the front, and put on his steel helmet.

Keeping low in the tall grass and weeds, they moved up to a group of Marines lying along a fringe of bamboo. Some of them had already scooped out shallow foxholes. They were peering ahead, watching for movements in the brush.

Several officers sat near a radioman in a hollow. This was the battalion command post. Private First Class Kearns reported in, and a runner was sent out to get the man who was being relieved. After several moments, a half dozen Marines hunched down and shoved forward through the bamboo. Fifty yards ahead, three tanks were moving around, like elephants, searching through the high grass and about the bases of breadfruit trees.

The corporal and the radioman crawled up to watch. The fringe of bamboo was lined by a row of spider pits, each filled with newly killed Japs. In one pit, two men huddled together, their heads pressed down against their knees. A grenade had ripped open the backs of both their necks.

A tankman came up to have a look. He leaned over and picked up a brown bottle, half full of liquid. He pulled out a twig stopper and sniffed it. "Gasoline," he said. "A Molotov cocktail." Similar bottles lay alongside each pit. None had been used.

A Marine sniper, Corporal John C. Evanich, of Youngstown, Ohio, kicked through the grass and came on the leg of a Japanese. It looked like a bloody hambone.

"That's part of the guy who blew himself up," he said. "The nut just stood up, took off his helmet, put a grenade on his head, put his helmet back on, and exploded. What people!"

Mortars burst suddenly on the right. The Marines hit the deck again. Two men lay on their backs, talking in a low voice. They were a single color, clay-red, from helmet to shoes. They saw Corporal Coulson.

"Witek just got it," they said. They meant Private First Class Francis P. Witek, of Chicago, a BAR man. "But he took thirteen Nips with him. Just stood up and sprayed them. Funny thing. He woke up this morning and said this was his day."

A shot rang out near by. A Marine ten yards away fell to his knees and slowly rolled on his face. Two men rose and, standing erect, pumped bullets at the source of the shot. Several others lifted the wounded Marine, and rushed him back to the aid station.

A man with a portable radio on his back tramped through the grass and greeted Kearns. He was grimy with dirt and had five days' beard coated with red dust. He took off the radio and helped Kearns put it on.

"Let's go," he said to Corporal Coulson.

A rifleman who had followed the relieved man waited for the new forward observer. Private First Class Kearns picked up his carbine and, motioning to the rifleman, started off. Those Marines in the clearing rose slowly, adjusted their gear, and headed for the road. The battalion CP was going forward again.

Corporal Coulson turned the jeep around and started back. The other man lit a cigarette.

"You were a little late," he said.

Master Technical Sergeant Alvin M. Josephy, Jr.

Chow

When lunchtime arrived on the front lines on Guam, a Marine automatic rifleman, picking off Japs caught in a pocket, mixed business with pleasure.

With precise rhythm, he fired, rolled over, took a mouthful of rations, rolled back, fired, rolled again to the food, ate, and so on, until simultaneously both rations and Japs gave out.

Master Technical Sergeant Alvin M. Josephy, Jr.

They Lived Through Hell

Shortly after 3 a.m. on the morning of July 26, 1944, an orange signal flare shot up from the Japanese lines. A singsong voice shouted into the night, and an avalanche of screaming forms bounded suddenly into view. With their bayonets gleaming in the light of sudden flares, they charged toward the Marine foxholes, throwing grenades and howling "Ban-zai-ai" like a pack of animals. That was the beginning of what was to become a frenzied, all-out Japanese Banzai charge, designed to hurl the Third Marine Division off the island of Guam and back into the sea.

The Marines had had no reason to expect that particular night to be any different from the preceding ones. During the four nights they had been on the island, the Japs had sent out a number of small patrols and harassed them with occasional grenades and mortars, but these had all been local skirmishes.

Meanwhile, the Japanese must have discovered that the Marines were spread thin. Five days of savage fighting in the hills above the beachhead had resulted in many casualties for the Third Division. The 21st Regiment, in the center of the line and under the command of Colonel Arthur H. Butler, of El Paso, Texas, had been particularly hard hit. That night of July 25, there were no more than 250 men manning the 1st Battalion's position in the center of the line—a position that ran for more than two thousand yards, a frontage normally requiring about 600 men. In the center of the battalion was Company B, under the command of Captain Donald M. Beck, which was down to approximately seventy-five men out of an original landing strength of two hundred and seventeen.

The Japs, from their high hill on the left, had no doubt seen the empty foxholes on the crest of the ridge that the Marines occupied, and noticed that the small groups of men were almost like isolated islands of resistance. There were plenty of holes through which the Japs could filter, even if the individual islands could not be overcome and blotted out. Moreover, a wide gap existed on the right flank of B Company, where a wooded gully separated it from C Company.

There had been some question in the minds of the Marines in the line that afternoon whether they themselves were going to attack again before darkness. However, they were not going to attack again without tanks, and there were no tanks yet on the ridge. Seabees had been pushing a road around the cliff for the tanks for several days, and it was not finished until five o'clock. When the tanks did appear, it was too late to begin an attack, and so the men were told to dig in again for the night. The tanks were drawn up in column in the draw, partially filling the serious gap between B and C companies.

As darkness approached, the men had eaten cold K ration and filled their canteens from five-gallon cans that had been lugged to the top of the ridge earlier in the evening. Private First Class Arnaldo Martinez, a thin, black-eyed youth from Los Angeles, had climbed into his foxhole with Sergeant Gordon Garner and Private First Class Grady C. Wimmer. A little to the right, past some empty foxholes and covering dead space for a pair of heavy machine guns, were Corporal John Dopp and Private First Class Edward G. ("Moose") Killian, who had once been captain of his high-school football team back in Rossford, Ohio. Both men were armed with Browning automatic rifles.

In a foxhole all alone on the left of the B Company line was Sergeant Werner H. Eubanks of Jacksonville, North Carolina, a 31-year-old acting machine-gun section leader. Eubanks was a tough old NCO who had first enlisted in the Corps in 1936 and had seen prewar duty in China, the Philippines, and the Caribbean. He was in charge of two light and two heavy machine guns in the line that night. The two heavies were a little ahead and on either side of his foxhole. The gun on the left was manned by four PFCs—Howard H. Kemp, Philip Toci, Joe A. Barcovic, and Steve K. Simon. Simon had been wounded and wore a bandage around his head. On the right-hand gun were Corporal Carroll A. Herzberg and Private First Class Edward R. Krejci.

Eubanks stayed awake all night, keeping an eye on the guns. Over to the right, Moose Killian fell asleep early. Corporal Dopp stood over him, peering out as the purple twilight deepened into moonless night. In the three-man foxhole, Sergeant Garner's team took turns on watch. Martinez drew an early morning relief and curled up on the red dirt floor of the foxhole until his turn came.

The hours went by, and it began alternately to drizzle and pour. The Marines tucked ponchos around themselves and squirmed sleepily into the mud. Toward midnight Eubanks noticed that the Japs were throwing grenades. On both sides of him, the Marines on watch were hurling other grenades back into the night. Many of them burst five and ten feet above the ground, and Eubanks listened to their fragments raining on the wet dirt.

The Japanese were no more than twenty yards in front of the Marine positions, along a road that ran parallel to the American front line. The road was protected from Marine fire by a high dirt embankment, and behind it the Japs had set up their mortars. Several times Eubanks thought he noticed noises on the road and in the patches of grass that lay between the road and the Marine foxholes. Each time, he called back for a concentration of American mortars. The mortars quieted the Japs for brief spells, but soon after each barrage he could again hear the grass being worked.

He was beginning to doze when the fierce Jap grenade and mortar barrage began soon after three o'clock. He heard the long drawn-out "Ban-zai-ai," and at the same instant noticed that his machine-gun crews were opening fire. In front of his eyes, Japs were jumping to their feet, yelling and shouting, and then falling again, as the Marine machine guns stitched their bodies with flaming bullets.

All along the line the enemy attack was on. Red tracers flashed through the blackness. Japanese orange signal flares and American white illumination shells lit up the night, silhouetting the running forms of the enemy. On the right and the left, the attack was stopped cold. As fast as the Japs came, they were mowed down. Their assault gradually focused on the draw, but here too they found fiery death. The parked tanks went into action, firing their 75s point-blank at the charging masses. At first the Japs attacked the tanks, firing rifles at the metal sides and then clambering up and over them in a vain attempt to get at the crews inside. They cursed and screamed and pounded drunkenly on the turrets, but failed to damage a single tank. Finally, like a stream, many of them flowed past the tanks, down the draw toward the beach.

The rest, cringing before the tank fire, moved to the left, hoping to break through the Marine lines and get to the draw farther down the ridge, behind the tanks. The front they now charged was that of B Company. Here, against 75 men, the full force of the Japanese attack suddenly broke.

In their three-man foxhole, Martinez, Garner, and Wimmer had maintained steady fire directly ahead, successfully diverting the first rush of Japs to other sections of the line. During a pause in the fighting, Sergeant Garner left the hole to go back for more hand grenades. Martinez and Wimmer were left alone. Around them they saw some of the other Marines withdrawing, sliding down the ridge to a secondary line of foxholes about ten yards to the rear. Here and there, in the light of the flares, they could see them pulling back wounded men.

Wondering whether to withdraw themselves, Martinez and Wimmer were confronted suddenly by the first wave of Japs from the area of the tanks. With bayonets fixed, the enemy came more slowly, throwing grenades and then falling to the ground to wait for the bursts. The first grenades exploded around the Marines without harming them. Then one shattered Wimmer's rifle, and the two men decided it was time to withdraw.

As they jumped out of their foxhole and ran and slid down the reverse slope of the ridge, they saw a group of screaming figures pour over the crest farther to the right and run headlong down the slope. This was the first indication that the Japanese had broken through. It would no longer be possible to tell friend from foe.

Martinez and Wimmer reached their platoon CP, which was nothing more than an old shellhole ten yards from the top of the ridge, inhabited by Second Lieutenant Edward W. Mulcahy, son of a Malden, Massachusetts, letter carrier. Mulcahy that night was commanding all that was left of two of B Company's platoons. When the two Marines reached him, he was trying desperately to make his field telephone work, but the wires to the rear had already been cut by mortar fire.

Wimmer slid into the hole beside the lieutenant, and Martinez lay on the forward lip of earth as protection with his rifle. The night was hideous with explosions, lights, screaming Japs, and running silhouettes. The lieutenant asked Wimmer what was happening on top of the ridge. Wimmer told him that most of the men left above were wounded.

The three men prepared to fight to the end where they were. Any moment, a wave of Japs might sweep down on them, and all they had were Martinez's rifle, the lieutenant's carbine, and a .45 automatic which Wimmer had been carrying in addition to his rifle.

They did not have to wait long for trouble. Against the sky line a handful of Japs suddenly appeared. Martinez fired, and they backed out of sight. A moment later, a string of hand grenades rolled down toward them. Most of them bounced harmlessly by to explode behind them. But one blew up directly in front of Wimmer's face. Fragments shattered Lieutenant Mulcahy's carbine and struck him on the left side of the head and body. He felt as if he had been slammed by a two-by-four plank. When he regained his breath, he saw Wimmer handing him the pistol.

"You take it, lieutenant," Wimmer said quietly.

The lieutenant protested.

Wimmer smiled. "That's all right, sir," he explained. "I can't see any more."

The lieutenant tried to bandage Wimmer's face. The noise from the top of the ridge showed that there were still Marines up there, fighting back. It gave the three men hope. The lieutenant began to shout in the night, like a football coach, "Hold that line, men! You can do it!" His voice became almost pleading. "Hold them. Hold them!"

But the Marine line on the crest had by now disintegrated into a few knots of men fighting together with the fury of human beings trying not to be killed. Killian and Dopp, still in their foxhole, were one such island of struggle. In front of their hole dead Japanese were already piled in silent layers. Steady fire and a continuous hurling of grenades had so far kept the enemy from overrunning their position.

Farther to the left, Eubanks's machine gunners were having trouble. A Jap grenade hit the left gun, temporarily putting it out of action. Kemp and the other members of the crew fixed it quickly and started firing again. A second grenade hit its jacket and exploded, knocking off the cover and putting it completely out of the fight. The same blast wounded Steve Simon. His old wound opened, and the bandage around his head began to drip blood.

His three companions moved him to a foxhole ten yards behind the shattered gun. Phil Toci jumped in beside him, and Kemp and Barcovic ran back to the machine-gun foxholes with their carbines. Heaving grenades like wild men, they managed to stall any Jap frontal charge for the moment. Soon, however, their supply of grenades ran low, and Eubanks decided to go down the ridge for more. He made the trip safely, but when he returned with a box of new grenades, he found Toci and Simon gone. The two men had decided to try to withdraw to an aid station down the ridge. On the way down, Toci was killed. Simon was later found in a clump of high grass on the hill and saved.

Eubanks was no sooner back in his foxhole than the Japs started coming over again. The new grenades temporarily held them off. Dividing the contents of the box between Kemp and Barcovic, Eubanks slid down the ridge a second time to tell the mortars to keep throwing flares over the top of the crest. The lights made better targets of the Japs.

While he was gone, hell broke loose around the right-hand machine gun. Killian and Dopp who were near by heard a sudden unearthly screaming from the gun position. By the light of the flares, they saw Corporal Herzberg leaning over Krejci trying to pull a Japanese bayonet out of his body. The same instant a wave of Japs appeared from nowhere and swept over Herzberg and the wounded man. Killian saw a Jap plunge his bayonet through Herzberg's back, then fall over him, as though in a struggle. At the same moment a mass of Japs came toward Killian. He emptied his automatic rifle in their faces, and they turned and ran.

Changing his ammunition magazine quickly, the Marine looked up again just in time to see a single Jap slithering toward him with a saber raised slightly in the air. Killian backed up, and the Jap slashed at him, hitting the barrel of the Marine's BAR and glancing off his arm. The force of his own blow twisted the Jap off balance, and he slid into the foxhole on his face as Killian let go a burst at him. The wounded Jap, bleeding from the head, pushed himself up and took another savage swipe at the Marine, nicking him above the right eye. Half-blinded, Killian threw his leg over the Jap's shoulder and pounded the stock of his BAR into his head. Dopp, who had been busy with Japs in the other direction, turned suddenly and, seeing what was happening, drove his bayonet into the intruder's body. It was still not enough to kill him. The wounded man sprang to his feet and with a wild yell plunged down the ridge in the direction of the beach. Lieutenant Mulcahy saw him coming and finally finished him with a shot from Wimmer's pistol.

Killian was still in trouble. As the Jap left, another group of enemy charged out of the darkness. Killian's BAR worked again, as he mowed them down. Dopp's automatic rifle jammed at this point, and he had to substitute a pistol. The Japs turned away and headed in another direction. Three of them stopped at Herzberg's silent machine gun. They tried to turn it around to fire at Killian. One of them pulled the trigger, and the bullets sprayed a group of Japs racing across the top of the ridge. Finally, the Japs tried to lift the entire gun and turn it, tripod and all. Killian blasted them with his BAR again, and the Japs dropped the gun. Two of them fell over the bodies of the Marine crew. The third pulled out a grenade and, holding it to his head, blew himself up.

During the comparative quiet that followed, Eubanks crawled back to his old position. He noticed that Herzberg's gun was silent and tried to wriggle toward it to find out what was wrong. A band of Japs, appearing suddenly from behind the gun, stopped him, and he ducked back into his hole. He could see several of the Japs stop and, as the others had done earlier, try to swing around the heavy weapon. Out of the darkness a lone, drunken Jap raced headlong at them, tripped over a body several feet away, and flew through the air. There was a blinding flash as he literally blew apart. He had been a human bomb, carrying a land mine and a blast charge on his waist. The explosion knocked out the Japs who had been trying to turn the gun, and Eubanks took advantage of the moment to withdraw.

Slightly to his left, he found that the remnants of B Company's third platoon had formed a new line on a tiny ridge that ran farther into A Company's lines. He and Kemp and Barcovic joined this line and remained there during the rest of the night. Shortly before dawn, a mortar shell landed close to them, and Barcovic was killed.

At the time of Eubanks's withdrawal, Lieutenant Ed Mulcahy, who had been keeping up his pep yells to hold the line, noticed an ominous silence settling over the ridgetop. Making the blinded Wimmer as comfortable as possible, he decided to crawl up the hill and examine the situation.

It was a painful task, dragging himself up the slope. His left side throbbed from the grenade fragments that had hit him, and he had to edge along on his right shoulder and hip over clumps of sword grass and coral hunks. When he reached the top, the first thing he saw was Herzberg's machine gun. In the gray light of approaching dawn, he made out a chaotic mass of blood and bodies. Near by, beneath a dead Jap, lay Herzberg. The lieutenant felt his face and placed his ear next to his mouth. He heard no breath and assumed that the corporal was dead.

At the same time he heard a wild yell and saw more Japs beginning to rush. He withdrew quickly. On the way down the hill he thought he heard two weapons firing back at the advancing Japs. He doubted his ears. It was almost too much to expect that there could still be Marines left on the crest.

But there were. Moose Killian and Dopp were still at it, all alone now on that ridge of death. They managed to stop some of the Japs, but herds of enemy stampeded past them and rushed down the hill.

As Mulcahy slid into his old shellhole again, Martinez suggested that they withdraw and try to join some of the others. The lieutenant said he would remain a little longer instead. He was thinking of the men who might still be on the ridge. Also, he knew what it would mean if that entire sector were given up. There would be a breach big enough for the whole Japanese army to come through. It did not occur to him at the time that the situation almost existed already. Only he and a few others were filling the breach.

Once again, Japanese grenades began coming down, bursting mostly behind the three men. One hit a man lower down on the ridge. He began to yell for a corpsman. The three men in the shellhole lay for a few moments listening to him, unable to do anything to help him. The man's agonizing screams gave way to a delirious laugh. Then abruptly the lieutenant noticed that the fire on the ridge had ceased. Either the last Marines had been overcome or they were withdrawing. He turned to Martinez and suddenly saw that the rifleman had been hit. Grenade fragments had smashed into his back.

Martinez was still capable of moving about, however, and the lieutenant ordered him to take off and get medical help. He suggested that Martinez could possibly direct a corpsman up the ridge to care for Wimmer and the delirious man on the slope. Martinez nodded and silently crawled away. He had gone only a few feet in the darkness when he bumped into a form. There was an instant of spine-chilling silence. Then a voice said, "It's Moose."

Martinez hugged Killian with joy, then called up to the lieutenant.

That settled Mulcahy's mind. He decided to try to contact other men along the slope and set up some kind of new continuous line. Wimmer at first pleaded with Mulcahy to leave him behind and not tie himself down with a wounded man. But the lieutenant ordered the blinded Marine to hang onto his ankle and, with Martinez as a guide, began dragging him back where Killian was waiting. They paused there. Killian found a small shellhole and pulled Wimmer in beside him.

A few moments later, two other Marines and a Navy corpsman, Hospital Apprentice First Class John J. Maloney, slid in from another direction and joined them. They no sooner arrived than another wave of Japs appeared at the top of the hill. The Marines fired as fast as they could. Some of the enemy paused and charged off in other directions. The main body drove pell-mell down the ridge, flopping over themselves and screaming hysterically. As they rushed by, Sergeant Andrew C. Hansen, one of the new additions to the group, stood up to his full height and, waving his fist at the enemy, roared defiantly at them, calling them every name he could think of. Lieutenant Mulcahy later remarked that Hansen at that moment reminded him of Victor McLaglen.

Several Japs at the crest of the ridge spotted the little band and resorted to the old trick of rolling grenades down on them. One burst near Maloney. The corpsman fell back injured against one of the other men and began to cry out in panic. He begged the Marines not to let him fall into the hands of the Japs alive. After a moment his cries subsided, and he became quiet.

Mulcahy decided now to try to establish a new defensive position. He ordered the men to withdraw farther to a knob that commanded the top of the cliff lying behind them. From the top of the knob the slope and line along the cliff edge could be covered. At the same time Killian volunteered to try to take the wounded men toward the left where they could still hear Company A putting up a good fight. He knew where their CP was and could probably get the men evacuated to the rear from that spot. The lieutenant agreed, and Killian prepared to leave the group. He locked Wimmer's arms around his neck and, telling him to hang on, grasped Maloney by the elbow and set off.

Dragging the two men along the rough ground quickly tired him. He paused in a shellhole to rest. A Jap mortar barrage fell near by. As he started to move again, shell fragments struck him in the arm and leg. He took hold of the two men again and shoved off. Once more he had to rest. When he set out a third time, he could pull only one man. He left Wimmer behind. A few minutes later he heard a voice call, "Jap or Marine?" He answered quickly and discovered that he had run smack into the CP he had been heading for.

There was shooting going on all around the spot, however, and he had to wait a moment before returning for Wimmer. He had scarcely caught his breath when three Japs suddenly appeared, charging straight toward him. Half a dozen shots stopped them but a few feet away.

The trip back to get Wimmer seemed to take an eternity. Killian was now ill from all the tension and excitement. He had a blurry feeling of numbness, as though nothing mattered any more. When he reached Wimmer and started back with him, it was beginning to get light. The blackness of the terrible night was disappearing, and in the gray of dawn he could go on again.

On his return to the CP with Wimmer, he found Martinez waiting for him. Martinez had become lost trying to follow Lieutenant Mulcahy down the ridge. His back had felt as if heavy rocks were falling on it, and there was a terrible taste in his mouth. He had to stop and rest several times. Finally he had wandered into the A Company lines.

The two men greeted the dawn together with almost hysterical joy. But the terror was not yet over. By the first streaks of gray, they made out a hillside above them covered with twisted Jap bodies. Here and there wounded enemy in torn, stained clothes were trying to crawl back to the crest. The air was heavy with the smell of blood and alcohol, for the Japs had been sodden with sake. The Marines took pot shots at the crawling enemy as they tried to squirm past their dead companions. Then an American mortar barrage lit into the area, and black fountains of death finished off the remaining wounded.

About 6 a.m., three hours after the attack had begun, a last wave of Japs suddenly charged over the top of the hill. It was the wildest, most drunken group of all, bunched together howling, stumbling, and waving swords, bayonets, and even sticks. Some were already wounded and were swathed in gory bandages. The Marines yelled back at them and chopped them down in their mad rush. In a moment it was over. The last wave of the three-hour attack died to a man.

But daylight revealed in all its seriousness how successful the earlier charges had been. About two thousand Japs were behind the American front line. B Company had taken the worst impact of the night assault, but other units had been having similar experiences, and in at least one other place the enemy had streamed through in great numbers. Now their furious attack began to hit the rear units.

Prompt action saved a potentially serious situation. The Jap plan had counted on driving the Marine line straight back into the sea, first piercing it so that the remnants would have to withdraw, and then fanning out in the rear, disrupting communications and disorganizing the elements on the beach. The attacking enemy, never well organized and from the start under the influence of alcohol, disintegrated once it got through the Marine front lines until it became a hodgepodge of wandering bands and individuals without leadership, communication, or well-defined aims. These small groups became easy prey for the many Marine mopping-up parties. By noon, most of them had been wiped out.

Meanwhile, on the ridge, a calm settled over the scene of recent slaughter. Marines sat by their holes, puffing nervously on cigarettes, their hands still shaking from the tension. Some made hot coffee. Others poked warily among the piles of contorted enemy cadavers. Stretcher bearers worked silently with morphine and plasma and sent a stream of bandaged men limping down the ridge. In the draw on the right, a tank's engine cranked up. As it started forward, a land mine blew off its tread. It was the only damage the tanks suffered through the whole attack.

Killian, Martinez, Eubanks, and the other survivors of B Company cautiously returned to the top of the ridge. The sight around Herzberg's machine gun was sickening. A score of broken Jap bodies lay piled about the gun. Krejci, with a bayonet still sticking in him, was mangled almost beyond recognition. A tattered enemy corpse hung over Herzberg's form.

Killian pulled the body away and discovered that Herzberg miraculously was still breathing. Sometime during the night he had come to, enough to take some sulfa tablets and tie his belt around his leg as a tourniquet. At the time the Jap human bomb had exploded, his life had also been saved by the enemy who had been lying across his body. He was evacuated, and it was later recounted that, besides a bayonet wound, he had 63 holes in one leg and 35 in the other. But he lived.

As the units re-formed their lines, it was found that B Company had almost been wiped out during the night. Captain Beck, who had had a bad time himself a little to the right of Lieutenant Mulcahy, discovered that he had only 18 men left out of his initial landing strength of 217. The number went down to 17 a few minutes later when they started to dig out Herzberg's machine gun. A Marine sat down behind the gun to see if it still worked. Before he could squeeze the trigger, a Jap sniper shot him squarely between the eyes.

It was one of the last deaths on what the Marines now began to call Banzai Ridge. Soon afterwards, the men of the Third Division were ordered to take the offensive and get off the ridge once and for all. Weary, red-eyed, and fighting mad, the leathernecks surged forward in an attack of their own. The Japs never again had a chance. Their last organized resistance snapped, and the island was soon secured.

Master Technical Sergeant Alvin M. Josephy, Jr.

Peleliu Spa

Water is where you find it during the early hours of invasion. Marines who didn't already know it quickly learned at Peleliu.

D day had faded into the morning hours of D day plus one. Stifling heat had marked the thirty hours of combat assault. Canteens had long since been emptied. Fresh drinking water had not yet been ferried from ship to shore to be trundled up to the front lines by rumbling amphibious tractors. Devastating Jap mortar fire on the beaches had knocked out many of the reef-climbing amtracs. Briefing instructions were correct—water was scarce on the 6-by-2 mile island.

Beside a battalion communications post that had been set up in a shallow ravine several hundred yards behind the front lines, a bomb-carved coral crater dipped. Its 20-yard circumference around the top rim narrowed to a 6-foot bottom. At the bottom was an eighteen-inch-deep pool of murky water into which coral rock rolled as it peeled from the sides of the shellhole. The water had seeped up through its coral bed to stagnate.

Huddled uncomfortably on the eastern slope of the hole, seeking shade from a rising sun and cover from Jap mortars were Marine Majors Richard T. Washburn of Hartford and New Haven, Connecticut, and John H. Gustafson of Las Cruces, New Mexico. Both were sweat-stained and weary from thirty hours under fire. Neither spoke. Mud-spattered enlisted men dotted the sides of the shelter. Some dozed. Others gulped, moistened their lips with their tongues and looked longingly at the bottom of the hole.

Almost all the Marines were members of an assault platoon that had already been called to the front lines on five missions since they first hit the beach. "Missions" meant almost any task in the face of direct enemy fire. The platoon's ranks needed replacements.

The sun rose steadily until its noonday heat stifled the air and the remaining corner of shadow slipped away.

Gunnery Sergeant "Sol" Jackson, from Ventura, California, yawned. "Wish I had a beer."

Drawing a large piece of coral from beneath his spine in order to settle into a more comfortable position, Corporal Harold L. Park, of Cortland, New York, shot back a rhyme: "Yeah, stateside brew at Peleliu—suds from Jackson'll speed the action."

A rock caught him squarely in the seat of his dungarees. Park winced. "Purple Heart," he said.

A Jap artillery shell crashed through a near-by communications hut, slithered along the ground, and came to rest twenty yards from the battalion CP. It was a dud. Platoon Sergeant Edward F. Lawanski, of

Binghamton, New York, remarked, "Guess they've run out of metal in making those popovers." Five minutes earlier a Jap sniper had nicked a packing case against which Lawanski was resting, splintering the board several inches above his uncovered head.

Corporal Earle L. Russell, Jr., from Clinton, Massachusetts, dragged himself over the rim of the pit and unslung his carbine. He dropped into the hole, sweat swimming on his brow, his dirty dungarees clinging to his body.

"Water come up?" he asked.

"Sure," replied Corporal Ernest A. Sansanio, of New York City, "we're purifying it down there"—indicating the murky water in which Matthew Konieczkny of Chicago was dunking his feet. "Help yourself."

Ignoring the sarcasm, Russell muttered, "Jimmy just got it."

"Where?" chorused four Marines.

"Through the stomach."

"Bad?"

"Bad?—He's dead."

Private Nick Giardina, of New York City, queried, "How're the First Marines doing on the hill?"

"They're finding out what the Peleliu surprise is, that Tokyo Rose promised us on the radio," answered Private First Class Elbert Satterwhite, of Washington, D.C.

The Japs' feminine radio voice was rumored to have broadcast several weeks prior to the Peleliu invasion that "when the First Marine Division lands in the Palaus our Imperial Japanese soldiers will give them a surprise." The "surprise" proved to be the Jap-infested caves, dug at staggered levels through solid coral and limestone which ran through hundreds of yards of Peleliu's treacherous hills and ravines. The First Marines were the men who hit them, suffering heavy casualties. Throughout the campaign hundreds of thousands of tons of explosives were thrown at the hills to level them and seal the caves.

From the base of the crater Private First Class Kenneth E. Krauss, of Roxanna, Illinois, threw up his blouse which he had just washed in the murky water. "Spread it out to dry," he yelled to the others as he emptied helmet after helmet of water over his sweating body. The water seeped back into its source, washing coral bits with it into the pool.

Over the brow of the shellhole trudged Naval Lieutenant (jg) Marvin P. Baecker, of Lawrence, Kansas. Dr. Baecker, attached to a Marine unit for the operation, had been treating the wounded close to the front lines for more than thirty hours. His bearded face was drawn in an anxious frown which advertised his unspoken need for fresh water. Peering at the muddy pool, he inched down to test its drinking qualities.

"How is it, doc?" The eager inquiry came from Sansanio.

"Well," replied Lieutenant Baecker, "I don't think it'll kill you, but it won't have the refreshing taste of an iced coke. You guys use plenty of halazones 'cause it'll take between six and a dozen per canteen an' give it time to settle—twenty minutes at least."

"Kinda doubtful recommendation," muttered Corporal James A. Hauer, of Fond du Lac, Wisconsin, as the doctor disappeared. "Guess I'll choke till the fresh water comes up."

Returning from the front lines, Corporal Chesley G. Gilbert, of Baltimore, Maryland, and Griffin, Georgia, lurched into the bomb crater and fell wearily to the ground. His six-foot-three, 200-pound frame sagged forward, grime and sweat oozing from his body. Gilbert had spent thirty continuous hours on assault missions, sandwiching in volunteer duty to carry ammunition to the lines through swamp and heavy jungle where vehicles could not penetrate.

"Someone gimme some water," he commanded.

No one moved.

"Who's got a canteen full?" asked the Georgia ball player, raising his head.

"Well, now," gulped Corporal Jacques C. Lewis, of San Saba, Texas, a battalion communicator who earned a meritorious promotion in the Cape Gloucester campaign, "you might phone the purifying plant, Gil, and tell 'em you're goin' to find yoreself another island if they're not more considerate."

"Yeah, I know you're a funny guy, but where's the water?" persisted Gilbert.

"Right down at ya feet where ya lookin'," barked Corporal Tom Duffy, of the Bronx. "Ice yaself a highball an' relax."

Gilbert let his body roll down the hill, carrying coral lumps with him, until his head and half his body were submerged in the murk beside Konieczkny's dunking feet.

"Hey, Gil," beefed the Chicago Marine, "don't splash!"

Withdrawing his head Gilbert shook his dripping face and gasped, "Anything that feels as good as that must taste okay." He stretched and gulped at the water.

"Hey, sucker," yelled the squad leader, Corporal Charlie Schneider, of Chicago, a demolitions man in the assault platoon, "Doc Baecker says if ya gonna take a chance ya gotta load it in canteens with halazones or you'll grab yourself a stomachful of germs."

"Yeah," drawled Gilbert. "Guess you're right—a guy can never be too careful," he added, lowering himself to take another drink. His thirst quenched, the exhausted corporal flung off his dungaree blouse and three minutes later was sleeping through the near-by bursts of enemy mortars.

"Jeez," whispered LeLacheur, "*That's* a Marine—I saw him work at Gloucester—he'll go through the same stink in this one and lose weight, but no Japs or germs'll ever affect his guts."

Sniper fire sang over the hole. Without pause Corporal Russell picked up his carbine and edged toward a near-by jungle plot, disappearing through the foliage toward the sound of the fire. Ten minutes later the distinct sound of a carbine replied to Jap machine-gun fire.

Minutes later Russell reappeared lugging a Nambu and a Jap flag. "He didn't even *have* a canteen," muttered Russell with disgust. "What the hell am I going to do with this thing?" He held up the Nambu machine gun.

"Send it back to headquarters," sang out a voice.

As late afternoon dragged into early evening the fading sun permitted a wisp of shade in which four Marines huddled. Lapping over the crest of the hole was the smell of Jap bodies, long dead. Huge bluebottle flies swarmed through the air and settled on the bare backs of the Marines and the crumbs of K ration. Listless conversation faded and finally ceased.

Men were dying near by and Marines in the crater thanked God that their only immediate need was water. And then, over the staccato of a Jap machine gun, a loud voice was heard beyond the crest of the hole. "Water's up! Water's up! Two canteens a man. Come and get it."

First Lieutenant Layton W. Bailey, of Dallas, Texas, who throughout the night had got ammunition to the front lines in tractors and on foot when necessary, was there with the precious relief. He apologized: "Couldn't get it here any sooner. All we had had to go to the lines. Mortars were raising hell on the beach—lots of amphibs knocked out. This may be a little rusty—it's had a long voyage—use it sparingly and give Doc Baecker what he needs first."

Canteens were filled and the parched Marines gulped the rusty, gasoline-tainted water and their exhausted bodies took on new life. Picks hacked away at the side of a crater, forming foxholes for the night's rest. The shadows lengthened and the last cigarette was blanked out and then there was darkness. Guards had been thrown out on all sides of the crater, each rifle carrying "one in the chamber." The water had cooled parched throats. And even though mortars exploded near by and the rattle of Jap machine-gun fire ripped the night, the exhausted Marines slept.

Early morning brought the word to "move up." Gear was readied. Packs were shouldered. The column started forward toward a new location, warily watching for sniper fire from the Japs who had infiltrated during the night. The last to leave the crater, Corporal Charley Draper, of Athens, Georgia, surveyed the coral pit, looked down at the muddy water, and sighed, "Ah—Peleliu Spa."

A Jap mortar got the range and planted one in the crater—dead center—but it was twenty minutes too late.

Staff Sergeant Walter F. Conway

The Valley at Night

For the past three nights we had had a line of defense running clear across Peleliu: from the beach road on the northwest side, up the precipitous first ridge, down the other slope and across the valley or "draw," then running up over the right-hand ridge and down into the flat land on the other side, whence the line slanted obliquely northeast. Up at the end of the draw were two saddle-shaped crags which commanded all this area.

The Japs were dug in there. They could not withdraw north, because our line went around the island. Sooner or later, if they survived, they would come charging down on this defense line, or so the Marines thought. At night each section of our line was posted before sunset. Two or three Marines lay in the rubble together so that they could take turns watching, and each little group was about five feet from the next. On the crest of the ridge on the left was a man with a BAR; next down were four riflemen, then three scouts with submachine guns, camouflaged under a broken Jap ammunition cart. Three feet in front of us, to the right, and a little below so as to be clear of our fire, were three men with Garand rifles, then a sturdy 50-caliber machine gun with its team. On the floor of the valley stood a half-track armored vehicle with a big 75 cannon pointed up the draw. Next to it was a low-lying 37-millimeter field gun; then more machine guns and rifle teams were strung up over the ridge on the right, and down across the clearing on the other side.

Marine Second Lieutenant Sidney Carl Beinke had charge of our section. He had walked the line and made sure each man had concealment and knew the night's password. The men were lying so that anything that approached had to be silhouetted against the sky.

At 6:10 it was dusk and Lieutenant Beinke said, "Last cigarette. Pass the word. The smoking lamp is out in ten minutes."

As the night closed down you could hear the men whisper and chuckle among themselves. Then they were quiet because they were watching and listening. The equatorial moon swung up behind you, lighting the rocks even through the rain.

Some friendly gun every few minutes lobbed a starshell, which popped softly in the air above the Japs' positions and hung for a long time in the sky. The strong magnesium flare etched the whole valley and hills in ghastly light. The two great humps of the saddleback hill where the Japs waited in the caves had no tree that had not been broken by fire, and there was hardly a patch of its coral cliffside that hadn't been split to a clean white surface by some explosion. The horizon all around was the bleakest picture of desolation—broken crags, dark gaping caves, and the entire floor of the draw littered with the ruck and waste of combat. Gustave Doré could have climaxed his career by etching such a scene—sinister, unearthly, Dantesque.

At ten minutes to twelve the guns were still. Up on the left-hand ridge somebody stepped on a loose piece of coral, slipped, and stumbled against a sapling which snapped under his weight. He fell to the ground. The coral tumbled down the hill, rattling against cartridge cases and sheets of iron roofing. At the same time the BAR man stood up against the sky line and said: "Give the password!" The BAR crashed out in the night.

It was silent again. You knew everyone was waiting, with weapons aimed at the noise. Then an animal was threshing around in the wreckage in front of our position, and a machine gun opened up on it from the right. Somebody threw two hand grenades which burst into red pieces in the dark like firecrackers. And there was no more noise on our line that night.

But two hours later there was great firing on the other side of the ridge to our right, where Major Joseph Edward Buckley, a leathery and tireless Marine, had the rest of his weapons company disposed much as we were.

During the night one Jap clambered into a foxhole and cut a Marine's throat before he himself was stabbed to death. Three Japs crept down the valley and set up a Lewis machine gun in front of the lines. Their first burst shot a Marine through the head before the gun on Major Buckley's half-track killed the three. And this morning, when the Marines walked out into the field of fire, they found two amazing things. Both of them were typical of the Japanese on Peleliu.

On the left-hand side of their slope Major Buckley's men found our Japanese where he had died, riddled through both legs. He wore the helmet and stained dungaree blouse of a dead Marine. The medical kit of a murdered corpsman was slung over his shoulder. After he'd been shot on our side of the line he had bandaged his wounds without battle dressings and sulfa. Then, as an efficient soldier, he had taken stock of the situation. He knew we were on the alert, and that therefore he could not knock out our gun.

Somehow, noiselessly in all that rubbish strewn across the draw, he had picked his way across the valley and over the ridge, intent on reaching Major Buckley's gun before he died.

The other discovery, also typical of these doomed but determined Japanese, set every Marine infantryman guffawing as he moved up the lines toward Ngesebus and the fall of Peleliu. It was a note pinned to the body of one of the three Japs dead at their machine gun:

AMERICAN BRAVE SOLDIERS WE THINK YOUR MUCH PITTIED SINCE LANDING ON THIS ISLE DESPITE OF YOUR PITTIFUL BATTLE. WE ARE SORRY THAT WE CAN GIVE YOU ONLY FIRE, NOT EVEN GOOD WATER. WE SOON WILL ATTACK YOUR ARMY. YOU HAD DONE BRAVE BY YOUR DUTY. NOW. ABANDON YOUR GUNS AND COME IN JAPANESE MILITARY WITH WHITE FLAG (OR HANDKERCHIEF) SO WE WILL BE GLAD TO SEE YOU AND WELCOME YOU AS COMFORTABLY AS WE CAN.

Staff Sergeant James Finan

The Landing

The tank dipped and fell off in the troughs of the sea and our motors idled, and we still swapped grins and gestures with the ship's crew while we waited for other tractors to emerge from the vessel lying off Iwo Jima.

The sun was high in the heaven and all the chill was gone from the air and everyone seemed more relaxed. I stood up and saw off to the starboard the Higgins boat that was the command craft for our wave. It swept by and our own motors roared and we turned to follow it and Boudrie said everybody get down. I sat on the mortar shell container again and saw that although my head was well below the top of the gunwale it was above the waterline as defined by the painted mark inside the tank, but I was comfortable and did not change my position.

Matchunis rummaged in the bottom of the tank and sat up with a manila-wrapped package in his hand. He unrolled the paper and displayed three sandwiches, one of which he offered to me. I refused.

"I'm about to starve to death," he said, "and I ate a hell of a chow. I don't know what's the matter with me."

I thought he was being ostentatious—*I* didn't feel as if I'd ever want to eat again—but he took a tremendous bite of one of the sandwiches, shifted the mouthful quid-like to his jaw and munched happily.

"My father," he said, "told me never to try to work on an empty stomach."

We new men grinned, but the veterans, those who had fought in the Marshalls and on Saipan and Tinian, paid no attention to him. And then I realized that we new men were lucky. Our minds now were invincible and immortal and indestructible, and although we said to ourselves this may be terrible, what we really meant was that it possibly would be awesome and exhausting. Of course we knew that fatalities might and probably would occur, but in our mind's eye we saw ourselves grieving over the loss of friends and we never could picture our friends grieving over us.

And the tank roared on, for we had reached the LD, which was the line of departure of each wave on its way to the beach; and the noise of the tank was everything, for the ordinary human sounds were replaced by the motor's activity and the battle before us had no sound which was good too.

Our air observers had seen what appeared to be a long row of oil drums buried in the sand of the beach and they had said those drums may hold explosives, or fuel to blaze up and hold you on the beach under the fire of enemy mortars, or they may be connected by pipes to the sea, and burning oil may be released onto the surface of the water as your tanks come in. But don't worry, they said, don't worry, for we have tested it out with live goats and we have found that they can ride through blazing waters in these tanks without being scorched. Just take these ponchos, they said, and wet them to put over the top of your tank and you'll be all right, and I wondered then which goats had dipped *their* ponchos into the water.

So we held three ponchos over the ramp and let them trail in the sea, and off our stern perhaps two hundred yards away the water spouted upward but I heard no sound of the shell that had fallen. We put the ponchos on the deck and forgot about them, for Boudrie nudged me and shouted in my ear, "Some tanks are on the beach!"

I stood again and looked and it appeared to me that they had even succeeded in scaling the first terrace which lay close to the water's edge. But before I could make sure Turlo motioned for me to get down and I sat on my mortar case again.

"Don't you think we ought to load now, Turlo?" Boudrie shouted.

Turlo failed to hear but in a matter of seconds he shouted, "Everybody load and lock!"

We peeled the covers off our weapons and I took a clip of ammunition from the side of my cartridge belt, tapped the black-tipped projectile ends on my rifle butt to make certain the bullets were aligned evenly in the clip, stripped back the operating rod handle, pressed the clip down on the follower and slide, and smashed the bolt home with a blow on the operating rod handle from the heel of my palm. I clicked the safety and placed the rifle between my knees, butt down, the muzzle pointing directly into the air. The man with the tommy gun cradled his weapon in his arms and the muzzle pointed directly at my head until I put up my hand and forced it around. He grinned apologetically and shifted it so that it pointed into the air.

I realized that Boudrie was shouting and waving and I saw that the tank on our right, which carried the company commander and our platoon leader and Summers's squad, had moved in until its radio antenna bobbed only a few feet beyond and above our starboard gunwale.

"Get that goddam thing away from here! Get it away! Do you want to draw their fire out here?"

No one in the other tractor could hear him, of course, but the antenna moved off to the right and it was impossible to tell whether that tank or our own had shifted positions.

The tank crewman left his position near the machine gun and worked his way quickly to the port side near the ramp and Turlo stood up and shouted, "Everybody take something! Everybody take something! We've got to get this stuff on the beach!"

The ramp controls ground in my ear and at the same time we bumped solidly and we had hit ground. The tank motors slowed momentarily, then roared again and once more idled and the ramp crashed and I saw without thinking that it led into the water and we hadn't been able to go over that terrace.

I turned to my right and grabbed the first thing I saw, which was a five-gallon can of drinking water, and someone started down the ramp treads on the right of me and another on the left, and I moved down the center, which was treadless and already wet from the surf, and my feet skidded from under me and I fell half sitting in the shallow water. Someone seized me under the right armpit and hauled me to my feet and my rifle was dry because I had almost by instinct held it above my head when I started to slide.

The roar of the tank was gone and there was another roar in its place but it was different, for where the sound of the tank was a oneness this was a conglomeration of all the noises ever heard but I didn't hear it until minutes or perhaps an hour later, for my mind said only run run run, get off the beach get off the beach, don't ever hole up on the beach unless it's absolutely necessary because they're sighting in on the beach and they'll get you sure as hell, get off the beach, put this damn thing down and get off the beach and run.

But I couldn't run because of the weight of the gear and the water can and because too of the sand into which I sank to my calves so that every step was a conscious uprooting of my feet and placing them one in front of the other and my weight seemed to grow, and I said to myself run but I only shuffled and staggered and something compelled me to look back and to my right (I don't remember any sound but it must have been there) and the beach sand spouted up like black water from a geyser and I knew that a shell had fallen close by, but it meant nothing to me because I had not been hit.

I saw someone in front of me drop the ammunition he carried and I released my grip on the water can and thus I had gone ten yards onto the beach from the water's edge. I moved faster when I had abandoned the can but only a few steps and I realized already I was tired and I was possessed with a desire for a drink of water for my mouth was so dry that the gum I had been chewing suddenly adhered to my teeth and gums and tongue and every surface it touched and it hung in maddening threads. With my tongue I worked most of it to my lips where it stuck until I bit it off and let it fall to the ground; tiny bits hung from my lip to my chin and clung there. All this happened as I ran and shuffled and stumbled, which was only a matter of a few steps.

Later that day I thought of the words I had read picturing such an attack and I knew then that the writers had seen too much. For although I had wanted desperately to form a picture of what it was like, what I had come through with was the recollection of my mental prodding and a few snapshots, disconnected in time and space, some of them faded as with age and out of focus and only one or two sharp and clear.

What I saw were dozens of figures running and stumbling aimlessly in all directions and they had to me neither faces nor uniforms nor weapons and were charged by emotions that I could never fathom. Perhaps no emotion existed and all the action was instinctive. But instinct would have driven us back, not forward; it is with the annihilation of such that training is concerned and it must have succeeded for although forms floated in front of me and alongside me none of them was going toward the rear.

But there was another picture which is as vivid to me now as it was then and with it is related the only clear sound I distinguished on the beach that morning. For as I ran toward the first terrace I heard to the left of me the cry: "Co-o-o-orpsman! Co-o-o-orpsman! Oh, co-o-o-orpsman!" It was a shout without being a shout; it was a wail that denied all the training of the trooper for in it was everything primeval:

fear, pain, and agonized terror. It was a wail without an end or a beginning but somehow it was repeated, and how I heard it over the furious sound of the beach I'll never know but I did.

I looked to the left and in a shallow hole against the terrace I saw the man sitting on his left hip and leaning on his left hand and his head was turned back and to the side and his mouth was open. I saw no motion of mouth or face or wide staring eyes but I knew it was from that mouth that those sounds issued. It was as a picture painted and hung against a gallery wall and in that instant I knew its every detail as if I had studied it for months.

To his left lay three Marines and I knew they were dead more certainly than if I had taken their pulses or listened for their breathing for they were heaped in the peculiar positions that death uses to distinguish its victims from the unconscious. Even the one man who lay curled on his side did not preserve the illusion of sleep for his head was turned sharply to the left and his face was thrust into the sand, and the second lay spread-eagled on his face with his hands and feet flung far apart as if they had been nailed there. The third was on his knees with his feet apart and his toes pointing inward and the weight of his upper body rested on his shoulders and the side of his head, for his arms were extended flat along the ground beside his legs. And the picture was so clear that I saw the tightness of his trousers across his buttocks and the bulge of some object in his left hip pocket and I saw that one canteen had twisted to the left so that it hung almost touching the ground while the other lay in the middle of his back and his poncho tucked under his cartridge belt was unfolded along the left side of his back. His helmet was not on his head.

I hurled myself against the terrace and my breath came in shallow wheezing gasps and I lay there and panted. My mental prodding to get off the beach get off the beach refused to recognize my physical anguish and I rose to a crouch and tried to sprint up the terrace wall, but my feet only bogged in the sand and instead of running I crawled, trying to keep my rifle clean but failing. At the top of the wall I pulled to my feet and saw directly in front of me a shellhole with another slightly farther inland and to the left and I decided to run to the second, but by the time I had passed the first my run again had become a walk and I said to myself I am a fine target standing upright here and I strained to run again but I succeeded only in falling down and I was so weak that instead of crawling I could only roll. I did until I rolled over the edge of the crater and into safety.

I sat up on the side of the hole near the bottom and my mouth was so dry that the roof hurt when I ran my tongue over it. I swallowed to try to renew the flow of saliva but the only thing I swallowed was my palate which seemed to have grown inches. I retched violently and the saliva began to flow so I swallowed again, retched again and felt better.

Private Allen R. Matthews

Iwo: the Red-hot Rock

February 19, 1945, was a clear and beautiful morning and the Fourth and Fifth Marine divisions went over the side into their landing craft at 7 a.m. The beaches seemed dead under dull columns of smoke, but they weren't dead. We saw an American observation plane overhead shudder and go down in flames. A light warship took a hit and began spouting water from the starboard side. There were sharp, crunching explosions and we saw the waterspouts around our landing craft. Then, as we came within a few yards of the beach, we heard the crack of bullets and the chatter of machine guns.

The island was alive. The Japs were waiting for us. They were on the terraces above the beach and on the tabletop airstrips and all through the ridges of the island in pillboxes, bunkers, and blockhouses. The smoke had hardly cleared from our own bombardment but there were Japanese firing at us at point-blank range. A mortar shell exploded twenty feet to our left, sending fragments whistling over our tractor. Behind us another tractor was blown out of the water. Marines who weren't thrown out by the force of the explosion were sucked under with their heavy packs. Men with inflated life belts struggled in the pounding surf trying to help others.

The beach itself was no more than ten yards deep, rising abruptly from the water, but it was treacherous volcanic ash and black cinders in which men and machines slipped and bogged down. A small precipice over which we scrambled led us onto a great sea of billowing sand interlaced by 5- to 8-foot-high terraces. When we had hit the beach the first waves had already scaled the first of these terraces and were face to face with the forward line of Jap defenders.

It was clear that every yard of the naked beach had been zeroed-in by Jap guns. Our casualties mounted steadily, especially among Major General Clifton B. Cates's Fourth Marine Division, which landed on the northern half of the beachhead with the job of seizing Airfield No. 1. There was something uncanny about the Japs' accuracy on Blue Beach Two where the Fourth Division was struggling to get more men and machines ashore close to a gutted and half-sunk Japanese transport which had previously been knocked out by American planes. Our spotters searched the hillsides but could find no point from which the enemy might be directing such accurate fire. Nevertheless, it continued, while the first waves fought to expand the 2-mile-long beachhead.

With flame throwers and demolitions, we blasted the enemy out of his pillboxes, many of which were connected by tunnels and trenches. On a 100-yard stretch we fought through the cross fire of fifty pillboxes and ten blockhouses, only to find that some of the Japs had sneaked back through those we had already passed, and were now firing on us from the rear.

The fighting became hotter as we moved toward the airfield. Each shellhole was a potential hiding place for a sniper, and we jumped into one only after throwing a grenade in first. On one bluff directly ahead, a Marine made a dash for three Japs in a trench but dropped before he had moved five feet. A minute later one of his buddies tried it and got to the lip of the trench before he was hit. Finally, a young private zigzagged his way up, shot one Jap and clubbed the other two to death with his rifle butt.

Not far away, a public relations officer who had sustained a wound in the early phases of the battle lay in a shellhole and tried to bring into focus the scene around him.

"At Tarawa, Saipan and Tinian, I saw Marines killed and wounded in a shocking manner," he wrote later, "but not like the ghastliness that hung over the Iwo beachhead. Nothing any of us had ever known could compare with the utter anguish, frustration, and constant inner battle to maintain some semblance of sanity, clarity of mind, and power of speech. Everybody tells me they felt as I did. As long as you could speak, you believed you had a slim chance to live. None of us would concede that death would have been a merciful coup de grâce. Everybody was seized with an insensate lust to live."

Second Lieutenant Benjamin F. Roselle, Jr., and a 6-man naval gun-fire liaison team had reached Iwo's blackened northernmost beach at H hour plus four. Laden with heavy radio gear, Roselle and his men scrambled through ankle-gripping volcanic ash at the precise instant the Japs launched a ferocious artillery and mortar barrage. The first mortar blast picked off one Marine. Roselle turned him over to the medicos and packed the casualty's gear upon his own back.

Striving to keep up with the combat troops, Roselle and his men plunged into the full fury of the barrage and managed to slough onward over a second terrace and to the brow of the third, some two hundred yards inland. This was as far as they got. Mortars plummeted down like hailstones—tearing, mutilating missiles that killed as they fell. Roselle was knocked sprawling with two of his men. The men got up. Roselle couldn't. His left leg burned and ached in vicious spasms. Only a slender thread of flesh held his foot and ankle to his leg, but he was brutally conscious. He told his two wounded Marines to strike out for the beach. They crawled away on all fours. The three remaining men put a tourniquet on the officer's shattered leg, applying pressure with a carbine magazine.

Then they hugged ground and took it. Roselle cracked wry jokes and damned the Japs. Fifteen minutes later an almost direct hit knocked out two more men and put four shrapnel gashes in Roselle's right leg. He didn't feel the steel bite, but the blood oozed out into the sand.

During the next ninety minutes, mortar salvos pounded the sector, but miraculously missed the leatherneck officer and the last remaining Marine crouching at his side. Then Roselle actually called the third mortar hit. "Hold tight!" he shrieked, as the high scream of the missile increased. It burst almost on top of them. The enlisted Marine's right leg was torn away, and Roselle was wounded the third time, in the right shoulder.

Without a word, Roselle's companion hoisted himself to his elbows and crawled off the terrace, working his arms and dragging the useless limb alongside the good one. That was when Roselle thought it was all over. He had never felt so utterly alone in his life. All he could think about was his mother and dad back in Royal Oak, Michigan. He almost went crazy thinking about them. Once he raised himself up for a look around. There wasn't a moving thing in sight—just dead Marines everywhere.

Soon the Japs began to walk their barrage up the terraces from the beach. Roselle simply lay there and waited. When the fourth hit came, he felt himself lifted by the concussion. By now he didn't care. Later, for some reason, he looked at his watch. But before he could reckon the time, a mortar smashed into the volcanic ash at his left side. The timepiece was shorn from his wrist and a gaping hole reddened his forearm just above the wrist.

"I was beginning to know what it must feel like to be crucified," Roselle said later. "God Almighty, I hurt! But I was so mad I think it kept me alive."

Then, when he thought he had reached the end, he saw helmet tops moving beneath the terrace brow parallel to the sea, headed north. It turned out to be a medical party moving toward Iwo's cliffs to evacuate front-line casualties. They found Roselle's left arm fractured, set it, then evacuated him to the beach. Within a matter of minutes, he was taken from the mortar-beaten beach, still under heavy fire, to an LST where his left foot was amputated immediately.

Private First Class Norman Pate, of New York, a Marine combat artist, abandoned his drawing gear as soon as he reached the beach and moved out with the fighting troops. His limited ammunition was

quickly expended and he began to help the wounded by seeking out
corpsmen. On his third trip, a mortar blast gouged his right shoulder.
He ripped off his dungaree blouse, applied his own battle dressing,
then helped haul ammunition forward, carrying litters loaded with
wounded on the return trips. He was struck by flying shrapnel and
didn't know his left arm was fractured. But, because he bled profusely,
Pate threw away his blouse to prevent infection. He was carrying
ammo when a sniper hit him in the thigh, ripping a long furrow
through the flesh. So he tore off his trousers and walked nude to the
beach for evacuation. That was enough.

Our tanks came ashore swiftly, but the soft volcanic sand trapped
them, and many floundered helplessly and never got off the beach.
Behind us on the beaches, the supplies we needed so badly began to
trickle in under the murderous Jap artillery fire. Landing craft began
to roll helplessly in the surf, and by late afternoon the beaches were
clogged with the wreckage of tanks, bulldozers, jeeps, trucks, and
half-tracks. Ducks, carrying artillery, were swamped in the high surf.
Their crews, many of them Army Negro troops, manhandled the guns
onto the beach. Casualties were increasing. One duck drifted three
miles out to sea after its propeller had been shot away. Its driver had
stuck with it because there was an artillery piece left, and he knew
it would be needed.

The need for ammunition became critical. A gunnery sergeant in
charge of a mortar platoon ran back to the beach to find an ammunition boat bobbing in the sea offshore because its coxswain couldn't
find a safe spot on the beach to land. One enemy shell would have
blown him and the ammunition sky high. The sergeant swam to the
boat and persuaded its crew to make a run for it. And they made it.

The fight for the airfield went on. The Japanese retreated slowly
from bunker to bunker and from trench to trench until they were
backed against the steep fill of the field. Then a strange thing happened. This remnant enemy disappeared completely. Suddenly, as
we climbed onto the edge of the airfield, we drew fire from these same
Japs. We stared momentarily in amazement. They had crawled

through the drains under the field like gophers, to pop up two hundred yards away.

A sergeant exclaimed, "The little bastards are coming back for more. Let's give it to 'em!" We did.

By nightfall we had established a secure foothold on the airfield. It had taken us a day to reach this objective which had looked so easy from our transports. The Fifth Division had swung south to attack Surabachi. We had lost several hundred men, and the landing beach was still under heavy enemy fire that continued to be uncannily accurate. No phase of the battle was more desperate than the continuous struggle to build up ammunition dumps ashore, to supply the advancing artillery and infantry. Marine Pioneers and replacement work parties hauled the precious ammo out of landing craft and up from the water's edge. Then the Japanese artillery methodically sent these dumps up in flames, killing and severely wounding dozens of Marines.

But the secret of the Jap artillery accuracy was about to be solved. A Marine—nobody ever got his name—was patrolling the shore where the gutted Japanese transport was beached at a crazy angle on Blue Beach Two. He waited for the next mortar burst and watched the stars. Something ghostly moved in the bomb-torn hulk. He listened. He heard a low, steady sound. He leaned over and stirred another Marine. They got a couple more. They crept up on the derelict ship. They made a rush, and there was a scuffle, and shots. There, in the empty black hull, lay a Japanese artillery observer, a radio sending set strapped on his back. He had been spotting the Marine dumps and guiding the deadly enemy fire. The Japs' accuracy decreased rapidly thereafter.

The struggle to cut off Mount Surabachi had begun on D day. The 28th Regiment from Major General Keller E. Rockey's untried Fifth Marine Division parted company with the rest of the line and, led by Colonel Harry B. Liversedge, bit into the approaches of the volcano on the south. The terrain leading up to the almost perpendicular cliffs ran from sand to boulders. Despite the tremendous weight of explosives showered on this cone, it spouted death from hundreds of openings.

The Japs had erected every conceivable obstacle along the approaches to the volcano base, from tank ditches to barbed wire. These had to be stormed by frontal assault. One of our boys perched atop a pillbox and leaped down on the back of a running Jap and killed him with his knife. Another lost his rifle and wrested a samurai sword from a charging Jap officer and cut his head off.

For the next three days, the 28th Regiment battled to scale and capture Surabachi. It was almost a foot-by-foot crawl with mortars, artillery, rockets, machine guns, and grenades making us hug every rock and shellhole. Rock slides were tumbled down on our heads by the Japs, and also as a result of our own naval gunfire. There were many pillboxes on the approaches and there were five main caves inside the mountain, in which a whole garrison of troops had lived. Some of these caves were on three levels. The largest had fifty openings and could accommodate three hundred soldiers. Scores of Japs eventually were sealed up in the caves. .

Around Surabachi, as elsewhere on Iwo, each pillbox was a separate problem, an intricately designed fortress that had to be smashed into ruins. Even after the assault troops moved past them, there was mopping up to do. Shocked and wounded Japs clung stubbornly to life amid the ruins, some of them half buried in dirt and shattered masonry. The walls of many began with 2-foot-thick concrete blocks, laced with iron rails. Then came ten to twelve feet of rocks, piled with dirt and the dirty ashes of Iwo. The rock and concrete roofs were supported by concrete pillars inside. Single entranceways, which were tiny, long holes, and one or two casemate openings were protected against direct hits or flying shrapnel by concrete abutments. The whole structure might look from the outside like a mound rising a few feet above the surrounding ground.

Once in the battle for Surabachi, a corporal asked for a flame thrower to attack such a pillbox. His lieutenant, trying to conserve fuel, hesitated.

"Only dead Japs in there," he said. "Try a grenade."

"I did."

"Well?"

"That blankety-blank dead Jap threw it back at me!"

Later, on the narrow path to Mount Surabachi, three Marines were surrounded at the mouth of a cave. There was not room to use rifles. One Marine made a flying tackle at the nearest Jap and, when felled, twisted the Jap's neck and broke it. Another plunged feet first on a Jap lieutenant, catching him in the groin. The third Marine leaped Tarzan-like from atop the cave, his jungle knife flashing. The Jap he landed on was stabbed in the heart before they hit the ground. There were no rules, no quarter, and no surrender.

It was in that manner that we took Mount Surabachi, and Lieutenant Colonel Chandler W. Johnson of Highland Park, Illinois, commander of the second battalion, 28th Marines, handed a folded American flag to Lieutenant Harold G. Schrier, and said, "Put that on top of the hill."

"Okay," the lieutenant said, and with Platoon Sergeant Ernest I. Thomas, of Tallahassee, Florida, and forty-two tired Marines, went up the battered hill, 750 miles from Tokyo. Japs were still in the caves but the Marines used grenades, flame throwers and rifles on them, and Schrier, Thomas, and Sergeant H. O. Hansen, of Boston, put the flag up early on February 23, just as the colonel had ordered. They used a piece of Japanese pipe they had found on the mountainside as a flagpole. The other men stood near by in skirmish line, but nobody said or did anything except watch for Japs.

Meanwhile, on February 21, the Third Marine Division, commanded by 48-year-old Major General Graves B. Erskine, began landing and immediately took a place in the center of the line, where the most obstinate enemy defenses were protecting Iwo's second airfield—Motoyama Airfield No. 2. This sector, an upsloping field of volcanic ash lying between the two airfields, resembled the surface of the moon. There was scarcely a yard not plowed by some kind of shell burst. It was bleak and windy. Coarse particles of sand, the size of buckshot, blew into our faces.

Our attack was aimed at taking an open stretch from one side of the central tableland to the other. We could go only as far as our tanks, which at that moment meant very slow progress. On the central plateau, Jap guns of all calibers, flaming from what looked like holes in the shifting sand dunes, laid down a wall of fire against our tanks. In addition to everything else, mortar pits dug six to eight feet into the ground with only tiny firing holes visible and mine fields covered by machine-gun fire combined to impede the tanks. From our shell-holes we could see several come to an abrupt halt as something hit them. Their hatches flew open and their crews scrambled out to keep from burning alive.

Our infantry push fared no better. As we struggled across the open dunes, the enemy hit us from the front and both flanks. For a Marine to leave his hole and dive for another was a brave act in this nightmarish battle. Mortar and artillery shook the ground like an earthquake. We saw men stagger and fall, some from sheer exhaustion and the strain of battle. Many Marines lost their lives in this field of stinking volcanic ash. Corpsmen and litter bearers crawled among the wounded, hauling them from hole to hole. Into this bizarre scene, a red rooster appeared from nowhere screaming and flapping its wings.

When the 24th Marine Regiment's 2nd Battalion reached the scene, they called it "the Wilderness," and there they spent four days on the line, with no respite from the song of death sung by mortars among those desolate crevices and gouged shellholes. The Wilderness covered about a square mile inland from Blue Beach Two, on the approaches to Airfield No. 2, and there was no cover. Here and there stood a blasted dwarf tree, here and there a stubby rock ledge in a maze of volcanic crevices.

The 2d Battalion attacked with flame throwers, demolition charges, 37-millimeter guns, riflemen. A tank advancing in support was knocked out by mortar shell. After every Japanese volley, Corsair fighter planes streamed down on the mortar positions, ripping their charges of bombs into the Wilderness. But after every dive was ended, the mortars started their ghastly song again.

Cracks in the earth ran along the open field to the left of the Wilderness, and hot smoke seeped up through the cracks. Gains were counted in terms of one or two hundred yards for a day, in terms of three or four bunkers knocked out. Losses were counted in terms of three or four men suddenly turned to bloody rags after the howl of a mortar shell, in terms of a flame-thrower man hit by a grenade as he poured his flame into a bunker. The assault platoon of flame throwers and demolitionists, spearheading the regiment's push through the Wilderness, lost two assistant squad leaders killed.

The Japs were hard to kill. Cube-shaped concrete blockhouses had to be blasted again and again before the men inside were silenced. Often the stunned and wounded Japs continued to struggle among the ruins, still trying to fire back. A Marine assaulting a pillbox found a seriously wounded Jap trying to get a heavy machine gun into action. He emptied his clip at him, but the Jap kept reaching. Finally out of ammunition, the Marine used his knife to kill him.

Forty-eight hours after the attack began, one element of the Third Division moved into the line under orders to advance at all costs. Behind a rolling artillery barrage and with fixed bayonets, the unit leaped forward in an old-fashioned hell-bent-for-leather charge and advanced to the very mouths of the fixed Jap defenses. Before scores of pillboxes the men flung themselves at the tiny flaming holes, throwing grenades and jabbing with bayonets. Comrades went past, hurdled the defenses, and rushed across Airfield No. 2. In three minutes one unit lost four officers—men died at every step. That was how we broke their line.

Across the field we attacked a ridge. The enemy rose up out of holes to hurl our assault back. The squads re-formed and went up again. At the crest they plunged on the Japs with bayonets. One of our men, slashing his way from side to side, fell dead from a pistol shot. His comrade drove his bayonet into the Jap who had killed him. The Japs on the ridge were annihilated.

The survivors of this bold charge covered eight hundred yards in an hour and a half. Brave men had done what naval shelling, aerial bombardment, artillery, and tanks had not been able to do in two days of constant pounding. What was perhaps the most intensively fortified small area ever encountered in battle had been broken.

This kind of fighting—hard, relentless, with the Japs under orders to stay in their positions to the death—characterized the days of battle for Iwo that followed. The Japs also were using a new weapon—a motorized 1,000-pound rocket. We dubbed it "Whistling Nellie" because of the screech and whistle that accompanied its launching and flight. One sergeant was thrown forty feet in the air and killed by a Nellie which left other Marines near by unharmed.

There were countless instances of bravery and of luck. An Iowa corporal, a machine-gun squad leader, seeking a spot to emplace his weapon, raised up from a mortar plastering that had him tense against the ground, to stare into the eyes of a Jap rifleman four feet away. The Jap's bayonet was fixed but his gun apparently had jammed. The corporal shouted, and a Marine with an automatic rifle shot the Jap while he was working frantically at the bolt of his own gun. The corporal, a member of the Fifth Division, then started a 10-yard dash to the gunsite and was plugged by a sniper, the bullet passing through his neck, grazing his larynx and missing his jugular vein.

The fight went on. The terrain north of Airfield No. 2 looked like the Dakota Badlands—barren except for ugly stunted palms with sulphur blowholes streaming at the bases of sharp, naked ridges that rose fifty to a hundred feet into the air. The ridges made perfect defense positions and the Japs had taken full advantage of them. Their tops were crowned with big guns, most of which had been knocked out by our bombings and naval gunfire. Three of these ridge formations—one on the left, one in the center, and one on the right—now held up our divisions. On the left, the Fifth Division passed up through the boulders and sharp rocks, in a frontal assault. In the center, the Third Division drove a wedge into the heart of the enemy defenses, which then shifted to the right where the third great battle was fought.

The scene of this battle was Hill 382—the highest point in the northern half of the island—and a vast amphitheater in front of it through which our men had to pass in order to assault the hill itself. The amphitheater became a grim battle scene with American and Japanese dead strewn everywhere. The Fourth Division launched attack after attack down its slopes, only to meet an incredible combination of fire from enemy weapons poised around the rim.

"It was like something weird," a corporal said, "with flares going up and tracer bullets and smoke, and some of the men coming out of there with blood streaming down their faces, carrying a few others who couldn't walk. It was like some scene in the movies."

The following day another of our companies reached the hill after running the gantlet of fire and swept the amphitheater. But the Japs had zeroed-in Hill 382 just as close as they had the beaches. We were forced to withdraw, and the enemy manned his positions again. A platoon from a company commanded by Captain Stanley C. McDaniel, of Duncan, Oklahoma, reached the summit of Hill 382 on the fifth night of the battle. They were cut off when fire in their rear became so heavy that supporting elements couldn't get through. We put down a smoke screen to get them out. Japanese fire was cutting them down mercilessly, and ten wounded had to be left behind.

The Japs infiltrated during that night. Captain Donald S. Callahan, of Springfield, Missouri, commanding a company that lost sixty men, said his outfit killed between fifteen and twenty Japs, many of them wielding sabers. One Marine lay for a day and a night on the side of Hill 382 with a broken leg, a dead buddy beside him. He was surrounded by Japs all night but was rescued the next morning when our troops regained the position. 55669

A battalion commanded by Major James L. Scales, of Stoneville, North Carolina, finally took a protecting ridge which was honeycombed with bunkers, pillboxes, and caves. The Japanese had set up machine guns and antitank guns in every conceivable protected spot, but we flanked them and then moved in frontal assault against the enemy. From our observation post we could see the Japs pop up from their bunkers and roll grenades down on the advancing Marines.

Our bazookas proved an invaluable weapon in this terrain. They were fired point-blank into enemy machine-gun positions with devastating results. After four and a half hours we held the most expensive —but the most valuable—hill on this island. The fall of Hill 382 punched a great hole in the Jap main line of defense across Iwo and gave us observation of all enemy terrain to the north, simultaneously denying them observation of our rear areas. There was plenty of hard fighting after that but it was downhill, and the odds were with us.

Master Technical Sergeant Alvin M. Josephy, Jr.
Second Lieutenant Cyril P. Zurlinden, Jr.
Master Technical Sergeant David Dempsey
Technical Sergeant Dan Levin
and Staff Sergeant Tony Smith

How It Was on Iwo

I was with the Fifth Marine Division and saw a little of what we did there and photographed some of it. On the ship the night before D day, it was like any night before a practice landing. I watched the others sweating through evening chow, and checking their gear and packs and weapons in the narrow aisles between the 5-high tiers of bunks. They looked the same and acted the same; there was no tenseness, no edge apparent in anyone. The main difference on D day morning was that breakfast was at 3:30 a.m. and we had steak, which made us feel the government was being pretty big about the thing.

Light had come and was growing when we moved out on deck and to our debarkation nets. There was only a little swell then, and it was easy getting down into the boat. I was in an LCM with about thirty other Marines and a half-ton truck. We moved away from the ship and circled with the boats that formed our wave. We were several miles from shore, but we could see the island clearly, and the battleships and cruisers lying close in, shelling it at point-blank range. The first waves, in the amtracs, were already going in. A guy sitting on the truck was reading a sheet of funnies from some Sunday supplement. I looked at the man beside me, and we shrugged. Whatever we had expected, it wasn't this. It was a letdown, somehow.

Now our boats formed their line and moved to the control boat, two thousand yards offshore. The sun was behind us, the light perfect for photography; I was shooting movies in color. We got our signal and started in. Very shortly the battleships and LSTs were behind us. Then we were down in the boat, bracing ourselves. We hit, and the ramp came down, and without getting our feet wet we were on the beach. The truck driver gave her the gun, and the truck rolled out, and three feet up the beach bogged in the coarse black bottomless sand. He hopped out and was gone.

The beach was fairly level for about twenty yards, then rose steeply for twenty more, and I moved across to this bank. By the time I had made the twenty yards to its top, I was exhausted. Not tired; just utterly limp and useless. It was that sand, as loose as sugar. I lay there five minutes before I had energy to run another twenty yards and hit the stuff again. If you did not reach a hole by the time you'd run as far as you could, you could make a hole pretty well by just lying there and wriggling; presently only your pack would be above the level of the sand, though this was a smallish comfort with Surabachi just to your left, from which they could shoot down at you. And did.

This was little more than an hour after the first wave had hit the beach, and more than fifteen hundred Marines were on that 300-yard-wide strip of sandy hill by then. And it was a hill, not a slope. But you saw only a few at a time, in near-by holes, or when they were up and moving. A little above me to the right, however, one was sitting on a sort of hummock, inspecting Surabachi with the reflective look of a gentleman farmer wondering whether he would have this field planted to corn or spring wheat next year. That was Colonel Harry Liversedge, commanding officer of the 28th Marines.

I made my way on up the hill and across it a hundred yards, and came upon some casualties. I made some shots as the corpsmen bandaged them and carried them on litters back down the hill to the beach. I spent the afternoon on the beach, as casualties were brought down and put into small boats for evacuation to the hospital ships. I saw no Japs, but you could tell they were around.

That was D day for me. On the whole, the thing I minded most was that exhausting sand. Which brings me to what I had wondered about most of all, along with a lot of others, I suppose: fear. There was no reticence about fear on Iwo. It was a familiar, almost a friendly topic; it was the stuff guys bragged about to each other—how full of it they were, this time or that.

I think several factors contributed to my not having a bad D day. One was that when I saw Colonel Liversedge sitting there so coolly, I did not know he was noted for being unconcerned under fire, so I thought that things couldn't be very bad. I guess the sight of him helped a lot of other guys too. Another factor was ignorance. For instance, up on the hill that morning I heard a rapid little popping that sounded like a child's toy machine gun, or small firecrackers. When a sergeant major in the hole with me said it was a Jap light machine gun, I thought it couldn't be as close as it sounded. Later I saw the emplacement—it was only about thirty or forty yards away. It would have made a difference, all right, to have known that on D day.

By far the most important factor, though, is that I was very busy most of the time. The few bad moments I had that day were only when I had to lie still for a time, and shells were landing not very far off. I had time to think then: "Maybe the next one will come here. Maybe I'd better move. Maybe if I do I'll get there just in time to meet one." But if you're trying to shoot pictures, checking your focus and exposure and camera angles and directions, or if your mind is fully occupied with how to take a pillbox, you haven't time to think about what might happen to you. When known risk is involved, you balance it against the worth of the pictures you may get, or the importance of the pillbox; but you don't paw it around with your emotions.

Up on the first airfield, after we had repaired it and were using it, I was sitting in a hole with some pilots when the Japs sent about a dozen large shells over. One was close enough to throw a load of dirt in on us—the closest a shell ever came to me. I knew as well as if I could see my face that beneath the dust and beard, around my eyes where it showed, my skin was a pale, damp green. I asked one of the pilots, and he said it was. He was grinning. The shell hadn't bothered him much.

It's just how your imagination works; men have different specialties in the line of fear. Mine is shells. When I thought of bullets, I thought of them as being unlikely to hit me in the first place, and of their going through a leg or arm, or shoulder, if one did catch me. A clean hole. Even a chest wound usually isn't too bad if you get prompt attention. But a shell—when I thought of a shell's hitting or landing near, I was thinking of no more me, of blankness, of that's all.

One of my friends, a movie photographer, had an unusual fear. It was the fear of being wounded and lying on the battlefield unable to move, and being run over by a tank or amtrac. He thought about it all the way to Iwo. On D day, neither shellfire nor anything else worried him—just the idea of being run over. On the morning of D plus one he was run over by an amtrac. He was asleep in his foxhole when he was awakened by the amtrac bearing down on him, only a few feet away. To make it as terrible as possible, he knew instantly and certainly what it was, had time to think, "My God, it's happening!" but not time to get out of the way. Its tracks ran over the hole and over him, over his head and upper body, driving him down into the sand. And stopped.

They dug in the loose sand under the amtrac and pulled him out. He had been sleeping in his helmet, and it is of a singular shape now, quite flat on one side. When he puts it on, there is just barely leeway to do so. The pressure on his chest and shoulders, which would have killed him if the amtrac had gone a few more inches, made it impossible for him to sleep except sitting up for the next week, but after that he was entirely okay, and went on shooting film all the time, quite unconcerned in some rather concerning spots he chose to work. Maybe he figured it had had a go at him and missed, so there was nothing further to worry about.

I had wondered what effect it would have to see men hit, men dying, and men dead. It's no good, but it's impersonal. You see with the eyes only, realize with the mind only; your emotions turn off. No human mental, nervous, and emotional structure could stand the impact of such feelings, I suppose, and so some automatic switch turns them off. It's bad, and you realize it, but you can go on with your work. But that's for the men you didn't know. For the few, for men you have known well, for close friends, then it's different. Then is when you're knocked all to hell inside, all dead and empty and mixed up.

Some men spoke emphatically on the way over of how happy they would be not to go in D day, or at all, and dwelt on the depth and size of the foxholes they would straightway dig and move into, if they did go in. I had wondered what they'd really do.

I saw them on D day carrying casualties on litters down that hill to the beach, through small-arms fire coming from both sides, through the bursts of mortar shells. You can't run very fast carrying a litter; you have to be upright; you have to stop for rest, in that sand; and when you do, there is rarely a handy hole to fit four men and a litter. So you make a dandy target. I heard others who, not having been sent in on D day, plead to go in D plus one; heard them later volunteering to go up to the front as replacements. It was about what I had expected of them, the phonies. They weren't exceptional.

I had wondered what it would be like on the front, of course. It's hard to explain, I'm afraid, for it's difficult to imagine battle without thinking of heroics and dramatics, of dashing figures and climactic spectacles. It is even difficult for me to do so now, when I have seen that it's not like that. It's like work. It *is* work. There are periods of urgency, certainly, demanding the right decision, made instantly, and split-second timing and desperate effort; and there are intervals when the tension is not at peak, of course; but these are merely parts of a whole, and the whole is no more or less than dangerous drudgery— mean, exhausting work at which men get shot and blown apart. And the only feelings evident are those of tiredness and anger and, when a mission has been handled with a minimum of loss, grim satisfaction. Oh, there's drama, but it doesn't seem such then; and there's heroism, and it doesn't either.

I landed with the 28th Marines and had good friends among them. Theirs had been the task of taking Surabachi at the first, the key to the operation, and they took it. Then, with a few days' rest, they were on the front lines almost steadily until the very end, and it fell to their lot to hit that deep gorge with its hive of caves which the Japs chose for their final stand. And chose well. I was on the beach when the 28th came down to re-embark. They had finished the gorge only the day before. They were cheerful, for they were getting off the island now, but they were quiet men. They would smile instead of laugh. You couldn't distinguish officers from men—all dusty, all weary, nearly all heavily bearded.

A battalion sergeant major stopped to pass a word with a sergeant I was talking to. The sergeant said he was looking forward to getting back into a camp and coming over to the battalion's sergeants' mess for a good meal once again. A battalion's normal complement of sergeants is sixty-nine. The sergeant major was silent for a moment. "Well, I got six now," he said. From sixty-nine.

I shall not forget our cemetery, with its rows of white crosses and its white picket fence the Seabees made from artillery ammunition cases; with a battery of big 155s firing over it intermittently; with Surabachi rising close behind it, from whose sides many of its tenants were routed here. Or the men walking through it, along between the rows of crosses, their eyes turned down, reading the names, looking for their buddies. (Is "buddy" a corny word? It had seemed so to me, but it never will again. It's the term they use.)

Casualties from the hospital, limping, with bandages on their heads, with their arms in slings. Men just down from the front, with maybe only an hour to spend before they go back up again. With their weapons, wearing helmets. With the dust of Iwo Jima caked on their faces until you cannot say whether one's skin is fair or dark, the dust of Iwo Jima matted in their weeks-old beards.

I won't forget their dirty, ragged dungarees, or their backs, or the way they walked. I won't forget their faces.

Sergeant Francis W. Cockrel

D Day

There was the faintest of grins on the faces of the Marines as they crouched in the landing craft that was bouncing toward the beach of Iwo Jima. It was D day and this was one of the initial assault waves.

On the inside of the ramp the coxswain had painted with bold letters and heavy brush: "TOO LATE TO WORRY."

Technical Sergeant Henry A. Weaver

Okinawa: Nightmare of Rain and Death

Okinawa's rainy season arrived while the fighting was still going on. Here is what it was like in one foxhole on the slope of a hill, perhaps seven feet long and three feet wide.

In it lay a Marine who at first could not be distinguished from the jellied terrain around him. He wore no poncho because it would have impeded him if he had had to advance.

He was soaked to the skin and the soft mud had been packed into clay over his face and clothing. He had spent a sleepless night, drenched in the water pouring steadily from the gray skies, and his eyes were red-rimmed with weariness. All through the night the Japs had kept up an intermittent artillery and mortar barrage into the area and for each dragging minute of that night he had heard the soft crunch of the deadly shells hitting the earth around him.

Occasionally there was a cry of pain, but he was too full of his own woes to think too much of it. Perhaps a hospital corpsman could break through in the morning to aid the wounded. Perhaps he couldn't.

The Marine had had a breakfast of sorts, only because he felt he should eat something. His rations were slimy, crusted with soft mud which had seeped into the small can of pork and egg yolks, eaten cold because a fire was impossible. Afterward he pulled a cigarette from the cache in his helmet, but that had been soaked, too. He lighted it carefully and tried to puff through the drenched tobacco.

He had his rifle under his body, although he knew he could never hope to keep it really dry. But he had it ready. His eyes stared ahead probing the blackness for a possible counterattack and wishing it would happen, yet hoping it wouldn't. In this war of opposing lines usually no more than fifty yards apart, the fighting went on regardless of weather conditions. The artillery duel was just as intense as it was two days ago, though the rain muffled the boom of the heavy guns into a shapeless roar.

"Don't let me be wounded in this mud," he prayed. "Don't let me get hit bad."

Suddenly an enemy mortar barrage was concentrated on that area. He ducked his head so that his chin disappeared under the surface of the muddy water. He counted the crunch-crunch-crunch of the shells. A short distance away a machine gun chattered and he carefully raised his head to see if the Japs were coming. Men near him had been hit and he was suddenly concerned. Now it was light enough to see the effects of the battle. He watched the slow movement of the first-aid men and wondered how he would let them know if he was hit. The rain still drummed against his helmet and pecked sharply at his face. Little pellets of mud shot into his eyes and clung to the lids.

The corpsmen were having a tough time with the wounded man near by. They slid around and dropped to their knees. Their feet crumbled the walls of the foxhole, causing them to fall in with their human burden. The injured Marine groaned softly and tried to wipe his face with a hand dripping mud. It dropped back into the yielding earth. The corpsmen finally placed him on their stretcher. Sliding and sinking into the mud, they carried their man back to the aid station. But they left behind them the quiet form of another man. The sudden realization that this man was dead was like an exclamation that popped in the brain of the drenched Marine in his foxhole.

The enemy barrage stumbled and came to a halt just as suddenly as it started. It was quiet now. The Marine became aware again of the mud and the rain. He noticed that his left arm was numb with the cold. He shifted to the right arm, tried to rub some of the rust off his carbine, and peered ahead through the rain, hoping it would stop and that someday he would go dancing with his best girl again.

Technical Sergeant Murray Lewis

End of Campaign

There was tragic irony in the burden carried by the Marine runner who was killed while taking messages from his Sixth Division command post to units fighting at the front on Okinawa. As he neared the front he was killed by a sniper. Clutched in his hands, along with battle reports and action messages, were the day's news sheets.

The lead story was a dispatch from Guam. It said the end of the Okinawa campaign was only a matter of hours.

Technical Sergeant George R. Voigt

The Flyers' War

Shot Down

My division was not assigned for flight so we volunteered to take the dawn patrol next morning. "Washing Machine" Charlie came over on the hour all that night and as we took off at five he came over once more to drop a stick of bombs on the field. It was still dark but there was a moon and, as I looked up, I could see his silhouette ten thousand feet above me.

We made a quick join-up and started after him. The boys came in close to me in order to see my wings in the darkness and I kept my eyes glued on the hazy blur in the distance that was the Jap Betty. From the first we knew we had a long chase ahead of us because he was speeding away and we had a long climb up to him. New Georgia was behind and we were almost over the mountains of Kolombangara before it became apparent that we were gaining on him. By then we were nearly on his level.

The plane I had grabbed checked out fine on the ground but, as we got over the water again, the fuel pressure gauge started wavering. The normal pressure is fifteen pounds per square inch and now the needle was down almost to eight. I checked over the gas supply and turned on the electric fuel pump but the needle kept going down. I called the division over the radio and told them I might have to turn back and asked them if they were able to pick up the bomber. They spread out a little to leave their attention free for the sky ahead, but the affirmative answer failed to come. I knew that the fever of the chase was just as strong with them as with me and I knew that I couldn't disappoint them by giving up while there was still a chance. We were on the same level with Charlie now and about a thousand yards behind. Our object was to get above and ahead of him before starting our attack but, as the little needle continued down, I wobbled my wings and started in from where we were. I wanted to pass the thirteen mark on my score.

I dove underneath him thinking that I could make one pass on his unprotected belly and then return to base. The boys could pick him up as I passed him. My intention was to attack straight up and miss the cannon in his tail that could fire down at an angle of forty-five degrees. The impression still remains in my mind that, as I came up, the bomb bay opened and a gun started firing down from that unorthodox position.

I was hit three times before I could wink an eye. All three shots seemed to center around the bottom of my cockpit and when I looked down, there was a small flicker of flame starting to take hold. All the reaction of months of combat surged up inside me and before I could think, I had my radio disconnected, the safety belt and shoulder straps unfastened, and the hood of the canopy thrown back.

It was when I stood up in the seat and attempted to climb over the side that thought returned to me. I was going to have plenty of time to think. My plane was pushing through the lower seat of air at more than three hundred knots, and its stream over my cockpit was like a steel wall holding me in. It would bend but it wouldn't break. The air whipping into the fuselage had fanned that spark into a blowtorch that swept up my legs as I sank back into the seat. I could not get out.

I will never be able to recall all the thoughts that ran through my head but one of them was: "How simple it would be just to ride her in." That thought grew until it excluded all others. The pain stopped in my legs and the turmoil in my brain subsided; complete satisfaction and contentedness engulfed me.

It seems that feeling was with me for hours, but I know that actually it was over in a split second. Then God came off his pedestal to give me one big boot in the seat of righteousness and I was free of the plane. What other explanation? I had been straining for freedom with my legs braced against the rudder bars and then the tail was coming at me. I raised my legs to clear the elevators and I was on my own. The plane was gone.

Then I remembered my parachute and wondered if it was still on me. I never felt it open when I pulled the ripcord but I noticed the risers braced against my back attached to something solid above. Almost at once I saw the plane crash in the water below. There wasn't a sound to be heard. The sun was just coming out of the sea and the water a few thousand feet below was like a peaceful dream.

I was brought out of it with a snap. The sock on my left leg was still smoldering and I began to feel it. I reached down and snuffed it out with my good hand. The rest of my clothes did not catch fire. I suppose they didn't have time. My legs were covered with a white ash that used to be skin but didn't hurt much at the moment. My face and right arm had not been burned so deeply and the surface nerves were still working nicely. My hair was all gone and pieces of skin hung around my lips. I hurt like the devil.

As soon as I got this inventory complete, I began to think of making a water landing in a parachute and as soon as I thought of it I did it.

The water was warm and with my Mae West inflated, it didn't take much effort to swim around and locate the bathtub size raft that was attached to the chute. I jerked the pin from the neck of the CO_2 bottle and turned the handle. The small raft squeaked like a toy balloom as it inflated. Too late I noticed that the guide rope had wrapped itself around the middle of the raft tying the two sides together. I swam around that darn boat for fifteen minutes working that rope loose so I could get in.

By the time that was settled, the thing was full of water but it made my legs feel better so I left it alone. I didn't feel like bailing anyway. The sun was well above the horizon and promised to scorch me good. I finally decided to throw my parachute over my head and make a slit in it to see through. It served very nicely.

The nearest island was Kolombangara and it was still Jap held, but I figured I probably wouldn't make it until night and I would find a fresh-water pool to wade around in until somebody found me. There was a fifty-fifty chance it would be a native. At any rate, I had to have something to do so I started paddling with my hands in that direction. I had to keep my right hand in the water anyhow to keep down the pain.

The rest of the division came back from the morning's work soon and as they headed straight for Munda, I knew they thought I had returned to base after the first pass and had not known of my predicament. A few hours later two planes circled the island near the shore and I knew they were looking for me. They passed twice—always too far from me—and started off. I knew the search was finished and to all intents and purposes so was I.

It may sound drastic but at this particular point I did not care. I was so exhausted that I could only paddle two strokes before I had to rest. The very best I could do was keep the raft facing away from the sun. My legs were starting to hurt more and I had fleeting wishes that I had stayed with the plane. To make matters worse, large fish were bumping the bottom of the boat making my legs all the more uncomfortable.

It was about 2:30 when the roar of a surface boat caught my attention. It was behind me, farther yet to sea and nearly out of sight. It was going down the slot toward New Georgia and I figured that it might be one of ours. It passed on from the point closest to me and I again turned towards the island. Almost five minutes later the dim sound of the motor stopped suddenly then broke into a more vigorous roar. I turned around and could tell that they were heading back to investigate me. As they came closer, a sailor held up the Union Jack and my subconscious fears were allayed. I suppose I was happy enough inside, but outwardly the situation registered and that was all. The PT boat maneuvered around me and I held up my left arm for them to grab. As I was hoisted aboard, all I could say was, "Be careful with my legs."

They were more than careful; they were tender. They laid me out on a hatchway and made a canvas shelter to keep the sun off. Someone cut my clothes away and gave me a shot of morphine. When he had taken my pulse and blood pressure he looked very surprised. I was going to be all right.

I was taken back to Munda where an ambulance picked me up. Harrison was with the ambulance and as they lifted me aboard, I said, "I sure look like hell, don't I?" From the expression on his face, I knew that he agreed with me.

The next morning I was taken by transport to Guadalcanal where a base hospital had been set up. In a few days, the boys came back from Munda on their way to Espiritu. From there they were going home. Avey told me that they had finished off the bomber and all its crew and that made me feel much better.

Just one year had passed since I last saw the mainland and though there were to be many times when I wished I had gone in with my plane, deep down I was grateful for the thought that I would see it once more. A good many of the best people I had ever known would not have that chance and it was fitting that I should at least suffer for the privilege.

I was glad to be alive.

Major James N. Cupp

Tactics

Young Sam Logan of Paola, Kansas, a member of the famous Wolf Pack Squadron, went out yesterday on an interceptor strike against fifty-eight Jap Zeros and bombers. He came back to Guadalcanal in a Navy rescue plane with his right foot gone and better knowledge of the tactics of the enemy.

Logan had been on the tail of a Zero. A second Zero whirled in on his own fighter. Before Logan could fire, the pursuing Jap emptied his guns. Logan's plane started to burn and he bailed out. He was at 8,000 feet. As he floated down, the Jap pilot evidently found his ammunition gone. He dove his plane on Logan, trying recklessly to clip him with the propeller. He dove twice. Each time Logan desperately yanked himself up by the parachute shrouds.

On the third pass, the Jap's propeller chopped off the Marine pilot's right foot and part of his left heel. Logan hit the water a few minutes later. Soon afterward, weak from the loss of blood, Logan was picked up and rushed to a hospital. His right foot was later amputated at the ankle.

"Each time the Jap made a pass at me," said Logan, "I thought he would hit me head on. I figure I'm lucky to get out with only my foot missing. That Jap did his best to kill me."

Technical Sergeant Harry S. Bolser

Song for a Pilot

Who plows the sky, said a wise man,
    Shows himself a fool;
But he went out to plow it—
    Taught in a different school.

Who sows the wind, says Scripture,
    Must reap and reap again;
But he went out to sow the wind—
    And reaped the bitter grain.

He took his death like charity,
    Like nothing understood;
He freshened all the oldest words
    With all his blood.

Captain Richard G. Hubler

Above Rabaul

The Avenger and its two Hellcat escorts circled above Rabaul, ignored for the moment by enemy fighters who were making things hot for the other carrier planes below. The Air Group skipper, Commander Howard Caldwell, was staying up high for the present to see how his boys were doing, and to give Photographer's Mate First Class Paul Barnett a chance for some good pictures. The 30-year-old photographer was taking shots of the havoc below as fast as he could work the shutter.

The Dauntlesses had already gone into their dives, screaming down on the ships in the harbor, their rear men shooting off enemy planes that managed somehow to get through a cross fire of antiaircraft to drop their fish. A few hundred yards away the other Avengers were peeling off. As the last of the group dropped away toward the harbor, the Zeros came in, concentrating on the lone torpedo plane and its escort. The Japs like easy pickings, and this looked like a setup. Odds were three to one.

Commander Caldwell put his plane into a dive, with the intention of joining up with the re-forming group, but the intention was never carried out. The three planes pulled out of the dive at little better than a thousand feet, fighting. The two escorting Hellcats took on as many Zekes as they could, but there were plenty left over for the bigger plane. They hit from all directions at once.

The pilot swung the bomber in frantic evasive tactics, watching for a chance to use his forward guns. In the exposed seat behind him, Paul Barnett snapped his camera shutter imperturbably. Ken Bratton, the Oxford, Mississippi, turret gunner, was having a busy time lining up his sights on one attacker after the other, the whine of his turret gears augmenting the sounds of the racing engine and the machine guns. Below, at the tunnel gun, Chief Aviation Radioman Bob Morey moved from side to side, trying to bring his gun to bear on the slim shapes that kept flashing by.

From overhead came the deep chatter of Ken Bratton's big 50, a long, sustained burst. Then a triumphant yell: "I got one!" Directly behind the Avenger, a Zeke was falling, out of control. Morey caught a glimpse of it as it hit the water astern; then he was too busy to watch any longer. There was a long nightmare of sleek shapes driving in endlessly, breaking away with a last defiant burst, then circling for a new attack. The air was heavy with the stench of burned powder and overheated metal. Now and then came dull crunches as slugs tore through the taut skin of the plane.

A splinter bit into Morey's forearm. He looked at it curiously, thinking in a detached way, "Why, you're wounded!" He rubbed at the bleeding spot and the splinter came out. Morey went back to the vital business of keeping the Avenger's tail clean.

Ken Bratton was swinging the turret muzzle, pointing at the most dangerous of the enemy fighters. Pretty soon he would have to call dawn to Morey for more ammunition. Then, without warning, the turret stopped swinging, and with an ominous rumble the whine of gear ceased. Bratton glanced up as a Zeke drove in, guns flaming. A jagged star blossomed on the bulletproof windshield. In the same instant, pain ground through his knee and hip. He gasped, "I'm hit!"

Morey glanced up into the turret in time to see Bratton's face twist with pain, but he couldn't leave his gun to help out, because more fighters were making their runs. One Jap, evidently noticing that the turret wasn't following him, came in with deliberate care and raked the Avenger before and aft. Slugs whined through armor plate. Morey heard one smash into the radio behind him and tried to call the pilot. The interphone was dead.

There were more fighters out behind, lining up to come in by turns. The Hellcats were battling heavy odds. The chief radioman said a brief prayer: "Please, God, help us to get out of here!"

Up in the turret, Ken Bratton was still fighting. The turret was out, his 50-caliber gun was useless. But the Mississippi boy wasn't taking the beating lying down. As Morey looked up to see how he was doing, Bratton pulled out his .45 automatic, and started taking futile potshots at the enemy.

Commander Caldwell was having troubles of his own. He had flown a zigzag course, following a generally southward trend through any cloud cover that offered, hoping to lose the Zeros. Instead, he had lost one of his own fighters. He pulled up abeam of the remaining Hellcat so that the two planes could give each other protection.

The loss of the fighter was not the only bad news. The left aileron was jammed, making it hard work to turn, and so much of the control surfaces was gone that the big plane was handling sloppily. Cold air blew in from behind, through holes left aft by enemy slugs, and the air was bringing with it a fine red mist, a thin spray of blood that was coating the windshield and making his goggles useless.

Morey turned for another look at Bratton. The turret gunner's arm was hanging limp, the pistol dangling from his fingers. He motioned weakly that he couldn't fire it any more. From the bottom of the turret came a film of red wetness that smeared the armor plate.

Morey started back to his gun, then turned again. Paul Barnett, the Texas photographer, was slumped over in his seat. But there wasn't time for an examination, not right then. He had to splice in extra rounds, working fast because a Zeke was making a run from astern.

Commander Caldwell spotted the Jap. It was high, too high for the tunnel gun to reach—and the turret was out. Morey was firing futilely under the enemy fighter, trying to scare him off with tracer. The Jap wouldn't scare. He knew the tunnel gun wouldn't reach him. He sent his rounds into the Avenger. The tunnel gunner felt something grate into his knee. At that moment the pilot shoved the nose of the Avenger down and the fighter was squarely in the sight. Morey depressed the trigger, saw his tracer bite into the Jap's engine, saw the engine explode, saw the wings rock as the Zeke fell off into a final spin.

But there were plenty of enemy fighters left.

Commander Caldwell watched one make a run on his remaining Hellcat, pouring burst after burst into the big fighter. The pilot must have been in trouble, because he took no evasive action. The commander tried to turn in, to take the Zeke off the Hellcat's tail, but the Avenger responded sluggishly.

The Hellcat staggered and rocked under the heavy fire from the Zero, taking all the enemy plane had to give. Finally the Jap broke away, his ammunition exhausted. Two more Japs were making runs on the Avenger astern. Morey threw tracer at them and saw them break away. He spliced the last of his ammunition into the belt.

Commander Caldwell scanned the sky. One left, high above his tail, out of range. As he watched, it made a long, slow turn, as though undecided, and broke off. The fight was over.

Twenty-five minutes had passed since the first planes jumped them

—twenty-five minutes of shuttling around the harbor, taking it from the Zekes every inch of the way. How about the crew? He had heard nothing from any of them for many minutes—and there was the ominous fact of the blood-soaked windshield and the useless goggles. He had no way of knowing if any of them were still alive.

As the last fighter vanished, Morey got busy. He ignored his own wounds, in neck, shoulder, knee and arm, until the others had been cared for. Bratton couldn't get out of the turret because of his shattered knee. Morey handed him bandages and morphine, then crawled forward to Barnett. The boy from Corpus Christi was slumped in his seat, blood staining his head and jacket. Morey ripped his sleeve away and injected a syrette of morphine. It left a hard lump under the skin. The tunnel gunner swallowed hard, and let the torn sleeve drop. Presently he crawled back to the aft compartment.

Bratton handed down a note. It would have been impossible to talk over the engine noise. "My knee is hit, also hip. You okay? Commander okay? Barnett?" The chief radioman pointed forward to where Barnett rested, his camera still clutched in his hands. He made a gesture the turret gunner recognized: the hand held stiff and drawn across the throat.

Morey scribbled a note to Commander Caldwell, debating whether to tell him of Barnett's death. He decided on half-truth: "Bratton and Barnett out of commission. You okay?" He took it forward, across the body of the photographer. Commander Caldwell didn't try to answer. He reached behind him and took Morey's hand and squeezed it tight. It told the chief better than any words what the skipper had been thinking.

Aft again, Morey lit cigarettes for himself and Bratton. There was another exchange of notes.

"We'll be okay now."

"Yes. For a while I didn't think we would come back."

Morey nodded. He looked around him; daylight showed through countless holes. He said softly, "Thank You, God."

And then they were over the carrier, getting a wave-off on the first approach. Commander Caldwell's lights showed only one wheel down. Signals from the ship confirmed it. Watchers could see the gaping holes in wings and fuselage, the ragged edges where great chunks of the control surfaces were shot away; the flaps needed to slow the big plane were fully closed. The plane was in bad shape for a tricky carrier landing, but dunking was out of the question with wounded aboard. He started in.

The Avenger came into the slot, well to port, out of the turbulent air behind the big smokestack. The landing-signal officer's paddles flashed and Commander Caldwell cut the gun and let the big plane sell out. The hook caught; the wing went down.

Howard Caldwell had brought the Navy's biggest carrier plane in on a pitching flight deck—and he hadn't even jolted his crew!

This was the aftermath: Ken Bratton went home to the States for hospitalization. A few days later Commander Caldwell and Chief Morey took off for another strike on Rabaul. Paul Barnett was buried at sea. The pictures he had given his life to take were complete and clear—and the last one in the camera told of the last thing Paul had seen: the perfect silhouette of a Zero, driving in for the attack.

Second Lieutenant Harold L. Goodwin

Behind the Lines

A squall burst suddenly against the Quonset hut that served as flight office for the Marine SBD squadron in the Marshalls. In a corner of the office several pilots stood around a portable phonograph and a rack of records. Someone selected a disk, placed it on the turntable and after a moment of scraping sound Dinah Shore sang "I Walk Alone."

The intelligence officer, a lean young man with a lined brown face, affectionately called "the Sad Sack" because he always met returning pilots with worried look and harried manner, said, "They're hitting Jaluit today. Pinpoint bombing. Gun installations. Supply area." Sixteen SBDs, each loaded with three 500-pound general-purpose bombs were about to set out for Jaluit atoll, once the administrative center of

Nippon's outer island perimeter, now a bomb-packed wasteland three thousand miles behind American front lines. The intelligence officer rubbed his palms together nervously. "That redhead loves it. He seems to think he has a one-man grudge against the Japs, and sometimes goes on extracurricular hops to get in an extra lick. And he flies that SBD as if he was raised in it."

The ebullient redhead from Bartlesville, Oklahoma, was Marine First Lieutenant Paul W. Norvell. He moved through the small crowded office toward the partitioned-off flight gear compartment. One of his buddies, a gangling ex-farmer from east Texas, called to him, "Hey, Red! This where you got that Jap power launch?"

The Texas pilot was standing with several companions before an enlarged aerial photo of Maloelap atoll pinned to the wall. They were looking at a red crayon check close on the lagoon side of the shore.

"Yeah," Lieutenant Norvell said. "Caught 'em by surprise . . . with a pair of roguish eyes. . . ." He was still humming the tune as he went into the other room and started to buckle on his Mae West and chute.

The Sad Sack said: "We keep a scoreboard with a tally of Jap craft sunk by our squadron. Early in the campaign we caught several small freighters, but there hasn't been a Jap ship of any size in the mid-Pacific for months. Besides our almost daily strikes we keep two-plane search patrols out over these by-passed Jap atolls. Occasionally the boys surprise some of the Nips out in small fishing boats or in power launches on the lagoon. Red leads; he has eighteen Nip boats to his credit."

The pilot with the sentimental streak wound up the phonograph and played "I Walk Alone" again. The other pilots began to cluster around the door, watching the rain sweep across the white coral runway. The driving drops made tearing sounds in the feathery palms leaning toward the breakers on the reef a scant two hundred yards away.

"Red celebrated this past December seventh in his own way," said the Sad Sack. "He was slated for search patrol over Mille and Jaluit that morning. So he stayed up half the night before, collecting empty beer bottles and writing out a message to put in them: REMEMBER PEARL HARBOR. He took along a score of hand grenades on his patrol and alternated dropping the beer bottles, strafing, and tossing the grenades over the side.

"Bombing cornered Jap garrisons in the Marshalls is a necessary duty," the Sad Sack went on. "But Red, like most of the boys in the outfit, wants in on the real thing. They feel sidetracked here. They want to be in the skies over the next beachhead when Marine infantry makes another landing. They want to be up there, punching at Jap Zeros when the boys go in for the next assault."

A jeep skidded to a stop in front of the flight office. Behind it a small carry-all truck ground to a halt. The pilots moved out and were joined by their gunners. The jeep and truck would take them to their parked SBDs whose engines were already warmed up by the silent, watchful mechs. On the eastern horizon clouds were turning pink. The trade winds blew steadily, rustling the wet palm fronds till they sounded like the long dry grass back in Kansas.

"They're one of the last SBD squadrons," the Sad Sack said. "Gunners and pilots—they're a vanishing breed. But they were quite a team in their heyday."

Lieutenant Norvell, Marine pilot, perched himself in the rear of the jeep. As it backed away and turned his voice drifted back. "A-bombing we will go . . ."

Technical Sergeant Peter B. Germano

A Man to Meet

The first Marine to hit the beach at Bougainville stumbled in the heavy surf, recovered and charged ashore. That first Marine is a man to meet, but our acquaintanceship was merely in passing. He had no time to look at me that hot November morning, and though I was looking hard for him, the glimpse was only fleeting. But I know I saw him. At least I saw a speck and a sliver of steel waver slightly in the haze of burning powder hanging over Empress Augusta Bay.

The first Marine was going his way, a few hard feet at a time, through the wet sand. I was going mine, snugly, riding at two hundred miles an hour in an Avenger bomber. We met there on the beach at Bougainville for, perhaps, a thousandth of a second. My watch said 7:23.

Someday I may get to shake the hand of that first Marine. He is a man to cultivate.

Captain Penn T. Kimball

Close Support Bombing

On a certain April morning, 1945, when the yellow mist began to rise from the sodden fields between the hills that guard the approaches to Gusakama Town, a battalion of a famous New York regiment was receiving extremely galling fire from the front, the right flank, and the rear. Their lines, formed in the darkness before moonrise after a day of the savage cave-to-cave fighting which marked the southern drive on Okinawa, lay in a lazy Z. Forward, in the direction of the advance, were the troops of Able Company, dug into shallow foxholes along an east-west road leading out of Gusakama. Hinged to their right flank, and running back along a line parallel to a little ridge from which the advancing troops had received only moderate harassing fire the evening before, was King Company. Its right flank in turn was attached to the left of Charlie Company, the bottom bar of the Z.

It was not a situation to make a commander lie down at night to sweet, untroubled dreams. Army Lieutenant Colonel James H. ("Gentleman Jim") Mahoney, of New York and Orange, New Jersey, had mulled the problem over in the night, as the flares brightened the sky and the enemy searched the crevices of the ground with mortar fire; and, as was his custom, he had chosen the simplest and most rational solution.

At dawn, Able Company would pour a steady mortar and small-arms supporting fire into Gusakama Town. King Company with similar fire would pin down the Japs on the ridge, and Charlie Company, covered by King Company's fire, would sweep along the ridge to command the high ground overlooking Gusakama. Then, while Able and Charlie poured their fire into the beehive village, King would move forward in the center to the assault upon the town.

But as the first light came, and men began to stir and tense themselves for the push, all plans became just so much paper, as plans often do in war. The Japanese, deep in their caves when King Company's flanking scouts had moved down the ridge the evening before, came out and laid down a devastating fire. It beat upon Able Company from the right flank, and from the rear. King Company was pinned to the earth under it, and Charlie Company, attempting its advance down the long axis of the ridge, found itself moving into a blizzard of flying steel.

Here was the time for another decision. From his forward observation post where he and his air liaison officer, Captain John S. Godley of Detroit, crouched in the opening of an ancient tomb, Colonel Mahoney looked over the field and made up his mind. Naval gunfire from the harbor would not do, nor artillery firing from the north, for to each of these there were unreachable spots along the ridge from which the heaviest fire was coming.

"It will have to be planes," he said to Godley. "How soon can they get here?"

"Thirty minutes at best," Godley said.

The colonel frowned. "We can be badly hurt by then. Ask them to hurry."

Godley spoke into his radio. "Hello, Speed Ball, this is Short Rock."

Back of the lines, in the Marine Air Support Control Unit, Captain Raymond A. Rogers answered. "Speed Ball to Short Rock. Go ahead."

Above the pound and chatter of the guns, Godley talked swiftly. First, from a map smoothed upon his knee, he gave the target squares located on the ridge. Then, his eye sweeping the terrain in front of him, he began to pinpoint, while Rogers followed him on an air photo. There in that gully, a machine-gun nest. See the big white rock there? Beneath it, in a cave, a DP (dual-purpose gun). He worked the face

· 123 ·

of the ridge, picking out the spots from which the hottest fire was pouring. Red dots—targets—speckled Rogers's photo as he followed the directions coming crisply from his phones.

Lieutenant Colonel William A. Kuretich, of Hope, Kansas, commander of Support Aircraft, glanced at the target form Rogers was filling out and began to scan his plane availability board. The evening before, like a housewife ordering groceries, he had ordered his strike planes for the day. A dozen Corsairs from Major General Pat Mulcahy's Second Marine Air Wing loaded with bombs for a strike on a Jap troop area. A dozen carrier-based Avenger torpedo bombers to do a little job for the Navy: a smashing strike at torpedo-launching stations along the coast from which the Nips had been harassing the Fleet. A dozen Navy Helldiver dive bombers, loaded with 1,000-pounders, to work over some stubborn cave guns down on the left flank. And, just to be on the safe side, four rugged Marine Corsairs loaded with bombs, rockets, and plenty of ammo for their 50-calibers, to prowl the front on call, ready to go to the aid of anybody who needed help in a hurry.

"Okay, Short Rock," said Rogers. "Help coming up." He passed the target data over to Major Jack Moore, support air director. "It's urgent, Jack," he said. "Push it."

Major Moore spoke to the Corsairs as they circled over the front. "Business for you, boys. Here's the word."

Even while he was speaking the gull-winged fighter-bombers were turning their noses toward the target area. The men went joyfully. For two successive nights, their pilots had lain in their foxholes beside the airstrip while Jap bombers roared over, laying daisy-cutters among the tents.

Huddled in his Okinawan tomb, Godley looked up to see them circling, and his eyes bugged. He had figured thirty minutes. Here they were on station, ready to go to work—in twelve. Through Moore, Godley began to talk them onto the target.

Then Rogers broke in: "Remember to give yourself time to pull back a little. We don't want a big one to go wild and pin your ears back.

Those are five-hundred-pound eggs they'll be laying. You are three hundred yards too close."

"Listen, pal," said Godley. "If I pull out of this hole, the Nips will really pin my ears back. I'm staying here. Your boys hit where they look. I'm not worried about 'em."

"Okay, okay," said Rogers. "But, for God's sake, give 'em some sort of marker to show 'em where you are."

In the tomb with Godley, Corporal Dick Winfield, of Doris, California, a tall, sad-eyed telephone lineman, stood up and draped a white panel down his back, knotting it around his neck like a cape. "Lemme get to that little ditch out there. I'll be the marker." He dived for the ditch and lay down, covering his head with his hands.

Moore passed the word of the human marker to Bob Hammond in the air. Hammond peered over the side of his Corsair and spoke to his pilots: "Little white speck down there. Marks the observer's post. Stay west of it, so you won't hurt any of our own folks. Got it?"

"Roger," said Lieutenant Marvin Van Salter.

"Sure," said Lieutenant Marion Crawford.

"Let's put the show on the road," said Lieutenant Stub Washburn, an impatient man.

Godley was talking fast now, through Jack Moore, to the planes. "See the little gully running east and west? The big white rock at the head of it? Gun position there. Now up a little, about forty yards. Little clump of trees. There's a DP in there. Machine guns all along the ridge. Both sides and on the crest. Give the whole hogback a good going-over with the bombs first. Then use the rockets on anything still kicking."

"Yowsah," said Hammond. "Got it. But let me give 'em a little dry run first, over that DP under the rock just to be sure I got it straight in my mind where it is. I'll waggle my wings when I'm over it."

He went down in the dummy run, his three planes following. In his hole, John Godley watched. Like a man having somebody else scratch his back, he gave directions: "Ea-sst a little. Now tell him west just a hair. Now they're on. Right there. Ahhh."

Crooomp! Hammond's first 500-pounder fell. John Godley gave minute corrections. Crooomp! Crawford came in. Whooomp! Kerr-rooom! Van Salter and Washburn followed him. Hammond was circling for his second run.

Croooom! Hammond's second bomb was in. John Godley, who had been cool and calm as he talked them on, was yelling now. In the control room, men around the table slid their earphones up to hear his voice as it shrilled in Moore's phone.

"Right on. Right on!" he was yelling. "Man, oh man, oh man, oh man! Is that letting them have it!"

Above the target the Corsairs were swinging in for their rocket run. Whooosh, Wham! "Oh, that's fine. That's perfect. Perfect, perfect! Right on the button. Right in there. Hey, Air Control, tell those boys they did a magnificent job. Tell 'em it was perfect. Tell 'em we said thanks a million."

"Thank you, Short Rock," said Captain Rogers. "We strike to please."

Down south, where the wrinkled hills lead to Gusakama Town, through the stinging smell of high explosives, and the debris of broken guns, Charlie Company, walking upright, moved swiftly up the shattered ridge.

First Lieutenant Harold H. Martin

F4Us at 2400

Corsairs with their wings pressed tight
Against their bodies, late at night
Look so much like birds asleep
I am tempted to stop and peep
To see if by chance they stand through the night
One wheel in view, the other out of sight.

Sergeant Henry Olczak

Visibility Limited

Guam's typhoon season, rivaling the Aleutians for foul flying weather, caught a night fighter pilot in a rain squall. Radioed to come in by the Orote Field tower, Lieutenant Malcolm G. Moncrief, of Prattville, Alabama, nosed down for a landing. The night was black. Pressure areas buffeted his Hellcat. Rain pounded on his windshield. He came in low over what he thought was the field and circled. He wasn't sure. He couldn't see much of anything. It was almost as black below as above.

The control tower men, hearing him twice come in and then zoom up again, called anxiously, "What's wrong? Can't you see the field?"

"Field, hell!" cracked back the exasperated pilot. "Where's Guam?"

Technical Sergeant Peter B. Germano

The Big Hairy Dogfight

Cy Dolezel said: "We broke out of the overcast at sixteen thousand feet, and dead ahead and two thousand feet above us was what looked like the whole Japanese air force. The thought flashed through my mind that they were Navy Hellcats because they were flying such beautiful formation. Then I saw those big rusty red meatballs, covering the whole wing tip. . . ."

"I knew them the minute I saw them," said Jerry Conners, "and I remember saying to myself 'Holy Cow!'"

"They were too pretty for ours," said Al Wells. "There's an old saying: 'If it's beautiful, it's a Jap,' and these were beautiful. Clean planes, not a bump nor an awkward line. Smooth round noses, slim fuselage, everything faired in smoothly—"

Charley Drake broke in: "That's right. Funny thing, the Jap seems to get the same perfection of line and detail in his fighter planes that the Jap artist does in these funny paintings; you know, every tiny little thing perfect and sort of delicate and beautiful. . . ."

Cy Dolezel said: "Everything but the camouflage. That's ugly. A sort of fishbelly bluish-gray below and a muddled blending of brown and green on top. Well, anyway, pretty or not, there we were and there they were looking down our throat with speed and altitude in their favor and us hanging on our props still in the climb. Maybe we should have ducked back for the clouds and run like hell, but that would have turned our tails to them and they'd have come down on us in a dive and it would have been murder before we got to the clouds.

"We'd been hitting a lot of old stuff, suiciders, low and slow on the deck, and we had been the ones with the advantage of speed and altitude. So we were sort of mentally conditioned to attack, I guess you'd say, and it didn't occur to anybody to run. We bored right on up and then they saw us. I saw them drop their belly tanks and here they came roaring down and we turned to get on their tails.

"They missed on their first pass and from then on down to the deck it was just a big wild, hairy dogfight, corkscrewing down and back up again. There's no way to tell it as one story for we were all split up then, and each of us went his way. It wasn't the way we were trained to try to dogfight 'em, but there was nothing else we could do. You couldn't find a man to join up on him because every time you looked there'd be a Jap. We were just diving and zooming and shooting every time one crossed our sights with our heads on swivels, and the Nips spinning on a dime and us yanking our noses up and down and left and right trying to get one in our sights for just a split second.

"Anyway, what happened to me was like this. When they missed in that first dive—and Lord knows why unless they were taken by surprise—I turned with the two that went past me and went into the cloud on their tail. We came out about two thousand feet below and one had drifted off to the left and was going on down in a diving spiral with me above him and off a little to one side. He came out of his spiral and leveled off and started to roll, and just as he turned on his back I gave him a quick squirt and he flamed.

"I went on down in my dive to about ten thousand, hunting for Drake, for I knew with the Japs flying in sections of two, and sometimes divisions, it was no sky for a single Corsair to be in who wanted to keep his health. But when I broke into the clear at ten thousand I didn't see Charley so I pulled back up to look for him and when I broke through again at sixteen thousand it was just like the playback of a movie scene.

"There were six of them waiting for me up there and when they saw me they flipped over in a dive. This time I made the mistake I didn't make the first time. I turned to dive back into the clouds below and just as I straightened out of my turn somebody hit me on the head with a baseball bat. It felt just like that, like somebody had hauled off and swung from Port Arthur and let me have one across the base of the skull about level with the ears.

"I went on down in an all-out dive with somebody playing 'The Bells of St. Mary's' inside my skull, and broke out again, this time about twelve thousand, and I circled around looking while my head cleared up. I began to figure by now what had happened. One of the Japs had caught me with a twenty-millimeter explosive bullet in the armor plate right back of my head and though the bullet didn't penetrate, when it exploded so close behind my head, the concussion had addled me a little. I wasn't scratched though, except for a bruised place on the back of my head. About this time I saw Jerry and I joined up with him and we reported back to Sleepytime who told us to come on home."

Jerry Connors said: "And they didn't have to tell me twice, either. Up till that time I wasn't so sure I was going to get home. They weren't coming in on me one at a time but two and three at once, right from the start. You see, I broke out a little behind Cy and Drake, when we spotted them, and the first thing I know as I start to the left in a steep climb trying to get on their tail, is these three making a section run on me. But they were too eager, for they overled me. I saw their tracers scooting past my nose but I didn't feel good about that.

"I grabbed my mike and yelled loud as I could holler to anybody who could hear: 'Hey, get these—off me,' and instead of going in behind them I started looking for Al, my section leader, to join up on him. But about the time I saw him, here came two more boring in on me from one o'clock, one high, one about level. I was behind Al and a little below, and the Zeke that was level must have figured on turning in on Al's tail, leaving me for his mate up high. So he whipped into a steep turn right in front of me. He filled up my whole windshield and I shot quick, a good burst, and he broke out of his turn, burning, headed down. But I almost scored double that time, for my tracers were whizzing right past Al's wing up ahead.

"The fellow who came in high I didn't see. He either didn't fire or missed. So I started trying to pull up on Al but just as I started moving up, Al got sight of one and firewalled after him, pulling away. Which left me lonesome as a lost chicken again, and here came two more, level, one dead on and the other from about two o'clock.

"The one head on and I started firing together at about seven hundred feet and he suddenly pushed his nose down to go under and I pushed over too and that brought him right through the pattern of my tracers. I saw pieces of his canopy flying off and he was smoking as he went under. I was doing all right so far but I still wanted company so I kept on hunting Al. When I spotted him again he was in the damnedest vertical ring-around-a-rosy you ever saw with a Zeke that was tying him in knots. Joining up with him would have been like trying to join up with two cats chasing each other around a barrel.

"I hung up there until they came out of about the fiftieth whirl, it seemed to me, and the Zeke didn't pull up again this time. He just kept going in on his back, into the sea. Then I looked around for Al and he was just disappearing into a cloud, climbing, and I lit out after him.

"When I broke clear, there was a Corsair off to my left, when Al should have been off to my right, but I figured maybe he crossed in the cloud so I joined up. Then I saw it was Cy, with a big hole in his canopy, and his radio antenna all wrapped around his stabilizer. He looked like he might need help and the last time I saw Al he was doing all right, except his radio was out, so I fell in on Cy's wing and we came on home. I didn't know where Drake was, dead or what, but about that time he called up and said he was all fouled up. He couldn't see anybody from where he was and his compass was out and—"

Charley Drake said: "You aren't kidding I was fouled up. To go back, though, what happened was, I lost Cy in the first tangle and as

I was looking around for him these Zekes whipped across my bow to the right. I took the inside one of the section and started firing, but I was too low in my seat and I couldn't use the gunsight. I was firing my tracers and was shooting astern of him. So I swung my nose a little and just walked them up his fuselage until they started going into his cockpit and he exploded, with chunks flying all around.

"I started swiveling my head around looking for Cy and trying to jack my seat up higher when I saw four more Zekes below. The two on the left were paying me no attention, but the two on the right were pulling up to make a run, so I went down on them, taking the inside man. He tried to turn and I got him right in the cockpit—a short burst this time because I could use my sight now. I pulled alongside him and looked in and his whole cockpit was a ball of fire that burned inside for a moment and then broke through.

"I pulled off and saw his mate falling away to the left and I came down on him beam on. It was a ninety-degree deflection shot—I am proud of that shot—and as I pulled away in a big wing-over to the left he was burning in the cockpit just like the other. They must have had some sort of gas tanks in there just forward of the pilot.

"What I needed most right then was company and I started looking around for Al or Cy or Jerry or anybody I could find. Then I looked in the rear-view mirrow and turned a thousand years old. I had company and I don't mean maybe. Two Zekes were coming in on my tail, one from each side and, brother, they really had me bracketed. I rammed the nose down and firewalled everything and goosed her with water and when I hit eight thousand feet, coming down from fifteen, I was indicating almost five hundred miles an hour and was still building up.

"I saw the Japs break off at seven thousand and pull up. I figured if I had all that speed there was no need to waste it, so I hauled back on the stick and roared up in a big hairy climb. Now a Zeke can turn like a Shetland pony, but he can't dive and he can't zoom like a Corsair, and I came up from below them like a freight train overtaking a tramp. I got the inside one in my sights for a second and poured about two hundred rounds into him and he started to burn in the cockpit just like the others.

"His wingman went off to the left in a sharp turn and I kicked left rudder and had him cold. I pulled the trigger and the guns went 'brrrrrrppppp'—maybe a hundred rounds, and that was all. I was out of ammo.

"I pulled up on him to the left and could see a little smoke coming from his wing roots, but not enough, I didn't figure, to kill him and he was flying all right. I was looking right down on him. That meat ball was big as a bed sheet, and I thought, if you want to confirm this one, kid, you better ram him. Then I happened to think how far it was back home and I pulled off and let him go.

"It was a good thing I did. I turned for home. Then I glanced at my gauges and the compass was going round and round, pointing nowhere and my gas gauge was out and I had no engine temperature or anything else. And I didn't know whether I was headed home or not. So I started yelling for help and raised Jerry, flying with Cy somewhere, and they tried to give me a steer but without a compass I didn't know north from Tuesday.

"I came over this little island which I didn't recognize and started circling, low, at about a thousand, trying to get oriented, and I looked up and off to the right at about five thousand there sat a Zeke. Well, I scrunched down in my seat and tried to look small as a seagull and I put her down on the water until I could taste salt, just about, and got out of there. I looked back and up and he was turning away, and I knew I was safe for then. But which way was home?

"I pulled up a little and tried to look around and the first thing I know, high above me I see these babies coming down. I figure this time I am dead for sure, but then I see something that makes me yell for joy. These are low mid-wing planes, not low-wings like the Zekes. They are Army jokers, P-47s. So I wobble my wings like mad and jink up and down so they can see my crooked wings, and they pull out of their dive.

"I call them up and tell them my troubles and they say okay and join up and they will take me home, and they finally did, thank God.

"I felt pretty good, with four kills for sure and one that might have gone in, and I knew Cy and Jerry were safe. But I was worried about Al, for the last time I saw him he was in this Maypole dance with a Zeke."

Al Wells said: "I could have used you. I could have used you and the rest of the squadron and a couple of sawed-off shotguns, for I never got into such a mess in my life, and why I got out of it as well as I did, I'm not quite sure.

"Like the others said, when we pulled up through the clouds the first time and they spotted us and started down in a dive, we held together for just a minute and then there were Japs everywhere, under us, over us, at both sides and cutting in front of us and behind. I don't know about the other guys but all I was doing was taking quick pot shots, just whipping my nose around trying to hold one long enough to kill him and not getting anywhere with it.

"I was afraid to try to pull in on one's tail for I knew if I straightened out that long, one would get on my tail, or maybe two or three, but I saw I'd have to do something, or I'd be out of ammo with nothing to show for it. Finally this one came shipping right in front of my nose and I turned with him, firing, and got a pretty good hit. He smoked and started to go down, but I had pulled around so tight it had stalled me out and I went down too.

"We went into the cloud layer below and as I recovered from the stall we broke out of that layer into the clear and there he was below me, still going down. I fired again and he started really to burn this time—all aflame in the cockpit.

"This second chase brought me out below the lowest cloud layer, at about eight thousand and I started to climb back up to see if I could find the fight again. But just as I started into the clouds I saw this Zeke, a little below and about a quarter mile away. So I stayed in my turn and went after him and he saw me and headed for the deck in a steep dive, with me coming right on his tail. I was giving it everything it would take, low blower, water injection—doing everything but waving my arms outside the cockpit like oars.

"I remember thinking as I closed to firing range, 'Well, you poor

· 133 ·

simple knucklehead, it won't be long for you,' when all of a sudden, as if he were jerked on a string, that Zeke went straight up. I mean straight, like a rocket, 'zoooom.'

"I yanked back on the stick to follow, but a Corsair can't make a square turn like that and the first thing I knew, from about fifteen hundred feet above me, head on and going like a bullet, here he came in a sixty-degree dive, on his back. I could see his guns winking. I could see the empty brass cartridge cases falling out of his wings. I was going up at about sixty degrees and he was coming down at the same angle and he passed ten feet above me. It was the closest I had ever been to a Jap in the air before. It was the closest I ever want to be. But he was missing and I was missing. His bullets were passing over my head and mine were whipping under his belly—under his back, rather, since he was flying upside down.

"I shipped over at the top of my climb and turned, and there below me, going straight away, was the Zeke again. So I lit out after him with everything jammed to the firewall again and just as I pulled in range—he did it again. Up and over and down on me, on his back, and I knew then I was in for something that might end very sadly for me. And we did it again, and again. And again.

"It was beginning to get ridiculous. It was like something we might have rehearsed together in flight school. It was like a play, or one of those dreams that are almost nightmares. I thought to myself, I wish I knew what frequency this cookie was on. I'd call him up and say, 'Listen, buddy, leave us knock this thing off and go shoot at somebody else, huh?'

"You know, always before, in air combat, it had been impersonal. It had been me against a plane, and you don't think of the man in that plane. But this was different. This was me against another man. And I was beginning to wonder if he wasn't the better man of the two.

"I had already figured out what one of us had to do, too, if we weren't going to keep on with that square dance forever. He had to nose down on me a little, to get me in his sights on the dive. Or I had to nose up a little, to get him. Either way, it was a hundred to one that that slight change in course would bring us together head on, prop to prop, and both of us would end up in little pieces of shark meat down there in the sea. But I had to do something. I was just about blacking out on every one of those steep dives and pull-ups, and I knew he was going to get me if we kept on. Seven times we had gone through that same routine—chase, climb, loop and dive. I said to myself, This time get him or quit.

"It was the same old rat race, he went up and I went up on his tail. He flipped on his back about fifteen hundred feet above me and in he came. My tracers were sliding right under him. I flipped the nose up quick and saw them go in just for the minutest fraction of a second and I shoved the nose down again and he roared over.

"This time he was closer than before, so close I could see the red glow of the flames that had started burning in his cockpit. I turned and watched him go. He stayed on his back, straight as an arrow, right on down to the drink. He didn't explode. He just went in. There was a splash and some ripples and that was all. I didn't feel much elation about it; I felt, somehow, a little regret. I felt I wished I could have met the guy. He could really fly that airplane, and for a long, long time he had made a monkey out of me.

"I saw a lot of spots on the water, where planes had gone in and the gas and oil had spread. I figured two of them might be Cy and Jerry, or Drake, for my radio had been out and I hadn't heard from a soul.

"I figured there wasn't much chance that the four of us could have gone into a tangle with all those Nips without some of us getting creamed. Then I went on back upstairs, to see if there was any fighting left up there. But I couldn't find anybody, so I started on home alone.

"I had gone a way when I looked up and there were four Corsairs coming down on me in a big hairy run, peeling off right on my tail. I saw them come on down, and I couldn't call them. I could just sit there praying that the dopes would recognize me before they shot me down. They did. They broke away at about two thousand feet. It was Joe Dillard's division, hurrying to the fight. Sleepytime had called them and they were tearing up the sky to get there.

"They were pretty sore when I turned out not to be a Zeke. So I joined up with them and we went back and hunted all over the sky for an hour, but we didn't find anything else, so we came on home.

"It was a good fight, and something to remember. But the best of it was not the fighting, but walking into the Intelligence Quonset to give Tilly the word on what happened, and seeing old Cy and Jerry there. And hearing from them that Drake was safe with them and would be home as soon as the Army refueled him. That was the best part. That was as good a moment, I guess, as I have ever known."

First Lieutenant Harold H. Martin

Casualty List

Bedside Manner

I was helping gingerly lift the wounded from the small boats to the deck of the ship. They had been evacuated from the beach by launch, their stretchers lying somewhat precariously over iron chains slung broadside across the small craft. Their wounds hastily dressed with enormous gauze patches, their torn "zoot suits" stained a fresh coat of red, the injured were on the initial leg of a swift passage to safety and treatment.

Down in the hot 'tween deck of this attack passenger destroyer, a chunky, red-faced, hairy-chested, balding doctor worked the sick-bay shuttle from Bougainville to Guadalcanal. Here under the dim, sticky battle lights, the wounded received their first promise of relief in the cocky, wisecracking banter of Lieutenant William S. Gevurtz, Medical Corps, USNR.

"They like rugged talk—their kind of rugged," he confided to me. "So I give it to them—in spades."

Stripped to the waist, sweating, swearing noisily at the improbable places a Jap missile can tear into a boy's anatomy, the doctor reigned over a compactly cluttered domain of precise medicine, rule-of-thumb psychiatry, home remedies, and prayer.

"I'm a chest man—studied the diseases of the lungs for five years. Now I'm running a first-aid station." He sighed and waved his hand in the direction of the male nurses known in the Navy as hospital corpsmen. They were busily engaged in disrobing the wounded and stowing them neatly in bunks. "Without these wonderful kids I'd go nuts."

He pointed to a blond, scrawny youth carefully undressing a lacerated back. "See that one? I picked him up off a gun crew. Came to me and said he'd like to help out. Look at him. You'd think he was that guy's mother." Then he squinted down the long compartment and raised his voice sharply. "You fellows ready for me yet?"

A corpsman hurried up the aisle, unscrewing his fountain pen. He took up a handful of hospital identification tags.

"All set, doctor."

"Okay. Let's go."

I followed him into the main compartment.

The APDs are 1918-class, four-stacker destroyers converted to two stacks and armed with 3-inch rifles, 20-millimeter cannon, and 50-caliber machine guns—all aircraft defensive armament. "They're falling apart" was the universal crew opinion, but they still squeezed out twenty-seven knots. As jacks of all trades in forward waters, they carried troops, supplies, and fire power to combat areas and evacuated wounded to base hospitals. Number One engine room had been torn out to make space for passengers and crew, and in the vacated area originally intended for ship's personnel were the wounded.

The compartment was not quite filled to capacity. Six long rows of three-tiered, blanket-covered, iron-springed bunks suspended on chains, supported the now entirely naked, grubby, bandaged men. We started at the far end. The doctor was joined by another corpsman.

"Get their names, serial numbers, diagnosis, and prescribed treatment."

"Yes, sir," nodded the corpsman with the pen and tags. The doctor sighed to me, "The Navy still runs on paper. Got to get everything down."

He stopped at the end top bunk. The corpsmen gathered on his flanks. I stood back.

The boy in the bunk hung over the side expectantly. His head was cropped almost to the scalp in prescribed battle fashion. It made him seem even younger than he was. He smiled and nodded vigorously at us.

"Hi, ya, doc!"

He thrust a hand out, then let it dangle in front of the doctor's face. The index finger was a reddened gauze patch. The doctor cradled the hand.

"My, my. How'd this happen?"

"Sniper got me," the boy announced—rather proudly, I thought.

"Did you get him?"

"Nope."

The doctor snorted. "Hell! You're no Marine. You're supposed to get three of them."

The boy looked indignant.

"I got my three before they got me! Would have got more except this is my trigger finger."

The doctor laughed. "Let's take off the bandage and see what's under there."

He reached a hand behind him and a corpsman slipped a pair of surgical scissors into it. Deftly he snipped the soiled rags, then gently began lifting the basic gauze pad.

"Now this is going to hurt like hell, so yell if you want to."

The boy tightened his jaws and watched the doctor apprehensively. Ever so slowly, the pad came away. The ugly wound was exposed. The boy blanched and turned his head away, sick.

"Hey, don't let that scare you," soothed the doctor. "That green color isn't you. That's what the medicine did." Without looking around he called, "Sulfa powder." A paper packet was torn open and slipped into the doctor's fingers. He shook its entire contents into the wound.

"See, now it's white. This stuff is great for you. Makes you feel like a million bucks. Here, let me see your muscle." The arm came farther out of the bunk. "Flashlight," the doctor ordered. He switched it on to see better in the gloom. "You must be a hard hitter, kid. Look at those biceps. Ah, there they are. Little bumps."

He nodded to me to come closer. I peered at the arm. There were indeed little bumps all up and down the forearm. His face turned solemn for a moment as his lips formed the words "blood poisoning." Then he stepped back into the jovial role. He turned to the corpsmen.

"I'm sorry, but I've got a crummy detail for you." He glanced back at the patient. "Not you—them. We'll make 'em work for their pay. Massive hot packs constantly. Forty-five grains sulfadiazine right away." The corpsmen groaned.

"I told you I'm sorry, but it's got to be done. Get going. See you later, son." The doctor nodded to the recording corpsman. "Tag him."

He crouched on the deck to get to the lowest man in the tier. "What's cookin', kid?"

A head and shoulders struggled into view. The eyes were bitter as they looked out over the lumpy bandages beneath them.

"What a hell of a place to get hit," the mouth said. "In the face! Son of a bitch!"

"What you worried about, pretty boy?" the doctor caroled cheerily. "Scars? What do you think you've been paying twenty cents a month to the Marine Corps for since you got in? Uncle Sam will fix you up like new."

The boy's eyes flew up with surprise and suspicion.

"Like new?"

"Better than new. Hell, you'll be knocking off those babes like nothing. Sit still while I get this off you."

The tedious business of removing the bandages got under way. A running conversation about "dames" crackled through the proceedings. The boy's spirits were on the upswing until the last moment when the final dressing came off.

"How's it look?" he asked in a strained voice.

It looked terrible.

The doctor assumed a thoughtful expression as though working out the solution to a puzzle.

"Well, I'll tell you," he pontificated. "It looks like some Jap tried to kill you with a hand grenade—but he muffed. Those bastards can't pitch worth a damn."

The kid's Adam's apple bobbed as he swallowed hard.

"Yeah. They stink."

The doctor barked out orders. "Sulfa powder—battle dressing—a big one—two grains of phenobarbital."

He held up the big dressing and exhibited it to the boy. "Do you know who made this dressing? Some doll sitting back in the States. When you have nothing else to do write a letter to the Red Cross telling them you got their bandage. Maybe you'll even meet the babe. Who knows?"

The bandage was being deftly applied. Finally the doctor straightened up from his squatting position and flexed his legs.

"Okay, Mac. See you later. Take it easy."

Our group moved up the aisle. A round red face and a chubby pair of shoulders appeared overhead.

"What's your trouble, lad?"

"Gee, doc. I got asthma!" The round face showed surprise and bewilderment at its own statement. The doctor reflected it instantly

"Asthma? You come seventy-five hundred miles from the U.S. to get asthma? You must be nuts!"

Everyone laughed.

"They'll take care of you down south." The doctor waved away the asthma case. He was already eying another boy.

"Where'd you catch it?"

A pale, tired face looked up from the middle bunk. "In the gut, doc."

"Why'd you let him do that to you?" He went to work on him quickly.

"I could see him up in the tree shootin' at me."

"Did you kill him?"

"Sure did. Killed him dead."

"Kicked his teeth out?"

"Well . . ." he hesitated apologetically, "I was feelin' pretty sick by then . . ."

"Sure. Hell with him." A new dressing had been applied and the ubiquitous sleeping potion was being administered. The patient gulped it down and made a face. The doctor wrinkled his nose in sympathy.

"Sleep tight, my boy. When you wake up a nurse will be looking after you."

The kid's eyes opened wide.

"A girl nurse?"

"Sure. They got them at the hospital now. You'll have to shave that beard."

The boy grinned dreamily. "Nurses! Well, what do you know?"

The perspiration was running in streams down our backs. The doctor paused at the cooler for some more water. Over the cup he mumbled at me: "Christ, they're young. They're so goddam young!" He shook his head and clucked his tongue.

I asked him if he ever had any doubts about his treatment.

"You mean do I make mistakes?" He reflected soberly. "I guess so, but I make as few of them as possible—and I never make the same one twice. My grandfather used to say: 'When a man cheats me in business once, shame on him. When he cheats me twice, shame on me.' It's the same thing."

We started down another aisle. A dejected boy sat on top of a bunk sucking hungrily at a cigarette. There wasn't a mark on him, but he was trembling violently.

"What's your complaint?" the doctor asked him.

"Nerves," the boy stated almost inaudibly. He turned his head away. He looked whipped and ashamed.

The doctor laid his hand on the boy's belly. "You're pretty warm. I'll tell you what we'll do. We'll give you a nice, cool sponge bath and then you'll go to sleep. What do you say?" The boy didn't answer. The doctor patted his knee, then nodded to the corpsman. "Take care of him."

He walked off a few steps, then turned a harried visage to me.

"Those combat fatigue cases get me. I don't know how to handle them. The first one I talked to, I made him cry. So now I leave them alone. I guess I'm no psychologist."

We moved along, the corpsman trailing us. A neat round hole in a thigh confronted us.

"What you got there, kid? A leg?"

"Yeah—and I don't like it."

"I know. I was shot once and it was lousy. Flashlight."

The boy watched him gravely as the doctor examined the leg.

"Is it bad?" he asked. His voice shook a little.

The doctor assumed a professorial manner.

"It's never bad when there are two holes. One is bad. Two is good. Remember that." He turned to a corpsman. "Okay. Wrap her up and take 'er away."

The procession carried on. Amoebic dysentery was laughed off with outhouse humor and an enormous dose of sulfathiazole. Dozens of tiny shrapnel fragments were dug out of a buttock to the accompaniment of ribald kidding. Sponge baths were administered like decorations for good conduct. Jokes were exchanged and repeated with each set of patients. Repetition didn't matter. The jokes were good, even the third time.

An officer appeared, cool and pressed in his khakis, obviously straight from the bridge. He held out a board with some papers clasped to it.

"I've got some bad news for you, doc. We just received these messages."

The doctor groaned. "On top of everything else I have to be the coding officer. Can't someone else do it? I'm snowed down here. Tell the skipper I'm too busy, will you, Henry?" His voice wheedled with the last phrase.

The officer nodded his head wearily. "I expected to do it again, but you can't blame me for trying." He smiled. The doctor shoved him playfully and turned to the next patient.

This was a six-footer, square and rangy. He had the long taut muscles of a first-rate swimmer. A homemade eye patch hung from his forehead, and he was fiddling nervously with the strings of his life preserver. When the doctor approached he leaped out of bed and addressed him tensely.

"Doc, you tell me the truth. Am I going to go blind?"

The doctor regarded him suavely.

"How'd you know I was the doctor?"

"Why—why—"

"You could see me, couldn't you? Then what the hell are you talking about?"

The boy rocked on his feet, then continued persistently: "Out of only one eye, though. And the other one's getting dim. I've heard of it happening before. One eye goes bad, then the other one blacks out. I can't afford to go blind, doctor. That'd be bad. Very bad!"

The doctor pushed him gently back on his bunk. "Let me take a look."

He stripped off the eye patch, shone the flashlight into the injured eye.

"Now I tell you what you do. Close the good one and tell me how many fingers you see." He held up one finger and waggled it back and forth. The boy strained at the vision. I could feel his passion to see —to be right in what he saw. Finally he blurted out the answer: "Four."

The doctor clenched his fist quickly. "Pretty close," he said triumphantly.

"There were five, weren't there? I thought there were five, but I couldn't make out the thumb very clearly. There were five, weren't there?"

"That'd be telling. I'm going to try this test on you later again. You don't want to know the answer, do you? Now let's wash out that eye."

Carefully he swabbed the eye with boric acid.

"How's that feel now? Can you see better?"

The boy squinted up at the electric light bulb.

"Yes—a little," he replied uncertainly.

"Okay. Now I'm going to cross you up. I fixed it so you could see a little—now I'm going to make it so you can't see nothing. Let's have the eye dropper, Ted."

Midway in the operation, the boy jerked back. He looked at the doctor beseechingly.

"Am I going to lose this eye, doctor? I've got to know. Please tell me."

The doctor sighed. "Look, son, you've got a hundred-to-one chance of losing your eye. It's a great gamble—but you'd gamble me anything at a hundred to one, wouldn't you?"

He pulled the boy's head back toward the light and applied a neat new patch. The boy closed his good eye tightly. His lips trembled. He seemed ready to cry. The doctor grabbed his shoulders fiercely.

"Now listen, dammit! Don't you know you've got the best doctors in the world looking after you? Do you think when you get back to the Canal you'll have some punk from Podunk taking care of you? You'll have the best damn eye specialist in America working on you. And I just gave him a head start. Now cut it out or I'll drop you over the side."

The boy stared at the doctor, shaken by the anger in his voice. Then he seemed to relax all over. He spoke very quietly. "I'm sorry, doctor. I guess a lot of fellows got it worse than me."

"That's a good boy. Now lie down and get some sleep." He turned away, then twisted his head around and spoke confidentially. "If it starts to get you down, yell for me. I'll fix you up."

We went to the cooler. We all consumed quarts of ice water.

"This heat's murdering me. I'm forty-two pounds too heavy for the Navy and I can't sweat it off. Maybe I ought to go back to Oregon."

He turned to his corpsman. "Is that all of them?"

The corpsman consulted his pad before handing it to the doctor.

"Check," he said, "except for those two appendicitis cases you looked at before."

"They're not hot, but keep 'em on ice." He frowned at me. "You know, sometimes a kid gets scared and he wants to get out bad, so he develops a pain—appendicitis. The doctors on the beach have no way of testing it, and they can't take a chance, the kid might really have a hot appendix, so they ship him out. I'm taking no risks either. They get ice packs every hour." He wagged his head despairingly. "It's that damn psychology again."

He hung up the board on a hook next to him, and breathed out noisily. "Well, that's that!"

I glanced at my watch. We had left Empress Augusta Bay only two hours ago. "Going to get a little sleep now?" I asked him.

He snorted. "Sleep! I haven't been to sleep since—" He paused and considered a minute. "Hey, Ted, what day is this?"

The corpsman wrinkled his face with concentration.

"Isn't it Wednesday?"

"Wednesday? It's Saturday!" Then uncertainly: "Or is it Friday?" He returned impatiently to me. "I haven't been in a bed for a hell of a long time and I'm pooped. I get letters from my partner back in The Dalles—that's just outside of Portland where I practiced—telling me how exciting it must be for me and how he envies me." He dropped into a brooding silence. "I'm a chest man. Worked for years at the State Tuberculosis Hospital. That's my field and I'm going back to it. I studied under the best lung man in the world. I can use a bronchoscope like you can drive a car. I have a collection of trophies I took out of lungs that would amaze you. It was interesting and it was my business. Now I'd sell my soul to get an inch of shrapnel out of some kid's knee."

A long, low whistle sounded from over our heads. We looked up. The combat fatigue case was snoring profoundly under his opiate. The doctor regarded me mournfully.

"Those nerve cases," he complained. "They're the one thing that gets me down. I don't know how to handle them. I'm just no damn good at psychology. Let's go up on deck."

Captain Milton Sperling

Saved by a Slit Throat

A Navy medical corpsman saved the life of a wounded Marine corporal at Iwo Jima by slitting his throat—a feat described by a doctor as a demonstration of the "most amazing presence of mind I have ever seen under fire."

Pharmacist's Mate Second Class Floyd L. Garrett, of Gadsden, Alabama, saw that the corporal was bleeding to death from a severed jugular vein and that it would all be over soon unless something was done quickly. Grabbing the end of the vein in one hand, Garrett slit the skin of the throat so that he could reach enough more of the vein to apply a hemostat.

A doctor explained that medical men often perform the same operation in hospitals, but pointed out that Garrett had no assistance, poor light, and was under fire from enemy mortars at the time. "Besides, it takes a lot of guts for a nonprofessional to start cutting on a man, even to save his life," he added.

Technical Sergeant Nolle T. Roberts

Atabrine

Atabrine, preventive of malaria, is undergoing the biggest advertising and promotion campaign in the history of the South Sea Islands. In jungle areas where the advertising salesman has yet to penetrate, in miles of newly developed servicemen's suburbs billboards proclaim only one product—atabrine.

The fall of the Philippines and the Netherlands East Indies early in the war stripped Allied nations of their major source of quinine. To combat malaria in tropic latitudes, service medical departments turned to quinacrine dihydrochloride derivatives developed in Germany, Britain, the United States—and possibly Japan. With British troops it's quinacrine. With Americans it's atabrine, proprietary trade name of Winthrop Chemical Company, Inc., New York, N. Y.

For months troops were suspicious of the bitter-tasting yellow pill. Fighting men are universally from Missouri and when medical officers began their "sales" campaign with speeches extolling "our new weapon against malaria," the men were at first merely apathetic. Then they became openly hostile to the new drug as rumors spread that atabrine "turns the skin yellow" and "causes loss of virility."

That's when some unsung advertising men in the ranks came forward with roadside signs, camp newspaper bulletins, radio blurbs. Army artists turned from camouflage with a will—to produce acres of huge signboards, usually depicting a voluptuous nude and the slogan, "Come Back to This—Take Atabrine."

Anonymous Pettys and Vargas decorated the sands of Africa, the woods of Italy, the jungles of New Guinea, with harems of leering lassies beckoning the eye-starved soldier. Duplicated ad nauseam was this questionable but appealing theme: "Two Reasons Why You Should Take Atabrine," with a picture of a maiden displaying Mae-westian mammary glands.

Marines in New Britain opened another new school of advertising—humor, and the pixillated use of established American advertising slogans. A jeep's-eye view of military roads revealed this barrage of promotion ads:

WITH MEN WHO KNOW MALARIA BEST, IT'S ATABRINE TWO TO ONE.

ATABRINE—GOOD TO THE LAST DROP.

REACH FOR AN ATABRINE INSTEAD OF A JEEP.

ATABRINES—THEY SATISFY.

MARINERS WISE ATABRIZE.

HEMORRHOIDS? GIVE ATABRINE A 30-DAY TRIAL. WRITE FOR FREE BOOKLET.

ATABRINE—NOTHING NEW HAS BEEN ADDED.

STOP EXCESS FALLING HAIR! USE ATABRINE.

But perhaps the classic of all was this promotion rub, harking back to the heyday of *Ballyhoo* magazine's sly digs at trade advertising:

WHY WEAR A TRUSS? TRY ATABRINE.

We can't help wondering just what the Winthrop company thought about all this.

Second Lieutenant Gerald A. Waindel

The Message

The first of the walking wounded at Iwo Jima came into the regimental aid station by himself. He didn't need to tell anybody what was wrong with him, for anyone could see that the flesh of his jaw was hanging by a piece.

Some men turned their faces and went on talking while Lieutenant Charles W. Hatch of Akron, Ohio, pulled the sagging flesh into place and wrapped a bandage around the man's head.

Above the bloody jaw a pair of clear blue eyes darted from face to face. Their expression was unreadable. He might have been trying to smile, or it might have been a snarl.

Two hospital corpsmen stood up to take the wounded Marine some two hundred yards down to the beach to be evacuated. He waved their hands aside and tried to talk, but only a strange and inarticulate sound came from what was left of his mouth.

He shrugged and knelt down, a big, powerful man with blond hair cut so close to his head that you could see his sunburned scalp. While the corpsmen crouched beside him the wounded man tried to write in the sand, the loose volcanic sand. But as fast as his finger wrote the sand filled in what he had written, until finally in disgust he gave the sand an indignant brush with his hand and stood up.

He was ready to go now.

Master Technical Sergeant Keyes Beech

Mobile Hospital

While the battle of Saipan was still being fought, the USS *Solace*, Navy hospital ship, unloaded 376 wounded Marines from the battlefield at a base hospital in the South Pacific. A month later, 374 of *Solace*'s wounded burden were on the way to recovery. Only two had died. That, the doctors said, was as much a tribute to *Solace* and her staff as to themselves. Yet, *Solace*'s work was only the beginning. Her men could do the emergency operations and treatments but the doctors, nurses and corpsmen of the base hospital did the miraculous job of mending shattered limbs, sewing torn flesh, and helping restore faith to the mentally sick.

The hospital staff by civilian standards was excellent. They had cut a swath in the jungle, long before the wounded of Saipan arrived, and they had put up their prefabricated buildings. They knew the lessons of war medicine the British and Russians had learned the hard way, and they had seen plenty of war medical experience too. They had attended wounded flyers, shot-up crews of PT boats, burned and maimed Seabees. They were using the latest equipment and drugs, including penicillin. More than that, they had the intangible assets of scientific humility before their task, and human sympathy and willingness to treat each man and his wound as an individual problem.

The medical stories of four of those Marines—wounded at Saipan— are not unusual, and they typify for hundreds of others the fateful thirty days that began in despair and ended in hopeful dreams of a return to peacetime usefulness.

There is the story of Cunningham and his pins, of the first full application in the South Pacific of the castless method of treating serious fractures. Private First Class Edward P. Cunningham, Jr., of Smithfield, North Carolina, is the son of a man who runs a small tobacco-drying plant there, and a stanch member of the First Presbyterian Church. Cunningham and many like him caused excited discussion in the hospital compound. "Dr. Sideman's pin-up boys," the staff called the ward where cases like Cunningham's were treated.

A Jap sniper got Cunningham the day his unit started up a precipice after some Japs who stood between the Marines and Garapan, Saipan's capital. It was late afternoon. The jungle around them was so full of snipers that he couldn't be taken back. For a splint, his buddies tied his carbine to his leg. A corpsman arrived, dressed the wound, gave him morphine, and covered him with twigs to hide him. When it got dark, his buddies dug a foxhole, and one of them stayed with him, whispered reassurance during the night, and, when Cunningham stirred, held the canteen to his lips. It began to rain just as the water ran out, and his buddy covered him with a poncho. Cunningham drank from the puddles that formed on the raincape.

Next morning he was taken back on a litter, after being given plasma and more morphine. He next awoke aboard the *Solace* when they put a cast on his leg. X rays showed that a bullet had gone through the thigh bone, shattering the shaft and embedding six pieces of bone. The leg was shortened four inches. Here, certainly, was a man who would limp.

Two days later, at the base hospital, Lieutenant Commander Sidney Sideman, USNR, in civilian life a Chicago bone specialist, took the cast off Cunningham and "pinned" him. Dr. Sideman described the castless method, the use of pins, simply. He said: "Instead of pulling the limb for weeks to get it in place and putting a cast on to hold it, pin it and pull it at the same time, then put the patient to bed and let nature do the healing." Bob Hope, the comedian, passing through the ward on his South Pacific tour, found another way to say it: "Instead of the man on the trapeze," Hope said, "the trapeze is on the man."

Lieutenant Commander Sideman inserted five stainless steel pins into Cunningham's thigh bone, three above the fracture and two below. They were connected outside the skin by metal rods, and fastened in a complicated vise called an "anatomic splint" in which the leg was manipulated until the bones were back to their normal length and position. This "pulling" would have taken weeks with the familiar pulleys and bars above the bed. The fracture was set; X rays proved that the pieces in Cunningham's thigh bone were in the right places. To hold them there securely until they formed what doctors call a solid union, clamps were put on the pins and the connecting rods were attached to them. During the next month Cunningham needed only routine postoperative care: sedatives and good nurses. Nature was doing her work; the bones were growing together. Cunningham, Lieutenant Commander Sideman said, would probably walk without a limp.

Aboard the *Solace* there were upward of a hundred men with fractures, men whose bones, shattered by land mines, mortar and rifle fire, looked under X ray like the broken and twisted girders of a bomb-devastated building. Twenty-one were "pinned," not one of them had an amputation, and not one will suffer any shortening of his limbs.

Lieutenant Commander Sideman frankly admitted that infection at the point of the pin's insertion is a danger in the use of this technic, yet not one pin was removed from those men for that reason. The answer is penicillin.

Pins can hold bones together, but they can't hold soft tissue. When a man is shot through the lung with a bullet, you cannot pull the hole together with an anatomic splint. To heal a lung, you make of it a kind of self-sealing gas tank, or use what doctors call "the conservative treatment of lung injuries."

Marine Private First Class Stanley F. Wilson of Dongola, Illinois, once he learned he was not going to die, began to worry about whether or not he could again play basketball. Wilson had been at Tarawa and had got shrapnel in his knee. That had healed long ago, long before he started to cross an open field full of Japs on Saipan.

His buddies were being hit, right and left. Wilson took cover behind a rock. He started out again. No sooner had he raised his head than the Jap got him. "Hit me like a sledge hammer," Wilson said.

Things became confused in Wilson's mind after that. He lost consciousness. He remembers awakening and trying to cut his pack off his lacerated shoulder. He thought of the Japs who must still be around. "I tried to lift my rifle and couldn't. I tried to call out to a corpsman, and all that came out of my throat was a gurgle. 'I am dying,' I thought. 'I am dying.' I prayed for my mother. I began to pass out again. I tried to stay awake. I tried not to die. I couldn't hold out.

"Then I woke up, and I was alive. I was surprised. I felt stronger, so I crawled back about fifty yards. The snipers were firing. My buddy helped me into the bushes, out of the way. Then I guess I passed out again."

Wilson was taken aboard the *Solace* where he had eight transfusions and was put into an oxygen tent. His left lung was bleeding into the pleural cavity, a sack that encloses the lung. Normally the cavity is empty and the lung has all the room it needs to expand and contract within it. But when a bullet goes through, the cavity fills with the blood that the lung pours off—that is, it fills unless you drain it. The men of *Solace* let the blood out of Wilson's pleural cavity with a needle. The hole in the outer skin was sealed with a vaseline pack. In other words, the outer hole was closed and the inside hole, the hole in the lung, was let alone. The pressure on the lung was relieved by removing the blood from the pleural cavity, "the self-sealing gas tank." Also Wilson was given 12,500 units of penicillin intramuscularly every three hours.

Daily X rays were taken of Wilson's lung, doctors looking for the "fluid level." That means they looked to see how much blood was in the pleural cavity, and whether the level was falling or rising. If it had risen, the cavity would have to be drained and they would have to start fighting something even more serious, the possibility of infection. So the first two weeks told the story of whether Wilson would again be able to play basketball or whether the lung would be permanently disabled. The fluid level went down, and down, and down. And as it fell the lung began to feel its oats, began to expand again. Wilson began to take full, deep breaths. At the end of thirty days his doctor, Lieutenant Richard L. Jones, USNR, Glen Cove, Long Island, told him that his lung was going to be all right.

Wilson was not the only one with chest wounds; there were many others, and not one died. Except for a relatively small number, all will again have full use of both lungs. Nature and penicillin won the battle of the pleural cavity; the doctors had the good judgment and the courage to let this formidable combination alone. That is why they call it "the conservative treatment."

Now take the case of Joe Marine. (That, of course, isn't his name.) He lost his memory at Saipan. You must know what these men went through to understand why a cure for a mental disorder is not simple. Commander J. W. Owen, USNR, formerly on the staff of New York's famed Bellevue Hospital, does not like to give statistics, but a significant number of men so affected from Saipan returned to their military units.

Joe and his buddy were in a foxhole. The order came to move ahead, and Joe started out. Just then a shell exploded near by and stunned him. After a moment of bewilderment, he looked for his buddy. He heard a moan in a foxhole. There his buddy was with his eyes and most of his face blown away. Joe lifted him across his shoulders and started to carry him back to safety. His buddy cried in anguish: "I can't see! I can't see!" They went on and on until Joe could no longer stand it. He lost his memory.

Joe's story came out through group psychotherapy. That's just a fancy way of saying that the doctors get these mentally wounded men to tell their stories in one another's presence. Joe told his as one of five Saipan men who were relating their experiences together. The principle is common-sensical. Most of them have some feeling of guilt about cracking up. When they talk before their buddies, they come to realize that not they alone did the kinds of things for which they now feel guilty.

Joe was not completely cured at the end of the thirty days, but his case was entirely hopeful. Group psychotherapy is no panacea; it is one of the many things the doctors at the base hospital were doing. "The men need confidence in their own aggression," Commander Owen said. "They want to believe they can fight again, that they can 'take it.'"

For example, the men were allowed to swim under supervision at a beach two miles from the hospital. Instead of going there in trucks, they had to walk. Basket weaving and other such handicrafts were rejected, and the men built things the hospital actually needed, things they could see being put to use. They built chairs, awnings, and the screen used for showing movies in the wards.

The mind takes time to heal. Time is just as important in belly wounds, but with a difference. It is blitz warfare; you must strike faster than lightning-fast peritonitis. When the intestines are riddled, let's say, with shrapnel holes, they pour out their infected contents into the abdominal cavity. Peritonitis comes quickly if something isn't done. When the large bowel, or colon, is damaged, the onset of peritonitis is prevented by a safe and quick procedure: simply loosen and lift the injured bowel out on the abdominal wall, where its infected contents drain harmlessly into a gauze dressing. The subsequent repair is simple and almost without risk. That is the grim, but fully successful, technic that saved the life of Lieutenant Alfred A. Pressick of Greenfield, Massachusetts. When a doctor from the *Solace* came down the gangplank with a list of men who were to get priority at this hospital, Lieutenant Pressick was high on the list. His stomach was distended and paralyzed when he reached the hospital, and his abdomen was filled with blood. He had eight perforations of the small intestine, and two in the large intestine.

Commander Harold E. Rhame, USNR, of Brooklyn, former associate surgeon at Kings County Hospital, opened the abdomen above the area of the injury and introduced a tube to drain and deflate the perforated bowel. Infected blood was drained from the peritoneal cavity. Then, two days later, he performed the operation of bringing the bowel out. "You forget your parlor surgery out here," Commander Rhame said, "and you stick to the simplest procedures you know." A month later Lieutenant Pressick still had a segment of draining bowel exposed through an operative wound in his side, but this was healing and he was going to be all right again.

Thirty days—and three hundred and seventy-four men recovering. Then word came that another mercy ship was on the way with the wounded of Guam aboard. The hospital corridors began to stir. "Pass the word along," one doctor told another. "All hands must be ready." The operating tables were prepared, skilled hands were scrubbed, soft beds had clean sheets, the galley set up a watch to keep hot coffee brewing all night for the next week.

"All hands" were ready to save as many lives as possible, and to do it again and again, until the coming of peace.

Technical Sergeant George McMillan

Medicine Hits the Beach

Long before they swarmed onto the beaches of Okinawa, the Marines had learned a grim lesson: To beat the Japs you have to exterminate them. That means you have to employ all the resourceful, step-by-step methods of the professional exterminator. It requires tactical planning complete to the smallest detail, reconnaissance of practically every square foot of enemy-held territory, an almost individual briefing of the fighting men. Such planning isn't unique, of course. The Germans developed it to a high degree; so did the Japs. But they often lacked an ingredient that saved the day for Americans: the initiative to cope with unforeseeable developments that send the planning awry.

One Navy hospital corpsman was to land with each assault platoon of Marines. The assault troops would widen out the beachhead and push inland; then the battalion medical section was to come in. The two surgeons and their pharmacists' mates would set up their sick bay, administer plasma, bandage the casualties, do rough surgery, and evacuate the seriously wounded men.

Soft-spoken Lieutenant Logan A. Spann, the 38-year-old Tulsa, Oklahoma, doctor in command of the section, assembled his men on the deck of the transport. His assistant, Lieutenant Jack C. Cooper, a 27-year-old Texan, helped divide the men and equipment among three amphibious tractors. In wartime you don't put all your eggs in one basket.

On the second of H hour the assault platoon rammed toward shore. Theory ended and practice began at the reef. The clanking amphibs, pushing the spray out behind them, crossed the reef into a full-dress Jap mortar barrage. The fire thickened as they came closer, reaching full intensity on the beachhead.

Ashore there was no place for a sick bay. The beach was the front line. The Japanese had let the assault troops through, and then pinned the succeeding waves to the fringe of the island with accurate mortar and artillery fire.

Side by side with the infantrymen, the medical officers and corpsmen crouched behind a sandbank, patching the casualties as best they could. To the left of the bank, a red and dusty road twisted away from the beach and up to the ridge where the advance elements of the battalion had dug in. After three hours on the beach, Lieutenant Spann decided to set up his sick bay at the base of that ridge.

The corpsmen wriggled the seventy-five yards to the road and joined a Marine unit waiting to make the dash. Loaded with their medical gear, they left cover and raced across the field. The Japs pinpointed the open space with accurate fire. Marines fell, and the corpsmen pulled them to temporary shelter in shellholes and behind oil drums, dressed their wounds, gave them morphine, and moved on.

Halfway across the field, a Jap sniper shot the first corpsman through the abdomen. A moment later a mortar shell burst near by, decapitating a Marine infantryman and severely injuring a second corpsman. The little party paused in the open to dress its two casualties. Lieutenant Spann was bandaging a Marine's leg. A shell landed near by. He dived for a foxhole, spraining his back and fracturing a rib. He pulled himself out of the hole, finished the bandaging job, and kept going for the ridge. Ignoring the warning shouts of Marines already at the ridge, the medical section charged across the final 100-yard stretch. It hadn't a trace of cover. The Marines stopped shouting and began to cheer.

Part of the medical mission was accomplished. With two of his corpsmen wounded, Lieutenant Spann started his work. There were plasma transfusions, bandaging, syrettes of morphine to ease the pain, probings for shrapnel, casualties to be fetched from the ridgetop, wounded to be evacuated. In the next four hours the unit handled sixty casualties. Three litter bearers were killed taking a Marine back to the beach through that open field swept by Jap fire, so Lieutenant Spann commandeered the amphibious tractors which were ferrying ammunition to the front lines. They made the return trips with wounded stretched out on their cargo decks. Evacuation proceeded smoothly.

"Nothing happened for the next few days," Lieutenant Spann said afterwards, "except that we worked all day and didn't sleep all night."

No, nothing happened except that the sick bay at the new position was set up close to a hidden Jap ammunition dump which was promptly blown up. Then the Marines moved on again to join another battalion. That meant a double set of casualties to be taken care of. Later the Japanese made a direct mortar hit on the piled-up stretchers, destroying them all. Casualties had to be carried on makeshift litters of ponchos and shelter halves.

Before the assault on the next ridge, the sick bay was pitched near a thicket. It seemed a safe location. The scene of action was moving farther inland and the battalion prepared to follow up. The medical officers and corpsmen began packing their gear again.

Then the thicket spoke. A Japanese grenade lobbed out. Its explosion signaled the start of a desperate enemy counterattack. Nine corpsmen were trapped in crossfire near the thicket. No one could reach the neatly packed medical gear. It had been stacked in several foxholes which were now cut off by the enemy.

Men wounded by the grenade needed treatment. Casualties drifted back from the front lines. There was one exit—a path back to the beach. The corpsmen skulked back along it, guiding the wounded to safety and returning with badly needed supplies. Soon the Japs discovered the path and tried to block it with their fire. But the corpsmen got through. They had to, for the supplies were chiefly plasma.

The battle lasted six hours. A brutally accurate mortar barrage ended it in our favor. Lieutenant Spann moved up to collect his equipment. Again the thicket came to life and a lone Jap machine gun sputtered sharply. A rifleman stepped forward and silenced it.

The exhausted corpsmen could scratch only three inches of dirt out of the hard ground for their foxholes that night. Too tired to care, they heard the Japanese throw a banzai attack against the Marine lines just in front of them. At first the screams and yells were very loud, but they died to a whimper as the Marine gunners cut loose. The organized resistance of the Japanese petered out.

Isolated groups of the enemy fought on until all had been killed or captured on the northern shore of the island. The Marines' job was virtually completed; the medical section had a chance to ease up.

When you come to measuring a fight, you get down to a casualty count—a hateful business of writing off your men. So it was in the medical unit. It figured out neatly: half of them were gone—killed or wounded. Of all the dead, the medical men agreed, none had given his life more valiantly than the corpsman who was cut down by Japanese machine-gun fire while tending a wounded Marine. His lifeless hands still clutched two of the weapons of his job: a pencil and a casualty tag.

Master Technical Sergeant Alvin M. Josephy, Jr.

Battle Scars

I don't see," said young Second Lieutenant Alvin W. Hoskins, of Mountain View, Missouri, "how so many of our men get wounds in the rump."

An officer of the engineers of the Third Marine Division, Lieutenant Hoskins was directing shore-party operations. The battle for Guam had just begun, and casualties were being brought through his sector for evacuation to ships offshore. He had scarcely made the remark when the Japs provided him with an answer. A mortar shell came whistling through the air. The lieutenant dived for the nearest hole. It happened to be none too deep.

After the explosion, he came limping from the hole. A piece of shrapnel had cut through his canteen and cover, and slapped him vigorously on the backside. A few hours later there was a huge, blue bruise, like the imprint of a mule's hoof.

Staff Sergeant Harold A. Breard

"You Still Living?"

It was not unusual to be greeted outside the blackened city of Naha on Okinawa by Sixth Division Marines with "Hell, you still living?" This was less a testimonial of your endurance or special skill in staying alive than to your luck.

You could get it walking on a road along which hundreds of trucks had rumbled without harm: "This kid, see, the one with the BAR, the one that dragged the other guys out of that valley. He stepped on one of the Jap land mines—blows his arms and one leg off. Naw, he ain't a basket case. He died 'bout ten minutes after it happened. Good kid, nice quiet boy."

You could get it after you'd escaped it a few times: "You know the major, the one whose walkie-talkie guys got hit by the snipers? The night before he got it, he was sayin', 'I'm a bad man to be around. I draw bullets and shells.' Next day he goes down to that little red house, thinkin' that's a good place for a conference. He's standin' there with his company commanders, they all talkin' away and pointin', and the major's orderly—you know, Connie—is standin' there, leanin' against a wall, and here comes this mortar shell. Just one lousy mortar shell, and lands right inside the house. Kills the major and some other officer. Yeah, Connie, too."

Men died here not in great concentrations as on Iwo or at Anzio. But they died, and their deaths were very close, because you knew them personally. There was a sharp pain in your side when you heard about "Pappy" or "Ski" being cut to pieces by machine-gun bullets. It was even sharper and deeper when you saw them go down, their arms flopping crazily as they fell.

And it was bad for your spirit to wander down to the battalion aid station, which had been moving almost as fast as the command posts. One night it had been in the court of one of the huge burial vaults. Some tanks moved in a hundred yards away. "A Jap observer must have spotted them," said a battalion surgeon, Lieutenant D. M. Thysell, of Duluth, "so pretty soon the shells start flying. Didn't hit us, but came mighty close."

Now the aid station was sheltered from the view of any observers, behind a cluster of huge boulders, but still only one thousand yards from the front lines. Down the road trundled a hospital jeep, dusty, dilapidated, and loaded with cargo. Three men got out without help, but they shook with a palsy. Others came out feet first, on stretchers. One was a corpsman. His left foot was dotted with holes. "Mortar shell exploded right near me and four other guys," he told Lieutenant Thysell. "Damn it, I'm the only guy that got hurt."

The lieutenant, a corncob pipe gripped in his teeth, took one swift look. "Take him to B Medical and get him there fast." When the corpsman was gone, he said, "They'll have to take off that leg."

The left side of one man's face, a lieutenant in a tank crew, was an ugly mass of blood and bits of flesh. Even before the first bottle of plasma had been administered, he died. A man in his crew, only slightly wounded in the leg, said in a dull voice, "We were going along there, and some little Japs run out from behind a building and throw what looked like a satchel right in front of us. One of them satchel charges—it blew us up bad." His eyes kept staring fixedly ahead of him as he talked.

Other jeeps brought in wounded and dead. Jack Riordan, of Columbus, Ohio, red-haired corpsman, his hand streaked with dried blood, bustled from one stretcher to another. "Hey, Jerry, for Pete's sake, how'd they ever get you?" he yelled at a Marine with a deep gash in his side. The Marine grinned. "Hi, Red," he whispered.

"Now's when your weight lifting is gonna come in handy. It'll really pull you through," assured Red. "Lookit those muscles!" While he talked, he worked deftly, applying clean bandages to the wound.

Then he went to another man. The Marine looked waxen. Flies swarmed about his blood-caked dungaree trouser leg. A bandage hastily applied at the front had slipped from his chest. A jagged hole showed above the heart. "Hey, fellow," said Red, "we'll fix you up in no time." Other corpsmen gave the Marine plasma and Red washed the chest wound.

The Marine whispered something. Red bent down to listen. He jumped up. "Nah, nah, kid, they didn't get your spine. What the hell gave you that idea!"

Hovering about the station were the inevitable "walking wounded," men with slight shrapnel cuts, bruises, scratches. They also suffered from sheer lack of sleep, but they would go back to the front after being taken care of here. While waiting, they exchanged experiences. "Right up this road, ya know where that stone wall is, well, there's where they started in to give us hell. Man, ah nevah saw so many of them bullets flyin' as flew in them three minutes!" "Listen, you can tell me all you want about brave platoon leaders, but this guy we got beats 'em all. He goes up this hill, see—"

When a corpsman approached these Marines, he was waved away. "Wait till you fix up the guys that really need it," said the walking wounded. "Take care of them first. We can wait."

An amtrac rolled up with more wounded. One man recognized another on a stretcher. "Hey, Joe, hey, they got Jennings—they got Jennings," he shouted wildly. The man on the stretcher raised himself slowly on one elbow and exclaimed, "Oh, damn it, damn it, I told that guy not to go off like a wild goose. Get him bad?" "I don't know," replied the other, "all I did was see him fall. They're having things pretty rough up there."

By nightfall, most of the wounded and the dead were taken to a rear area. Dr. Thysell found time to light his corncob pipe. "Sure hope they don't start shelling us again tonight. I don't like it much."

For a moment you are away from death—you think. You walk down the road, away from the Asato River front, farther from the sniper bullets and the chatter of the Nambu machine guns. You pass Marines lighting fires to heat chow, others digging their foxholes deeper. Then suddenly, some three hundred yards ahead, there is a blast in the air and a black cloud of smoke; a Japanese air burst, scattering its chunks of steel all over the area. You cling to the side of an embankment until four of these insidious things go off. Then you scurry a little way down to the regimental command post. The first sergeant looks up. "Hell," he says, "you still alive?"

Technical Sergeant Herman Kogan

The Corpsman

A few Marines on the Orote Peninsula front at Guam saw one sight they will not easily forget. In skirmishing formation, one squad was moving slowly through dense brush to clear out an enemy position when enemy fire broke out all around them.

When one of the Marines, wounded, called for aid, a Navy medical corpsman with the unit began crawling across a small clearing toward the wounded man. As he reached the edge of the clearing, a rifle shot hit him in the face, passing through both cheeks, and destroying the sight of one eye. He fell to the ground, out of reach of the Marines pinned down by a spray of machine-gun fire.

Again the wounded Marine, unaware that the corpsman was hit, called out for help. Blinded by his own blood, the corpsman dragged himself to his knees, fell, rose again, and began crawling in the direction of the voice. Another Marine was finally able to reach the wounded medical man, dragged him to cover, and had to hold him to keep him from going any farther.

Master Technical Sergeant Murrey Marder

The Agreement

Casualties were so heavy among Navy hospital corpsmen in one Sixth Marine Division sector on Okinawa that the men agreed all their wounded would return unaided to the medical station some two hundred yards back.

"We refuse to let any more corpsmen risk their lives for us," a Marine told Navy doctors and corpsmen who took him into an operating tent. He had been shot through the chest by an enemy sniper. Then he saw another leatherneck lying on an operating table. "Hey, Mac, did you keep our agreement?" he asked.

The other Marine raised his head. "Yeah," he said, "I made it back." His left foot had been blown off by a mortar shell.

Staff Sergeant Elvis C. Lane

Letter Home

August 2—I have already written one letter, but I doubt if it was mailed, so I shall repeat what I said there.

I was wounded on Guam at 0300 the morning of July 22. The Japs counterattacked, and though we beat them back, one of them managed to throw two grenades into my foxhole. The first one I was able to throw back at him, but the second went off in my face. My sergeant, who shared the hole with me, was killed. I lost my left eye and three front teeth, ruptured both eardrums, and suffered burns and shrapnel wounds of my face and hands. They found me at dawn and evacuated me in a hurry to the ship and flew me back to the Hawaiian Islands, where I now am mending rapidly and already am able to walk around. My right eye is all right, thank God, and my hearing will improve. There will only be a few minor scars on my face, and a glass eye should find me looking pretty much the same as ever. So do not worry. I should be home in a couple of months, and after that I don't know.

I can't tell you where we landed, but you can guess. The action was very severe. Nearly all my friends with whom I went through Brigade School in Samoa are dead. There were only two officers left in my company when I was hit, so you can see things were pretty rough. I find it hard to believe that so many of the people I knew and served with for so long are gone now. I feel a little out of place among the living and shall never complain. Those others have paid their last debt. I had great good luck during the day's fighting as I had five bullet holes through my dungaree jacket and not one touched the skin. One bullet cut a cigar I carried in my left breast pocket in half. Providence, luck—call it what you will.

I hope everything goes well with you and that you have not worried too much. I look forward to seeing you both again after all these months. What a lot we shall have to tell each other. All my love to you both. I am quite cheerful and really feeling fine, so do not worry at all.

August 6. I continue to improve daily and my hearing is better. My right eye has a few coral fragments in the corner but they are getting them out. Every day, I wonder more at my extraordinary luck at being alive at all. It was a close thing at that. I shall never forget the doctor on the ship, when I first got there, saying about me to a corpsman, "I'm afraid we're going to lose this one." I could hear but neither move nor speak, but I felt like saying, "The hell you are!" Five units of blood plasma did the trick.

Write when you can, and it won't be long now.

August 13. Every day, I see many here who are far worse off than I —limbless, sightless, and yet cheerful, joking, infinitely hopeful. None of them wish to be pitied or feel they should be. Yet for the blind I have enormous respect. For a week or so I feared I was to be and I don't know if I could have endured it. It's the narrowest and blackest of prisons. I think I'll make a point of always giving to the charities that care for them.

I don't think back much yet, and just drink my fresh milk, think about the snow falling at home, and admire the many pretty nurses. Mine is called Miss ——— and she looks like one of Vermeer's Dutch girls. I call her "Fräulein" and try to talk German with her, but she says in a Low German accent, "Ich kann nicht verstehen." The view out of my window is a famous one and I wish you could see it.

All in all, though, I see my present condition as close to a miracle. Three weeks ago I was damn near dead.

Write often and much love.

Cord

Captain Cord Meyer, Jr.

They Do Rest in Peace

A friend wrote from the Pacific. He didn't have much to say about the war. He told of a Sunday morning walk he took.

"After church services," he wrote, "I walked alone down the winding road toward Red Beach One, the D-day designation we had for that stretch of shore. There in a quiet glade the chaplains had laid out our Marine Division cemetery.

"Something about its solitude reminds me of Hilton's Shangri-La. By some strange twist of terrain here, too, it is secluded and untouched. There is no turmoil here, only peace.

"Here it is cool. Here the sun's strong rays seem canted as if bent in a celestial canopy. Here is a small stream at the top of the tropical glade, reminding me, somehow, of the Little Beaverkill at the bend where we used to get those rainbows . . .

"I walked between the rows of white crosses, straight in their long lines and evenly spaced. The paint was fresh and white, the names plain-lettered. Here a major, there a private, all quietly resting. And the flowers—they are here for all.

· 165 ·

"The foliage is strange and exotic to the eyes, but a palm frond and a bougainvillaea bloom seem as peaceful here as the upthrusting oak and spring flowers in an Ohio country churchyard. And if the road leading here is hot and dusty—still this rude road over the knoll is the one they came down together. And the sky, it is the same sky. The same stars come out at night. The same sun shines on these new graves as on the old at home.

"Names I knew and their faces come swarming back into memory. Call them Smith and Jones and Brown. Add a 'ski' or jumble the letters around. Men I fought with; yet, I don't feel sorrow. Rather it is that I miss their ways of kidding, or of smiling, or the phrases and inflections they used to gripe about the chow. But I couldn't feel sorry for them, not here.

"For a man dies and that's that. If I die, here is where I would want to be—with the others, the men I fought with.

"In dying, these men—these friends of mine—made this bit of soil forever American. They are in no strange land. They are buried in no strange grave.

"As I look out over this quiet burial place and down the broad vistas of the island hills to the sea, I wish that those who loved these dead could know this place, could know amid what tranquillity their sons have found their final resting places."

Master Technical Sergeant Gene Ward

Death

Death is a quire of red tape.
It is posting a name in the MIA column.
It is dropping a name from the OD roster.

It is listing the contents of a field trunk
And sunning the blankets.

It is a routine call for replacements
And the curse of a corporal.

It is a good word said by silence
And an extra bottle of warm beer.

Captain Richard G. Hubler

Memorial Address
AT FIFTH MARINE DIVISION CEMETERY AT IWO JIMA

This is perhaps the grimmest, and surely the holiest, task we have faced since D day. Here before us lie the bodies of comrades and friends: men who until yesterday or last week laughed with us, joked with us, trained with us; men who were on the same ships with us, and went over the sides with us as we prepared to hit the beaches of this island; men who fought with us and feared with us. Somewhere in this plot of ground there may lie the man who could have discovered the cure for cancer. Under one of these Christian crosses or beneath a Jewish Star of David there may now rest a man who was destined to be a great prophet—to find the way, perhaps, for all to live in plenty, with poverty and hardship for none. Now they lie here silently in this sacred soil, and we gather to consecrate this earth in their memory.

It is not easy to do so. Some of us have buried our closest friends here. We saw these men killed before our very eyes. Any one of us might have died in their places. Indeed, some of us are alive and breathing at this very moment only because men who lie here beneath us had the courage and strength to give their lives for ours. To speak in memory of such men as these is not easy. Of them, too, it can be said with utter truth: "The world will little note nor long remember what we say here. It can never forget what they did here."

No, our poor power of speech can add nothing to what these men and the other dead of our division who are not here have already done. All that we even hope to do is follow their example. To show the same selfless courage in peace that they did in war. To swear that by the grace of God and the stubborn strength and power of human will, their sons and ours shall never suffer these pains again. These men have done their job well. They have paid the ghastly price of freedom. If that freedom be once again lost, as it was after the last war, the unforgivable blame will be ours, not theirs. So it is we the living who are here to be dedicated and consecrated.

We dedicate ourselves, first, to live together in peace the way they fought and are buried in this war. Here lie men who love America because their ancestors generations ago helped in her founding, and other men who loved her with equal passion because they themselves or their own fathers escaped from oppression to her blessed shores. Here lie officers and men, Negroes and whites, rich men and poor—together. Here are Protestants, Catholics, and Jews—together. Here no man prefers another because of his faith or despises him because of his color. Here there are no quotas of how many from each group are admitted or allowed. Among these men there is no discrimination. No prejudices. No hatred. Theirs is the highest and purest democracy.

Any man among us, the living, who fails to understand that will thereby betray those who lie here dead. Whoever of us lifts his hand in hate against a brother, or thinks himself superior to those who happen to be in the minority, makes of this ceremony and of the bloody sacrifice it commemorates an empty, hollow mockery. To this, then, as our solemn, sacred duty, do we the living now dedicate ourselves— to the right of Protestants, Catholics, and Jews, of white men and Negroes alike, to enjoy the democracy for which all of them have here paid the price.

To one thing more do we consecrate ourselves in memory of those who sleep beneath these crosses and stars. We shall not foolishly suppose, as did the last generation of America's fighting men, that victory on the battlefield will automatically guarantee the triumph of democracy at home. This war, with all its frightful heartache and suffering, is but the beginning of our generation's struggle for democracy. When the last battle has been won, there will be those at home, as there were last time, who will want us to turn our backs in selfish isolation on the rest of organized humanity and thus to sabotage the very peace for which we fight. We promise you who lie here: We will not do that. We will join hands with Britain, China, Russia in peace, even as we have in war, to build the kind of world for which you died.

When the last shot has been fired, there will still be those whose eyes are turned backward, not forward, who will be satisfied with those wide extremes of poverty and wealth in which the seeds of another war can breed. We promise you, our departed comrades: This, too, we will not permit. This war has been fought by the common man; its fruits of peace must be enjoyed by the common man. We promise, by all that is sacred and holy, that your sons, the sons of miners and millers, the sons of farmers and workers, will inherit from your death the right to a living that is decent and secure.

When the final cross has been placed in the last cemetery, once again there will be those to whom profit is more important than peace, who will insist with the voice of sweet reasonableness and appeasement that it is better to trade with the enemies of mankind than, by crushing them, to lose their profit. To you who sleep here silently, we give our promise: We will not listen. We will not forget that some of you were burned with oil that came from American wells, that many of you were killed by shells fashioned from American steel. We promise that when once again men seek profit at your expense, we shall remember how you looked when we placed you reverently, lovingly, in the ground.

Thus do we memorialize those who, having ceased living with us, now live within us. Thus do we consecrate ourselves, the living, to carry on the struggle they began. Too much blood has gone into this soil for us to let it lie barren. Too much pain and heartache have fertilized the earth on which we stand. We here solemnly swear this shall not be in vain. Out of this, and from the suffering and sorrow of those who mourn this, will come—we promise—the birth of a new freedom for the sons of men everywhere.

Lieutenant Roland B. Gittelsohn

The Men

Twelve Hours AWOL

The official records of his regiment disclose that Private First Class Gareld Thomas Shelton was AWOL for twelve hours. A serious enough offense in itself, there was this added ominous notation . . . "during combat."

The story of Private First Class Shelton, a lean, quiet, red-haired, red-bearded Marine from the Cascades country of the state of Washington, properly begins when somebody handed him a tommy gun out of a wrecked amphibious tractor going into the beach at Tarawa on D day. Red was a communications man and he knew his business from antenna right through the alphabet. Not that he didn't stick to his communications job. When his Higgins boat was wrecked by a near miss from a Jap antiboat gun—and we began to find out just how tough Tarawa was going to be—Red pushed the watertight radio cart over the side, swimming behind it the last hundred yards to Red Beach One, under fire. And he set up his radio net, shore-to-ship. Routine stuff . . . with Red.

Still, as the sound and fury of battle unfolded about his ears and the snipers' bullets clipped off the palm fronds above his head, Red couldn't keep his eyes off the tommy gun. He fondled it, found time to oil it between sending and receiving there in the regimental command post and finally, when the captain told him twenty-four hours without sleep rated a breather, he picked it up and slung it over his shoulder.

Technically, Red was AWOL the moment he disappeared over the

On your way to the next beach . . .
wondering whether it will be better or
worse than the last one.

4

It's bad enough and once you hit the beach the thing is to get off it.

5

So you get up and go

6

if you can

the best you can

and keep moving up.

By this time you're getting support.

But wherever your position is

it's subject to change without notice.

The stuff is pretty well ashore now,

and if you're lucky

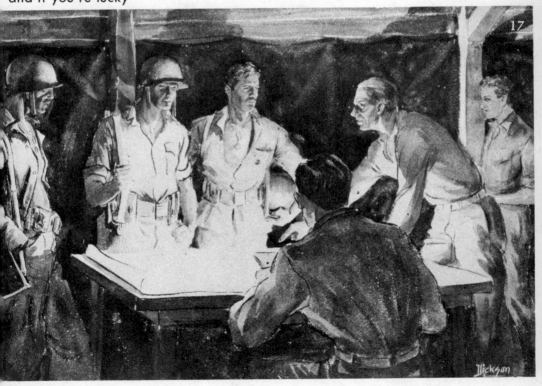

things are proceeding according to plan.

You keep going,

never knowing what the next ten seconds will bring.

The casualties start coming back

Jackson.

as the fight goes on . . .

and there's water,

blood,

aid,

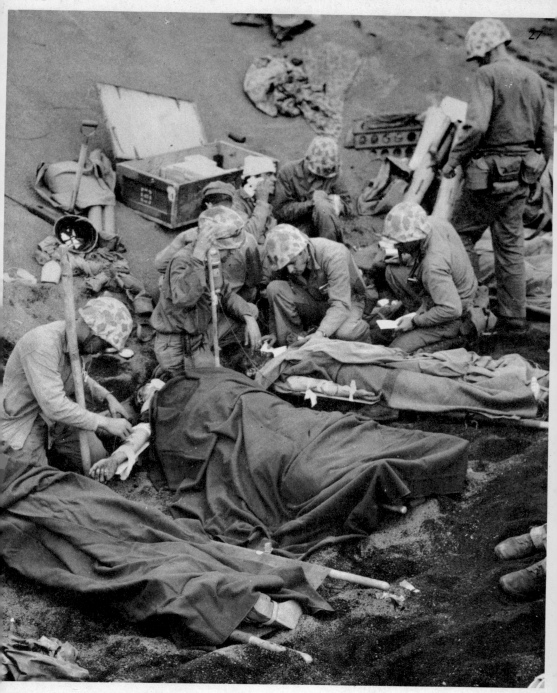

and some comfort for those who will fight no more.

28

When you get some terrain you can move on,

29

you really go places;

32

you've got them licked

and they know it.

Your flag goes up

and the gun barrels cool.

Later there will be time for a wash,

DASH-RITE
-INN-
THRU·THESE·PORTALS
PASS·THE·FASTEST
MEN·ON·EARTH

a rest,

maybe a movie if you're around long enough.

You've cared for your wounded,

buried your dead,

For a Pal —

left another beach behind you.

And you're a marine so you know you'll be going along somewhere . . . soon.

shoulder of the debris-littered sand dune toward the battle raging on the airstrip. Several hours later, with Red and the tommy gun still missing, it wasn't just a technicality. AWOL "in combat" is a serious matter, very serious. In fact, it is a life-and-death affair. "Desertion in the face of the enemy" is the official phrase applied. So later Red was the subject of investigation and an official report.

What Red headed for after he left the CP was written into history as one of the worst battles in which Marines ever have fought. He negotiated the airstrip with one, continuous broken-field run, arriving in a hail of lead amid the foxholed Marines on the far side. Five minutes later he was piloting a wounded buddy across the airstrip to the beach evacuation station.

"Helped to evacuate a casualty," stated the testimony in the report.

Red's meeting with his first Jap came a few moments after his return trip to the front across the airstrip. He had just arrived on A Company's left flank when a Jap soldier popped out of an underground tunnel waving a dirty piece of rag and gesturing wildly for mercy. While Red struggled to make a decision the Jap made a grab for his pistol. The tommy gun barked briefly.

Later the dead Jap was taken into consideration. "Killed one of the enemy," the report read.

Company A and its self-attached member had run into a deep vein of Jap pillboxes about this time and from one of these concrete-and-steel emplacements six Japs staged a mad rush in Red's sector until another and longer burst from the tommy gun laid them to rest.

"Six or seven [the report wasn't positive on this point] of the enemy were killed by the subject named man just before dusk of the second day."

In the subsequent melee, A Company pushed its lines three-quarters of the way down the airstrip, Red and the tommy gun pushing with them. He must have presented quite a picture there in the dust and debris—the red blood trickling down through red hair into a red beard. The report mentioned that "he [Shelton] had been wounded in the head during the straightening of our lines just prior to sunset of the second day."

· 171 ·

There was still light enough left for a lot of Jap activity in that particular sector, and a heavy concentration of machine-gun fire was coming from a demolished Mitsubishi approximately a hundred and fifty yards down the airstrip. That became the tommy gun's next target and, along with another Marine who had a BAR, Red ducked and crawled to a vantage point behind a smashed Jap truck. A sniper nicked him across the shoulder blade en route, although this wasn't noted in the testimony. However, the report mentioned, "a Jap machine-gun nest in a wrecked plane was wiped out by a two-man detail with automatic weapon fire, at approximately 1800."

Later, as the many fires began to throw tricky shadows amid the devastation, the Japs began their usual infiltration tactics. Silhouetted against a sudden larger flare from an exploding ammunition dump, a cluster of them rose out of a shellhole at the extreme end of the airstrip. The situation called for grenades and Red secured them from his BAR buddy. He crawled forward out of his foxhole and let fly.

The unwounded Japs, flushed into the open by the explosion, surged forward with banzai screams, firing as they came. The tommy gun and the BAR barked side by side until suddenly the former fired alone. Red's buddy was down, shot through the leg.

The official report continued: "At approximately 1930 subject named man aided in repelling enemy counterattack with grenades and automatic weapon fire."

Dropping quickly behind the ruins of a log emplacement, Red seized another grenade and poised to throw it. A terrific impact knocked him back but he got rid of the grenade "on target," as his BAR buddy later testified by affidavit from his hospital bed. The impact was that of a Jap 31-caliber bullet hitting the left side of Red's face, entering just in front of the ear and emerging below the left eye.

The report mentioned a fourth wound "through the nose, laterally, received while aiding a BAR man with a shattered leg to the beach evacuation station."

The doctors on the beach took one look at the half-blinded Red as he staggered up with his charge and then promptly tagged him for immediate evacuation. Just twelve hours had elapsed since he had slung the tommy gun over his shoulder and crawled away over the sand dune from the regimental CP.

It was one day several weeks later at the division's rear area "rest" camp that Red stood at attention before a stern-mouthed group of officers, his face expressionless, his usually bronzed skin still white from his hospital sojourn.

In the senior officer's eye, as he looked up again at Red, there was the suspicion of a twinkle. Then he took up a pen.

The final words he scratched on the AWOL report were:

"Charges, in the case of Private First Class Gareld Thomas Shelton, withdrawn."

Master Technical Sergeant Gene Ward

Incident on the Natamo

The kid was already a legend in Company B. He entered the war with the flamboyancy that was part of his nature, simply by stowing away on a plane at a South Pacific base and arriving at Guadalcanal in time for a spectacular share of the Matanikau fighting. He went out the same way—with courage and aplomb and a grin when he saw the war was over for him.

Two hundred men watched him die. And some of them died to save him.

The dawn was still a promise of red in the eastern sky when Private First Class Cecil Bruce Dunthorn, a 22-year-old Marine of Nutley, New Jersey, went out on patrol along the mouth of the Natamo River. The ten-man squad commanded by Sergeant Arthur C. Falla, of Arlington Heights, Massachusetts, paddled a rubber boat across the dark, sullen waters where the Natamo meets the sea. The men dispersed through the curtain of jungle, scouting the Japanese position known to be there.

From deep in the jungle came echoes of a machine-gun burst, instantly alerting Marines poised along the river. Rifle fire punctured the stillness. Then there was quiet, a silence that lasted until 11 a.m. as the burning sun arched overhead.

Private First Class Dunthorn raced to the beach, into the open, onto the sandspit of Natamo. Two hundred men on the other side sensed his message. The patrol had discovered the Japanese position, had been intercepted and pinned down. These were the Japanese who took Bataan; they knew how to fight.

A sharp burst of enemy machine-gun fire shattered the quiet. The running figure neared the rubber boat. Private First Class Dunthorn fell and was still.

Its presence unsuspected, another machine gun covered the river mouth only a hundred yards from the men awaiting the signal to cross. The Japanese gunners had craftily held their fire half the day. Now they sprayed the Marine position, driving to cover the men who wanted to rescue Bruce Dunthorn. Beyond, the trapped patrol was fighting its way back to the beach. By ones and twos they slipped into the river, wading and swimming to safety, evading the enemy at the river mouth.

It was noon. Only Private First Class Dunthorn was still out there. He was moving now, and Dr. William B. Kintzing, a naval lieutenant of Hanover, Pennsylvania, examined the lanky, blond kid through his glasses. Lieutenant Kintzing was refused permission to swim out through the hail of bullets to rescue him. There were spontaneous volunteers from every foxhole. They knew Bruce Dunthorn and they knew he would do the same for them, any time, any place. They talked of what he did along the Matanikau "on The Island." Then Private First Class John S. Sunny was selected.

Sunny is a huge, muscular veteran of five years in the Marine Corps, from Brownsville, Pennsylvania. He strips. His tanned body glistens with sweat. Around his waist is a strap with two hand grenades tied on. Flotation bags are looped to his shoulders to keep Bruce Dunthorn afloat.

He slips into the water. There is a splash behind him. Another Marine is swimming alongside.

He is Private John J. Whalen, Jr., of St. Albans, New York. Private Whalen is a buddy of Bruce Dunthorn. He has slipped away from his mortar position to help rescue a pal.

As bullets flay the water surface, obscuring the two swimmers, Private First Class Sunny is hit. He reaches shore and staggers to Dunthorn's side. Through the glasses Lieutenant Kintzing sees blood on Sunny's back, sees him favor a leg.

Private Whalen makes it unscathed. The three men huddle on the sand as a second Japanese machine gun, nearer than the first, opens up directly ahead. Escape is impossible now.

First Lieutenant Perle W. Vaught of North Terre Haute, Indiana, sends a patrol headed by Sergeant William F. Lawrence, of New York, on a circuitous route to flank the enemy guns from the rear. It, too, is pinned down by enemy fire.

The minutes pass. Bruce Dunthorn has been out there three hours. Private Whalen is tearing Dunthorn's clothing for bandages.

Tensed men watching the drama relax as time wears on. They sprawl in hastily scooped foxholes, raked by bullets a few minutes ago. Soft waves lap the beach and the water is a translucent blue and green. The rasping music of cicadas in the trees comes and goes in monotonous cadence. Major William H. Barba of Kinston, North Carolina, is impatient for the flank patrol to withdraw. He wants to lay a mortar barrage.

The men who were with Bruce Dunthorn this morning cluster together and talk about him. Murphy passes a pack of cigarettes. The machine gun opens up again. Murphy isn't his real name. Even a war correspondent can't tell the name of a man who dies like Murphy died. He was an Irish kid from Florida who had been out there with Bruce Dunthorn this morning.

The cigarettes have just been lit. Murphy gasps and the red blood spurts over his lips and his cigarette goes out. He has been hit in the lungs and the abdomen. Lieutenant Kintzig crawls over. He whispers:

"Murphy doesn't know it, but he's going to die. Ten minutes, twenty minutes, maybe."

· 175 ·

The machine gun rattles again and the bullets sing overhead. The cigarette Murphy lit for me is burning my fingers.

They give Murphy blood plasma and you can't help wondering whose blood it is. A girl, maybe, back in the States. The last rites are administered by Father Charles M. Eggert of St. Paul, a Navy chaplain. Ten minutes, twenty minutes, and Murphy's blood wells from his lips and we cover his body with a jacket.

It's 2 p.m. The enemy's guns are barking every few minutes. Private First Class Alex C. Fraser of Little Falls, New Jersey, jokes about the bullet that sliced his thigh. He clings to a bullet-creased cartridge magazine he is carrying in his pocket.

Through the glasses it appears that only Private Whalen is moving on the sandspit. Dunthorn and Sunny are still.

A landing barge is brought into the river, attempting to screen a rescue party. Heavy machine-gun slugs rake the control deck. The awkward craft wallows in the surf and limps off. The barrage continues as First Lieutenant John E. Williams, Jr., of Wellesley, Massachusetts, takes a platoon aboard a barge for a diversionary landing behind the enemy lines. A Japanese heavy machine gun opens up on the barge as the ramp is lowered. We scramble in the surf, dropping and running for concealment in a coconut grove ashore.

Working on a sniper is Private Donald Booth, Jr., of Milwaukee. The overhead fire ceases. We advance slowly down the beach. Suddenly the radio reports that our strategy has worked. The barrage and the surprise landing have turned the enemy flank and our men are preparing to cross the Natamo.

Down the beach we see men going out for Dunthorn, for Sunny, and for Whalen. Dripping and exhausted Whalen is making his report when we get there. Sunny lies on a stretcher, blue lips smiling as plasma is injected in both arms.

Private Whalen explains: "Dunthorn died just before the boys reached us."

He doesn't say any more.

The rescuers are being congratulated. They are from a machine-gun outfit who strung empty cartridge belts together for a life line and got Sunny across the river. They didn't crow over their feat.

It's 5 p.m. and the sun is searching the horizon. In silence two hundred Marines who have waited all day under fire, who have watched Dunthorn and Murphy die, move across the river.

It wasn't a battle; just an incident along the dark waters of the Natamo.

Second Lieutenant Gerald A. Waindel

The Last Thing

The Marines who knew Corporal Ethan Allen Farrar on Guadalcanal say there seemed to be only one thing he ever wanted to do after his brother was killed.

"I never heard him say a word about his brother or how he felt," a friend said. "He never even told us his brother's name. But I knew that after that Farrar seemed to live for just one thing—to kill Japs."

The friends said they got used to seeing Corporal Farrar, a tall, quiet man of 25, volunteering for patrols even when he was so weary he could hardly stand—volunteering for any job that might give him a shot at a Jap.

"I guess he was the only one who knew how many he killed, and he never said. But he must have got a lot of them. He was the kind of shot who hit what he aimed at. He had a funny habit, too. I don't know how many times I saw him do it. His mouth would be tight as he took aim, as he squeezed off his shot. Then he'd smile."

It was the same way when the outfit came fighting its way through the jungle and the kunai grass flats of Cape Gloucester. Corporal Farrar's squad was held up by a troublesome sniper. It was a tough job locating him. It was a tougher shot once he was spotted. Corporal Farrar seemed to aim a long time before he fired. He got the sniper. At that moment, a bullet got Corporal Farrar.

He couldn't have felt any pain. It was too quick. They saw he was still smiling as he lay in the grass. The last thing he'd known in life was that he'd got another Jap.

Technical Sergeant Asa C. Bordages

Halt Led the Blind

The slug entered Robert E. Gass's head between the eyes and he slumped alongside the concrete Jap emplacement he had started out to take. Consciousness ebbed and returned, and the thought dominant in the mind of the 22-year-old automatic rifleman was to "get the hell out of here."

Miraculously the slug, even though it had torn into his head, had stopped short of his brain. But it had blinded him. He clung closely to the concrete wall and tried to figure things out. He had landed with the first assault wave. Pretty rugged going. But he had accounted for two snipers and then left his heavy rifle to rush a pillbox and knock it out with a grenade. Next this second job—this second pillbox. He had had the grenade in his hand, was all set to pull the pin, when—smash!—the slug tore into his head. And now here he was, right under the gun port in the pillbox—blinded, bleeding, and not knowing what to do, what direction to take.

And at that moment he felt something smooth being slipped around his wrist and a whisper. "Just hang on, mate," the whisper seemed to say. There was a tug and he crawled with it. Dizziness and a feeling of extreme nausea swept over him, but he held on grimly while the fight raged around him, continuing to inch along on the coral sand. Years, it seemed, went by before he passed out from exertion, pain, and the sun's blazing heat.

When he came to, a Navy medical corpsman was giving him first aid on the beach.

"What . . . what happened?" he asked.

"You're a lucky guy, Joe," the medic said. "Some crazy Marine came along and put his gun sling around your wrist and led you down here outa that mess."

Gass just shook his head.

"Who was he, what's his name?" he asked.

"I dunno," said the corpsman. "But his legs—both of them—was broke from shrapnel. Couldn't even walk. Just had to crawl and lead you. We got him out to the hospital ship."

Technical Sergeant Henry A. Weaver

The Marine Who Wouldn't Give Up

Two Marines on New Britain were sent out on patrol in advance of a big push to be made against the Japs on the following day. Returning from their job, one of them stepped on an enemy booby trap. The explosion shattered both his legs. Realizing that he was too heavy to be carried back to camp, he persuaded his companion to go on alone. The second Marine treated the wounded man as well as he knew how, then reluctantly started back. Fears that the Japs would find his companion plagued the Marine, but he continued to camp and turned in his information.

As scheduled, the attack on the Japs was made the next day. The enemy was soon withdrawing in disorder. When the Marines came to their wounded buddy they were horrified. There he lay, silent and motionless and about his body and up and down the length of it were tangled wires. Evidently the Japs had come and rigged him up as a booby trap.

No one dared touch him. This was a job, a delicate and dangerous job, for an engineering unit. Suddenly the "human booby trap" opened his eyes, grinned feebly, and whispered, "Hey, fellas, get these damned wires off me. An' help me up." The Marines stepped forward and removed the wires. There was no blast, no explosion.

· 179 ·

Knowing that the Japs would be attracted to the spot by the first explosion, the Marine had painfully wired himself up as a booby trap with wire from the one which had wounded him. The Japs had come. They took one look and fled. And the quick-thinking American had lain undisturbed until his companions found him.

Captain Seymour Arnold Gross

First Sergeant Falzone

"Let me out, doc. My boys are catching hell. They need me."

First Sergeant James P. Falzone stood waiting for the Navy physician to answer. Both could hear the rumblings from Saipan's front lines. Slowly the doctor shook his head.

"You're badly wounded, sergeant. I can't do it."

The topkick, an 11-year veteran from Waltham, Massachusetts, stepped back, snapped to attention. "Sir, you had better have a guard watch me. I can't leave my boys up there alone."

The tired doctor gazed at the crowded sick bay. "Corpsman!" he called. "Corpsman," the physician told a youthful sailor, "get a jeep and drive this Marine as near to the front as you can."

Falzone grinned. "Thanks, doc!" But the physician was already tending to another casualty.

As they left, the first sergeant saw one of his men. He leaned over. "How ya' feeling, kid?"

The youth grimaced, then smiled. "Okay, top. Doesn't hurt much."

Falzone patted the youth's shoulder. "You're going back to the States, kid. Isn't that great?"

"I can stand anything to go back to the States," the other Marine laughed.

The jeep driver hunched over the steering wheel every time a sniper's bullet whined overhead. "Want me to drive you right up to the front?" he growled.

"Yeah," replied Falzone. "Riding beats walking."

"You're crazy but I'll do it," the driver said, gritting his teeth.

Falzone jumped out, raced for the nearest foxhole. The driver quickly turned the jeep around and disappeared in a smoke screen of dust.

"The top's back!" someone yelled.

"Keep your heads down!" Falzone ordered.

"Think we need you, top?"

"Naw," Falzone answered. "I just want to watch how good you guys are."

"Shorty's hit and won't leave, top."

"Where is he?"

"Two foxholes on your right."

Falzone peered out, then ran to Shorty's foxhole.

"Think you're tough?" he asked. "You're going to sick bay, kid."

"What about the shrapnel in your back, top?" Shorty snapped.

"Just a scratch."

Shorty smiled. "I'm as tough as you are, top."

"Sure you are, kid. Tougher. But don't be a fool. You get good chow at sick bay and a bed to sleep in. Besides, you've done more than your share. We've plenty of men."

"Sure you don't need me, top?"

Falzone hugged Shorty. "Positive, kid."

A mortar shell exploded while Falzone returned from helping Shorty to the rear. He rose from the ground spitting dirt.

"Bet yo' wish yo' was still on recruitin' duty in Boston," a Southerner drawled when the first sergeant crawled in beside him.

"I sure do," Falzone said.

Jap snipers then opened up from a near-by cliff. "Hold your fire, men, until you see your target," Falzone ordered.

The leathery topkick, watching the cliff, ignored the bullets which tore up the earth only a few feet away. Then he saw a movement. He squeezed the trigger. A Jap toppled off the cliff.

A Marine in the next foxhole fired. Another Jap spilled off the cliff. Soon the snipers were silenced.

A lieutenant crawled up, and asked, "Where's the officer in charge?"

"He was wounded and evacuated, sir," Falzone answered.

The lieutenant studied the section. "Everything's in good shape," he remarked.

"Yes, sir," Falzone said. "These kids are on the ball. Don't have to tell them anything. They anticipate everything."

The lieutenant said, "Fine," and left.

"What a snow job!" someone hollered at Falzone.

The topkick laughed. "Don't you guys think you're good?"

"Know what you remind me of, top?" a Marine yelled from an adjoining foxhole. "A fussy old hen looking after her chickens!"

Several men commenced clucking like chickens.

Falzone yelled, "Keep watching for the Japs or you'll find out I'm a mean old rooster!"

Someone crowed.

Even Falzone laughed.

Staff Sergeant Elvis C. Lane

Retreat, Hell!

The Corps's proudest tradition and a Negro Marine corporal who believed in it stood the acid test together eight days after Saipan was officially secured.

The corporal was Joseph Gogins of Chicago. A caveful of Japs staged a surprise attack on an Army working party north of Garapan. A volunteer group of Marines and sailors, some armed only with rocks, went to their rescue. The unarmed members of the conglomerate group decided to withdraw after a Marine was wounded by rifle fire. Nineteen-year-old Corporal Gogins, himself unarmed, rose to the occasion.

"You come back here," he shouted. "Don't you know the Marines never retreat?"

Soldiers, sailors, and Marines stood their ground together, killing eighteen Japs and capturing two before they ran out of ammunition.

Master Technical Sergeant Gilbert Bailey

Line Company Men

I'd like to tell you something of the line company men. We know now that some men do walk right at enemy machine guns and sometimes they keep right on walking when the men around them go down. For instance, on Saipan, and it must have been the same in the Palaus before the American flag was raised, some line companies were fighting at half strength, which means that up front you had a fifty-fifty chance of being shot. The line company men were "in the assault" on Saipan twenty-four times in twenty-five days. They occupy most of the room in the newest and largest American cemetery in the Pacific. Because they are the ones who get close enough to the enemy to kill him, they get killed themselves.

The line company man makes the long marches, his pockets jammed with grenades, his chest crossed with bandoliers of ammo clips, a light machine gun on his shoulder. At night he digs in to form a line of defense for himself—and everyone else behind him. The magazines never show him as dirty, as tired, and as worn as he is. After two weeks on Saipan, he looks "rugged," like a sandhog who has long gone without a shave or a bath. His tired eyes are the mark of an inner struggle between dread and courage.

He carries his souvenirs with him: a bullet hole in his helmet, a crease in his canteen, a bayonet cut in his dungaree jacket, or a slight wound which "doesn't amount to anything." When there is nothing else to laugh about, he laughs about that. He doesn't jump into a foxhole when a bullet whines over. By the time he has fought his way across the first ridge, his attack position is a slouching walk, and it puts a lump in your throat to see him keep on walking when the men next to him go down.

The public makes little service distinction between a man who faces death every day and another who is simply overseas. They all wear the same ribbons and tell the same stories. The line fighter knows this, but he doesn't care very much, for the moment, what the public thinks.

He has everything to live for. A second lieutenant with a pretty wife,

4-year-old son, and a good job waiting for him at home runs out in front of his company alone to meet a Jap banzai charge. He lives through it, but others are not so lucky. Some true stories sound like sentimental fiction when you write them. A 23-man patrol holds a mountaintop all night against an encirclement of Japs, refusing to withdraw and leave their dead and wounded. Five come out alive.

These men would be legendary characters if history could absorb them—unnoticed people who for the first time in their lives heard the call of greatness and glory, and recognized it when it came. Like the unnoticed corporal who was wounded three times, but always talked his way out of the hospital to "get back to my outfit." Stories will never be written about most of them. There are too many, and what they do has come to be taken for granted.

Master Technical Sergeant Gilbert Bailey

Foxholes

I shall grow fur like moles
From darting into holes.
And, like the mole, grow blind,
Eating what I find;
Sleeping where I light,
When I think it night;
Loving only earth
Fitted to my girth;
Mistrusting sounds apart
From the ticking of my heart;
Fearing every sign
Of movement except mine;
Considering every breath
Potentially death.
I shall learn to live
On what a grave can give;

Lie in my narrow lair
And grow my coat of hair—
Already on my features—
Like all the hunted creatures.

Major Raymond Henri

The Difference

The Kid was scared. He stood alone at the rail on the fantail at sundown, facing the sun. Guam was just over the horizon. He'd be landing on that beach at dawn. He was only eighteen or so, with sun-bleached hair and that curious pallor under the bronze of his skin.

It was while he was staring there that his shoulders shook a little.

A large hand dropped on his shoulder, there was a gruff "Hi, kid," and he was joined at the rail by a tall, heavy-shouldered sergeant, a man young in years too, but already battle seasoned.

"Get the kinks outa that bazooka, kid?"

"Yeah, sarge."

"Guam's dead ahead."

"Yeah."

"Y'know, I'm scared, kid—it's a big show."

"You scared, sarge?"

"Sure, scareder'n anything! It's always this way. Hands shake, belly feels funny . . . can't help it. Wish I could, but I can't."

"I . . . I feel it, too."

"There isn't a man aboard that don't, kid—or else he's lying if he says different."

"They all afraid, sarge?"

"Afraid? No, kid, scared. Lots of difference. A man that's afraid would want to quit, now, without tackling the job. A man that's scared—he kind of wishes it was over and he was cleaning his rifle, but he's going to stick it out. Y'see?"

· 185 ·

"Yeah, sarge. Guess I'm just scared."

"Sure, kid." The big hand closed on the kid's shoulder again.

"Let's go check your bazooka again."

They strode across the deck together.

Technical Sergeant Ward Walker

Chonito Cliff

This story was written by Sergeant Cyril O'Brien. He had fought in an earlier campaign with the men he describes. But for the accident of a recent transfer, he would have been with them in the fight for Chonito Cliff. The cliff was taken, with the help of another Marine unit, but not until almost all the men in O'Brien's company had been killed or wounded.

Nearly half my old company lies dead on the barren slopes of Chonito Cliff. Four times they tried to reach the top. Four times they were thrown back. They had to break out of a twenty-yard beachhead to make way for later landing waves. They attacked up a 60-degree slope, protected only by sword grass, and were met by a storm of grenades and heavy rifle, machine-gun and mortar fire.

The physical act of forward motion required the use of both hands. As a consequence they were unable to return the enemy fire effectively. Most of the casualties were at the bottom of the slope. They had been hit as they left cover.

There was Pappy, his name stenciled on his canteen cover. A bullet had ripped away the first "P" in his name.

My former assistant squad leader was beside him. He often had me on his working parties. I had seen those arms of his, which in death still clutched a splintered rifle, throw full ammunition cases about as if they were empty.

There was the first scout of my squad. We had shared the same tent for months, when I was second scout. He was always promising

· 186 ·

himself "a white Christmas in 'forty-five." He was facing the sky, his hands at his sides. You'd think he was dreaming.

Willie, who volunteered for mess duty so he "wouldn't have to stand inspections," was lying halfway up the slope. His feet were dug into the dirt. His arms were bent as if he were ready to charge again. But his Garand rifle was empty and thrown aside. The pistol in his hand was empty too. Perhaps he intended to club the enemy with the empty weapon.

The "Beast"—we called him that because he was so big—had charged his big frame to within five yards of an enemy machine-gun nest. He caught a blast in the chest. The fancy lettering he always placed on the back of his dungaree blouse was torn by bullets.

There was Frankie, who had received a shiny, chrome-plated pistol from home. He had boasted he would get many Japs with it. Now the sun's rays from over the ridge glinted on the handle. The pistol was still in its holster.

Peter had a strong voice in camp. He had it in the face of death. He was halfway up the ridge, yelling something about the "bastards" on the top, when their fire cut him down.

The lieutenant we called "Chicken," because he seemed so young, was the only one to reach the crest. A grenade smashed in the side of his head. Those skinny legs which had led me so often to exhaustion were white in the dried grass. Two Japs, five feet in front of him, had holes in their heads. An American grenade which the Chicken evidently had thrown was lying between the Japs. How often the lieutenant had drawled in his slow hesitant tone: "Now, a grenade— it explodes five seconds after you heave it." His hadn't.

Eddie was lying in a bed of mountain flowers. He was fond of flowers. He used to put them in his helmet for camouflage when others used grass. The hand that was not on a rifle was crushing a flower.

Behind the lieutenant, his face anxious as if awaiting an order, was Angelo. He loved to sing—but couldn't. He and I were penalized once for singing "Put on Your Old Gray Bonnet" after taps.

The company was still under fire when, on the ridge, I talked to the men who had made it. Private First Class Leon Slicner of Perth Amboy, New Jersey, tried to tell me how "Smokey" could have been saved had they been able to pull him out of the fire lane in time. His words came slow. Finally, he stopped in the middle of a sentence, leaving the story in mid-air. He really didn't want to talk. Besides, he was pressing low into a foxhole, and he couldn't breathe well, for a machine gun was spitting fire over our heads.

Sergeant Cyril O'Brien

Master Gunnery Sergeant

This is the story of how Navy Pharmacist's Mate Virgil Warren, of Oakland, California, came to sing "God Bless America"—not very well, he admits—on a hot beach-head at Guam. It happened during the fiercest fighting there. Marine Master Gunnery Sergeant Israel Margolis, of Los Angeles, had been hit trying to man a machine gun. No one knows how Margolis got there. He was a weapons expert. A man with that job usually is to be found somewhere in the rear. But Margolis must have seen the wounded streaming back. He knew what was going on. All of a sudden, he was on top of the 100-foot cliff above the beach, looking for action.

Margolis was 48 years old, not young for a front-line fighter. But, like many Marines, he was a professional. Born in Volkovisk, Russia, he had fought as an officer of the czar in the last war. After the Russian Revolution he had joined the American Army in France, then had come to the United States, been naturalized and joined the Marine Corps. Margolis was short and wiry, with a square-cut head. He had been all over with the Marine Corps. His record book showed service in the Caribbean, China, Iceland, New Zealand, the Solomon Islands. He was in action on Bougainville before Guam.

The Japs had that clifftop on Guam well marked. It was flat and open. The Marines were trying to bring enough strength together there to launch an attack. Machine guns were holding them up, sweeping the position with murderous fire. Just after Margolis was first seen there, Jap machine gunners spotted one of our guns. In succession, five Marines tried to man that gun and each was hit. The fifth, though wounded, tried to drag the gun to a new position.

Margolis went to his aid and began to man the gun himself. The Japs caught him immediately. Bullets cracked his legs and hips and he fell. Warren pulled him to the cliff edge, but there was no way to get him down. He dressed the wounds. It was useless. Margolis was dying. He knew it and pleaded with Warren to leave him. The corpsman looked around helplessly. If there were only a block and tackle, a sling to lower the wounded man down the cliff. But men were just beginning to fashion a sling. Margolis' life wouldn't wait.

Final thoughts must have crowded the man's mind as he lay there —the St. Petersburg cadet school, the Czar's Uhlans, the AEF, his eighteen years in the Marine Corps, his adopted land he would never see again. Suddenly he opened his eyes. Warren asked if he wanted anything. Margolis nodded. Warren knelt by him. "Please," Margolis whispered, "please sing 'God Bless America.'"

The corpsman swallowed. He tried. "God bless America, land that I love . . ." Warren sobbed. Muddy Marines, shaken by battle, crowded around. Warren tried again. "Stand beside her and guide her . . ." Lumps came into the throats of the men. One, then others, knelt. "Through the night with the light from above . . ." Margolis' eyelids fluttered.

"From the mountains and the prairies . . ." On the clifftop above the beachhead there was a hush. "From the oceans white with foam . . ." Now the corpsman lifted his voice: "God bless America, my home, sweet home."

In the silence that followed, the tough little soldier, U.S. Marine, and naturalized American, died.

Master Technical Sergeant Alvin M. Josephy, Jr.

The Kid

We were sitting in a command post, a tarpaulin strung between two bomb-splintered coconut trees. He edged forward to speak to me. He was Marine Private First Class William L. Sellers of Cairo, Georgia.

"You ought to write," he said, "a story about the Kid."

Wise was the Kid's name. He was port machine gunner on their armored amtrac—an ungainly alligator mounting a 37-millimeter cannon—and Sellers was Wise's crew chief. A shell penetrated their "trac" as they were crossing the jagged coral reef of Peleliu to blast the way clear for Marine assault waves. "It's my leg . . . they got me in the leg," Sellers had heard Wise cry in the interphone. Soon a small stream of blood came eddying down from Wise's perch.

"But he propped himself up, and kept firing . . . firing and cursing the Japs," Sellers said.

The Kid's blasts of profanity, added to the steady splutter of his machine gun, strengthened the crew's hatred, defined their determination. "We listened to the Kid and fired all the faster" was the way Sellers explained it. As the huge vehicle lumbered out of the water and across the beach, it took another hit, and they were forced to abandon it. When Sellers got to Wise, he had passed out. His torn leg was dangling.

Well, that was the story about the Kid, Sellers said, and he looked at me questioningly, as if to see whether I shared his feeling about Wise.

"It's a good story," I said.

He got up to leave. I didn't have Wise's address. Sellers remembered it: Private First Class Charles L. Wise, Fullerton, California. As I wrote, I wondered aloud, "What happened to Wise?"

"We got a corpsman . . ." Sellers paused, and looked reluctant to go on. I grew curious.

Sellers, then, if I must know, had devised a plan. "We set our minds the Kid would live," he said.

The mangrove swamp into which they had run was infested with Jap snipers who, unless they were distracted, would pick off Wise when Sellers lifted him out of the turret. Sellers sent two of the crew out forward with their rifles to draw off the Jap fire, another for a hospital corpsman. Still another gave Wise morphine, and put on a battle gauze. The last man ducked behind the amtrac to lay a poncho for Wise—where the Kid could be given plasma in comparative safety.

When the corpsman arrived, Sellers went out, jumped down the side, waited to help Wise. Consciousness regained, Wise pulled himself up and out, and rolled himself down the side. Sellers caught him. They were both covered with Wise's blood when Sellers put him down behind the amtrac.

The plan was working with a vengeance. The riflemen were getting fire—too much of it. So Sellers went back inside, loosened a machine gun, and with it ran forward to the other flank, laid it on a coconut log, held it down with his hand and began firing.

It seemed an endless time that they fired, there in that Jap-stinking swamp, Sellers said. The barrel of the machine gun got blistering hot —it burned the skin off his palm. Finally he saw the corpsman hail another amtrac, lift Wise up over the side. He watched till it got back to the reef, to safety.

"After that we found foxholes until things cooled off," Sellers finished.

"Why did you call Wise the Kid?" I asked.

"Oh, he was only nineteen," Sellers said. "The rest of us are twenty."

Technical Sergeant George McMillan

The Marine

The Marine with whom I live today is a character I'll never forget. He answers to many names and at times I've put my head on a pillow and prayed I could wake tomorrow and find him gone. I've grown sick of his face, sick of his voice, sick of his family. Still every day he grows nearer to me, and every day I'm more sure that I'll never forget him nor lose my affection for him.

I don't suppose anybody really cares what I think of him, least of all he himself. My country, suffering from an analytical binge, has described him a hundred different ways. He used to be considered as simple a problem as two plus two, but he has grown as complex as relativity. Suffering from nothing more than a cold in the nose he is being treated for lobar pneumonia.

He has a sense of humor that enables him to laugh aloud at the amateur psychiatrists who plague his life. The tear-jerking commercial advertisements that have flooded his reading matter verge on a stupidity that is mildly amusing. When politicians have the disgustingly poor taste to resurrect his former tentmate, call him GI Jim, and be presumptuous enough to get out a crystal ball and read his mind, he is insulted. However, he also enjoys this Americana—in much the same way as he would the circus.

He laughs at the story that tells him the country has provided a flock of new national cemeteries for himself and his loved ones, and with mock sincerity he congratulates himself upon his luck.

He isn't a dashing, devil-may-care hero; nor is he a frightened, worried creature. He has long realized that the thin line which supposedly separates genius from insanity is even thinner when it gets between bravery and stupidity.

At times he can drive you to near insanity. On occasions he can prevent you from reaching that goal under your own power.

His complaints have received nation-wide attention. His little wants are supposed to be the wishes of a nation. In truth, nine-tenths of his complaints spring from boredom and an ever-present sympathetic audience. He has proved that his complaints diminish with enemy activity. His "beefs" and desires grow with inactivity.

He doesn't like death, but he can grow more upset about a cut finger or a sick pet at home. He has been heard to say after the death of a friend, "Well, we aren't playing for marbles."

In his foxhole, he wonders out loud as to what manner of maniac would make a one-man bombing attack on a clear moonlit night. For the life of him he can't figure the mental operations of his opponent, but laughingly he admits that it doesn't make a helluva lot of difference whether he kills them or they kill themselves.

He wonders why a pair of female tramps who became embroiled with a couple of Nazi prisoners of war should receive international publicity, while literally millions of perfect wives and sweethearts are regarded as candidates for a Ripley drawing. He wonders who at home is designated to send that tripe into a war zone. People say it will hurt his morale. As a matter of fact he really doesn't give a damn.

Trouble doesn't mean much to him because its familiarity has bred contempt. You may wear his clothes, spend his money, borrow his books, and share his food.

You can't touch his personal pictures, you can't bother him when he has mail from home, and you can't touch his personal weapons. The rules for getting along with him are simple and easy to follow.

Sometimes his voice gets loud and stern but you never see him raise his hand in anger against his companion. Silent contempt is just about his strongest attack in his own group.

He wants to return home, but not as a conquering hero nor like a person who has been away on a long fishing trip. He doesn't think the country owes him anything, and he'll tell you that there isn't enough money in the nation to pay a man for the sort of work he has been doing. The one thing he doesn't want is to be treated as a laboratory test tube.

He can laugh or be grouchy and wonders why that should surprise anybody. He can be hungry, thirsty or romantic, but there is nothing new in that. Loyalty and co-operation have become second nature to him.

He wants a few mental problems to face for himself because he is tired of other people doing nine-tenths of his thinking. He has no complaint about the fellow who didn't get into the war and often sympathizes with his repressed enthusiasm. In spite of all his complaints he considers himself lucky to be part of the big show.

His great wish is that he be excused from the role of guinea pig by a country full of amateur and professional psychoanalysts. He wants his family again, but he still doesn't want them as much as he wants his country to win this war. I'll never forget him. And neither will you.

Staff Sergeant John F. Slocum

The Japs Couldn't Get Him

Gil had just set up his camera to get a picture of the whole-blood transfusion process when we saw them bring in Big Gus. Of course, Gus isn't his real name. That's what some of the boys call him up on the lines and that way we can get his story past the censor. Seeing Gus there in the hospital was a shock. You get funny ideas when you've been through three campaigns with a division; and one of the funniest and strongest we've nourished for a long time is that the Japs might shoot every Marine in the Pacific but, by golly, they'd never get Gus.

Many a night we've sat up and talked about it. And pretty soon we came to believe it. Gus would always be there, no matter how much lead the Japs threw at his company. Gus would walk right into a wall of shell and bullet. Everyone else would fall, but not Gus. Maybe Gus believed it himself. He used to share our joking, and said he was "too damned mean" ever to get shot. Anyhow, it seemed to us there was a surprised look on Gus's face when they brought him in, as if he didn't really believe he was there on the stretcher. Maybe we sold Gus too strong on the idea that he was a modern Achilles.

You'd think, when you saw them bring your best friend in on a stretcher, you'd rush right to him. But we didn't. We stood there and tried to figure out what we were going to say to him. We knew that if we went over there looking like a parson at a funeral, Gus was going to be sore as hell.

When we did go over, we just grinned and said, "What goes on here?"

Gus took a stronger chomp on his big cigar and looked pained; as if he'd hoped we wouldn't see him wounded. Gus probably wanted us to go on believing he was immune.

"Damned if I know," he said. "Someone said I got shot."

We followed the formula after that.

"You're a lucky stiff, you know that, don't you?"

"Sure I do. They're going to evacuate me. You've got to sit here on this damned island until it's over. Why don't you go up and look things over and pick up a little bullet like I did?"

There was nothing more said. Gus let go of his cigar and added:

"They got Roy, you know."

We didn't know that.

Gus winced while the doctor probed his wound.

"This is going to hurt," the doc said.

Big beads of sweat popped out on Gus's brow, and when he could talk, he said, "Bill's dead, too."

We figured the conversation was getting too serious, so we slapped Gus on his good arm, and said:

"You lucky stiff! When you get out to the ship, kiss one of the nurses for us."

We walked off; but two stretchers away we met the padre.

"Gus is down there," we said.

The padre looked as if we'd slapped him in the face. Maybe the padre had believed it, too.

"Where?" he said, and we led him back to Gus. It seemed to us that the padre also was wondering what to say.

"Hello, you big ape," he finally got out. It didn't sound convincing.

Gus was biting hell out of his cigar. The doctor was really into that wound.

"Got the press and the church with me now," Gus cracked. "Ought to make it in good style. Padre, don't never let them damned Japs put one of them slugs in you. It hurts to beat hell."

"I won't, Gus," the padre said.

Gil walked up, and Big Gus had an idea.

"Hey, you," he said to Gil, "I want a picture. Right here. I want

· 195 ·

the padre and the press in it with me. I want to prove to that kid I'm going to have when I get back that I was wounded on Iwo Jima."

The doc was still probing the wound. And Gus was worrying about his boys up there in the hills.

"Only Sam's left," he said. "You know, this is the first time I've ever been away from them boys, as much as a single hour, since we landed in the Marshalls."

No one said anything.

"Damn it," Gus said, "they're throwing everything at them boys. I hope Sam knows what to do."

"Sam knows plenty, Gus," the padre said. "You taught him."

"Yeah," Gus said. "Yeah, Sam's okay."

"Sam's a winner," we said.

Gus jumped when the doc dug deeper into his wound.

"You know something, padre?" Gus said. "You really want to know something?"

"Sure we do, Gus."

"It's the truth, padre. I really believed the Japs couldn't get me. Funny, ain't it? Funny now, anyhow. But I really believed that. Honest I did."

"We did too, Gus," we said.

First Lieutenant Jim G. Lucas

Ie Shima

Twelve of us sat on the ground beside the tent in the deep evening shadows, all staring at the officer's clothing roll among the gear in a far corner of the tent. No one would go near it.

It was just a plain clothing roll, mud spattered, and on its side were ink-written letters no more than ¼-inch high spelling out the name "Ernie Pyle." You thought of other clothing rolls you had seen, with big-lettered names and "War Correspondent" stenciled all over in bright-colored letters, to ensure the gear finding its rightful owner.

But this name had been hand-printed with a fountain pen, the way a schoolboy marks the cover of his book.

Five minutes before we had been notified that Ernie Pyle was instantly killed that morning by a hidden Jap machine gun on Ie Shima, the little flanking islet that we could see in the distance during the bright part of the day. Now we could occasionally hear the sound of naval gunfire from that site. The low, hollow rumble was a funeral dirge to our ears.

We had been pleased when we learned that Ernie Pyle would land with Marines for the first time. For months and months we had heard Marines in the field wondering aloud "if Ernie Pyle will ever come out here and write us up."

We were a public relations unit and Ernie had lived with us. We had found him a place to sleep, fed him chow, arranged a spot for him to write in, gave him transportation around the island. Like everyone else we had fallen in love with him. It was very easy to do, because we had all been in love with Ernie the writer long before meeting Ernie the person.

We had just sent off our first letters telling folks back home how swell it was to have an easy landing with few casualties and to know that your friends were not dead and wounded as at Iwo Jima, Saipan, Tarawa, and Peleliu. Now we felt miserable about the elation in those letters. We knew that every man on the island had lost a dear friend, a friend he held in common with his buddy and his family and his friends and even people he didn't know.

This writer landed on the same beach that Ernie did on L day. Pyle wrote his beachhead story there and submitted it for transmission by ship's radio. He was very gay and talked incessantly of how pleased he was at not seeing any dead or wounded. He laughed a lot and repeated how he had enjoyed a picnic lunch of turkey wings and fresh oranges on the beach 350 miles from the Japanese homeland. A few days later he came to live with us in our shell-pocked house in the town of Sobe, not far from where he first landed.

One evening we had to cover a large pile of refuse in the yard of the house. Ernie said he felt like some exercise (he'd only been tramping around all day), so he picked up a shovel and spaded earth for half an hour with the general duty men. You can imagine how they loved him.

We got a few cots in for war correspondents, but Ernie designed his own pallet with his collection of blankets and sweaters and odds and ends of gear and slept on the floor with the men. He was that kind of guy.

He went back to the front and lived for five days with a company of the 5th Marine Regiment. When he returned he was very tired-looking and badly in need of a shave. He sat on the ground with us and mapped out his plans. He said that he wrote very laboriously and that he wanted to go to a ship to write his stories in some degree of comfort. He said he would leave his gear with us and return in about three or four days and have us attach him to our Seabee units.

As we were sitting there he told us that he felt very lucky about getting back from the front this time. He said he had had a close call. The company he was with had rested in a small clearing, and a few minutes after they all sprawled out, smoking and talking, someone discovered two Jap soldiers, only twenty yards away, with rifles and hand grenades.

We didn't hear from Ernie again until another officer brought us word that he was still writing columns and resting, that the ship he was on would join the forces striking Ie Shima, and that he would "go for the ride's sake." Then he would come ashore and join us.

We all knew what must have happened then. The landing was easy at Ie Shima and Ernie, even though he wasn't covering that outfit, just couldn't resist going in the next day to look for story material. Some credit could be given to the men who would be wounded and dying on a small island that might not get much public attention.

We sat there by the tent that night talking for an hour about Ernie. Later there was an air-raid alarm and we spent the next hour in a bomb shelter, all huddled together. Most of us were recalling favorite Ernie Pyle columns and passing the time and forgetting the discomfort by reciting the passages we could recall from the columns we liked best.

A general-duty corporal who had chauffeured Ernie on the island, remarked, "It seems a shame such a big guy had to get it on such a lousy little island."

Another man said, "I sure was glad to see him with the Marines this time, but I guess as long as it had to happen it was best he got it with the Army boys over there on that island. He sure loved them and they sure loved him."

The next morning we checked Ernie's clothing roll. It held just his shoes, underwear, caps, sewing kit, some public relations releases, khaki trousers, flashlight, belt and canteens, socks, felt-lined slippers, some toilet articles, and several spools of the dental floss he always used each morning and night.

There was only one intimately personal item—some pretty little colored seashells strung on a silver-colored chain. He had probably got it at our staging area, where the island natives sold them, or else it was given him by some Marine or sailor aboard ship. It was something he had stuffed away to take home as a souvenir of this trip, his last one.

We wrapped up the shell necklace at once and sent it on to be delivered to Ernie Pyle's "That Girl."

Captain John N. Popham

Epitaph for a Young Marine

It was on the island of Saipan, the morning after a particularly trying night of heavy enemy mortar fire that had caused numerous casualties in our front lines. I was walking along the road when I saw some of the dead being loaded gently into the backs of several trucks that had been drawn up to take bodies to the division cemetery. I looked to see if I recognized any of the dead Marines. There were half a dozen stretched out, some on their backs and several face down. One of the latter was a young, fair-haired private who had only recently arrived as a replacement, full of exuberance at finally being a full-fledged Marine on the battle front.

As I looked down at him, I saw something which I think I shall never forget. Sticking from his back trouser pocket was a yellow pocket edition of a book he had evidently been reading in his spare moments. Only the title was visible—*Our Hearts Were Young and Gay*.

Captain John H. Magruder

The Words They Spoke

Never again would they talk the same way.

The jokes they made in battle would come to them later, and they would wonder, with a sense of fright and amazement, how they could have spoken them, how they could have wisecracked then. The Marine who snapped back at his superior officer would be militarily proper—later. The Marine who dallied a moment to equivocate with a Japanese soldier before shooting him would shake his head ruefully as he remembered.

Here are some of the accounts that recall their words in and out of combat, their stories and their jokes.

On Cape Gloucester, a Marine patrol stumbled on a group of Japs. One of the enemy, it developed, could speak some English. As the guns cut loose, the Jap screamed:

"I'm shot!"

The patrol included a sergeant from Brooklyn, Philip Mettola. He was a stickler for accuracy.

"Shot, hell!" he shouted. "You're dead!"

And it was a fact. The sergeant saw to that.

By mistake—almost a fatal mistake—another Marine, Private First Class Richard J. Butler of Des Moines, Iowa, won credit for one of the prize understatements of the war.

It was midnight on Tinian, and the Marianas were slowly slipping out of the Japs' grasp. They counterattacked. In the blackness, a Jap officer leaped into Butler's foxhole, brandishing a sword.

Butler saw the man's outline and mistook him for a Marine. He saw the sword glint and mistook it for a bayonet. He pushed the sword blade aside.

"Be careful, Mac," he whispered. "Be careful or you're liable to hurt somebody with that thing."

The startled Jap leaped out of the foxhole and ran. Another Marine promptly shot him down.

Sergeants Hans R. Johansen and Herbert Schultz

Another notable understatement was heard March 18 on Iwo Jima which, for one hour in the midst of combat, was the happiest spot on earth. American weapons were turned away from the enemy and aimed instead into the air. Machine guns, antiaircraft guns, carbines, rifles and even pistols—the only festive equipment handy—roared their jubilation.

The war in Europe was over. Germany had surrendered. Or so they thought.

The dismal truth came quickly.

A soldier operating a walkie-talkie had become bored in his solitary foxhole.

He had decided to play radio announcer with a buddy a few foxholes away.

Near by, in a truck, another operator was typing military messages radioed from San Francisco.

By some freak of the battlefield, the frequencies became tangled. From the official operator's set came a tension-charged voice with the electrifying message: "Germany has surrendered unconditionally."

The operator got the news to headquarters. In ten minutes all the island and ships offshore had the word.

Hearing all the shooting and shouting, the foxhole "radio announcer" grew worried. He went to his commanding officer with his historic utterance.

"Sir," he said, "I think I've done something wrong."

Technical Sergeant Frank Devine

Mention Cape Gloucester to a Marine and he may tell you of the rain and mud. If he is disposed to talk of combat, he may mention the snipers—they were everywhere. He may discuss the enemy planes which contested the American advance. And, if he feels like reviving battlefield jokes, it's a safe bet that eventually he will get around to stories concerning the fabulous observation post, the one in charge of Sergeant Tucker and his seven staff "commentators."

The observation post was five hundred yards beyond the front lines. Swept by tropical storms, beset by snipers, it was as uncomfortable a spot as you could find on Gloucester.

The boys at the post had a field phone connected to G-2 (Intelligence). In addition to their duties of reporting enemy ground activity, they had assumed the burden of providing reports on Japanese bombing raids, extremely unofficial reports. Each one was awaited by G-2 with as much eagerness as a prizefight broadcast.

One memorable report was made on an evening when the audience was enlarged by a colonel and his staff who, chancing on the open wire, had tuned in just when Japanese planes came into view at the observation post. Sergeant Tucker's staff didn't know that. And it wouldn't have mattered if they did. Corporal Lester W. Bachran was at the field phone for the event. He sailed into the broadcast with characteristic gusto.

"This is Graham McBachran, coming to you from the Ridge OP on the road to Rabaul. We interrupt our program of Sergeant Tucker's snoring with a special bulletin, direct from the newsroom of Station USMC. Bit-dit-da-da . . . Three enemy bombers are approaching from the southwest.

"It's a beeotiful night on Cape Gloucester. A perfect bomber's moon beams down and tracer bullets create gay patterns in the starlit sky. Our blow-by-blow descriptions are a nightly feature . . . The bombers are coming low . . . they're circling low . . . off to the west . . . they're circling again . . . here they come!"

There was a chill at the command post. Corporal Bachran bellows: "Bombs away!!"

Half of the CP burrowed into convenient foxholes. Others—including the colonel—stood where they were, fascinated by the running account of the raid.

"Missed us," breathed a listener as the bombs crash to the south. Corporal Bachran's voice comes through again:

"One . . . two . . . three . . . four. There they go, into the ocean. Those guys couldn't hit a politician at a national convention.

"We've got one in the searchlights. He won't catch us with our ack-ack down!"

Suddenly, the raid was over. The All Clear sounded. The calm, suave voice of Corporal William J. Walden came in.

"It's never too late to choose your mountain resort. Why not escape the heat? Make the observation post your last resort. American plan with hot and cold running Japanese throughout!"

There are other tales concerning these boys beyond the front lines.

One day the CP grew solicitous. A major telephoned:

"You fellows getting enough to eat up there? We can make arrangements to bring you one hot meal a day."

Private First Class Edwin Boyd of Selma, California, was on the phone.

"Eat?" he said cautiously. "What kind of chow have you got down there, sir?"

"Beans and corned beef, I guess," said the major.

"Well," said Boyd, "you can keep it, sir. Here's our menu at the Club Outpost. Breakfast: fruit juice and pancakes; coffee and fresh doughnuts. For lunch there's potatoes au gratin, beans en casserole, and creamy hot chocolate. For supper . . ."

"How in the holy cow do you manage that?" the major shouted.

"Combat patrols, sir. Combat patrols."

Then he explained: "You know that Army engineering outfit repairing the airport? Well, valiant two-man Marine patrols are successfully infiltrating the quartermaster's lines nightly. Better come up here for chow, sir. We've got hot biscuits with gravy tonight."

There was a pause.

"You were saying, major?"

The major's voice was weak. "Never mind," he said, "I didn't say a thing."

One night, that same observation post was lashed by a severe electrical storm. The wires were filled with static electricity. Private First Class Erwin Kane of Miami Beach, Florida, tried to pick up the phone. The shock spun him off his feet. Amazed, he grasped the phone again.

When he picked himself up the second time, he turned to a buddy.

"Here," he said. "You take the phone. I think I've got Warden Lawes at Sing Sing."

Second Lieutenant Gerald A. Waindel

Informal broadcast versions of combat were not limited to ground troops. One day over Rabaul, New Britain, a Marine Corps fighter pilot started another form of exuberant commentating. It wasn't long before anyone tuning in on the fighter frequency would hear broadcasts strangely reminiscent of home. They went like this:

"I'm the Green Hornet! Bzzzzzzz ! Bzzzzzzz! ! Watch me sting this Jap . . ."

"Wheeeee! I'm Dead-Eye Dick! I nev-ver miss!"

"Here comes Jack Armstrong, the A-a-a-all American Boy! Rat-a-taaaaaat! Rat-a-taaaaaaat!"

"Which way'd they go, sheriff? Thataway, pardner. Yippeeeeeee! The Lone Ranger rides again!"

"Avast, ye villain, I'll pay the mortgage. Take that . . . and that . . . and that . . ."

"Dick Tracy's the name. Flat-top . . . you're a goner—Rat-a-a-taat! Rat-a-taaaaaaaaa!"

First Lieutenant William K. Holt

The mocking of radio commercials kept leathernecks stationed on islands in the Pacific from going "rock-happy."

In one tent on Guam, where the Third Division was based after the island was secured, a group of men were just about to go to sleep after a particularly rough day.

Suddenly, a weary voice drooled: "Are you fed up with the setup? Then, my friends, join the Marines and see the world—through a peepsight!"

A second asked: "Are you nervous in the service?"

As the other tentmates started firing articles of clothing at the impromptu announcers, a final saccharine message was heard, poignant and inspirational: "Be terrific in the Pacific."

The boys groaned and went to sleep.

Washington's alphabetical agencies found a staggering counterpart in the Pacific where Marines tangled their tongues on Navy abbreviations. One phone conversation at a jungle island air base sounded like this:

"Hello, COMAIRNORSOLS? Gimme Sergeant Slocum, please."

"Sorry, he's not at COMAIRNORSOLS any more—been transferred to COMTHIRDPHIBFORS."

In other words, the sergeant no longer was assigned to Commander Aircraft, Northern Solomons, but had been transeferred to Commander Third Amphibious Force.

There were other examples: COMCARDIV (Commander Carrier Division); COMPHOTOSOPAC (Commander Photography South Pacific); COMGENSOPACBACOM (Commanding General South Pacific Base Communications); SUBORDCOMSERVPAC (Submarine Ordnance Commander Service Pacific); COMMTBRONSO-PAC (Commander South Pacific Motor Torpedo Boat Squadron); COMFWDAREACENTPAC (Commander Forward Area Central Pacific); and COMARBASEDEFAIRWING 4 (Commanding Officer Marine Base Defense Air Wing No. 4).

First Lieutenant Milburn McCarty

An apocryphal tale made the rounds of infantrymen as well as airmen. It concerned a southern pilot in a dogfight. The pilot's voice was calm as it came over the radio.

"Heah come three bogeys . . . I'm a-goin' aftuh them."

Moment's silence.

"Spla-ash one."

Another pause.

"Spla-ash two."

Then: "Spla-ash three."

The slow accents suggested mild surprise.

"Well, what do you know? Heah come fo' mo!"

Silence.

"Spla-ash fo'."

Short pause.

"Spla-ash five."

His drawl still belying any excitement, the Marine said, "Heah come eight mo'."

Quickly, yet calmly, he added, "You bettah send some moa boys up heah or you're gonna lose one helluva hot pilot, 'cause I'm a-comin' home."

Technical Sergeant Claude R. Canup

Another Marine flyer, Captain Dan Johnson of Neosho, Missouri, was patrolling over the East China Sea when he heard a fellow pilot put in a call to headquarters.

"Where am I?" the lost flyer asked. "I'm all fouled up."

An angry officer at headquarters barked back.

"Who's that Marine pilot who doesn't know where he is? What's your plane number?"

The lost flyer cagily drawled his answer: "I'm not *that* fouled up."

Captain John N. Popham

A Corsair pilot was on his way home from a raid and was having trouble finding his way back to his base, since his instrument panel had been badly shot up. He came down through the overcast in an attempt to get his bearings and spotted a battleship below him. He got on the radio:

"Hey, you, in the boat. Can you give me a bearing to Saipan?"

"Whatsa matter, are you lost, ace?" the battleship wanted to know.

"Yeah, can you give me a bearing?"

"Just a minute, ace, and we'll see what we can give you, ace. How about two-seven-o True. Think you can find it now, ace?"

"Sure, thanks, you guys."

"Any time, any time, ace. Only next time don't call us a boat."

Second Lieutenant Frank X. Tolbert

Once or twice the Marines were confronted by news more significant than the news they were making in their island battles. One such day came as expeditionary forces were moving to assault the Marianas Islands. Games and idle chatter were helping to erase thoughts of the passing hours that were bringing them closer and closer to the island beaches. In the wardroom of a ship, three games were in progress. The men were playing bridge, cribbage and chess. In a corner, an officer was reading a book. There was a low buzz of conversation. Silence fell as three crisp words crackled over the loudspeaker:

"Now hear this!"

A short pause.

"The invasion of France has started. That is all."

In the silence that followed, the men heard the throb of the ship's engines. It seemed the first time they had listened. They kept listening in that silence, as though it would tell them something more. Then a voice said, "Thank God!"

The officer in the corner slowly put down the book he had been reading, deliberately blessed himself, softly uttered a moment's prayer, and blessed himself again. Then he returned to his reading.

The others watched him, and without a word shuffled their cards again and resumed their games.

On deck, veterans of other Pacific campaigns squatted in small groups. Some walked below to smoke cigarettes nervously in corridors. Others gathered on the mess deck for coffee.

One man shouted, "I've got two brothers with the infantry there!"

A young Marine turned to a buddy. "My kid brother is there," he said. "He's a machine gunner."

The next day the tension had worn off. The men talked of nothing but the invasion. The statements of President Roosevelt and General Eisenhower attracted knots of readers where they were posted. The men laughed and talked eagerly of being home for Christmas. They formed long lines at the PX. All over the ship, they offered candy to each other. Thus they celebrated the assault on Hitler's Europe.

Ahead of them, only a few hours away, was the bloody battle of Saipan.

Captain John N. Popham

On the eve of the assault on Saipan, a medical officer summoned a Marine artillery unit and warned them of the island's perils to their health. In the surf, he said, were hazardous sharks, barracuda, sea snakes, anemones, razor-sharp coral, polluted waters, poison fish, and giant clams capable of snapping on a man as tightly as a bear trap.

Ashore, he continued, the men must beware of leprosy, typhus, filariasis, yaws, typhoid and paratyphoid fevers, dengue fever, dysentery, a wide assortment of skin and eye infections, saw grass or saber grass, a variety of insects, snakes and giant lizards. Eat nothing growing on this island, the medical officer cautioned the Marines, and do not drink its waters or approach its inhabitants.

Finally, the horrendous recital was ended. The doctor asked if there were any questions. A private raised his hand.

"Sir," he said, "why don't we let the Japs keep the island?"

Technical Sergeant John B. T. Campbell, Jr.

It was during the Marianas campaign that the Marines changed a slogan and proved themselves uncanny prophets.

In the dark days of Guadalcanal, leathernecks in the Pacific had dourly predicted: "Golden Gate in '48." And they had their fingers crossed.

But at Saipan and Tinian, as they read reports from the Philippines and the European front, they took a more hopeful view. They gave voice to a new slogan: "Home Alive in '45."

Staff Sergeant William B. Allen

In combat, there always seemed to be one man who could find a way to make his buddies laugh. One man fighting on Saipan was typical of many men in other battles. He was a member of a mortar platoon which had been dueling with Japanese mortar units all the way across the island. Shell fragments swept the canefield where the men lay preparatory to an attack. One Marine looked up.

"Three times in the past four days," he muttered, "my wife has almost been a rich woman. I could see them counting out my insurance, ten bucks at a time, the wife riding downtown in a new Packard roadster with a spotlight on each side."

The section leader heard him. To a combat correspondent he said, "That guy talking, he's our morale."

Then the mortar platoon moved forward to attack.

Master Technical Sergeant Gilbert Bailey

Not even the most grueling battle could carry their thoughts very far from home. There was Private First Class Michael F. Stile, who was recounting his experiences on Tarawa and Saipan where he had been a machine gunner. His gun had been far from quiet. He was taking a rapt audience through the two battles, burst by burst, when suddenly he interrupted his recital.

"You know the most unusual thing about me?" he said. "I live in Brooklyn and I'm a Yankee fan."

Staff Sergeant Harold T. Boian

It wasn't in combat alone that they were able to laugh at their own discomfiture. Once, during a rest period at Ulithi, in the Western Carolines, a movie was being run off. It reached a scene where a man said to a beautiful but addlepated blonde:

"You're so dumb you haven't enough sense to get out of the rain."

Laughter rocked the Marine audience.

Theirs was an outdoor theater.

And it was raining.

Technical Sergeant Claude R. Canup

During the mopping-up operations on Saipan, Private First Class Bert A. Kopcho did something he was at a loss to explain later. He awakened a sleeping Jap soldier. It happened one morning after a night of alerts. As it grew light, he saw the enemy soldier lying in front of his foxhole. On an impulse, for no reason he knew, he reached out, tapped the Jap on the head, and said, "Wake up, Tojo."

The Jap rolled over and looked up at him.

This, Kopcho said, surprised him. But he wasn't too surprised to shoot before the enemy soldier did.

Technical Sergeant Frank Acosta

On Guam's Mount Alifan, Marine Corporal Roger Spaulding, a farmer from Sheridan, Indiana, plopped to the ground and found himself face to face with a Jap officer.

The Hoosier turned to his platoon leader. "Hey, sarge," he shouted, "there's a Nip here staring me in the eye."

"Shoot him!" the sergeant hollered.

"I can't, my gun's jammed," the farmer answered.

At this, the Jap rose from the ground and charged Spaulding with a large samurai sword. Gripping his rifle with both hands the Marine rose to meet the charge. A shot rang out. The Jap fell, a victim of another Marine rifleman.

"Why'd you do that?" Spaulding called to the Marine. "I was just fixin' to club him to death."

Technical Sergeant George R. Voigt

· 211 ·

Even the wounded Marines hold their sense of humor almost as dearly as they hold their lives.

One Marine lay wounded and silent in front of the lines throughout a Jap attack. When the stretcher bearers got to him, he began to complain. They asked what was the matter.

"Aw," he said, "how'd you like to lie here wounded all day and then have three ugly guys like you come back to pick you up?"

In the eerie, tense and agonizing early days of Iwo Jima, the mortar and artillery fire seemed endless. Just as bad were the land mines, which the Japs had sown cleverly throughout the island. Thinking a mine field was cleared, one battalion (10th Amphib. Tractor) of Marines bivouacked in the middle of it. After they were there for a day, a leatherneck, digging a hole to enlarge a fire pit found a mine attached to a 250-pound aerial bomb. All day, a GI can of coffee had been cooking within three feet of the bomb, the fire going constantly.

A few moments later in the "cleared" mine field, another bomb was found beside a foxhole in which Marines had spent two nights under Jap shelling.

If it hadn't been for Private First Class Dwayne R. Hilbert of Salt Lake City, that battalion of Marines might have hesitated to move an inch. But Hilbert broke the tension.

"Somebody would think," said Hilbert, "that they didn't want us around here."

Jap artillery and mortar shelling on Iwo was so heavy at times that Marines huddled in foxholes and dugouts found their vocabularies limited to three words.

When a salvo of Marine artillery cut loose, they would assure themselves: "That's ours."

When an explosion would rock the ground and send showers of sand into their shelters, someone would remark, "That's theirs."

The morning after was a time to dig shell fragments out of sandbags and out of the timber roofs of dugouts. "Close," the men would say. "Pretty damn close."

News came to the men from the beachmaster who was using a loud-speaker to direct unloading operations. On D day plus four, the Marines heard from him the first news that Japan's little Gibraltar, Mount Surabachi, had fallen. The speaker blared:

"Mount Surabachi is ours. The American flag has been raised over it by the Fifth Marine Division. Fine work, men."

The weary fighters turned their eyes toward the hill and saw the flag fluttering atop the 546-foot rock. They looked for a moment, then turned back to their rifle sights.

"We have only 2,630 yards to go to secure the island," the loud-speaker said.

"Only . . ." came a Marine's voice. "Only . . ."

Staff Sergeant Jack Vincent

Almost every man was an unpaid Junior Chamber of Commerce for his home town, and the debates on the wonders of trees and crisp air of Prairie du Chien, Wisconsin, as against the theaters and busy streets of New York were endless and inspired. Two of the most eloquent eulogists were from Milwaukee. They prated about the nation's brewery capital until the rest of the men groaned in anguish. They even dug a foxhole together. Having found several heavy 6-by-2-inch planks they used the lumber to build what was probably the best frag-mentproof shelter on the beach. After one barrage, proud Milwau-keean Private First Class Joseph L. Hart said to proud Milwaukeean Private First Class Lloyd R. Christensen, "We're going to put up a flag or sign saying this is the Milwaukee City Hall."

Within earshot was a Texan who had grown weary of their praise of Milwaukee.

"Oh, hell!" he said. "Just put a beer bottle on top."

Staff Sergeant Jack Vincent

Every island had its signposts. Iwo Jima was no exception. On grim, bloody, forbidding Mount Surabachi, for instance, there was the sign advertising:

SURABACHI HEIGHTS REALTY COMPANY
Ocean View
Cool Breezes
Free Fireworks Nightly!

At a cave entrance, there was a poster:

ICHIMOTO'S INN
Under New Management
Soon Available to Personnel
of the U. S. Army (We Hope)

A deep sympathy for home-front problems (not to mention a blunt blow at the company's cook) was expressed in another sign, saying merely:

COOK WANTED

One leatherneck was more verbose. His sign said:

NOTICE: This Foxhole is Privately Owned
And Was Not Constructed With the
Help of the Federal Housing Administration.
Not built for comfort but for Speed.

Long arguments were provoked by another sign problem: what name to give to the much-shelled strategic road that ran along the island's perimeter. One of the most popular suggestions was "Seaview Boulevard." The debate never was settled to anyone's satisfaction. But long after the last shots were fired on Iwo Jima, most Marines who fought there found it hard to refer to it as anything but "that damned road."

Technical Sergeant Charles B. Cunningham

At a Marine and Navy recreation pavilion, facing the beach of one lonely Pacific island, a sign read: "Shady Acres Rifle and Gun Club, 'Where Life Is a 155-mm. Bore.'"

And a similar, though more extensive complaint, was registered on Kwajalein Atoll where one sign spoke the thoughts of thousands of men:

HOTEL ATOLL

No Beer Atoll
No Women Atoll
Nuthin' Atoll

It was a phenomenon of the sign-painting art that, as island after island fell in the Pacific, the city limits of Los Angeles grew. California's metropolis took its last great stride of the war at Okinawa where a lavish signpost sprouted at a crossroads outside a Marine CP. It read:

Berlin .... 4,182 miles
Tokyo .... 401 miles
Chicago .... 9,008 miles
New York .... 9,762 miles

The signpost concluded with the inevitable: Los Angeles City Limits!

(The Marines on Okinawa weren't as far from their homes as they thought. Actual distances were: Chicago, 7,120 miles; New York, 7,510 miles; Oklahoma, 7,000 miles. From Okinawa to Berlin is 5,760 miles, and to Tokyo, 910 miles.)

Staff Sergeant James Finan

Soldiers and sailors pounced on a song which suddenly cropped up anonymously. It poked fun at the "glory hounds" that many thought the Marines were. They were considerably deflated later to learn that the author was Marine Captain Earl J. Wilson.

The Marines, the Marines, those blasted Gyrenes,
Those sea-going bellhops, those brass-button queens.
Oh!! They pat their own backs, write stories in reams.
All in praise of themselves—the U.S. Marines!

The Marines, the Marines, those publicity fiends,
They built all the forests, turned on all the streams,
Discontent with the earth, they say Heaven's scenes
Are guarded by—you guess—U.S. Marines!

The moon never beams, except when the Marines
Give it permission to turn on its gleams.
And the tide never rises, the wind never screams—
Unless authorized to by the U.S. Marines.

The Marines, the Marines, in their khakis and greens,
Their pretty blue panties, red stripes down the seams.
They thought all the thoughts, dreamed all the dreams,
Singing "The Song of Myself"—the U.S. Marines.

Chaplains came in for their share of the humor. On Guam, after 40-year-old Commander Alvo O. Martin, a Navy chaplain from Manistique, Michigan, outdistanced a field of eight to win the 880-yard run in a Third Division track meet, one sergeant remarked to a buddy, "Sinners don't have a chance in this outfit. If the chaplain can't reach 'em with sermons, he can run 'em down."

Staff Sergeant Francis X. O'Donnell

One group of Fourth Division Marines, after lying for six successive days in open shellholes as American naval guns dueled Jap artillery on Iwo Jima, used titles of songs to identify each type of shell whizzing over their heads. When a flat, crackling barrage sprayed the area with shell fragments, they would bellow, "It's Mortar, He Says." The nightly air raid brought spectacular displays of ack-ack fireworks, and a chorus of "Mighty Flak A Rose." Most touching of all was the song title applied to the sound of massed Marine artillery shells, rockets and ships' guns sweeping overhead—"Going My Way?"

Technical Sergeant Robert Cook

One evening on Iwo Jima, a combat correspondent recorded the conversations of a group of men around him. These are the things he heard:

"My wife's birthday comes this month . . . she's eighteen."

A platoon sergeant spoke. "If there's any justice, it won't rain tonight, so those Nips can't get fresh water."

A husky man walked up to his lieutenant, said, "Here's a letter they found in M's pocket right after he died."

A tired-looking Marine approached. Someone shouted, "My gosh! There's Smitty! Hey, Smitty, I heard you were dead. Damn you! I was feeling sorry for you."

A man who was on outpost duty said, "You shoulda heard those Nips yelling last night. When they sealed up that cave, they hollered and squealed all night."

A plaintive voice: "Say, sarge, you think we can secure this rock in a couple more days? Boy, the Army's welcome to this place. I'd go nuts if I had to stay here long."

A corporal grinned. "Had some coffee today. Feel like a million now."

Sitting near a cluster of men, a lieutenant spoke, almost to himself: "All the officers I came overseas with are gone now—all killed or wounded."

One of the men answered quietly. "I know how you feel. Trinkler and I are the only ones left out of our tent now."

Another Marine said, "Mind if I hole in with you fellows tonight? My buddy hasn't come back."

"God! Listen to that barrage our artillery is sending over. Glad it's going the right way."

"Any of you guys get souvenirs? Me, I'm through souvenir hunt-

· 217 ·

ing. The other day I reach out for a Jap rifle and a sniper almost takes off my hand."

A languid voice broke in. "Anybody know of a good abandoned pillbox? I'm tired of foxhole life."

"Comb that hair, boy! Comb that hair! There's nothing that will help win this war like the combing of your hair!"

A few men smiled.

"You say today's Sunday? I lost track. Meant to go to church today, too."

"Where's that guy who said we'd take this island in five days anyway? I hope he's on the front line right now."

"Oh—oh! Looks like that Jap mortar hit some guys over yonder."

"Reckon they'll banzai tonight. 'Bout time for a big one."

There was a sudden quiet. A mortar shell whipped overhead. Then an exclamation.

"Look at this, Charlie! Wonder when that bullet landed here? I'm moving. You guys can stay here and get picked off by a sniper if you want to. I've got to go back to the CP."

"Tell my 'wife' not to shoot me when I come back. I'll be back in an hour."

"Those rats stomped around our pillbox all last night. They musta wore horseshoes."

"Well, well. I got two Christmas cards in the mail today."

"Huh! I got seven letters today . . . and an ad from a roller-skating rink in L.A."

"I told that guy not to park that 'weasel' out there. No wonder he got hit. Some guys never learn."

"When they start buildin' monuments after the war, they better build a couple for the jeep and the bulldozer."

Silence, then . . .

"There are only two kinds of Marines on this island—the lucky and the unlucky."

"Let's hit the sack. It's seven o'clock."

Technical Sergeant Frederick K. Dashiell

Before the Okinawa campaign, an officer was briefing his men on the strategic importance of the island. "From there," he said, "we can bomb the Japs anywhere—China, Japan, Formosa . . ."

A rasping voice came from the rear.

"Yeah," said the sergeant, "and vice versa."

Technical Sergeant Stanford Opotowsky

Then there was the story of the Marine general who was driving at night. Since he was a general, he had a driver. He also had headlights on and the Japanese were expected soon in their nightly air raids.

"Put those goddam lights out!" bawled an antiaircraft gunner as the jeep scuttered past.

The driver obeyed.

"Put those goddam lights on," instructed the general in a less vociferous but no less forceful manner. The driver obeyed.

"Put those goddam lights OUT!" shrieked the antiaircraft gunner in the distance.

"I *can't* put the goddam lights out!" yelled back the driver, who knew fully as well as the general what lights on during a Japanese raid would mean. "I've got the goddam general with me!"

And there is the apocryphal one of the colonel getting into a jeep. The sergeant standing at attention suddenly unlimbered and kicked the colonel soundly . . . While the colonel was still trembling from this unexpected treatment, a private first class rushed out of a near-by foxhole and kicked him again. Both were court-martialed. They asked the sergeant if he had any reasons for his mad action. The sergeant said he did: the colonel had inadvertently trod on his foot. He had a very tender corn. The sergeant's agonized reflexes had done the rest. It seemed possible but not plausible. They turned to the private. Had he any . . . ? "I ain't got no excuse," he said. "Hell, I thought the war was over!"

The Nature of the Enemy

These Nips Are Nuts

Wherever they have fought in this war, the Japs have shown an amazing aptitude for the queer and fantastic. They have staged solemn funeral processions in the midst of hot battles. They have blown themselves to bits with hand grenades, have stabbed themselves with daggers, sabers, bayonets, and even with scythes. They have plunged forward in stupidly blind banzai charges, and they have danced wildly atop ridges while exposed to American fire.

Some of these acts are part of their ancient philosophy that it is glorious to die for the emperor. Some are designed to terrorize and demoralize the foe, so that he will respond with a burst of rifle or machine-gun fire and thus reveal his position. And some are so freakish that they defy explanation. Whatever the motivation, these strange things have been etched sharply on the minds of the men who have witnessed them in every campaign of the Pacific war and who have been chilled, angered, puzzled—and even amused—by them.

In the third week of the battle for Saipan, Marines had fought their way to within sight of Makunsha village. Then the Japanese began one of the most furious—and futile—counterattacks of the campaign. One of the few who witnessed this banzai of banzais was Marine Lieutenant Colonel Lewis B. Rock, of Dayton, Ohio. From his vantage point high on a mountain, he saw thousands of Japs headed for the American defensive positions. At their head were half a dozen soldiers bearing a huge, blood-red naval flag.

"It was like a throwback to medieval battle scenes, gripping and dramatic," said Colonel Rock. But what followed in the wake of these front-line soldiers was even more startling.

"It was an unbelievable spectacle. Following these troops were the enemy's wounded. There were men with bandaged heads, men without arms, men on crutches, the great majority of them unarmed. They were tagging along, sometimes a mile or so behind the fighting troops, to participate in this last banzai charge, to have the privilege of dying for the emperor."

Two days later, the ground between Tanapag and Makunsha was covered with the bodies of these Japs who had made the vain assault. And on the Saipan coast line lay the huge red naval battle flag, now a prized Marine trophy.

On a smaller scale, but no less ferocious or crackbrained, was the exploit of a Japanese officer on Guam who led nine men in a suicidal attack on a forward CP in the Tumon Bay area. In the light of a full moon, they leaped from the jungle, shrieking and stomping wildly. The enemy soldiers were cut down instantly by grenade and rifle fire. But the officer, clutching a wound with one hand and waving his saber with the other, lurched on. He staggered into a medical aid station and wounded four corpsmen before rifle and pistol fire finally ended his foolish foray.

Such saber rushes are common in front-line fighting in the Pacific. A Jap troop leader, either to impress his own men or to frighten the enemy, has often leaped out of a foxhole and rushed singlehanded against his adversaries.

The Marines who fought on Guam will not soon forget the "Dancing Officer" or the "Trumpet Player." The first appeared one day on the crest of a hill about 1,400 yards from the American lines.

"There he was," related Corporal Donald S. Griffin, of San Jose, California, "jumping up and down, cutting this way and that. Maybe he was exhorting his men, but it's my guess he was going through some sort of ritualistic dance. Or maybe he was trying to impress us with his bravery by doing a dance while exposed to the enemy."

The Trumpet Player was a Jap who pulled a similar stunt on Guam, except that he stood on the hill and blew on a long horn, similar to the kind blown at New Year's Eve parties.

Several other Japs also showed our men some fancy didos on Guam. During the heavy fighting on the Agat front, they suddenly ran out of an emplacement. All were shirtless. First they paraded solemnly in single file in front of the Marine line. Then they moved forward again. They executed this step several times before they were shot down. And there was another Jap on Guam with more nerve than sense. Just before the opening of a banzai attack, this Nip jumped to the crest of a ridge above the Marines.

"One, two, three, you can't catch me!" he shouted.

Two dozen 30-caliber bullets promptly proved him wrong.

This eccentric could easily have been first cousin to the Jap on Eniwetok who took a shot at Private First Class Richard Kyhill, of Brooklyn, and missed. So irate was he at his poor marksmanship that he threw his rifle away and waved his hands in the air.

"He started hollering and screaming," said Kyhill. "He was really sore. And then he started swearing. Bad language always annoys me. So I shot him in the head."

Sometimes these weird things the Japs do verge on the near-heroic, although, in a military sense, they constitute useless expenditure of life. On Guam, several waves of Japanese infantry charged a squad of huge 34-ton medium tanks. One of the infantrymen drove his bayonet into the periscope of a tank driven by Sergeant Joe Rzesutek, of Oxford, Connecticut, before he was mowed down. Another jammed a grenade down the barrel of a 75-millimeter cannon and held his hand over the cannon barrel so the grenade would not drop out. The explosion blew his hand off.

There are other incidents Marines will always remember with a puzzled brow. There was the group of Japs who stormed a hill on Cape Gloucester, shouting, "Gimme back my hill; gimme back my hill!"

There was the attack by a band of Japs on one of the Marshall Islands in which each wore an oversized gas mask and uttered hideous cries. The "crazy howls" were first heard on Guadalcanal. They came at night—shrieks and bloodcurdling yells from the darkness of the jungles. They were intended by the Japs to frighten the Marines into a state of complete inability to fight. The battle cries of the Japs' have become familiar to thousands of Marines, too. "Banzai!" and "Marines, you die!" and "Marines, we kill you!" and "More blood for the Emperor!" were common enough, but on Cape Gloucester one unit of Japs tried a new one. As they stormed a Marine strong point in a hopeless attack, they yelled, "To hell with Babe Ruth! To hell with Babe Ruth!" This cry, however, was no more profitable for the Japs than the others. Marines wiped them out.

Technical Sergeant Herman Kogan

Ex Libris

One little Jap whose worldly woes are at an end, apparently whiled away the long, dull days on Cape Torokina before the Marines came by studying English verse.

The flyleaf of his book was found in the ruins of a pillbox. It bore this inscription in a painful Japanese version of English penmanship: "I am get this book at Is. Bouganfil at 20th day May 2503.— K. Kumana." The poem on the opposite page was apparently his favorite, because the sheet had been torn from the book and folded. It was: "Dainty Wee Daisy."

Technical Sergeant Frank Devine

Marpi Point

I have just returned from Marpi Point, at the extreme northern end of Saipan, where, with thousands of Marines, I have been eyewitness to one of the most sickening and unbelievable orgies of death any group of men has ever been forced to watch.

Many of the things we have heard from others who have seen them I had not believed possible. For that reason, I will not repeat them. I am certain they would not be believed back home, where our own people have no experiences with which to compare them.

Hundreds of Japanese have killed themselves and their families. Marines have seen Japanese women throw their children into the sea, and jump in after them. Hundreds of wounded and maimed boys and girls under ten years of age are now in our field hospitals—not one of them wounded by shrapnel or bullets, but the victims of their own people, usually the parents. I saw today a Japanese woman and girl, their tongues cut out. The girl had been stabbed. Their murderer was the father and husband, who took his own life.

Civilians have reported they were warned by Japanese soldiers that they would be shot and killed merely for possession of surrender pamphlets dropped by our planes. There have been instances in which we know that natives have been killed for trying to give themselves up. At Marpi Point this morning, I met another Marine, so sickened by all that he had seen that he was actually begging to be taken back to the rear. He had gone through twenty-four days of bitter fighting without flinching, but he was made almost hysterical by what he had seen.

"You don't want to go up there," he told me, pointing to the cliffs ahead. "It's too horrible. You can't write what you see."

I agreed that I did not want to go. I did not tell him I had already been up there. Without exception, the attitude of Marines is one of dismay—of sick horror. They cannot understand or grasp the psychology of such people. Certainly, it is not their intention to harm little children, yet they have seen children marching in front of Japanese troops, who have tried to attack behind them, and they have seen children forced to run through cane fields to draw our fire.

For the first time on Saipan, I cried today. It is more than many of us can stand to see horribly maimed boys and girls who look at you with eyes which do not register fright, which show no fear, but which are so old and tired as a result of all they've endured that the children simply do not care any longer. This afternoon, I saw a husky Marine sitting by the side of a road, brushing flies from the face of a 6-year-old Japanese girl. Tears were streaming down his face. Near by, another group of Marines tried to look after a week-old baby, rescued from a cave beside the dead body of its mother.

I have no idea how many of their children the Japanese have killed, nor how many we have saved, but all of us pray we will never have to witness this sort of thing again.

First Lieutenant Jim G. Lucas

Strange Battle

One of the strangest battles of the war was fought one night on Saipan island. It was not a battle of bullets, or shells, or bayonets, or grenades. It was a battle of ideas.

The contenders were a Marine and a Jap prisoner. At stake was a man's life—the Jap's.

The Marine, Private First Class Joseph Berger, of Superior, Wisconsin, was a Japanese language interpreter with the Fifth Amphibious Corps. The Jap—a 26-year-old doctor who had been helping attend wounded Japanese prisoners since his own capture by the Americans—was despondent and decided to commit hara-kiri.

The Japanese prisoner and the Marine had worked together for several days among the wounded Japanese prisoners at a Marine stockade. And the Japanese had come to like and respect the American. Therefore, when he decided to commit hara-kiri, he came to the Marine one evening with a request. He wanted the Marine to take the role of his best friend. Traditionally, when a Japanese commits hara-kiri, his best friend stands by and finishes the job by cutting off the suicide's head.

Private First Class Berger listened while the young and despondent Japanese explained that he felt guilty because he had allowed himself to be taken prisoner. He had disgraced himself and his country. Life held nothing for him. Facing him was only imprisonment and dishonor. It was better to die and thus fulfill his vows to his country and his emperor.

"You are wrong, my friend," the Marine told him. "You are young and you have much to live for. You have not disgraced yourself or your country."

"My life is over. Of what use am I now?" the Japanese cried.

"You are of great use this very moment, taking care of your wounded countrymen and helping them survive to the day when a free Japan is born. You are learning what democracy is. When the war is over you can return to your country and help your people both as a doctor and as a man who has learned about democracy."

The young Japanese thought about it.

"I still think I must perform hara-kiri," he said reluctantly.

The American presented more arguments against suicide.

Another Marine interpreter and an Army doctor who understood Japanese came nearer to listen to the strange debate. They also urged the Japanese to choose life instead of death. It grew late in the evening. The other interpreter and the doctor went to another part of the tent and went to sleep. Still Private First Class Berger and the Japanese wrestled with the problem.

"You are not brave if you choose to die," the Marine finally charged. "You are a coward. If you choose to face life and to help your people now and after the war, you are really a brave and modern man. Japan will then be grateful for your decision."

The Japanese could not think of a good reply. His arguments grew weaker. It was now the deepest part of the night. He sat silent a moment.

"Perhaps you are right. I am all confused. All my life I thought differently about these things," he said. "I will try your way."

The Marine and the Japanese lay down to sleep. When the Marine awoke in the morning, the Japanese was hard at work, cleaning and bandaging the wounds of his captured fellow countrymen.

Technical Sergeant Dan Levin

To the Last Man

He was an extra-small Japanese soldier. His uniform hung limp like a scarecrow's trappings. A Marine on Orote Peninsula asked him why he surrendered.

"My commanding officer told us to fight to the last man," the prisoner answered.

"Well?" queried the Marine.

A look of wounded innocence spread over the Jap's face as he declared, "*I* was the last man!"

Master Technical Sergeant Murrey Marder

Busted Disguise

An apparently feeble old woman hobbled out of a cave along with a band of natives on northern Okinawa. A pair of Japanese Army regulation pants, which protruded from the woman's torn kimono, aroused one Marine's suspicions. Pretending to help the decrepit old soul, the leatherneck ripped off the tattered kimono and a full rag bosom toppled to the ground.

After the disguised Japanese soldier was captured, the Marines tossed for one of the unique souvenirs of the war.

Staff Sergeant Edward F. Ruder

Some Japs Surrendered

In the latter days of the fighting on Guam we thought we could speed the process of straggler elimination by inducing Japs to surrender. It meant a new relationship between ourselves and our enemy—an incongruous relationship that bewildered a lot of our men. From the early days of Guadalcanal we had learned not to trust Japs who wanted to surrender. There had been too many cases of treachery. We all knew some of the terrible stories. One concerned Japs who surrendered in pairs. Just as they reached the Americans, one man would fall on his hands and knees, revealing a light machine gun strapped to his back. His companion would man it quickly, shooting down the startled Americans. In battle, therefore, we learned to live by the rule of kill or be killed. We refused to risk our own safety to test the good intentions of Japs who indicated a wish to surrender. In face-to-face encounters we knew that the man who shot first won—and lived.

That is not to say that we never took prisoners. During our initial landing on Guam, for instance, we found a Jap sitting on the beach, dazed by our D-day bombardment. It was a simple and safe matter to take him back to one of our ships as a prisoner. We also captured many wounded Japs during the fighting on Guam—men who were too injured to put up resistance. And, finally, we were beginning to bring in sick and starving men who could hardly stand up without our help. Our patrols were finding them lying in cave entrances or in the jungle.

But to most of the Marines, our new policy was puzzling at first. We dropped leaflets from airplanes into the jungle areas and tacked them to trees alongside paths. They told the Jap survivors in their own language that they could keep their lives and honor by surrendering.

"Do not be afraid," our notices read. "You will not be harmed. Advance alone and unarmed to where American troops are located with your hands up, stripped above the waist, carrying this leaflet and walking down the center of the road. Those who do so will receive food, water, and medical treatment."

The Japs must have been puzzled too. The results were not encouraging. Few of the enemy took up our offer. Those who did were mostly frightened civilians who had fled from their businesses and homes in Agana and had taken refuge in the jungle with their troops. They were not so disciplined as the others, and our leaflets made more sense to them than staying in the woods and starving to death. They sneaked away from the small bands of fanatic soldiers with whom they were traveling and, following our orders, gave themselves up. But the bulk of survivors—Army and Navy men—continued to hold out.

We decided the Japs needed proof of our promises and began to use sound trucks—regular transport trucks rigged with a loudspeaker system. Jap prisoners who had received good treatment from us volunteered to go along. As the truck toured slowly through the mazes of jungle roads, the prisoners talked into a microphone in Japanese telling any Jap who could hear the blaring loudspeaker that the Americans lived up to their promises.

The results were better. The Japs heard the voices of men they knew. In greater numbers they began appearing on the jungle roads, stripped to the waist and waving copies of our leaflets. Our old veterans were astonished. They referred sarcastically to the truck as a "vote-getter truck" and complained that it broke up their ambushes. One of our patrols heard the sound truck coming through the jungle one day. The patrol was hiding in the brush near a hut which showed signs of recent Jap occupancy. The infuriated patrol leader sent a runner to the road to tell the truck to get away.

"Damn it," he called, "they'll scare all the Nips out of here."

Some of the Japs surrendering told us that most of the survivors were hiding in the dense coconut groves and rugged terrain below the cliffs lining the northern shore. It posed a new problem for us. We had to get to where the great numbers of them were, yet it was a particularly wild and inaccessible area, cut off from the rest of Guam by sheer 600-foot coral cliffs. There were no roads into the area, so we couldn't get our sound truck in. The only way to reach them was from the water.

We took over an LCI, a small green landing craft that had launched rockets at the Japs all through the Guam battle. There were two old salts aboard: Chief Boatswain's Mate John D. Henderson and Boatswain's Mate First Class Ernest L. Adamson. Between them they had seen action in almost every naval engagement and amphibious landing since Pearl Harbor. Henderson had been with the Asiatic Fleet when the war broke out and fought in the early disastrous battles around Singapore and Java. Adamson had been in the Central and South Pacific and had been in all the Solomon Islands fights. He rated sixteen battle stars. After so much action against the Japs, the two regular Navy men felt funny when they were told that their little gunboat

was to be used to lure enemy survivors on the northern coast into surrendering. They watched us when we came aboard and rigged our
public address system in one of the gun tubs, and pointed all the guns
of the ship skyward instead of shoreward, and hung colored signal
flags and pennants to all the lines.

"Damned if it ain't a peace ship," Henderson said.

The name stuck; she was the "Peace Ship" from then on.

Our plan was to cruise back and forth along the reef opposite the
coconut groves where it was suspected Japs were hiding. A Jap
prisoner, who had volunteered for the job, would call to his fellow
countrymen through the public address system with the same sort of
appeal we had made from the trucks. As an added measure, two other
prisoners would be rowed across the reef in a dinghy from time to time
and left ashore by themselves, to enter the coconut groves, find some
Japs and try to prove to them that the Americans were acting in good
faith. We could hardly have been more liberal in showing the enemy
our good intentions, for we were actually releasing two prisoners of
war who might very well choose not to return to us.

Henderson and Adamson's astonishment soared when the first Jap
came aboard and was quartered in the same hold in which they slept.
He was a little, brown-skinned fellow with big, pouting lips. He was
a comical-looking monkey and at first the seamen stared curiously at
him and laughed. Then he, too, began to grin and chatter in English.
He knew a lot of our words, particularly our slang, which he had
learned from the Guamanian people. He told the sailors his favorite
people in the world were Babe Ruth and Judy Garland, and he amazed
them by quoting American big league baseball batting averages for
past years. He immediately became popular aboard the ship. The
sailors gave him free run of the vessel and named him Joe.

The other two Japs were quieter and more reserved. They were the
ones who had volunteered to be rowed ashore, while Joe would do
the hollering through the loudspeaker. One of them, whom we will
call Nito, had been a schoolteacher in Saipan and then a civilian pay-
master for the Jap Navy on Guam. He was about thirty-five and spoke
German and English. He was slightly effeminate in his gestures and

· 230 ·

manner of speaking and acted as if he had not wanted any part of the war. He was still somewhat shocked at the experiences he had gone through on Guam, particularly our shelling and the days he had wandered around starving in the northern jungles. Although he had surrendered voluntarily, he had been frightened not only of us, but also of the other Japs—particularly the fanatical Navy officers. He was afraid they would kill him if they ever caught him. Oddly enough, that is why he had volunteered to go back into the jungle. He would show himself to them as a gesture that he had not lost all his honor. If they killed him he would be receiving his just punishment. If, instead, they chose to do what he had done and surrender, it would again be what fate wanted to happen.

The third man we named Taki. He was a slight youth with long hair and delicate features. He had been a soldier, used to taking orders. He had little to say and did his best to stay out of everyone's way. When we passed him, he bowed low. When we looked at him, he smiled apprehensively and glanced quickly away, as though he expected an ax to fall suddenly on his neck. He had come from a poor peasant family and had had little schooling. Nito was teaching him English.

We went aboard the LCI and set out that evening for the northern coast with orders to stay out three days. Early the first morning we sighted smoke from a campfire, rising above the coconut trees. Joe manned the public address system and began calling on the Japs to come out of the grove and surrender. He had a high, strong voice that carried over the water.

"Nipponese!" he shouted. "Come to the beach and give yourselves up to the Americans. The battle is over. The Americans are treating those who surrender with honor. Do not starve to death. The Americans will give you food and water and medical care. I have surrendered and can promise you all these things."

A solitary Jap poked out of the bushes and stared at us. Then he disappeared. We decided to put Taki and Nito ashore to try to talk to the Japs personally. Ernie and Henderson rowed them across the reef in a little dinghy and landed them on the sand. They told the two Japs that the LCI would sail out of gun range to show that we meant no harm. Then, in a couple of hours, we would come back to pick them up. Nito said that he would try to have many Japs waiting for us on the beach when we returned.

"If we are not here," he said stoically, "you will know we have been killed."

When we returned two hours later we found three Japs waiting on the sand with Nito and Taki. They were proud of their accomplishments, and they were also happy that the other Japs would see that the Americans had kept their word and had returned and saved their lives.

We picked up more Japs in the afternoon. Ernie and the chief kept rowing them back to our fantail. They would be hoisted aboard, scared that we were going to kill them. We would make them undress, and that only added to their terror. But then we gave them soap and hosed them off with salt water and they knew they wouldn't die immediately. We gave them clean Navy skivvy drawers and shirts, and our pharmacist's mate looked them over and dressed their wounds and jungle sores.

They were all in bad physical condition. Some of them had been living on nothing but coconuts and breadfruit for weeks. Their bones showed through their skins, and their stomachs were distended. Many had open wounds which they had been unable to clean or dress properly. A young soldier had a mortar fragment wound in his shoulder, which was full of maggots. The prisoners were also filthy dirty from their days of living in the bushes. Their matted hair was full of lice. Their legs and feet were covered with running sores. We sprinkled them with everything from sulfa powder to the new DDT which had just come out to the Pacific.

Before throwing the Japs' clothing overboard, we searched it and told the prisoners they could keep their personal articles. The only things the Japs wanted were their little prayer books. We gave them a full meal of rice, chile con carne, corn, coffee, and canned fruit. They gobbled it up and smacked their lips appreciatively. Then we put them on the forward deck and they squatted down out of the way and studied their tiny prayer books, still believing that sooner or later we would kill them.

By the end of the first day we had talked sixteen Japs into surrendering. They were quite a burden for our little LCI. We would gladly have returned to our base and given them over to the MPs, but we had orders to stay out three days. Also we wanted to get an early start again the next morning, which would have been impossible if we made the round trip back to the harbor. So we looked all over the cramped ship for a convenient place to quarter the prisoners during the night. Finally Ernie suggested putting them down in the hold where we slept. Henderson and I didn't like the idea very much. The prisoners were still covered with dirt and sores, and they smelled like bad fish. One gnarled old fellow—a Navy worker—had a terrible case of dysentery from the coconuts on which he had been living. Ernie compromised with us and quartered the old man in another compartment where the pharmacist's mate could look at him every so often. The others were herded down the ladder to our clean, whitewashed hold and shown where to lie down against the bulkheads on either side.

Our Jap interpreters, Joe, Nito and Taki, didn't like the presence of the prisoners any more than we did. Joe, who had thrived on the way we had accepted him, was jealous of his position and wanted no competition from other Japs. Nito and Taki were uneasy over being quartered with the men they had urged into surrendering. They were still nervous that some of them might develop a change of heart in the middle of the night and try suddenly to murder them.

We put the prisoners on the opposite side of the hold from Joe, Nito and Taki, and placed a member of the LCI's crew between them as a guard. Ernie gave the prisoners life belts for pillows and blankets and, using Joe as his interpreter, ordered the prisoners to stretch out beside each other. Nito and Taki sat on their bunks across the way, watching the men nervously. When I took off my pistol belt, Nito urged me to keep it next to my pillow. Joe heard him and laughed at the schoolteacher's anxiousness. We were inclined to agree with Joe. The prisoners looked harmless. Most of them were still nervous and scared, but gradually as Henderson, Ernie and I began to talk among ourselves

· 233 ·

and as the guard stopped watching the prisoners and took up a magazine, they became less tense. A little later they began whispering among themselves. Out of the corners of our eyes we noticed that they were sitting up, admiring a metal ammunition can that Ernie had brought down to use as a wastebasket. As the jabbering increased, Henderson turned to Nito.

"What's bothering them?" he asked.

"The metal," Nito said with his polite smile. "In Japan metal is scarce. It surprises them to see it used as a basket."

"We've got lots and lots of metal, millions of tons more than Japan thinks we have. You tell that to them," Henderson said.

Nito digested the thought, then told the prisoners. They listened eagerly and, when he was finished, there was a murmur of interested "Ahs." The reception encouraged Henderson to have Nito pass on some more facts. He began to tell Nito about our great war production, the thousands of tanks and guns and planes and ships that the Americans were turning out, the big war factories spread over thousands of miles in the United States, and the stream of equipment that would arrive to be thrown against Japan as soon as the war in Europe was over. Nito nodded and passed each item on to the prisoners. They sat up slowly and murmured and shook their heads as if it were all too much to believe. They turned to each other and began to argue and then asked Nito for more information. Henderson passed it on eagerly—about our big convoys, getting larger each month, about all the new kinds of American landing ships, and about our great army that was tearing across France.

As Henderson talked, Ernie got out a pony edition of a recent copy of *Time* that fortunately had some convincing pictures. He showed Nito a shot of GIs raising an American flag in Paris. Nito exclaimed in surprise and passed it eagerly among the other Japs. It somehow made him feel better, as if it helped to justify his own surrender and the urging he had done to make the others give up.

Suddenly one of the prisoners startled us by speaking out in English. He was a tall, thin man with a wispy black mustache that curled down over his lips.

"I wish to thank you for telling me all this," he said in a sharp voice. "I have no doubt that you are speaking the truth for I know America too. I was a cook on a ship that went to the United States. I was in Galveston, San Francisco, New York, and I have been in Washington, D.C. I have an uncle who owns a restaurant in New York City. I would like to go there after the war."

He glowered at the other prisoners as though he expected them to lunge at him. After a moment, during which we tried not to look startled, he turned back to us and announced that he knew all along that the Japanese leaders had lied to the people.

"They are bandits," he snapped. "They lie to us all the time. The American Fleet is sunk, they say. The American Army is destroyed. Japanese soldiers are in Washington. And all the time they wage war through us for the gain of the Mitsuis and Mitsubishis. They are the only ones who gain. The people suffer."

The cook was an intelligent addition to our dramatic bull session. The incongruity of what was occurring—a frank, uninhibited discussion between captors and prisoners, men who had been used to fearing and hating each other—was lost in the closeness of the little hold. Ernie, delighted by the Japs' willingness to talk, passed around a pack of cigarettes, and some of the prisoners nodded their heads politely and accepted a smoke.

"No doubt," Ernie said, "the Japanese lied to you about the treacherous way your navy attacked us at Pearl Harbor?"

The cook looked puzzled. He puffed silently on his cigarette, staring at Ernie.

"I do not understand," he said.

"Don't you know that Japan attacked the United States without warning at Pearl Harbor and Wake Island and the Philippines?"

"While your so-called ambassadors, Nomura and Kurusu, were talking peace in Washington?" Henderson added.

The cook hissed thoughtfully and nodded. "Ah," he muttered. "We were told the United States Fleet was coming to attack us in Japan. We struck back and halted the Americans." He turned to the other Japs and spoke quickly to them. Then he looked back at Ernie. "Please tell me. Am I wrong?" he said.

"I should say you are wrong," Henderson said. "Tell him, Ernie."

While the Japs waited for a translation, Ernie told the cook of the anger aroused in the United States by Japan's sneak attacks.

"The whole U.S. was united against Japan," Ernie said.

The cook nodded and translated to the other prisoners what Ernie had said. They whispered excitedly.

"So," the cook said. "I have cooked for the deceitful Japanese Navy. I would like to cook for the United States now."

Ernie laughed. "I'm afraid that's impossible," he said. "But after the war you can go back to Japan and tell all the people there the truth."

The cook's face fell and he became silent.

"We can never return to Japan," Nito said. "None of us. Ever."

"Why?" Henderson asked.

"Because we have surrendered. We are dead men," he said. "We can never return."

Joe saw our puzzled looks. It gave him a chance to get in a word. "It is this way in Japan. When a Japanese surrenders it is felt he commits dishonor. One must forget him completely. His wife and his poor mother and his children erase him from their memories. There is no memorial placed for him. It is not that he is dead. It is that he never existed."

"Silly," Ernie said.

"More," Taki nodded with an awesome look on his face. "After death—no paradise."

"You go to hell?" Ernie asked.

"Hell?" Joe repeated. "No hell." He shook his head. "There is no hell for the Japanese. But no paradise either for him who surrenders. Nowhere to see again one's wife and mother and friends. There is nothing. Everything is finished. It is terrible." He paused, looking seriously at us. Suddenly he smiled. "I do not believe any of that. I don't care what they do in Japan. I don't want to go back."

Nito and Taki launched a stream of Japanese at him. Joe hissed back at them, then looked at us again and grinned. "They still believe it," he laughed.

The cook cleared his throat authoritatively and hunched forward. "It is true," he said. "One cannot return to Japan."

"But look, fellow," Henderson said, trying to make the thing clear to them. "If everybody back in Japan surrenders, then there is disgrace for everyone—no?"

None of the Japanese answered. It seemed too hard for them to comprehend.

Henderson tried again. "Now you agree, your leaders lied to you about the war—right?" The cook nodded slowly. "All right. Maybe they lied about your not being able to go back to Japan."

The cook stared at him. Suddenly Nito said, "Ah, yes. Maybe."

In the silence that followed, as the prisoners tried to understand what Henderson was telling them, I could see for the first time some of the mental torture through which these men were living. In a moment of weakness and spiritual confusion they had surrendered. They had committed a dishonorable, cowardly act which they could never undo. I thought back to the many cornered Japs I had seen fighting like wild animals from the Guam caves. The issue they had faced became suddenly clear. To die honorably and go to paradise or to surrender and face eternal damnation? I looked suddenly at Nito, the aesthetic schoolteacher. A few days before he had been something dangerous and hunted, a Jap enemy, stumbling wildly through the Guam jungle. To us Marines he had been one with all the weird, half-human visions of men who live in caves on fish and rice and shoot Nambus at passing Americans, and then blow themselves up with their one remaining grenade.

"Do you have any children?" I asked Nito.

He drew out his wallet and handed me a small, yellowing studio picture pasted on a card. It was a family portrait of a young-looking Japanese woman in a flowered kimono, and two small children in robes with bangs over their foreheads. The man in the picture was Nito. He was stout and was wearing a civilian suit.

I handed the picture back to the schoolteacher. He was smiling

· 237 ·

modestly. For a moment, it was impossible not to think of my own family, my wife and year-old daughter, back in Washington. Suddenly I had the urge to ask Nito the one question that had been shaping in my mind during our discussion.

"Tell me, Nito," I said. "If you had it to do all over again, would you have committed suicide instead of surrendering?"

He looked around embarrassedly. The other Japs didn't seem to understand my question. Nito dropped his eyes.

"If you give me a knife, I will kill myself now," he said.

"Good Lord, fellow!" Henderson exclaimed.

Nito looked up and saw that we were shocked. He thought he had offended us.

"I will kill you too," he added. "Then we can all go to paradise together as friends."

We Americans laughed, but we felt uneasy. I glanced around to be sure that my pistol belt was still on my pillow.

"He thinks that he would be doing us a favor," Ernie exclaimed.

Henderson leaned forward, puzzled. "Why do you fellows believe in this hara-kiri business?" he asked. "Maybe that's more lies, huh?"

Joe drew back startled, and I laughed. It looked like we had suddenly stumbled on ground sacred even to Joe.

"It is bushido," he whispered in a tone of reverence.

"Bushido," Henderson said. "You explain that, huh?" he pointed at Nito.

Nito shook his head sadly. "Please," he said. "I could argue with you all night trying to convince you that Christianity is all superstition and untrue and that there was no such person as Jesus Christ. I might even force you to say you believed me. But in your heart you would not be swayed. You have been born to it and raised and educated to it. In the same way you can argue with me all night that bushido is wrong, that hara-kiri is senseless. But you cannot convince me. It is my faith and my spirit. I am Japanese. I was born and brought up Japanese. I cannot change."

After a moment Henderson got up.

"I guess we getter get lights out," he said. He turned to the guard.

"They won't make any trouble. But don't let one of them make a move."

I climbed into my bunk and lay in the darkness, listening to the heavy breathing of the men around me. One by one the prisoners fell asleep. I began to wonder if these people could change, so that some-day we could live in a world at peace with them. They had a lot of strange ideas—big ideas that had been drilled into them all their lives. It seemed to me, though, that there were bigger ideas in the world—ideas like freedom and democracy and justice and truth. With patience we could change the Japanese—and more quickly than most people thought. Even our little bull session had begun to work a change among the handful in our hold. Truth has a peculiar power over human beings. Myths—perhaps even the myth of a sun-god's descendant—give way before it.

This was the present, though, and these were still Japanese enemies. Our look into their minds could be no more than a prelude to what would come after the war. Before falling asleep, I put my pistol beneath my pillow. It was bulky, but it made me feel better.

Master Technical Sergeant Alvin M. Josephy, Jr.

Prisoner of War

American prisoners of war broke each other's arms and hands and produced chronic leg ulcers with soap and lime to escape the oft fatal slavery of Japanese coal and copper mines on Kyushu. Even these desperate measures failed when the Japanese, noting that the broken bones were on the left arms of right-handed men, ordered that the prisoners would work even with broken arms.

This story was told by Marine Private First Class John S. Kliss, Jr., of Chicago, whose own left hand showed a badly healed fracture of the little finger and three small bones. He also showed an ulcer scar on his ankle. He credited the ulcer with saving his life. By keeping it a running sore, he said, he was able to stay on the sick list for months.

"For most of the men," he said, "it was simply impossible to do the work required on the amount of food provided—and live. There were a few men who could stand it, but they were only a few and I wasn't one of them. Others who tried just simply lost weight until pneumonia or some other disease picked them off."

Kliss demonstrated how his hand was broken. He put the heel of his hand on a table, with the fingers resting on a book.

"The guy who's helping you," he explained, "picks up a club and you turn your eyes away and say, 'Let 'er go.' The guy that did it for me didn't do a very good job. He broke my little finger and three other bones. One break would have been enough."

Technical Sergeant John B. T. Campbell, Jr.

Propaganda

An Okinawan boy, about twelve years old, was looking through a back issue of *Life* magazine given him by a Marine warrant officer. He came to a series of pictures of demolished German cities with U.S. tanks rumbling through the debris. He scanned the photos with a knowing air, then turned to the warrant officer, pointed to the pictured ruins, and inquired politely, "America?"

Technical Sergeant Robert W. Harvey

Memo to Californians

During the Japanese occupation of Guam, Jap soldiers showed the Guamanians snapshots of themselves in fur-lined clothes and earmuffs. They explained that they had been taken in California. In reality, the pictures were from northern Manchuria where the Japs had been stationed before coming to Guam.

Master Technical Sergeant Alvin M. Josephy, Jr.

Kazuyuki Sugai Comes Home in a Box

When the Japanese submarine I-14 came in from the sea with an American prize crew aboard, she bore in the cluttered hangar on her deck a jumbled cargo of bales and boxes, straw suitcases tied up with rope, and rag-wrapped bundles of assorted shapes instead of the planes she supposedly carried. The assortment looked no different, and smelled no different from the other musty piles of gear lying about in the bowels of the submarine —a Jap submarine being a combination of floating junk shop, rat-ridden grocery store, flophouse, and neglected septic tank. Some of the stuff was obviously cased sake, in green bottles. Some of it was no-ticeably canned fish, a few cans of which, poorly sealed, had burst their tins to release their noxious gases. Rice spilled from sacks the rats had gnawed into, and mingled with the rice grains on the deck were the flinty bits of hardtack that is the Japanese K ration.

Consequently, when Commander John S. McCain, Jr., who was to sail her home, took over, his first order to the Jap bosun in charge of the working parties was:

"Get that junk out of here."

The Jap bosun, who looked like the Mongolian idiot brother of Fu Manchu, understood no English, but the gesture was unmistak-able. He bowed six times to Commander McCain, went "hissh, hissh, hissh" through his teeth, turned toward his blank-eyed laborers, leaped three feet off the deck, and bellowed an order in Japanese. Before he had come to rest solidly on the deck again a line of fifty-odd bandy-legged sailors of Nippon were hurrying into the hangar and out again, like a stream of oversized ants.

Commander McCain strolled aft, munching his cigar, well satisfied that in fifteen minutes he could return to find the hangar clear, ready for the scrapers and scrubbers and the sprayers of paint. His con-fidence was somewhat shaken later though, when a sailor came pant-ing up.

"Sir," he said, "them Nips unloading that gear are bringing out the sake and the chow and loading it on the barge alongside, like you said, but every once in a while they dig a box out of the pile and put it back in the corner, handling it like it was a baby, and when we tell them to get that stuff on outta here, they just shake their heads and jabber."

Commander McCain went forward. The Jap bosun rushed up, bowed four times from the waist, and delivered a speech just four words shorter than the first six chapters of *Gone With the Wind*.

"Get me a language officer," said Commander McCain. "Get me two language officers and a box of aspirin. Get me another cigar."

Lieutenants Ferguson and Clark and the cigar arrived.

"Now," said Commander McCain, "what is the holdup here? Find out from them what is in those boxes they are handling as if they are something holy and find out why they don't bring them out of here."

Lieutenant Ferguson spoke briefly to the bosun. The bosun delivered the first fourteen chapters of *Anthony Adverse* in Japanese.

"He said," translated Lieutenant Clark, "that these boxes contain the ashes of Japanese dead which they brought from Truk. The suitcases and bundles contain the personal effects of the deceased. He requests that we do not put these things ashore with the chow and stuff. He wants us to notify the Japanese authorities so they can take care of the ashes properly."

The bosun ripped a slat from a box and took out a small wooden monument, set on a wooden base. He handed the monument to Lieutenant Clark, making motions that he wished him to read the inscription. Lieutenant Clark read:

"This is the soul of Kazuyuki Sugai. He is dead—20th year of Showa —16 June—of sickness."

The bosun nodded violently, took the monument back, and pulled the upright part from the slot which joined it to the base. He drew out a small slip of paper from a niche in the slot and unwrapped it. The assembled company peered. The soul of Kazuyuki Sugai was half a thimbleful of coarse black hair clippings. The bosun darted into the hangar and came out with a small box, hefting it to show it was light. Lieutenant Ferguson studied the inscription on the box.

"Sugai's ashes," he said.

The next afternoon a motor launch headed shoreward from the I-14. Aboard her were the ashes, the hair clippings, and the personal effects of Kazuyuki Sugai and 499 more of the dead from by-passed Truk. Accompanying them as a guard of honor were Lieutenant Masotoshi Masuno and Chief Petty Officer Kosuku Hamada of the once Imperial Japanese Navy. Accompanying Masuno and Hamada as a guard, but not of honor, was Ship's Cook First Class Elza E. Morton, armed with a carbine. In charge was Ensign Francis Wertz of Portland, Connecticut, so that no suspicious Marine sentry would seize the party in the belief that the ship's cook was making off with a boatload of souvenirs all neatly boxed for shipping.

Lieutenant Masuno was a round-faced, bull-necked youth whose long black hair fell in a cascade down his neck and over his collar. For the occasion he had donned his new uniform jacket of coarse green cloth. The silver cherry blossoms of his insignia had been newly shined; his trousers, stuffed into soft black leather half-boots, were stained and shiny with wear. Chief Petty Officer Hamada wore a green uniform of similar shade but cheaper cloth. His shoes were canvas-topped split-toed tabis. He was middle-aged and incredibly ugly, with a coarse mass of Dundreary whiskers. Both of them sat upright against the roll of the boat, their small caps with the short bills perched exactly amidships and set squarely fore and aft on their heads.

"What did they die of?" I asked Masuno, nodding toward the boxes of ashes forward.

"Bomb," he said. "Bomb, and hungry."

That seemed sufficient answer.

Ashore, Wertz took Masuno to a telephone near the Navy Yard gate. Soon a mustard-colored Jap truck arrived, gagging and hiccuping, like all Jap vehicles, on its fuel of alcohol. The commander and the two lieutenants who arrived in it were more formal than the submarine party. They wore white cotton gloves. And now, it seemed, a problem had arisen. The ashes made quite a load and with the exception of the truck driver there was no one present to do the menial work of unloading. There was a fast quacking of Japanese. It evidently was decided that labor such as this—the moving of a companion's remains—would not degrade an officer. Led by the commander, the crew fell to and moved the boxes of ashes, the straw suitcases, and the ragged bundles from the dock to the truck.

At the foot of the high hill on which the temple sat the driver pushed the throttle to the floor board and the truck lunged half-heartedly at the slope. It made it halfway to the stone steps leading to the temple, coughed and died, then started rolling back. Despite loud warning yells of "Hai" and "Hoi" by the Japs, it kept rolling, and Japs and Americans alike scrambled frantically over the side just as the tailboard smashed into a telephone pole. The truck was too old and too full of alcoholic asthma to make it to the top. The ashes, somewhat tumbled about, were unloaded on the spot and the Japs trudged up the hill to the temple with the boxes on their shoulders.

Grass was green around the temple and crickets, their voices sweet as the song of birds to men who had been long at sea, sang in the trees. At the entrance the Japs laid down their boxes, held their arms stiffly at their sides, bowed low and kicked off their shoes before they took up their burdens and went into the temple. From the door a priest returned their bows. He had the wrinkled, ageless face of the old lama of Shangri-La. His shaved head shone like old mahogany, and he wore black-rimmed spectacles. His snowy white robe hung to his sock-tops. Over it was a calf-length robe of soft purple, and over that a flowing gown of sheer white material on which was worked a pattern of birds and leaves in gold.

The temple was open on three sides and a cool breeze swept through it. Its floor was of mats, plain on the sides but woven in geometric designs down the center toward the altars. Against the back wall hung a bamboo screen and behind it, seemingly in a deep niche, a huge golden Buddha could be dimly seen. On each side of the screen, in niches high off the floor, were fat, squatting gods in black and red lacquer. To the right, in an anteroom all its own, was a three times life-size figure in dark-red lacquer, with shining golden eyes and a snarling mouth of gold. Instead of the bland countenance of Buddha it had the hawk nose and the heavy bone structure of a Mohawk chief. It looked like a drunken cigar-store Indian sitting down with a blue and silver drum major's shako on its head.

A spindly little Jap in a blue sack suit who wore a band on his arm announcing him as "K. Ihara, Interpreter," explained that this was "Imma, king of Buddhist hell." Imma seemed an admirable selection for the job.

Amid all this gaudy hodgepodge the boxes containing the ashes stood out in bleak simplicity on a table of new unpainted pine before the altar. The white funeral cloth that had been thrown over it was too short to conceal the rough two-by-fours of the table legs.

When the last box of ashes was on the table and the ash-bearers had taken their places near the entrance, the old priest went over to the left of the entrance and knelt on a pillow of emerald-green silk. In front of him, on a short-legged black-lacquer table, padded by a red pillow and a green one, was a bronze urn-shaped gong, four feet tall. To his right, on a wooden block, was a hollowed-out noisemaker of dark wood, the size of a coconut in the husk. He lifted his head and began a slow singsong chant, his right hand beating a soft accompaniment with a felt-wrapped mallet on the wooden shell. The chanting increased in noise and pace and just as he reached a point where Gene Krupa would have had to pause, he stopped, took up in his left hand a wooden club, shaped like a bowling pin, and beat the big gong three times. The sound was deep and mellow, and as it died away he dropped the big club and picked up a tiny mallet. He tapped a little gong on his left. It went "piiinnnngg." He chanted some more and beat on the wooden shell some more, working up to another climax of three more "BONGS" and a "ping." Then he went up to the altar and bent over the ashes and took something from a little red wooden box. He wafted it about and the faint smell of incense drifted sweetly on the air. He came back and knelt at his gongs again and gave them a good working over. This went on for about half an hour, while the ash-bearers stood reverently with bowed heads, and the Americans began to feel their feet going to sleep.

Finally the priest finished and rose from his silken pillow. He came over to the Jap commander and bowed and hissed at him sharply and the Jap commander bowed back and hissed and then they both hissed together and the commander went up to the altar to pay his respects to the departed. He must have been quite a boy in the Jap Navy, for he had a chestful of ribbons, but his pants were so baggy in the seat he seemed to be all thighs from his hips to his ankles. He gave an almost perfunctory bow. When Masuno went up he stood at sharp attention for a second, head high, his black mane hanging down over his collar and his thick shoulders straining at the too-narrow coat. Then he bowed very deeply and held it a long time, which gave the congregation ample time to observe that there was a big hole, not torn, but worn, in the seat of Masuno's trousers, with the back flap of his G string poking through. Then K. Ihara, the interpreter, went up to make his bow, and his pants had long since passed the stage of Masuno's, for two round white patches stared like eyes from the seat of his blue trousers, and these patches were wearing through.

Then when Ihara had retired, the priest hissed goodby at everybody and everybody hissed goodby at the priest, and we all put on our shoes and went back to the consumptive truck.

And I wonder if it occurred to the Japs to consider that this was what their dream of greatness had brought them to—the best of their manhood only ashes in a dirty box. And they themselves, proud and arrogant men, under guard of a ship's cook before the altar of their temple—with the seat of their pants in rags.

First Lieutenant Harold H. Martin

The Role of the Conqueror

Two Things

The bow got them.

The Marines were standing outside the wire-enclosed stockade and the Japanese women, children, and old men were inside the enclosure. One Marine, just returned from the front, squatted and beckoned to a Japanese child who was sitting on the ground with a woman, presumably his mother. A stocky kid, about four or five, wearing a Jap soldier's cap, came bustling forward. He stopped at the wire and stood foursquare, his legs firmly set and wide apart, his eyes level with the Marine's. The Marine reached into his pocket for a bar of chocolate, broke it in half and dropped one piece into the cupped, outstretched palms of the child.

Then came the bow. The child stiffened, clutching the chocolate in one hand, and with mature dignity bowed quickly, wheeled, and raced back to the woman who was sitting on the grass. It was the bow that got the other Marines who were standing around. They had just returned from a fire fight and had seen several of their mates killed and badly wounded. They were dark eyed, bearded, dirty and tired looking. But when the Jap kid bowed their eyes lightened and they went nearer the stockade.

A photographer focused his movie camera while a second Marine took the other half piece of chocolate and went up to the wire. Instantly the Jap kid bustled forward again, grave and courteous, but obviously confident. The second Marine, a Mexican who wore a long handle-bar mustache, looked like a tougher, wilder Trader Horn.

The Jap child and Trader Horn regarded one another seriously for a moment. The boy proffered his cupped palms, and the Marine placed the chocolate in them. The camera ground. The boy made his courtly but jerky bow and raced back with his second triumph.

The child was tried a third time, but there was no more K-ration chocolate; so a third Marine advanced with some Japanese candy drops. The camera was set. The Marines stood with rapt faces, and the Marine who was offering the candy beckoned. The boy came charging forward, his brown hands stretched out. The candy was dropped into them. And then the boy turned and raced back, without any bow! Everybody began to laugh.

"The little bastard!"

"He's learning fast!"

"His own candy ain't worth it. He wants that K ration!"

Everybody was laughing and kidding, the Japanese women in Japanese and the Marines in English, but everybody knew that everybody else knew that the kid had crossed everybody up by not bowing the last time.

One of the Marines, who had been fighting in the canefield that morning, suddenly got mad, and bitter. His face went dark.

"Don't forget what you saw out there this morning," he said. "Don't forget it."

Another Marine turned to him. "That's two different things, Frankie."

Trader Horn said, "These kids don't have anything to do with it. Or these women. It's not their fault. They're innocent."

"I hate the bastards, I say kill them all," Frankie mumbled. "Don't forget those two Marines with their heads all bloody, dead in the cane there."

"That's two different things," the second Marine insisted.

"What happened out there hasn't got anything to do with what's going on here," Trader Horn backed him.

"I wouldn't mind having that little kid for my kid brother," a third Marine told him defiantly.

"We got to forget that," Trader Horn said. "Out there we kill them or they kill us but now it's over and they're the same people we are. Look at that little son of a bitch."

They'd found some more Japanese candy and the child came rushing out again, like a star player rushing back into the game. Everybody waited to see if he would bow this time. His mother had been coaching him. The guns were booming hollowly a couple of miles away, but nobody heard the guns.

Technical Sergeant Dan Levin

The Gentle Marine

A new kind of Marine hero emerged from the conquest of the Marianas. He is not a barrel-chested, hell-for-leather assailant of pillboxes, stormer of beaches. He is a little stooped, nearsighted man of thirty-six, whose marching gait is a compromise between a meander and a shuffle. It is safe to say that on Saipan and Tinian islands he conquered more Japanese through love and sympathy than any Marine disposed of with the latest automatic weapon.

Private First Class Joseph Morris Berger is from Superior, Wisconsin. He majored in ancient Greek at the University of Minnesota, found no opening to teach Plato and other classics, and so went into insurance. He came into the Marine Corps as a Marine of the line. An insatiable curiosity about things and people caused him to start studying Japanese while still stationed in this country, and he ended up as a language interpreter. In that capacity, attached to the famous Fifth Amphibious Corps headed by Lieutenant General Holland M. Smith, he hit the beach on Saipan Island.

Assigned to a first-aid station of the Fourth Marine Division, hard by the beach, Joe Berger saw his first civilians—Japanese men past military age, women and children—shattered and stunned by the guns of war. They were brought down to the beach in stretchers, often by Marines and Navy corpsmen who had just seen their own buddies shot to pieces by Japanese artillery. Other civilians came under their own steam, suffering from shrapnel wounds, shock, exposure, or scorched by flame throwers. Some had wounds from attempts at suicide. Others were only frightened. They had been told that the bearded American devils would cut their throats or torture them to death.

Some of the other translators and interpreters had laughed at Joe Berger because he insisted on learning colloquial Japanese. But now the sick, the frightened, the wounded, the dying, and the bereaved found in him one who really understood what they said in Japanese— one to whom they could come with their problems. He worked day and night as a combination confidant, confessor, male nurse, errand boy, doctor's helper, interpreter, and all-around angel of mercy.

First he was stationed at the improvised stockade near the beach on Saipan, then at a new composite stockade, finally near Charon Kanoa at the Thirty-first Field Hospital. The work of caring for the Japanese and Chamorro civilians who came to the hospital soon became too much for the doctors, corpsmen, and Joe Berger. Chamorro and Japanese girls were the logical ones to help them, Joe reasoned. A few had been tried out as assistants, but had not wanted to do the unpleasant work that has to be done around the wounded and sick.

Joe approached Magdalena, a Chamorro girl who had been a nurse under the Japanese in Garapan for six years. He had got permission from the Army major who headed the hospital unit to try five girl assistants again.

"I do not think the girls will come," Magdalena said.

"They will be well treated," Joe assured her. "They will have food and clothing."

Magdalena came herself the first day and brought one friend. Joe assigned their work—changing dressings, changing sheets, all the routine labor of a hospital. He gave them his own K rations and insisted that they eat with him and the other members of the hospital staff. The next day Magdalena and her friend brought three other girls. Joe insisted that they wash their hands frequently when tending the patients. Water on Saipan was precious, but he saw to it that there was water for washing. And in a few days he had arranged the incredible—a shower out of a steel cask, so that the girls could be clean

and fresh each morning and also each evening after the day's work.

When word got around that the girls ate at the table, with the doctors, that there was a shower, that they were treated with respect, there was a rush of volunteers. Because the work was more than the present staff could handle, the five-girl limit was waived and the volunteers were accepted. One of the first was a Japanese girl named Yoshiko. After Joe talked to her, he turned to the major and said, "This will be a good girl. I vouch for it."

The next morning Yoshiko did not show up. Joe felt humiliated. He went to the camp and found her sitting forlornly on the ground among the other civilians. She had on only an old torn skirt and a towel wound around her chest. The dress worn the previous day had been borrowed for the occasion. She had no other garments and had been ashamed to come to work without decent clothing.

From a warehouse, Joe got an armful of clothes for her as "hospital issue." Later, he requisitioned skirts and blouses and underclothes for others of the girls. Yoshiko came to work. The next day she, too, brought a friend.

The number of girls who volunteered swelled rapidly until finally there were forty-five nurses in all. Magdalena was No. 1, in charge of the hospital routine. She was Joe Berger's good (and pretty) right arm. Terechan, a Japanese, was No. 1 girl over the volunteer nurses. The number of civilians to be cared for (mostly Japanese, a few Koreans and Chamorros) also multiplied, as hundreds surrendered daily. They came streaming in—unwashed and filthy from hiding in marshes or crouching in caves, bleeding, with broken bones, shocked, grief dazed, and often starving. Joe Berger, the forty-five girl volunteers, the doctors, and corpsmen worked twelve to fourteen hours at a stretch, slept a few hours, worked again.

A typical case served by the hospital was that of a woman brought in with her throat slashed. Joe asked her whether Japanese or American soldiers had done it. She tried to speak, but blood gushed out. He asked her to write her answer, but she could not grasp the pencil strongly enough. Finally he wrote out the Japanese characters meaning "American soldier" and "Japanese soldier" and placed the pencil in her fingers. The staff stood around while she painfully drew a circle around "Japanese soldier."

Another Japanese woman who was brought in had been stabbed and her two small children slashed. At first she blamed American troops, but her story showed contradictions. Finally Magdalena and one of the Japanese nurses got the facts and reported them to Joe. The woman had wanted to surrender to the Americans, but her husband had refused to let her. They had quarreled, and he had stabbed and slashed her and the children. She had hidden the truth because it would have been shameful to reveal that she had dared contest her husband's will.

The amphibious assault on Tinian saw Joe Berger landing to establish his own kind of beachhead. He fought with junior commissioned officers for permission to allow Japanese and Korean civilians to construct decent sanitary facilities. He organized another volunteer nurse corps. He gave water out of his canteen to the crippled and old. He gave his K rations to the volunteer nurses, who carried them as great prizes to their parents and relatives living at the civilian camp. And in the course of all this he contracted a fungus affliction, so that for weeks after his return from the Marianas his body and hands and feet were grotesquely discolored by the medicines prescribed to cure it.

A high-ranking Army officer told the Marine, "I think you've done more than any man on Saipan or Tinian to build good will for America among the people who live here." And later the officer in charge of the garrison area of Saipan wrote him:

"Your unselfish conduct, your untiring energy and patient consideration of the suffering civilians deserve the thanks of the command, which I now extend to you."

Joe Berger's face glowed as he read those words. "Now," he said hopefully, "maybe I'll make corporal. Then I won't have to do mess duty on the ship when we move out again."

Then he dropped his eyes to the Chinese grammar on the desk before him. The Marine sensei had already started to prepare himself for new beachheads.

Technical Sergeant Dan Levin

"Who Do They Think We Are?"

Masalog Point is a wild, rocky promontory, a labyrinth of chasms and tangled undergrowth, on the Japanese island of Tinian, which is one of the lesser members of the Marianas group. An assault force of United States Marines invaded Tinian last summer and after several days of hard fighting captured it. The point was by-passed during the battle, but when things quieted down a bit, someone decided that Japanese stragglers who had been unable to escape from the island might be hiding there. A detachment of five Marines, led by a lieutenant, was assigned to explore the point. I went along, in my capacity as a combat correspondent.

It was hard going all the way, and it became harder when we reached the promontory. There the land fell away toward the sea. Clinging to vines and branches, we let ourselves down over jagged coral outcroppings to a narrow canyon. We were all sweating and jumpy as we worked our way; it was an ideal place for an ambush. The Marine in the lead was a thin young man with a long, tired face and red hair. I walked a few feet behind him. The lieutenant was a little to my right. Suddenly the man in the lead stopped. At the same moment, I saw what he must have seen. Something was moving in the brush at the edge of a small clearing just ahead of us. The red-haired Marine shouted in a high, uneasy voice, "Don't move—and get those hands up!" A stocky Japanese civilian, wearing a dirty shirt and even dirtier shorts, rose abruptly from the undergrowth. His hands were stretched rigidly above his head. I had never seen such a look of fear on a man's face. The lieutenant ran up to the man, searched him, and found that he was unarmed. I was several yards away from the Japanese, but I could hear his breathing. It was quick and gasping. No one spoke for a moment. And then, in the silence, we heard what sounded like a baby crying. The sound seemed to come from a cliff beyond the Japanese and to our right.

"What's that?" the red-haired Marine said sharply. Nobody answered him. We were all looking at the Japanese. He was bowing to the lieutenant. His hands were still stretched above his head, so his gesture was something like a salaam. Then he bowed to each of us in turn. It seemed to give him confidence, or at least hope. After he had finished, he began to speak rapidly in Japanese. When he realized, from our silence, that we could not understand what he was saying, he broke off and bowed to each of us again. It was somehow embarrassing. The lieutenant said, "All right," and gestured to the Japanese to lower his hands. The man's arms dropped stiffly to his sides. He spoke again, then pointed in the direction from which the cries had come. "We'd better take a look," the lieutenant said. He motioned to the Japanese to lead us.

We followed the man through the underbrush to a dark cleft in the canyon wall. The lieutenant walked close behind him with his pistol in his hand. The rest of us had our carbines at the ready. The cleft was the entrance to a narrow chasm. After we had taken a few steps into it, a sickening stench struck us, but what I saw almost made me forget the smell. The chasm was full of little shacks, huts, and lean-tos built of palm fronds and twigs and scraps of corrugated sheet iron. The settlement looked deserted.

The lieutenant ordered the Japanese to stop and moved down the chasm a few yards. "Day-tay-coy!" he shouted, which means "Come out! We won't hurt you." He waited a moment and then shouted again. For what seemed like several minutes nothing happened. Then a frail old Japanese with a sunken, toothless face and a wisp of beard thrust his head from a low opening in one of the huts. He stared at us and then at our prisoner, who said something that I suppose was a reassurance. The old man crawled out of the hut and stood up. Several naked children crept out of other huts. Then a few women, carrying babies strapped to their backs, came out. They stared at us and we stared at them. Some of them began to cry, apparently from fright. More and more Japanese appeared; they seemed to rise out of the ground—elderly men, women of all ages, and children. I realized then that the stench was the smell of filth and people packed together in squalor. All of them were in rags, all of them were dirty, and all of them were emaciated and terrified. It was obvious that they expected us to attack them. Their fright made me realize that in our own astonishment we had forgotten to lower our carbines. I slung my gun over my shoulder and the others did the same. The lieutenant hesitated and then put away his pistol. He ordered one of the Marines to explore farther down the chasm. Everyone, including ourselves, relaxed a little. A boy of abour four sidled up to me and timidly touched my dungarees, then slowly inspected my carbine, my cartridge belt, and my helmet. He smiled warily. I smiled at him, and he grinned.

At the lieutenant's order, we herded the Japanese toward the entrance of the chasm. They backed away before us, pausing every two or three steps to bow ingratiatingly to us. The red-haired Marine gave a snort of irritation. "What's the matter with these people?" he said to me. His voice was as unsteady as it had been when he shouted to the first Japanese. "God damn it, who do they think we are?"

I shook my head without replying, but I knew what he meant. The group continued to grow as we moved toward the entrance. The Marine who had gone down the chasm to explore came trotting back, followed by more people. He reported that there was still another chasm, connected to the one we were in, and that it, too, was filled with huts and frightened Japanese.

It seemed to me that there must be at least four hundred in the crowd in our chasm. (Later, I learned that there were actually seven hundred and eighty living in the two settlements.) The lieutenant pulled out a package of cigarettes and lighted one. Before he could return the package to his pocket, he was surrounded by grinning faces and outstretched hands. The people surged around him, bowing. His cigarettes were gone in a few seconds. I passed my package around and so did the rest of us, and our cigarettes vanished, too.

The red-haired Marine suddenly shouted, "God damn it, stop bowing!" There was an instant of terrified silence. Then the people began to bow even lower. One bearded old man dropped to his knees and pressed his forehead to the ground. The red-haired Marine shouted again, I couldn't hear what, and pushed his way through the crowd

· 255 ·

toward the lieutenant. His face was pale and streaked with dirt and sweat. "Lieutenant!" he shouted. "For Christ's sake, do something! Make them stop bowing to me! Tell them who we are!"

Technical Sergeant George H. Mattie

Takara Sensei

Always there was fear. The Okinawans had seen the mighty fleet, stretching from horizon to horizon, enter the East China Sea. Then came the planes to strafe and bomb and the big ships to shell. There was invasion and thousands and thousands of fair-skinned giants had stormed through their towns and villages. Had not the truthful radio in Tokyo described these Marines as barbarians?

So the people sat in their caves and trembled. They talked of these Americans and of rape, torture, and death. All but a few old men of learning. And among them was Takara Sensei.

Takara Sensei was found by a Marine patrol. He was sent to the rear, fed and given clean clothing. When I first met him, he bowed as if a strange American covered with dust and armed to the teeth was the most natural thing in the world. Takara was still not ruffled when these Marines wore their shoes indoors, sat in chairs and ate from a table. He apparently was amused no end (to save their "face") when they forgot and leaned against the wall. Our men seemed forever to be falling through the paper-and-glue sliding panels.

Takara bowed again as he accepted a cigarette. His eyes twinkled out of his alert, 70-year-old face. Then he could not longer contain the question burning inside. "What will become of Okinawa and her people?"

"We do not know," the Marines told him. "We are still fighting a war. To us civilians are a problem. If you like, Takara Sensei, you may help your people and help us."

And so Takara Sensei, former municipal secretary in Osaka, Japan, ex-schoolteacher and "Panama" hat manufacturer, became his people's ambassador to the Marine forces of conquest. His work for his people was Takara's compensation for his lack of information concerning his own family. Takara, like others, was separated from his wife, children and grandchildren. "The whole," he said simply, "outweighs a small part."

Takara was a believer in democracy—which brands him as a wild Japanese radical. He was visionary. This is what he said: "You tell me the United States will remain a great sea and air power after war. Then why are you surprised when I suggest the United States establish a protectorate over Okinawa? Here we can give airfields. There are great anchorages for your ships and submarines. In this place you will control the East China Sea and the Western Pacific. You will control Japan. You say the United States has no imperialistic aims, but would you give us back to Japan?

"We do not have much to offer, but we are a minor market. In times of peace our farmers have perhaps four hundred yen each year to spend for nonessentials. For necessities we barter among ourselves. We could use forty thousand American-made suits now. Thereafter, we would buy two thousand such suits a month. We have heard of your kitchens and iceboxes with electricity. We do not like to cook on brick furnaces either. . . . Our homes are destroyed. For three hundred fifty of your American dollars, we could construct a comfortable dwelling. There are fifty thousand people in Naha and Shuri now without a roof. There will be more. Rebuilding and reorganizing alone will take two years.

"It is true we have no gold or silver. Japan has confiscated all that. But we have our little industries. We can make hats. We make cloth. Our fishing is good. Our lacquerware is excellent. We make pottery. With these and other things we can pay. We would like America to help us with our educational system. In three years we could wipe out the fear of the United States. We could reorient our soldiers.

"You say it is strange to hear a Japanese talk like this? For thirty years I worked in Osaka for the municipal government. . . . The Japanese were making fools of Okinawans. They use us and tax us but they do not accept us as citizens. We do not wish to return to

Japanese rule. We would be suppressed again. With the help of the United States we could, in years, be a responsible people capable of taking a place in the United States governmental organization such as is now enjoyed by the Philippines. We, too, would like to be happy. For us, 'Nippon Ga Maketa' . . . Japan Is Finished."

Second Lieutenant Bem Price

The Banquet

In a native village on the east coast of Guam, where the sword grass is higher than a man's head, a company of Marines "found some of what we're supposed to be fighting for." On August 3 the Marines, on patrol, reached the village of Aslucas, where fifteen hundred Guamanians who had been interned by the Japanese since this island fell to the enemy greeted them in wildly demonstrative happiness, cheering, shouting and weeping in joy.

"It was the most touching, heartwarming thing I have ever seen," said First Lieutenant Frank A. Kemp, Jr., of Denver, a veteran of fighting in the Solomons, who led the patrol.

"Old men, women with children in their arms, and young girls in dresses they had saved for two and a half years—just for that moment —came out to shout greetings and kiss the hands of our men. Some just threw their arms around us and cried."

As the Americans entered the streets of the village, edged with thatched shacks and small frame buildings, the people burst into a song they had composed for the occasion. The song, which has now spread all over the island, is sung to the tune of "Silvery Moon."

> Sam, Sam,
> Dear old Uncle Sam,
> Won't you please come back to Guam?

The Marines had carried only enough rations for one day when they began their patrol the day before. Even this information, however, had preceded them. In the center of the village, wooden tables sparkling with flowers had been set in banquet fashion. It was the Marines' turn to be bewildered as the people urged them to sit down while a meal was prepared.

"To us, dirty, tired, unkempt, the whole thing seemed like Shangri-La," said First Lieutenant John S. Greenwood, of Bryn Mawr, Pennsylvania. "When we came the village had supplies remaining for only about three days, and what they gave us was special food, carefully saved from the Japanese."

Before the Marines the Guamanians placed a banquet of steak, hamburgers, soup, and coffee. Japanese cigarettes smuggled from the enemy were on the table.

"But the crowning touch was yet to come," said Lieutenant Greenwood. "Ceremoniously, a man brought out four bottles of Canadian Club whisky, as the people whistled and shouted. That was almost too much for us. We knew that it had been hoarded all these years for what they regarded as this great occasion. We were just numbed by the whole thing."

"It all seemed like a dream," said Corporal Robert S. Wilson, of San Jose, California. "Everyone kept smiling and staring at us while we ate. Some of the children kept coming up to touch our uniforms, and we just about choked up."

As the meal progressed, the people quietly explained how they had lived under the Japanese. The last of the Japanese guarding their village camp, they said, had fled the day before. A regular guard of only three Japanese armed with machine guns had been maintained at the village.

All of them, they said, had been forced to work for the Japanese, for which they were not paid but given only the most meager food rations. Concentrated in the village, the people had been gathered from the neighboring area, some from Agana, Agat and Sumay, the largest towns on the island. For lack of quarters, many had been living in caves.

"During the banquet," said Lieutenant Kemp, "there was a continual round of toasts. The first was to the President, then one to the armed forces, especially they said 'to the United States Marines.'"

At noon, the banquet closed at the request of Lieutenant Kemp, as the company had to move on. Before the men left their tables, however, the priest led the people in a prayer "for the servicemen who died to liberate Guam."

To the singing of "God Bless America," the Marines filed out of the village to a campground a mile away. Small patrols, which searched the area, rounded up one Japanese soldier and found an abandoned heavy machine gun.

"That night," said Lieutenant Kemp, "a party of Guamanians from the village came to our lines. We could hardly believe it when we saw what they were carrying. In their arms they had their few blankets, which they offered to us for the night."

An officer was assigned sixteen men to lead the Guamanians and others to a rear area where a settlement camp had been established.

On August 4 a strange-looking procession set forth from Aslucas. A handful of Marines walked down the mountain trails with some fourteen hundred civilians in every kind of attire, carrying all the possessions they could bear on their backs or pack on their few cattle. The caravan wound through the hills, small children running beside the trail, and a few old women sitting somberly astride water buffalo. Few turned to look back. As their Father Oscar had told them the day before, "We must try to forget what has been—and start a new life."

Master Technical Sergeant Murrey Marder

Moving the People

Roger, the interpreter, who had been born in Honolulu and spoke fluent Japanese, explained the matter to the mayor, who had been the postmaster before the Americans came to Okinawa. The mayor was a slender man in a white shirt, the only one in the village, and a pair of khaki trousers. His white straw hat had once been a Panama, but because of many rains now flapped shapelessly about his ears like a rag. He listened intently as Roger explained that the people must be moved, bowing slightly at the end of every phrase, not the deep bow of courtesy that is made from the waist, but a short nod of the head and a droop of the shoulders to show that he understood. And at the end of each sentence that Roger spoke, he drew in his breath sharply through his teeth in assent.

Roger explained everything in much detail, as the Military Government people had told him he should, and when he had finished it all was clear. In the morning, at daylight, the people must assemble at the building which had been the town hall of the village, where the rationers of food would parcel out to each representative of a family the half pound of rice for each of its members, and the handful of dried seaweed, and the black gummy paste made from soybeans, and the cabbage, and the dried beans. They must bring their slips with them showing the names of the members of their family, so that all would receive food, and no one would get more than his share.

When the food was distributed, the people should then place all their belongings together, the sleeping mats of thick straw, and the cooking and washing pots and tubs, and the little tables at which they sat to eat, so that the gear might be transported in the two-wheeled carts, drawn by the short-haired cart ponies. No one should be afraid to leave these things for the carts to carry, for the Military Government people would see to it, through the native police who were known by their silver helmets, that no person should steal another person's goods, and all would be redistributed properly at the village to which the people were to be moved.

The life of the village went on unchanged. The women went to the public well for water, carrying their water tubs on the poles across their shoulders. They smiled and bowed to MPs who sat by the well at the guard tent, and the MPs nodded back and did not smile, for they tried to observe to the letter the Military Government rule that these people, who were of an enemy race, should be treated with fairness and firmness but not with cordiality. It was hard, though, not to help when the very old came to the well and struggled to draw up the heavy buckets, or when the little kids, with their funny ducking bows and their half-frightened smiles, let the empty bucket down and filled it too full and could not get it up again.

In the village, behind the white stone walls of the courtyards, so old that gnarled trees grew in the crevices of the stones, life went on as if it could go on forever the same in the same place. Women tended cooking fires in the courtyards, and at the stone-paved wash places bathed babies, or trod on wet heaps of clothing with bare feet, their feet slapping against the wet heaps in a sort of rhythm. Men sat without speaking, smoking the tiny pipes of metal that hold only a pinch of dusty, fine-shredded tobacco. Younger girls, in shirts of bright stripes and trousers full in the waist and gathered close from the knee to ankle, sat combing each other's hair, searching for the fleas they had brought from the dank, goat-ridden caves in the hills.

The children were kimonoed like their elders or garbed in odds and ends of salvaged military gear. The little boys with shaved heads, the little girls with heads shaved high up the back and sides with only a mop of black hair on top, wandered about, climbing on things and jumping off, tugging and shoving each other, squabbling over some fragment of broken toy. They ran about, getting underfoot and being bumped out of the way with affectionate impatience, wailing when they were washed about the ears, and in general behaving like children anywhere.

Evening came, and with it a dying of the wind. Under the blanket of smoke from the cooking fires was the smell of the village. In the houses with their thin-paneled walls of wood, their red-tiled and thatched roofs, on the grass mats of the floors, the people squatted, each family huddled in its corner, about the evening meal.

When an American military policeman passed they looked at him without suspicion, and without seeming rancor, all the family, down to the small children, bowing low to the floor and smiling. If he stopped, they moved as if to lay a mat for him, and gestured for him to join them at their meal. When he shook his head and moved on, they bowed low again and smiled. How to respond to their courtesies and at the same time maintain the required aloofness from them was a problem to the MPs.

"It makes you feel like a German or something not to smile back at them when they are always smiling and bowing at you," one MP explained. "You feel like you ought to say 'H'ya, pop' or something just to let them know you aren't going to shove them around or muscle them up any. You can't help feeling sorry for them too, sometimes, the old folks and the kids particularly.

"These old women and men carrying big loads and looking like they wonder what the hell is going on! Then you see how nasty they are in some ways, going to the toilet just anywhere, until we stopped them and made them use the latrine. And how mean they are to animals. You see one driving a horse to a cart with big sores on his back or gashes all on his legs or lame in one leg and you want to knock their brains out for being so cruel to a dumb beast.

"You ever see them butcher a goat? I saw it once and I wouldn't look at it again for a hundred dollars. They build a big bonfire and then catch them a goat and twist its head over a log and cut its throat just enough to cut the vein and hold the goat head down until most of its blood runs out into a bucket. Then while the goat is still kicking and bleating they throw it on the fire, hair and all. When it's charred all over they take it down to the salt water and scrape it off a little and draw it and take it home to make stew out of. You see them do something like that you quit feeling sorry for them. You just say 'The hell with it' and play it like the book says—treat them firm and don't abuse them, but don't try to be nice to them."

By eight o'clock the village was dark and quiet, everywhere except in the house on the outskirts where the geisha live. Here was the sound of chattering talk and singsongy chanting, one favorite song, a piece that school children sing at graduation, to the tune of "Auld Lang Syne." When the patrol returned sternly to order silence, there was an impudent chorus from the dark interior.

These are not true geisha, the Military Government officers explain, but stolid, gold-toothed peasant girls who served the Jap Army as prostitutes. Military Government found out about this when they sent some of the "geisha" to the fields to gather food, and the respectable married folk of the village refused to work with them. So the geisha were given the custody of the orphaned babies, and the very aged who had no family to care for them, and the arrangement worked out very well.

Their attitude toward authority varied from sullenness to obscene flippancy expressed in gestures, and they alone of the village people expressed open sympathy for the Japanese cause. They would inquire of the interpreters how the battle to the south was going, and when told that many Japs were being killed they would bow their heads into their cradled arms and moan as if in grief. Many of their number, the authorities said, followed the Japs in their retreat to the south, and would probably die with the soldiers.

After the geisha had been quelled for the night by the threats of having their food ration withdrawn, the curfew was complete. There was no sign from the village, and no sound of movement, even when an MP, late in the night, cut loose with a long burst from his tommy gun to kill a dog that had butchered five kids in the goat corral.

Long before day, though, the people were up, gathering their goods together for the journey, and by the time the sun was well up they were lined up in the yard of the one-time city hall. All their possessions were wrapped in bundles and stacked, waiting for the carts, except those things they had been told they could carry themselves. These often made a larger package than the one which was to go on the cart. There was some delay, for many of the old women, though seemingly too bent and feeble to walk, had bundled up their own gear and protested shrilly when told to get on the trucks.

"Tell them all right, they can walk if they want to," the Military Government officer told the interpreter. "But tell them they have got to keep up and not lag behind."

The children—the smallest ones—got into the trucks willingly enough, but when they found out that their fathers and mothers were not going to come with them, they began to cry and hold out their arms and scramble down. So they were permitted to walk too, and the trucks moved out loaded with only the more adventurous small fry, the 8- and 10-year-olds who could have walked the distance with less strain than those who refused to ride. When the carts and the trucks were loaded, and the people had filed past the rationers to get their careful measures of rice and beans and had lined up beside the road, and an MP on a high-headed, frisky black Okinawan pony nodded to a bandy-legged, gold-toothed native policeman in a silver helmet.

"Okay, Joe," he said, "move 'em out."

Joe didn't understand the words but he got the idea.

"Tah-teh," he yelled, meaning "Get up."

Down the long line the other policemen, stationed every twenty yards or so, took up the yell. "Tah-teh. Tah-teh. Tah-teh." The squatting line rose as one man, stooped in unison for its burdens, swung them up and moved out behind the MP riding on his horse. They carried their burdens on balancing poles slung across their shoulders, or in towering baskets on their heads. Across the backs of both men and women tiny babies clung like spiders, supported by straps that crossed under their arms, and beneath their buttocks. Even the smallest children carried burdens. Little girls hardly big enough to walk carried tinier children on their backs. A tiny boy came by, grimly lugging two huge GI shoes. They did not trudge or amble but moved swiftly, in a bent-legged trot. They made no sound as they moved, no talking, no sound of their bare feet on the road, no clink and rustle of gear.

"They are the slowest workers and the fastest walkers I ever saw," said an MP. "I reckon it's because they figure that when you are carrying something heavy the quicker you get there the quicker you put it down. I've tried to heft some of these bundles they're carrying. It's all I can do to lift one. Even the little kids can carry a load that would break a man down."

The road out of the village, which was a fishing village on the flat plain of a peninsula jutting out into a shallow bay, crossed a long stone causeway over the tidal flats, wound through the swampy marsh of rice paddies, and sloped gently upward to the new villages to which the people were being moved. The new farming villages were tucked into folds of the earth at the foot of low hills that were emerald green with potato and grain and sugar-cane patches, and gold with the tints of ripening soybean vines. In the middle of the long causeway a Military Government officer watched the procession pass.

"You can almost read their history in their faces and their dress," he said. "That little old man that just passed—the one who looked dwarfish even among all these tiny people—he's almost aboriginal. Probably an Ainu, a race whose origins are lost in history. His forefathers were stunted, stupid, dark of skin, and short and crooked of bone, and hairy all over. See that red headband there. That's Malay in origin, probably. And that old goat-whiskered fellow there. His great-grandmother was probably brought here from the coast of China by Jap pirates.

"Look at their clothes. Mixed Oriental and modern, civilian and military. Straw cone-shaped coolie hats and hard-brimmed flat straws, the kind you can buy for ninety-eight cents on any side street in America. Twisted head rags and old felts. Those high-crowned caps and wrap leggings are Jap soldier gear. We had to mark all that stuff MG for military government, so the sentries wouldn't think they were spies.

"Poor devils. They've always lived hard. The Chinese shook them down for a thousand years, for taxes and soldier levies. Then the Chinese and Japs together worked over them. Then the Japs took over exclusively. We think of them as Japs. But the Japs don't. They always looked upon them as a lower race. They used them for laborers around their airfields, here and at Saipan and Tinian. And a few of them for soldiers. But an Okinawan never could be an officer. Even the Jap officials who lived here and ran all the government and what little industry there was kept themselves apart from the natives. The people just worked like dogs—they are wonderful farmers. There wasn't an acre of eroded land on Okinawa when we got here—and then the Japs took what they needed and left Okies the rest."

The long line stopped. The people stood still, with their burdens on their head and the poles slung across their shoulders.

"Rest halt," said the MG officer. "They don't quite get the idea. We have to make them put their bundles down. They had rather keep on going, I guess. An hour's walk is nothing to them. But the book says fifty minutes marching and ten minutes rest. We aren't going to have

Tokyo Rose yelling any lies on the radio about death marches and abuse of civilians."

The people rummaged in their gear and brought out short stalks of sugar cane. They peeled the sugar cane with their teeth, chewed, and spat the dry shredded residue in the roadway. Around each squatting person a circle of sugar-cane pulp appeared. Babies, sleeping on their mothers' backs, heads lolled back as if their necks would break, woke and fretted. Without removing the band that held them the mothers swung them under their arm around to the front and gave them the breast. One mother fed four this way, the last a boy who seemed at least eight years old. The men puffed their tiny pipes, gazing out over the salt flats toward the bay. The MP who had spoken of the Okinawans' cruelty to animals came up, hopping mad.

"One of them gooks tied a goat on top of his wagon and the goat slipped off and was hanging head down over the side, bleatin' its head off. He was just driving on paying no attention. I wanted to bust his head."

"Did you?" asked the Military Government officer.

"Hell, no," said the MP. "I just made him fix the goat comfortable. But I ought to have."

There were shouts of "Tah-teh," down the line. The people rose with their burdens. The line moved on. Before there was another rest halt they had come to the first of the villages where they were to find their homes.

The mayor gathered the Han-Chos around him, pointing out to them the houses they should occupy. In family groups they moved out, pawed through the duffel to find their own, and each family went to find its house. In an hour the open space where they had gathered was cleared. Working parties were headed for the fields to find food. At the schoolhouse, men moved out the wooden desks and tables, the piles of books, the weights and balances and test tubes and retorts of the chemistry and physics classrooms, the stuffed birds and snakes and squirrels of the biology room. They removed thick folders of pictures, beautifully colored, showing legendary battles of Japanese mythology between horrendous-looking knights in gold and silver armor, alter-

· 267 ·

nating with modern water colors showing great land and naval battles with the Rising Sun, naturally, triumphant.

Young women with buckets and scrubbing brushes came through, washing down floors and walls so that the building could be turned into offices for the Military Government, and for the interpreters, the mayor, the native police, and the military police.

Down in the narrow streets of the village there was the smell of wood smoke as the tiny cooking fires flickered under the iron pots. In the houses, mats were on the floors, and the short-legged tables of red and black lacquer, about which the people knelt to eat, were out. There was the slap, slap of the women's bare feet, washing clothes, and the shrill protest of a baby being scrubbed, and the laughter of children who swung in a swing that some MP, who liked kids, had hung to the limb of an ancient tree.

Life was going on again, as serenely as it could go on amid the back-wash of war. The people had moved, and on their journey there had been no shouting and no cursing and no abuse and no prodding with bayonets. All had been done quickly and quietly, without trouble, and all the orders on which they had acted had come down to them through their own people, or people of their own blood who under-stood their language and their customs even though they wore the uniform of the United States.

First Lieutenant Harold M. Martin

The Islands and Their People

New Zealand

Drop thousands of well-paid, free-spending Marines, soldiers and sailors into the metropolitan area of a nation with a total population approximating that of Connecticut and the result is a slightly violent volcanic upheaval in the social and economic life. That is precisely what happened in New Zealand, home of the kiwi bird, cheese, sheep, and some of the best fighting men in the world.

Picture a country engaged mostly in the primary industries, that is, farming and the processing of farm products, and with only a drop in the bucket manufacturing output. Visualize a nation where poverty is all but unknown. There are poor, to be sure, but the government sees to it they are fed, clothed and given a certain amount of medical care. By the same token, there are few who are rich by U.S. standards. To the Yanks pouring ashore to train for the first offensive against the Japanese, the cost of living was low. To the New Zealanders, however, living costs already were high.

When the Americans arrived—the Marines and sailors first, the soldiers later—they found a country all but stripped of able-bodied men. It is safe to say that one-tenth of the entire population was in the armed forces. Before the Yanks arrived, New Zealand was a placid, proud little country interested mostly in sports, reading (there are an amazing number of book clubs and book stores) and the radio. Generally speaking, there was no such thing as night life as we know it in the States.

There were public dances, of course, but they in no wise resembled the night clubs of New York, Chicago or Los Angeles. When you go to a dance in New Zealand, you go to dance and perhaps indulge in tea or an ice-cream soda. All bars closed at 6 p.m., save in hotels where, by some peculiar quirk of the law, guests and their friends may obtain drinks until midnight. Incidentally, while the Americans were in New Zealand in force, whisky was all but unobtainable, and the pubs served mostly weak beer and light wines.

About the only direct contact the people had had with America outside of books, magazines and a few businessmen, was the Hollywood product—a fact which leaves room for some amusing misconceptions, although New Zealanders are surprisingly well informed concerning the United States.

All in all, the war had seemed pretty remote to most New Zealanders despite the tremendous sacrifices they were called upon to make, and the too-frequent arrival of terse cablegrams announcing deaths on the sands of Africa, the mountains of Greece, Italy, and the shores of Crete. All this was changed when Japan bombed Pearl Harbor and the war was brought perilously close to home. New Zealand, her fighting men overseas, watched anxiously as the Philippines fell— Hong Kong, Singapore, the Dutch East Indies, the Solomons. From Guadalcanal to Auckland is but a hop, skip, and a jump.

Many New Zealanders feel that had the Yanks not arrived, they were next on the Japs' timetable of conquest. There was no panic at the time. The New Zealanders mustered what men they could, taught the women to shoot, built road blocks, pillboxes, gun emplacements, and prepared to pit their inadequate air force against hordes of enemy Zeros. Then one morning in 1942, New Zealand was heartened by the news that U.S. Marines had stormed ashore on Guadalcanal and Tulagi. The attack was not altogether a surprise, though, for the New Zealanders long had known something was afoot by the enormous amount of supplies and men pouring into their little island commonwealth.

The usually phlegmatic New Zealanders felt as if the Marines were saviors and greeted them as such. They opened their hearts and homes to these strangers from across the waters. No nation could have been more hospitable. After the first novelty of being in a strange land wore off, the Marines, healthy, happy-go-lucky lads with pockets that jingled, began seeking entertainment.

In the two major towns, Auckland and Wellington, milk bars—soda fountains to us—began appearing like magic. Great beef eaters, the Marines demanded steaks, and restaurant owners, anxious to please, gave them what they wanted while the national meat, mutton, took a position on the bottom of the menu. Tipping was not a widespread practice until the Americans arrived. It was considered an act of snobbery and no self-respecting waitress or waiter would accept a tip. Soon, however, many were discovering that the Americans attached no stigma to the practice.

Hotels, the drink situation being what it was, soon were doing a land-office business as Marines and soldiers came and brought hosts of friends. Reservations had to be made weeks in advance. Taxi drivers found Americans the answer to their prayers. You can't tell a New Zealand hackman there's no Santa Claus.

And the boys met the girls. The Marines wined them and dined them, took them out to the movies, showered them with candy and flowers. In a matter of weeks, Marines had taught the girls to jitterbug and wisecrack à la United States. In brief, the Yanks set out to transplant their own social pattern. At night, the streets of the two major cities were crowded with Yankee khaki and green. The boys crowded into milk bars, movies and eating places with their dates, sometimes to the practical exclusion of the residents. Naturally—and it is thoroughly understandable—some of the New Zealanders were inclined to be resentful, but in fairness it must be added that the majority gave up their places cheerfully.

On the economic side, the Americans put thousands of dollars daily into the hands of the shopkeepers, and farmers were called upon to supply enormous quantities of all kinds of foodstuffs and milk products. Further, in order to alleviate the strain on shipping, New Zealand's factories worked mightily to provide the fighting men from across the seas with as much of their essential gear as possible.

Perhaps the best indication of the impression this sudden flood of Yanks and money made on the smallest member of the British Commonwealth of Nations is found in the conversation of New Zealanders who often and unconsciously measure local events "before" and "after" the arrival of American forces.

Second Lieutenant Bem Price

The Little Chief

Hardtack will be a mighty chief someday who will rule his people in Samoa with wisdom and justice. He will be faithful to those he will rule, because once his heart was broken by one who was faithless; by one who considered the spoken promise lightly and of little importance.

I was a Marine captain of infantry in command of a company of Marines on Samoa during the early days of the war. The camp area was an isolated spot, for the only access to the bay, except by boat, was a precipitous trail over a mountain. And my mission was to resist enemy attempts to land and to continue troop training for combat.

I was on the assignment a few days when I received a box of hard candy from the States. Tropical heat does odd things to hard candy, not the least of which is the fact that it makes it soft as butter and as sticky as glue, and to get rid of it I gave it to the first native boy I saw. He acceped it gratefully and, to my amazement, said, "Thank you, captain." Recovering rapidly, I engaged him in conversation, and found that he was the chief's son, that he had picked up a smattering of English from a missionary, that few of the natives spoke or understood my language, and that he would like to go and eat his candy. I patted his bare shoulders and told him to go ahead, but to return later in the day, as there were many things I wished to talk over with him.

Not more than fifteen minutes had passed when I noticed that the native boy was coming in my direction. Watching him, I was impressed with his poise, his bearing, the way he carried his head on youthful brown shoulders and the straight, sturdy legs which brought him before me.

"Okay, captain, I ready," he said.

"Ready?" I asked.

"You tell me to come back. I here," he answered.

"Oh, yes," I replied, "but don't tell me that you have eaten all that candy! There must have been two pounds of it!"

"I eat and I back" was his reply, and he drew up his little body stiffly, as if to say that white man knew nothing of eating, that he was the eater of all eaters.

The interview that followed will live with me a long time, for our friendship began that morning. He told me his name was Hardtack and that it had been given to him by Marines who were stationed in the bay before I arrived. The name was chosen, he said, because he could eat more hardtack at one time than any Marine. He told me of his people, of the fact that he was the son of the chief, and that he, too, would someday be chief. He added that his people had been great fighting men and that his father had led them in a tribal war only twenty-five years before.

It was then that I started, unthinkingly, the great deception. I said, "Hardtack, let's you and I work with each other. I will attach you to my staff. You will be my runner. Wherever I go in this area, you will go. If the Japs land, you will be able to show me the hidden approaches and the hidden trails, and we will fight them together. You will organize the boys in the village and train them. You will train them to be jungle scouts. I will inspect them every seven days, and you will be their corporal. Whenever you meet me, you will salute and I will return the salute."

Hardtack gazed at me as I was talking, and I could see a great hope being born in his eyes. I should have stopped right there. But I was in good form, and I pictured for him all the glories of war. When Hardtack left me, his brown shoulders were broader and his head was reaching to the sky. I really sold him a bill of goods that morning—a bill of goods I would give a great deal to recover at this writing.

The days which followed saw great activity among the native children. Hardtack was everywhere, organizing, choosing and equipping his troops with weapons ranging from clubs to homemade knives. Finally he had about fifteen boys formed into one oversized squad. The little fellow was observant, and from watching guard mounts and the like he had picked up the rudiments of the basic close-order formations. Also his position as the chief's son gave him the same prestige with the youngsters in the village that his father had with the older ones. He could act with authority, and did.

When the day came for me to inspect the squad for the first time, Hardtack formed his men outside my tent and, as I went out, he barked "Tenshun!" and came to a smart right-hand salute. I returned it and gave the necessary command for him to prepare his detail for inspection. He was perfect, and his squad members, dressed in white lava-lava cloths tucked in around their waists and hanging below their knees, with their weapons tied to their right sides, presented a striking appearance. Barefooted and bare from the waist up, their brown skins shone with coconut oil. I completed my inspection, had Hardtack dismiss his squad and invited him into my tent.

"Your men were in good shape this morning, corporal, with a single exception, and that was the second from the left in the first rank. Do you know the one I mean?"

"Yessuh," he replied. "I know, hair mess."

"See that it does not happen again, corporal," I continued. "Dismissed."

Hardtack saluted, did as pretty an about-face as you would want to see, and left the tent. I never did figure how he could pivot on that bare right big toe.

Two hours later Hayes, my gunnery sergeant, entered the tent and said, "Sir, if you don't mind, I think you should be careful the way you handle those kids. Just a minute ago I prevented Hardtack from drowning a boy who did not pass your inspection this morning." I warned Hardtack against doing anything as drastic as drowning one of his troops for a slight infraction of the rules, giving him at the same time an idea of the way we treat similar cases. He accepted my reprimand stoically, but he seemed to be puzzled, probably at what he considered our indirect methods of correcting a bad situation. His way of removing a source of irritation was more direct.

Hardtack was with me constantly from that point on, except when he was with his own squad, for about five months. If reveille was at 5 a.m., he would meet me coming from my tent and stay with me for the greater part of the day. Whenever there would be Condition Red, which indicated that the enemy was thereabouts, Hardtack would be at my side, asking with his eyes for errands to run or messages to deliver. His own troops would be standing by, trying to anticipate his every thought and faintest signal. I used him and his squad members many times to carry messages to my platoon leaders, and the way they would disappear into the jungle, sure-footed as cats, was uncanny. I began to rely on that 8-year-old, and it led me to make him a promise I did not intend to fulfill.

Hardtack and I were hiking along a trail in single file on our way to visit a Marine camp in an adjoining bay. Hardtack pulled up alongside, touched me on the arm and stopped. I stopped, too, and looked down at my companion. For the first time I saw a smile on his face and his teeth shone like ivory.

"I your friend," he said, looking up at me. This was the first time he had indicated his feeling toward me in all the months we had been together. Previously it had been all business—and military.

"I am your friend too," I replied. Feeling good because I had at last broken down his reserve, I went on, "We work together well, son. If the Japs ever land on this island, the two of us will really cause them trouble. By the way, how would you like to go up to the Solomons with us, if we ever get orders to go in the lines up there?"

The boy knew about those islands because our fight for them was raging at that time, and Hardtack had been around Marines. He looked at me intently for a minute, then "I go with the captain. I his runner."

I did not think it important at the time to tell him that if I left the island, he could not go with me. Maybe I thought that he would consider it all a game, and that I was merely playing it out with him to the last full inning. Anyhow, I let it go at that. From that point on, Hardtack redoubled his activities and, as I would train the troops under my command, he would train the boys under his. He was learning as much military as he could, and learning it well.

Finally the great day came. We were going on up north to fight the Japanese. Of course, we were not told that, but we knew, as all fighting men have known when they were going to war. This was the day we had been waiting for. With our combat packs and weapons on our backs, we started up the trail. Suddenly I remembered that I had not said goodby to Hardtack, and stopped the column. I did not have far to look, however, for he was about fifteen yards away, saying goodby to his squad. It was then that I knew I was in trouble. For the first time I realized what I would have to do to that boy.

There he was, with a little homemade pack strapped to his back and an old rusty machete slung from his right side and dangling to the ground. He was going with me to fight the Japanese. He was going to show those fighting ancestors that he, the son of a long line of warrior chiefs, was the greatest warrior of them all. He was going with his captain, because once long ago the captain had told him so. Hardtack had not forgotten and, of course, neither had the captain, for had not the captain, time and again, said that he was indispensable and was needed?

Hardtack fell into the column near me, and as we started moving, I stared stupidly at him. Although the trail to the top of the mountain was steep and took a long time to climb, now it seemed short and easy. I just didn't want to reach the summit, because I knew that there Hardtack would have to be told. It would have to be done, for I had been responsible for opening the gates of high adventure to an 8-year-old boy, and it was up to me to close those gates in his face.

We reached the top and stopped for a breather. We could see the transports in the harbor below. Gathering my courage, I called Hardtack to me. He approached rapidly, stopped before me and came to a right-hand salute. His eyes were shining and his heart was high, for he had seen the ships too. He was a perfect picture of the native fighting man in miniature. What an unthinking fool I had been.

"Hardtack," I began, then stopped—I could not go on. The little

fellow was quivering with eagerness to do the errand he thought I was
going to ask him to perform. Then, with a rush, came the words: "I
cannot take you with me. I should have told you before. I want you
to be a great chief and rule your people wisely, and I will think of you
often. Please think of me. I—"

He stared at me, it seemed for hours, then a great rasping sob shook
his body. Tears, floods of them, blinded his eyes, and he swayed before
me. Suddenly the heartbreaking realization fell upon him, and he was
gone. I saw him, half stumbling, half running down the trail we had
just ascended. He fell, picked himself up and continued. My last
memory of Hardtack was of him disappearing around a bend in the
trail, his little pack bobbing up and down on a shiny brown back. He
was still stumbling as he made the turn.

Major Robert Simpson

Midway's Birds

Midway Island is inhabited by more than a million
birds. Men stationed there are glad to have the
birds for companions. There is, for instance, the bosun bird, which
flies backward just for fun. The bosun is a beautiful white bird with
two thin tail feathers. Ordinarily it flies forward, but to attract attention it will pull into a stall in mid-air, then fly straight backward.

Slightly larger than the bosun birds are the boobies, the "dive-
bombing" members of the Midway avian family. Boobies like to soar
over the water. Bosuns and boobies are constantly badgered by the
local king of the skies, the poaching frigate bird. Frigates are large
black birds, with powerful, hooked beaks. They cruise over Midway
at about a thousand feet, waiting for bosuns and boobies flying home
with food in their mouths. When a frigate sees one, he screams down,
and gives the bosun or boobie a rough body block that knocks the food
out of its mouth. Then the frigate catches the food before it hits the
ground.

Also at the mercy of the frigate birds are the terns—the sooty terns and the fairy terns. The sooty terns have sooty-colored backs and wings. The fairy terns are pretty little white birds that balance their eggs on tree branches rather than build nests. When the egg hatches, the baby tern immediately grabs on to the branch to keep from falling.

Noisiest birds on Midway are the moaning birds. They give off, particularly at night, with terrible wailings that a newcomer to Midway might mistake for a mass bull slaughtering. This is said to be their love call. But best loved of all birds here is the famous Midway gooney. The gooney, which is an albatross, is one of the most graceful of all birds in flight. But on the ground it is downright comical. It's a black-and-white bird, about the size of a goose, with a funny hooked beak, web feet, and a 6- or 7-foot wingspread.

The gooney dance always gains an avid audience among the servicemen. Two gooneys, approaching each other, agree on a dance by making certain little bows to each other. They square away by crossing beaks and necks. One will then emit strange cackles while the other rubs his beak under his wing. A routine of beak snapping follows, then both stand on tiptoe, stretch their necks, and give each other a Bronx cheer.

First Lieutenant Milburn McCarty

Guadalcanal

Guadalcanal is an island of striking beauty to anyone who does not remember the battles that have bloodied its soil or the men and ships that lie beneath the waters off its shores. Blue-green mountains, towering into a brilliant tropical sky or crowned with cloud masses, dominate the island. The dark green of jungle growth blends into the softer greens and browns of coconut groves and grassy plains and ridges. Much of the shore line is rough with coral that cuts men's feet and rips the bottoms of landing boats, but there are also good beaches of soft sand. The water is always warm. It is clear and clean too, except when flotsam from wrecked ships—oil, crates, stinking bloated sides of beef, papers—washes ashore.

In three distinct ranges, the central one reaching a height of eight thousand feet, the mountains cut across the island. They rise steeply from the southern coast, fill the central part of the island from one end to the other, then diminish toward the north. From Cape Esperance to Marau Sound, ninety miles away, they form the backbone of Guadalcanal.

From the high jagged mountains fingers of coral ridges, many of them grass covered, reach into the coastal plain on the northern side of the island. The plain, too, is covered with tall grass, about the height of a man's shoulders, and swift-flowing streams feed lush tropical growth and groves of great trees. In the dense jungle of such lowlands and coral ridge slopes the bitterest fighting of the Guadalcanal campaign took place.

The northern coastal plain is the most important part of Guadalcanal in both war and peace. There the peaceful life of the Melanesian natives centered. From the Matanikau River eastward to Taivu Point, a distance of about twenty miles, there are grassy fields on the plain ideal for the construction of airfields. Farther east the plain is swampy or covered with dense jungle.

Native villages dot the shore line—little groups of fiber huts and gardens where the natives of Guadalcanal lived a simple life before the war reached them. They grew fruit—bananas, limes, oranges, and pawpaws. Unfortunately none of these fruit trees grew inside the tiny airfield area first occupied by the Marines and fresh fruit was a rarity in Marine messes. Occasionally, however, a patrol or scouting party going far down the coast would bring back a bunch of bananas or helmetful of limes given them by friendly natives.

A traveler skirting the northern coast of Guadalcanal on a ship, southeastward from Cape Esperance, sees a succession of points reaching out into the sea. They are barely distinguishable against the dark, dominating background of soaring mountains, but a man familiar with the coast line can pick them out for the newcomer. Each has its story to tell of men fighting against each other and the jungle.

Rounding the northwest end of Guadalcanal and heading southeastward, as the Marines did, the traveler sees Savo Island—rugged, high, and almost circular—about ten miles off Cape Esperance. Savo became a name rich in sinister connotation for the Marines on Guadalcanal: the deep water around the island is the graveyard of the three American cruisers and the Australian cruiser sunk by the Japanese in the night battle of August 9.

From Cape Esperance to Taivu Point, forty miles away, the shore now is littered with the wrecks of landing boats and barges. Some are American, especially in the central area, but most are Japanese. Between Esperance and Tassafaronga—a stretch of coast which was a Japanese beachhead on the island for five months—are the wrecks of Japanese transport and cargo ships, gutted by fires and explosions and run up on the beach by men desperate to save anything they might from the hulls that had fallen victims to our bombers. Farther east are beached American ships, the victims of Japanese torpedoes.

Still going southeastward, beyond Tassafaronga, the traveler sees the unmistakable outline of Point Cruz, a coral spit reaching out into the sea. It was once a vantage point for Japanese observers watching activities at the United States Naval Operating Base at Kakum across the bay and a forward position for Japanese guns.

Just east of Point Cruz, between the coral spit and the mouth of the Matanikau River, is a half mile of beach, coconut palms, and jungle that was once upturned, burned, and blasted as few spots on this earth have been. By now surely the quick-growing jungle plants have thrown a coat of green over those scars of battle, inflicted by the concentrated fires of both belligerents on this most fought-over spot on all Guadalcanal. For more than four months the Americans and Japanese surged back and forth over this bit of land.

The Matanikau River is muddy and deep. A sand bar extends across the river's mouth and, except when the river runs high, only a little water trickles through a narrow shallow channel to reach the sea. Across this sand bar the Japanese launched a tank attack late in October, the first thrust in the crucial land fighting of that month. Their shattered tanks can still be seen on the sand bar and shore to the west. The Japanese planned to receive the surrender of Major General Vandegrift on the banks of the Matanikau in October. The general, accompanied only by an aide, was to walk along the beach toward the west until he came to the mouth of the Matanikau, where the Japanese commanding general would receive him. The enemy's surrender demand was never delivered. Instead of overrunning the airfield, the Japanese forces attacking in October were driven back with shattering losses, and Major General Vandegrift never made the mournful journey to the river's mouth.

From the Matanikau the shore line sweeps seaward again toward Lunga Point, formed by the delta of the Lunga River. That river was as important to the Marines on Guadalcanal as the Nile is to Egypt. In its swift waters, flowing through the center of our position just west of Henderson Field, the Marines found some respite from the strain of battle and the heat and dirt of Guadalcanal. The river was drinking fountain, bath, and laundry. In the early days all our drinking water came from the river above the bridge which the Japanese had built half a mile inland from its mouth. Below that point the Marines swam and washed their clothes.

About three miles east of Lunga Point is the Tenaru River, a sluggish stream with a sand bar across its mouth. The coconut palms all along the shore from Kukum to the Tenaru and a bit beyond are shattered and ripped by shellfire. The grove of coconuts just east of the river and the sandy beach were the scene of the bloody battle of the Tenaru River when more than seven hundred Japanese were encircled and annihilated August 21.

The next river the traveler sees is the Ilu. The Marines first landed on the beach just east of the Ilu. Our traveler, looking at Beach Red where the Marines swarmed ashore on that historic day, can see a large hill rising above the line of palms that fringe the shore. A grove of trees on the hillside describes a rough L and makes it a familiar landmark. This is Mount Austen, or "Grassy Knoll," as it was known among the Marines. It looks as if it were near by, but actually it is about four miles from the beach. In the early days, when the Japs were free to roam the jungle around the tiny area where the Marines had dug in behind defensive lines, new arrivals on the island occasionally asked, with mixed heartiness and anxiety, "Where are the Japs?" The oldtimers took delight in pointing to Grassy Knoll, which appears to rise from the very edge of the airfield, and saying, "There they are." The inquiring newcomer usually was incredulous—and noticeably more nervous.

Captain Herbert L. Merillat

Robert Louis Stevenson's Island

Abemama—"Land of Moonlight"—lies only eighty miles from Tarawa, but it is difficult to imagine that they are in the same world. Tarawa today lies a blasted shell, with hardly an inch of its coral soil unmarked by the surge of battle that devastated it for three horrible days. Abemama is the Hollywood director's dream, the perfect South Sea island. One expects to find a movie star back of each waving coconut frond, and the tinkle of soft guitars from the beach of each blue lagoon.

Here it was that Robert Louis Stevenson lived for years among the Gilbertese, an island he described as a "treasure trove of South Sea Island beauty." And apparently the gods willed that war should touch only lightly on the Land of Moonlight, for the Marines' occupation of this Central Gilberts atoll, five days after the first shells roared into Tarawa, was as calm and peaceful as our previous experiences had been brutal and punishing.

Twenty-five Japanese defenders—a handful isolated by the annihilation of their main garrison on Tarawa—chose hara-kiri before we arrived, so that not a shot was fired as our men waded ashore.

Today, at a formal ceremony attended by Major G. L. Holland, British director of education for the Gilberts, who returned to his post with our troops, the native government formally ratified our offer of protection and officially welcomed the white man's troops which had destroyed the invading Japanese troops.

Major Holland's return was in the nature of a triumphant homecoming. Natives, from old men and women to small children, flocked about him wherever he went, some of them anxious only to touch his clothing and to hear him speak in Gilbertese, a language he described as "one of the most beautiful in the world."

"The Japanese," he told the assembled native chiefs, "told their men the Marines could not drive them out in a hundred years. They were right. They are still there." The natives, whose sense of humor is highly developed, laughed and applauded for fully five minutes.

As at Tarawa, it was necessary to wade for more than five hundred yards to reach the beach. Our reception, however, was vastly more friendly. On Tarawa we were met with Japanese pillboxes and machine-gun emplacements which killed hundreds of our men. On Abemama we were met by grinning native families, anxious to become our friends.

Our boys were shy, reticent. It was difficult to imagine that these were the same men who, forty-eight hours ago, had been blasting away at men in foxholes, completing their destruction of the Jap's big Tarawa garrison. Long before we landed in the Gilberts, each boy was handed a booklet describing native customs and religions. They were warned not to step between two persons engaged in conversation, not to touch a native about the head, not to refuse his offer of a gift, and not to touch anything that might be personal property, down to and including a single coconut.

Their desire to follow these instructions to the letter was almost pathetic. Marines who picked up so much as a dry coconut frond were set upon by their fellows, frowning and whispering, "Be careful."

Their reserve soon was broken, however, and I recall one big Marine private exclaiming:

"I love these people! They're friendly! They don't meet you on the beach with a gun and try to kill you. That's how people should be!"

As we stepped on the beach we met our first Gilbertese family, an old man, two old women, two younger girls, and four small children, three boys and a girl. They chattered wildly, in a lather of excitement at the sight of our boats and guns, and kept running into the bush at the slightest commotion. One of the old women—I nicknamed her Grandma—left no doubt that she was head of the house. "Granny" gave orders with the air of one who is accustomed to being obeyed. She herded the family back and forth from the beach to the comparative safety of the bush as she thought the occasion demanded. Once she spotted one of the older men—I called him Grandpa—smoking a pipe. From Granny there came a wild chatter, and Grandpa cringed as a child who had been discovered with his hand in the cooky jar. Grandma pounced on him, took the pipe, and calmly smoked it. Later, she handed it to one of the younger women, giving Grandpa a malignant glare.

When Major Holland came ashore, more of the natives appeared. Daniel, one of the major's boys, told us that many of his people were still frightened and hiding, for they had heard the shelling of Tarawa eighty miles away, and had experienced bombing since the start of the war.

"Now that they see a government officer, they will know it is all right," Major Holland said.

He was right. By nightfall our camp was full of friendly natives, willing to trade for anything, anxious to dispose of their few meager possessions. A single piece of hard candy was a treasure, and a cigarette was priceless. I gave one native a cigarette, and offered him a light. He refused. Daniel explained:

"He wants to take it back and show it to his people."

The natives quickly set up the Gilbertese equivalent of a soft-drink stand. A 13-year-old boy skinned agilely up a coconut tree—at a pace that left us breathless—and began throwing the fruit to the ground. One of the women set up a sharp stake in the ground and quickly stripped them of their husks. Another cracked them open with a single deft blow of a native hatchet and passed out the open cups for us to drink our fill. We gave them chewing gum, cigarettes, malt drops —whatever we could find in our rations.

It was the good neighbor policy at its best.

Early the next morning we borrowed Domingo, one of Major Holland's boys, for a tour of the island. We found it a place of enchanting beauty, an island paradise populated by bronze-skinned, friendly people.

At night, we got our real treat. Nearly a hundred natives visited our camp, and entertained us with their music. Many of them had beautiful baritone voices, and their strange chants had a mysterious appeal.

Our boys, in turn, entertained them with songs, including "The Beer Barrel Polka" and "God Bless America." Each group loudly cheered the other. The program was climaxed when natives and Marines joined together to sing "Silent Night, Holy Night." It was one of the most stirring and touching scenes I have ever witnessed. It was brought home suddenly to all of us that we were about to spend another Christmas thousands of miles away from home.

Today, we left Abemama—Robert Louis Stevenson's enchanting Land of Moonlight. We have enjoyed ourselves here as only the veterans of a battle such as Tarawa could have enjoyed a bit of paradise.

First Lieutenant Jim G. Lucas

Bougainville

Bougainville, November 1, 2, 3, 4, 5, 6, 7 (Delayed).— It rained today.

Technical Sergeant Frank Devine

Taitos of Tabal

His name was Taitos. He was thirty-two years old, though he looked fifty, a short-legged, long-bodied, mahogany-brown man, powerfully muscled about the arms and shoulders. For ten years, during the Japanese occupation of the Marshall Islands, he sailed as a seaman on Japanese vessels plying between Yokohama and the little copra ports of the Marshalls. He later was a scribe for the Japanese.

Today, under the Americans, he is headman of the island of Tabal, one of the minuscule chunks of palm-shaded coral which make up the atoll of Aurh, in the Ratak, or Sunrise, Chain of the Marshalls. He is, in addition, the finest of all the native scouts who in outrigger canoes and yellow Navy rubber boats creep in on moonless nights over the

· 285 ·

reefs where the wild surf bellows, to harass and spy on the Japs in their by-passed island strongholds. He takes prisoners, and he kills when it is absolutely necessary, and from every expedition he brings back to the Military Government officials information of Japanese gun emplacements and troop concentrations that brings the Marine airmen of Major General Louis E. Woods's Fourth Wing—the Jap stranglers of the Central Pacific—thundering to the attack in their Helldivers and Corsairs.

War came to quiet Tabal, where the palm-thatched cottages of Taitos's village huddle away from the sea winds beside the blue lagoon, without the agony and death which it brought to tortured Kwajalein and Eniwetok farther north. The Japanese had never made the copra atoll of Aurh a military strongpoint. Only a few Jap traders were there, and they had gone with the sight of the first American patrol plane over the area.

"But before they left," said Dwight Heine, missionary-educated Marshallese, interpreting Taitos's soft gutturals into quaintly phrased but precise English, "they tell the people that when the Americans come they all shall die, for the Americans will kill the people. They will shoot the men, and take the women, and throw the babies into the sea. So when the people see American soldiers coming ashore with their rifles they are frightened, and gather together in one place, so they may die together.

"But when the Americans see there are no Japanese there they seem very happy. They make shouting and laughter. Then they place their rifles in little pyramids on the beach and come where the natives are standing together, and shake hands with them and give them chocolate. And Taitos, seeing that his people are not to be killed, wishes to sing a song of praise to God. But he is afraid to sing, for he fears that the Americans may be like the Japanese, who do not permit the natives to sing since they have driven the missionaries away, but make them set up little altars in their houses to the Japanese god, and bow before it every morning.

"But one who speaks a little English asks the Americans if they may sing and the Americans say 'Helyiss,' which mean 'Okay.' So, there on the beach Taitos compose this song which is called 'Song of Praising Him for His Grace' and the people sing it together, even the little children.

"Then soon the Americans go away to other islands where there are Japanese who must be killed, and Tabal is quiet again, except now and then there are people who come in their canoes to tell of terrible things that are happening on other islands. And one night there are three Japanese come from the island of Maloelap, which is ten miles up the wind from Aurh, and they tell the people that the American planes have come and destroyed their food, and the people of Tabal must make food for them.

"And Taitos greet them with great courtesy, and tell the people to make food for them. But when he is telling the people to make food he also tell them that when they eat, and he shall say the word 'kio,' which mean 'now,' then the young men shall rise and help him seize the Japanese to hold them prisoner.

"So he sits down with the Japanese and make polite talk with them in their language and he offers the leader of the Japanese a cigarette. And when the Japanese reaches for the package he sees that it is an American cigarette which the soldiers have given to Taitos, called an Old Gold.

"When the Japanese see the American cigarette he is greatly excited, and he spring to his feet saying: 'What is the meaning this?' And Taitos say, with great dignity: 'It mean that this island is American island now, and you are American prisoner of war.' And the Japanese grab for his pistol, but Taitos, who is so quick he can catch the fish in the water with his hands, seize his throat with the one hand and with the other he grab the pistol. But the pistol is also tied to a lanyard which is around the neck of the Japanese, and Albina, who is the wife of Taitos, must come and cut the lanyard. And as Taitos seize the Japanese by the throat the young men of the village fall upon the other two Japanese and take them prisoner. And the three are tied with cord of coconut fiber, and they are placed in the old copra warehouse the Japanese have built, until American ship shall come.

"And when the Americans come they learn of what Taitos has

done and they say to Taitos: 'Taitos, will you come with us to be scout and to go to the islands where the Japanese are to find out where they have hidden their guns, so we may bomb them? Are you afraid to do this?'

"And Taitos say: 'I am not afraid. I will come with you.'

"And Taitos say goodby to the people of Tabal and go with the Americans on their ship. And they take him to the islands where the Japanese are, at night. And in the canoe or in the rubber boat of the Americans Taitos goes into the islands at night when it is dark. And sometimes Niembuk go, and sometimes Jetnil, or Jenathen or Aknej. But it is always Taitos who lead for there are none who are so bold as Taitos, and nobody who can take the canoe in over the reef at night like Taitos.

"But he is not bold without smartness. He is also clever. For when the canoe creep along the edge of the reef at night and they see somebody fishing which they cannot tell if it is native or Japanese, Taitos say in Marshallese: 'Ek kokke?' which mean 'Are they biting?' for he know that the Jap will not understand this Marshallese word, but will say 'eh?' Then Taitos will say in pidgin-Jap 'Ik? Elon?' meaning 'Fish? Many?' and the Jap will understand this and will think Taitos is a native of the island looking for a place where the fish are biting.

"And Taitos learn when he go into the islands at night that the Marshallese who are there are abused by the Japanese. And Taitos tell the American people of the Navy that the Marshallese wish to leave the islands where the Japs are, but they cannot get away. And they tell him they will come in their ships and take the people away, if Taitos will tell them to gather at night on the little islands of the atolls where the Japs do not live. And Taitos tell the people, and they go across the reefs at night and in the mornings the ships come and send in boats through the surf. And while they are doing this the planes come and cast bombs upon the Japanese islands, and make them stay in their foxholes so they cannot fire upon the American ships and the people as they come through the surf to the ships.

"But sometimes there are Japanese, maybe four, five, six, on all the little islands of the atoll and the people do not know what to do. So

Taitos show them how they can take these Japanese prisoner, and they listen to Taitos, and do this, but they are afraid, for they are long time a peaceful people and are afraid of the Japanese. But Taitos give them courage.

"And once on a little island from which the people are to escape they tie up five Japanese. But when the day come and they see the ship off the reef they all rush to the beach to go to the ship and leave the prisoners without guard. And when Taitos, who is with the ship, go ashore to get the prisoners, they have untied themselves and have escaped into the bushes. So Taitos, with August, go into the bushes to get the prisoners, and one of them see Taitos, and throw the grenade at him. But Taitos only call to him to surrender and does not shoot him. For there is a strange thing about Taitos. He is great-grandson of men who hunted heads, and who pierced their ears and were savage. But he does not wish to kill, for he is long time Christian even though he is not Number 1 churchman like many Marshallese, for Number 1 churchman cannot drink the jukuru, which is made from the sap of the palm, nor smoke cigarette nor sing and dance, and Taitos love to do these things.

"So Taitos only call to the Jap to surrender, but he throw more grenade and Taitos must duck behind palm tree. And Taitos keep begging him to surrender but he will not and Taitos must shoot him. But this does not kill him, and August come with his knife and open the Jap's stomach, which Taitos does not wish to do.

"And the Navy ship take the people to the villages on the islands where there are no Japanese and which the Americans protect. And all the people who are already there come down to the beach and there is much happiness, for there is meeting of sons and daughters and fathers and mothers and brothers and sisters who have been separated by the Japanese when they take the men away from their villages to work for them.

"And the young men climb the coconut trees and get coconuts so that the Americans may have coconut milk to drink. And the women give them woven mats, and fans which they have made. And that night there is a gathering of all the people in the town hall of the village, to dance and sing the songs of the Marshallese people. And always they sing Taitos's 'Song of Praising Him for His Grace.'

"And that is how Taitos help the Americans, and his people."

First Lieutenant Harold H. Martin

Mussau Boys

Emirau is a small island in the St. Matthias group down South Pacific way. Over a year ago, the Marines sent some troops ashore, met no opposition, and in a matter of days, the Seabees ripped up the jungle. Since then the tide of war has swept toward Japan. By now, the only deadly thing about Emirau duty is boredom and loneliness—and this encounter with three dusky natives by four Marines.

It started with about five pounds of precious ground beef. How this delicacy was obtained is nobody's business, but around it was built an excursion to the palm-fringed, coral beach. The smell of hamburgers was incense and myrrh. Evening time, and the beat of the sea! Just beyond the reefs which churned the swelling waves into foam and froth, three curlyheaded "Joes" bobbed and dove.

We would see a head, the flash of glistening black arm clutching a spear, then hear a wild, triumphant yell and see a flapping fish slide down to join other speared brethren on the 5-foot weapon.

"Well, I'll be damned," said Master Technical Sergeant J. P. Mc-Lemore. "Around Meridian, Mississippi, we didn't get fish this way, but let's give it a whirl." (Did I mention the two cases of beer we had?) Anyway, in short order we had cut spears from the brush, stripped and waded over the sharp coral to the fishing grounds.

It didn't work out. The salt water kept pouring into our mouths at most unexpected moments. It burned our eyes, and the fish were swift. We admitted defeat after a bit of a go, and returned to the hamburgers and brew.

The fish were probably poison anyway . . . we said . . . but when these three grinning Joes timidly came to our fire and mutely offered us eight still wriggling specimens, we took them with thanks. And they were strange, some brilliant red, purple, and two of them with perfect golden sergeant stripes down their shimmering black sides. We must have shown our doubt because the natives quickly chorused, "Him okay. Him good guy fitches." They grinned.

So we cleaned them and into the frying pan they went. The squatting Joes looked on with interest. Master Technical Sergeant Manuel ("Stumpy") Roy, a gentleman from Tampa, Florida, graciously pulled out his pack of rare cigarettes and with a flourish passed them around. The natives shook their curly heads: "Cigarettes no good. We Mussau boys. No smoke. Bad!" And they pounded their chests to show us where the devil nicotine burrows into the meat of the noble white man and speeds him to his coffin. Stumpy had just lit his own smoke, and he choked on that speech. He is usually pretty flip, but now he almost shamefacedly tossed the fag away. "Well, well," was his snappy rejoinder.

The Joes, little guys, mind you, who were at least a foot shorter than we were, stood or squatted and grinned. Here we were, United States Marines, feeling slightly uneasy at the turn in events.

Bancroft tried. Now Sarge Bancroft used to sell Buicks before he joined the Corps, so with the finesse that characterizes the master, he dug into the box of Ten-in-One rations we brought along and pulled out a packet of soluble coffee and offered it with prescribed gestures and technique: 'This very okay guy. Simple. Take hot water and. . . ." But he got no further. One of the short curlyheaded rascals, who up to this moment looked absolutely incapable of anything but grinning, tossed off with Oxonian clarity, "Oh, we understand these things." With brilliant diplomacy he added, "Me savvy. Me Mussau boy too."

"What the blankety blank hell is this 'Mussau boy' detail?" I wanted to know. Being new in these parts I turned to my companions. It seemed Mussau is an adjoining island where missionaries for many years . . . But my buddies were interrupted. "Pardon me," said this character, "it is true. We are from Mussau and we do not smoke . . . or swear [I blanched under that look]. The good missionaries have taught us many things. We are Christians. May we use your fire?"

We snapped to and took our fish out of the pan and offered the works to these strange lads who so far were just one jump ahead of the Marines. But the proffered pan was refused. This Joe who could speak English as well as any of us lapsed into the pidgin stuff. So help me, he didn't want to embarrass us! "Me throw on fire," he said and they did. Heads, tails, scales and all, they tossed the fish into the coals. There was burning, twisting and curling, and in a few moments our guests snatched their supper from the fires and discreetly withdrew a little way, and ate the mess with apparent relish.

We looked at each other and chuckled. Who ever heard of cooking like that? How stupid of these people! We felt better. The Joes thanked us, gave us a few more finny Sergeants, and wandered off.

Well, so we did toss them into the coals, heads, tails, scales and all. And so they did taste better than any fried variety. The charred skins and scales pulled off and underneath was flaky whiteness, steaming and delectable. We argued about who would get the extra fish when the count came out uneven.

We were full . . . pleasantly so . . . but just a little rankled. The assortment of greasy pan, dirty plates and forks, and the crawling ants in the whole mess, mocked us. McLemore took it all in, then scooped the wreckage and refinements of civilization into a box and heaved it into the ocean.

"Me Mississippi boy," said Mac.

Technical Sergeant George H. Mattie

Quakes

Marines are plagued not only by the Japanese, but by the Japs' ancient curse, earthquakes. Recently the men on Bougainville were subjected to a 5-minute temblor which rattled men around in their foxholes like dice in a cup, displaced logs before machine-gun positions and caved in dugouts.

To amuse himself, this writer kept a box score on quakes for a couple of days:

FIRST DAY

6 A.M.—Severe for five minutes.
6:20 A.M.—Slight.
7:30 A.M.—Moderate.
12:50 P.M.—Heavy.
2:20 P.M.—Slight, very short duration.
4 P.M.—Very sharp, three minutes' duration.
5 P.M.—Tiny tremor.

SECOND DAY

8:30 A.M.—Very slight.
10:30 A.M.—Moderate shake.
3:30 P.M.—Fairly heavy.
3:35 P.M.—Heavy for two minutes.

Master Technical Sergeant Theodore C. Link

Pangilan's Gift

We dined on the sala, the great open porch of the beautiful plantation home that Don Robinson had built for his wife, Ann, when they came to Basilan in the Philippines thirty years ago to carve a coconut plantation out of the deep jungle that covered this green island lying off the tip of Zamboanga. By any standards it was a meal to marvel at. To Lieutenant Burnham Litchfield and to me, both of us accustomed to the rough fare and the rougher service of Marine chow halls, it was a miracle. There was a tablecloth of lacy beauty, a treasure from Ann Robinson's hope chest. There were, unbelievably, napkins of linen, monogrammed, and a centerpiece of tropical flowers. There was fine old China in the design the Cantonese call "the Little People," and old silver, heavy and lustrous.

Two deft, immaculate Filipino girls served, their bare feet noiseless

· 293 ·

on the wide ipil-wood boards of the floor—boards thirty feet long and thirty inches wide without a knot or flaw, hard and shiny as some dark plastic. The food was the kind that a man might dream about if he had ever experienced it before. Paco, a salad made of the fern-fiddle, the tender curling tops of the jungle fern. Suman-rice cooked in coconut milk, broiled chicken, tender and sweet, with mango chutney, lychee nuts, and huge golden slices of pineapple, fresh picked that morning. And for dessert a coconut pie, soft, sweet and creamy on a flaky crust that melted in the mouth.

It was a Sunday noon, and the wind blew cool through the sala off the deep curving river that formed one boundary of the wide green lawn. Birds sang in the tangled branches of the balete, the strangler fig, and beyond the lawn the stately columns of the coconut palms marched in ordered rows toward the blue hills in the distance. On the white sand road northward toward the little village of Lamitan, Moro men in their brilliant costumes walked with their fighting cocks under their arms, Moro women carried their baskets to market, and Moro youngsters drove their big-wheeled carts, shouting. It was the Christian's Sunday, the Mohammedan Moro's market day.

In keeping with the spirit of the place and the mood of the day, the talk was of small and pleasant things, and not of war. We had talked of war already, for Don and Ann Robinson had seen their share. There was first Bill's going, and then his loss when his plane went down over Java. And then there had been the coming of the Japs, and the flight of Don and Ann to the hills, and their three years of wandering among the Moro tribes who hid and sheltered them. And then their return, a few months before, to find that, though the Japs had been there and had used their house as quarters for officers, they had, remarkably, destroyed nothing except the beautiful gardens of ground orchids that had surrounded the house, and had failed to find the hidden cache where Ann, in the last hours before they fled, had buried her treasured silver. Nor had they found where the Moro families to whom Ann had entrusted her linens, and the smaller pieces of her furniture, had kept these things safe alike from theft and jungle mold. We had talked of how Don, a tattered ghost, building house after house of bamboo and thatch to shelter his wife as they incessantly moved from place to place, had finally become so ragged he could not afford to be seen except from the front, and how Ann had knitted incessantly, using any scrap of thread she could find, to keep from going mad.

But that had been the night before, and today we spoke of lighter things. Ann told of the teas and the parties and the dances of Zamboanga in the placid days when Army officers and their wives sought relief from the boredom of garrison life. Don spoke with humor of his wandering, footloose youth, that took him from Indiana around the world, ofttimes broke, but never disturbed by that, and of how on a flip of the coin, one night in Bozeman, Montana, he chose the University of Texas instead of the University of Chicago, and there met the gay, vivacious, tiny girl, fresh from the study of violin in Berlin, whom he finally married and brought with him to the Philippines—choosing this place for no reason perhaps except that he remembered the smoky blue of the hills of Basilan and the colored striped sails of the Moro fishermen as they sailed in their needle-slim vintas and their broad-bellied wallowing kumpits out of the mouth of the Hondo across the straits to Basilan.

So we talked of small things like these, and war was very far away on this sunny Sunday noon. Until the Moros of the plantation, the women in their bright shawls and tight silk trousers, white lace at their throats and gold buttons shining on their tight-sleeved jackets, began to stir and chatter where they leaned on the rail of the sala, watching us eat.

Soon the one called Mondiaran, Don's private guerrilla, spoke to Don in the Yakan tongue. A quick frown shadowed Ann's face as he spoke. Don translated for Litchfield and me.

"He says that Pangilan, from Tipa-Tipa, has come with a gift." He rose from his chair. "Like to come along?" he asked.

"Don't you think you should have your dessert first," Ann said, and there seemed to be a faint stress of accent on the "first."

"Maybe," Don called back to her, as we went down the broad stair to where Pangilan waited, "it won't be so bad this time."

It wasn't so bad. As Pangilan unwrapped the banana leaf and proffered his gift to Don, the Jap's head had a waxy, fixed-staring look, like the head of a clothing dummy in the window of a store. The blade of Pangilan's barong had taken him just above the shoulder blades, and he had died in an instant, without alarm.

Pangilan was slender of body, massive of shoulder, erect, and one could tell, vastly proud. He had long black hair which flowed over his shoulders from beneath his red and green and yellow turban. A crimson sash bound his waist, and from the silver box which hung there, he took a betel nut, touched it with lime juice from a little silver vial, wrapped it in a pepper leaf, chewed for a moment and spat delicately a gobbet of rusty red in the dust. He had found the Jap an hour's walk away, he said to Don in Yakan, busily digging for camotes, the native potato. He had come upon him quietly, and there had been room for a clean swift stroke. There had been other Japs near by, but he had not molested them. The head was a gift for Don.

Don thanked him heartily, and shook his hand. We shook his hand, and looked, in some awe, at the shining white steel blade, with its handle of silver, in its case of shiny dark wood set with mother-of-pearl. When the thanking and the handshaking was done, Don told Pangilan he was deeply grateful, but he thought that the people at market should see the head too, so they could know what manner of man was Pangilan. Pangilan agreed that this was so. He took up the head and wrapped it again in the banana leaf and went on to market, followed by an admiring retinue.

"That makes five they've brought by," said Don, as we returned to dinner.

As we sat down, Ann lifted an eyebrow at Don in faintest inquiry. His nod was equally unobtrusive.

The dessert was delicious and, as we ate, Ann told us the history of the magnificent silver platter that held the centerpiece of flowers. It was made for her, it seems, long years ago, by a Chinese silversmith in Manila.

First Lieutenant Harold H. Martin

· 296 ·

No Grass Shacks in Kealakaku

The Hawaiian Islands are a land of green roses, sands that bark when you walk on them, and grass skirts imported from the mainland for sale to the thousands of servicemen who are currently stationed there. It is also the home of the hula. During the months I spent on one of the islands with a detachment of Marines I was able to see at least two hula shows a week by merely walking from my tent to the camp theater or the nearest USO. It was in this way that I became acquainted with the Holokai family, which consisted of four sisters, who danced, their father, who accompanied them on a guitar, and their mother, who acted as chaperon. Through the Holokais I got to know something about the Hawaiian people in general and the hula in particular. Joseph Holokai's principal ambition was to revive the lost grandeur of his island for the benefit of American servicemen, who were at that time almost as numerous as the natives. He hoped to do this by means of the hula, though when I first met him he had had little success. In slow, precise English he would tell his audiences that the meaning of the dance was in the motion of the hands and not in the hips. Frequently, however, someone in the audience would yell "Shake it up!" at the height of the Holokais' performance and the mood of the dance would be—for them—completely spoiled. I gathered from the Holokais that "swish" had come into the hula only after haoles—foreigners from the mainland—had begun to take over the dance.

This corruption of the hula may explain why a permanent look of sadness clouded Holokai's pleasant, tawny features. His wife, Lizzie, looked more cheerful. She was a buxom woman who often likened herself to Madame Pele, the Hawaiian volcano goddess, who could only be propitiated by the sacrifice of silk handkerchiefs, money, and roast pig. Like most of the Holokais' visitors, I was chiefly interested in the daughters. They were not beautiful, even by native standards. Julia, the oldest, was plump and shy. Winona had coal-black hair and eyes the color of guava jelly. Gloria had a reticent charm that tended to overcome the homeliness of her too-large features. Thelma, the youngest, was still slender. She had an ingenuous smile, lips as red as the hibiscus blossom, pretty legs, and a cream-colored skin that set off her dark hair and eyes.

Since giving performances at various camps, USOs, and island festivals provided a poor livelihood, the Holokais also took in laundry. Their price for washing and ironing a khaki shirt was twenty-five cents. The results left something to be desired but those of us who were stationed in the mountains far from town had no choice but to patronize them.

After several visits, I became friendly with Thelma Holokai. She was shy in the presence of haoles like myself, and our friendship was a model of Victorian decorum. We met in the sitting room. The Holokais' bedroom was next to the sitting room, separated from it only by curtains hung in a doorway. Not only could our conversation be overheard by Thelma's mother and three sisters (who retired to the bedroom for that sole purpose, I felt sure), but whenever there was any prolonged silence between Thelma and me the curtains parted and Mrs. Holokai's chubby, suspicious face appeared. She asked some senseless question, then withdrew. So it became necessary for us to carry on our love-making in the midst of a continuous brisk discussion of irrelevant topics.

This was rather awkward. Once I found myself holding Thelma's hands in mine, gazing into her dark eyes, and saying, "Doesn't the noise from the machine-gun range scare you sometimes?"

"Yes," Thelma replied with a coy look. "Dad's even afraid to go down to the lower pasture because of stray bullets."

I squeezed her hands a little tighter and said, "You're lucky the mortar range isn't near here."

We never grew very ardent. Most of the time I sat across from her and gazed at her trim, bare legs and at her feet, which had acquired thick calluses from dancing. On one visit I hit on the notion of discussing the hula with Thelma. I thought this would permit her to take a livelier part in the conversation and, since most hulas are accompanied by love songs, would enable her to enact with appropriate gestures any words I failed to understand. I hadn't foreseen that the hula was a subject over which no member of the family would grant another undisputed authority. Before long, the whole family entered the sitting room to share our discussion.

There is a saying in the islands that if a haole would love a native girl he must first learn to love her country. Though I had no intention of falling in love with Thelma, my actions were ambiguous enough so that I became not a suitor but a sort of protégé. On one occasion the Holokais took me to a native luau, or feast, where I was fed pig roasted in banana leaves, raw cow's liver, salted seaweed, roast coconut, and a native liquor called okolehoa, which is made from the root of the ti plant. The Holokais had a great many ti plants in their yard, as they were popularly supposed to keep away ghosts. The Holokais used their leaves to make hula skirts. I was told that a person who drinks okolehoa almost invariably gets the impression of witnessing a violent rainstorm. Holokai told me that the leaf and root of the ti plant do not mix, and that there is a tendency at luaus for the men to go around setting fire to the skirts of hula girls. At first, the territorial government ordered that all skirts be made fireproof. "But there was nothing," Holokai said, "that could put out the fire in the head of a young man who had drunk okolehoa. They finally had to outlaw the drink."

The Holokais urged me to establish among my friends a deeper appreciation of the hula. This was a big order, for most servicemen seldom saw anything but hapahaole, or half-white, shows. Holokai did not regard these as authentic, and he put the blame on the USO, Dorothy Lamour, and the Honolulu radio stations. "Most of the Hawaiian songs they broadcast," he said, "were composed by men who sit around in New York, where the only palm trees are in hotel lobbies. How can you get inspiration from a palm tree that is used to put out cigarette butts?" Holokai always became excited when he talked of the New York brand of Hawaiian music. "That song—'Take Me Back to My Little Grass Shack in Kealakaku, Hawaii,'" he said. "There is no grass shack in Kealakaku. There aren't any grass shacks anywhere in the Hawaiian Islands, except the one the government maintains for tourists in Honolulu. There never have been any grass shacks. But that Dorothy Lamour! She has made you mainlanders think we are a people who do nothing but live in grass houses and wriggle our hips."

I was expected to get such notions out of my head before I could hope to be taken seriously by the Holokais. There were other notions that I was supposed to put into my head, and the most improbable of these was a belief in menehunes. The menehunes are the "little people" of the Hawaiians and, though the younger generation was inclined to scoff at their existence, Holokai and his wife spoke of them with reverence. Holokai described them as "night workmen." "They are no taller than a man's knee," he said, "and they have bushy eyebrows and long beards. They love to sing, they love to dance, they love to fly kites. Oh, and they love to slide down grassy slopes, spin tops, play checkers, and fish and swim!" There were menehunes living in the woods near his property, Holokai assured me, but they could be seen only by those who had menehune blood in their veins. Furthermore, since they slept all day, they could be seen only at night. "A freckle," Holokai told me once, "is a menehune's kiss. They are planted on the noses of good children on the night after the full moon." Holokai glanced at his daughters and smiled. "They love Hawaiian children so much," he said, "that they are just one big brown freckle."

Many of the island superstitions were expressed in the Holokais' dances and songs. Their singing was, of course, in Hawaiian, in order to combat the singing of American songs like "Sweet Lilani." There was only one exception to this rule, a hula which described the plight of those whom the gasoline shortage had turned into hitchhikers. The last verse of the song was in English, perhaps out of spite, and ended with the refrain, "Going my way, mister? Step on the gas." An upraised thumb was the motif of this dance, which was very popular with the islanders.

Before giving public performances for servicemen, the Holokais tried out their act at a luau attended only by natives. When they finished, two old women came up to them with tears in their eyes. They told the Holokais that they had been hula dancers some sixty years before. "They had been afraid that the hula was a lost art,"

Holokai said to me. "Seeing us brought back memories of their youth. It is something for a couple of old hula girls to weep because their hearts are full of gladness. Our own hearts were very full of gladness that day." The Holokais revived a number of ancient forms of the hula, many of which were accompanied by special instruments composed of iliili (pebbles), puili (bamboo), uliuli (gourd), ipu (drum), or kalaau (sticks). In addition to his guitar, Holokai had a trumpet made of a conch shell and a flute which he played by expelling air through his nostrils.

I was lucky enough to watch the rehearsals of some of these ancient dances. The house shook and hummed like a machine shop. Kneeling, the girls clacked the pebbles in their hands, slapped the lengths of bamboo against one another, rattled the gourds, beat the drums, and cracked the sticks on the floor in a tattoo which sounded like that of a light machine gun. To this accompaniment they sang a plaintive song, and Holokai played his nose flute. "If this doesn't take the soldiers' minds off the hips," he said to me as the sweat ran down his cheeks, "nothing will."

Holokai never succeeded in persuading the servicemen on the island to think of his daughters as an embodiment of an all but lost Hawaiian culture instead of as hula girls. I had gained his confidence, however, and he and his family were sorry to hear that our outfit was moving away. I had been a good customer and a willing listener. I even fancied, when I told them the news, that Thelma might make some gesture of affection, but it was Julia who went outside, stripped a ti plant of its broad leaves, and quickly wove me a skirt as a souvenir. Then Holokai gave me a drink of okolehoa. "With the goodbye," he said, "you can mix the root and the leaf." He raised his glass. "Aloha," he said. "Aloha," I repeated.

On my last visit to the Holokais I took Thelma a bouquet of the most beautiful blossoms I could find. She smiled gratefully. Julia, Winona, and Gloria squealed with delight. There was a good deal of laughter as we said goodby. Winona placed a lei around my neck, but Thelma did not kiss me, as I had hoped she might. Instead, she went into the kitchen and brought out my laundry.

When I got back to camp, I found that my khaki pants had been starched to a brittle stiffness and creased to the fineness of a knife's edge. Into each shirt had been ironed a military pleat. Not since leaving my own country had I seen such beautiful khaki.

Master Technical Sergeant David Dempsey

A Real Town

One of these days in the South Pacific, we're going to capture a town. Maybe not a large town—just something with a few blocks of real houses, paved or even cobbled streets, and one or two buildings like a post office or village store.

Starting with the August 7, 1942, landing on Tulagi and Guadalcanal, the Marines have been hoping that someday, somewhere, they would occupy an area that resembled civilization. A small town, perhaps with a village square and one or two two-story houses. Something you could point to with a little pride and say, "Look, we've taken back a lot of swamps and jungle, but here, look, a real town," and it would be akin in a small way to Podunk or Pleasantville.

In a year and one-half of jungle fighting, the Marines have been looking forward to that day which dwindles as island after island falls away from Japanese control.

"Huts, damned thatched huts," you hear the men say, "and what the maps call a road turns out to be an overgrown trail you couldn't coax a cow through."

Guadalcanal, the Russell Islands, the New Georgia group, Vella Lavella, the Treasury Islands, and a portion of Bougainville have come under Allied control—and still no town.

"We read about the troops in Africa and Italy," said one town-capturing-conscious corporal, "they take real honest-to-God towns, with streets and electric lights and water systems and brick buildings and bars and gardens and people. What do we get—grass shacks and lizards and swamp 'gardens' of slimy banyan trees!"

Master Technical Sergeant Murrey Marder

Hizzoner, the Mayor of Okinawa

In some ways Taira's city council, the first in the Ryukyus under American military government, is not unlike the city council in Chicago or New York. The local aldermen are called hanchos, unlike the "paunchos" of America. But, like them, they often snap sarcastically at one another. They demand that the chief of police clear the streets of bums, children, and stragglers, suggest that the commissioner of sanitation haul away the garbage, and, in traditional aldermanic fashion, occasionally doze off when a statistical report is being read.

The hanchos had little or no legislative experience before they were picked by the town's military administrator, Army Captain Warren McAllister, an insurance adjuster from Cedar Rapids, Iowa. Four were farmers, three were bank clerks, three were salesmen, one owned a grocery in Naha. Despite these varied backgrounds, they have helped immeasurably to establish a rudimentary communal organization among some ten thousand frightened and bewildered Okinawans here and in neighboring Nakaoshi.

In the first days at Taira, practically the only effective link between the military officials and natives was sly little Yi Ikimeyga, who had learned English in 1937 at the Shanghai Y.M.C.A., but whose favorite expletive was "Goddam!" When I recently sat in on a council session, I found that Yi was now mayor of Taira, bubblier than ever over his new authority. "Ev'body say to me, 'Hi, Misser Mayor.' Ev'body know me. Goddam! I feel like king," he snickered.

Mayor Yi and his hanchos held their meeting in the upstairs room of a former brokerage house. A torn paper lantern hung by a string from the half-open ceiling and a battered funeral urn lay in a corner. Up front was an Okinawan poster reading, EVERY MAN SHOULD HAVE A STRAIGHT HEART. "This mean," Mayor Yi explained, "we no want no crook heart heah. On'y straight-heart men—'es, 'es."

When the session started, only nine of the fifteen hanchos were present.

"That's our biggest problem," said Captain McAllister. "We tell them to be here at one o'clock, so they decide that two will do just as well. Must be the Oriental mind. Hey, mayor, where are the other hanchos?"

"Aah, goddam!" snapped Mayor Yi. "They late again. No un'estan' Amewican speet. Amewican too fast do thing, fast like hell." He grinned at Captain McAllister. Then he motioned for the councilmen to be seated. Yi, Captain McAllister, City Clerk Yosuke Gushumi, a Mr. Koshi, the sleepy-eyed commissioner of sanitation; K. Makayima, a baldish schoolteacher; Y. Nobulu, commissioner of agriculture; and S. Tuma, a local lawyer, ranged themselves in a row facing the aldermen. All sat on very low wooden chairs salvaged from the wreckage of the local kindergarten. The tiny Okinawans seemed comfortable enough, but Captain McAllister, a big handsome guy built along the lines of a football tackle, kept shifting uneasily on his little stool.

After Captain McAllister distributed cigarettes, the men lit up and Mayor Yi cleared his throat. But before he could speak, Captain McAllister looked around the room. "Hey," he called, "where the hell's the chief of police?"

Everyone shrugged when Mayor Yi repeated the question in the native tongue. "Maybe he out on bisness," he said. "Go start now?"

Captain McAllister sighed. "Gosh, the chief oughta be here. There's a lot that concerns him. But I guess we'd better begin. Well, mayor, the first thing is about these wives and girls and kids hanging around the labor compound where the men are standing by to go to work. We can't have it. They get in the way, the men want to talk all day, and we get all fouled up, see? Now, let's tell them we'll have regular visiting hours, from six in the evening till dark. See how that suits."

During the captain's speech, Mayor Yi had listened intently, interrupting once or twice with a softly hissed " 'es, 'es." When the captain finished, Mayor Yi turned to the aldermen and talked rapidly for five minutes. "Listen to him go," Captain McAllister said admiringly. A hancho in a tattered silk robe, Jap soldier leggings, and a Marine's undershirt raised his hand. Mayor Yi listened impatiently. "He wants know," he translated, "can womens bring package, box, clothes?"

"Yes, but only during visiting hours," Captain McAllister replied. "Tell them the other night one of the men escaped and got into the hills and there are Japanese soldiers in those hills. Understand what that means, if they take those clothes and stuff to the Jap soldiers? It'll be rough if they do that, see?"

Mayor Yi nodded and briskly explained. The men mumbled, "Hei! Hei!"—Japanese for "Yes." They nodded too. "Okay now," said Mayor Yi, with a languid wave of his hand.

"Okay," said Captain McAllister, referring to his notebook. "Here's something they'll like. We got a spot picked out for some playgrounds for the kids. The schoolteacher here and the city clerk will take a detail out and start getting wood for teeter-totters and stuff like that. How's that?"

Mayor Yi relayed the information. Smiles broke out on the drawn faces of the hanchos and there was agitated jabbering. "They like. They say iss good, good," the mayor grinned. "Keep kid, little bebby off street, no get hit by ummmm-oh, oh—auto'bile." Several children, he told me sadly, had run in front of jeeps and trucks on the road cutting through the town.

A lank fellow with the inevitable black-rimmed spectacles arose and spoke quite passionately for about three minutes. Some of the others stared at the floor. It developed he was criticizing the chief of police for not keeping the streets clear.

"Well, the chief isn't here," said Captain McAllister, "but we can take that up again when he comes. Anyway, we're going to have playgrounds."

At this point there was a clattering below and a little man with a round face and scrubby beard ran up the stairs. He stood at the head of the steps and bowed to the assembled hanchos. They bowed back. He wore a long white linen coat at least three sizes too large for him, green trousers, and a Marine's helmet with CHIEF in black letters against a white background. This was Sadeo Futamai, once a construction engineer, now chief of police of Taira.

"Where's he been? Ask him!" said Captain McAllister. "He's an hour late."

Chief Futumai, with head cocked and a smile on his lips, listened to Mayor Yi's nervous tirade. Then he slowly removed his helmet, laid it on the floor, and replied. First there had been the inept traffic policemen he had appointed. "Country bumpkins!" he snorted. "They sat down and didn't know what to do. They had never done this sort of work before, so they had to be told again. You see, I am a conscientious police boss. I don't do things in little spurts. How can I tell when I called away from my duty?" snorted the chief.

"Okay. Let's get going," said Captain McAllister.

In succession, the council discussed such matters as how many carts Mr. Koshi could get in the morning to carry fertilizer for the sweet-potato patches, the need for soap, and the influx of more civilians into the settlement. At this point a hancho read a statistical report on recent additions in his district, and Mr. Koshi fell asleep. When the hubbub of voices suddenly woke him, he promptly slipped in the sage suggestion that such reports henceforth should be shorter.

"Now, here's something up the old chief's alley," said Captain Mc-Allister. "There have been a few troublemakers around, people who hang around the compound all the time, who wander around at night —dammit, they get shot accidentally that way!—and who don't clean up their houses. Stuff like that. Well, we're going to set up a court, and you, chief, and you, mayor, and the lawyer in the village will be in charge. The better people behave, the less work you'll have."

Mayor Yi's head bobbed as Captain McAllister spoke. He was obviously pleased with the added power. "I be good judge," he promised.

Next, Captain McAllister and Mayor Yi held a 5-minute symposium on the need for keeping streets clean and for digging deep drainage ditches. Several hanchos related what was being done in their sections. One testy old man boasted that even the women in his district were working at these jobs. The others sniffed at this show of pride and mumbled demands to get on with the meeting.

It was now Y. Nobolu's turn to tell of the program for planting sweet potatoes. In a dullish voice he outlined how each district would begin preparing the earth in the morning. He droned on and on at some length, and again Mr. Koshi's head dropped on his chest and he snored very quietly. This time, two of the hanchos joined him in irreverent slumber. They were awakened by the excited voices of three hanchos, silent up to now. These were the farmers, who had little interest in the urban problems discussed earlier. They gabbled away, obviously overjoyed at having their first say in the meeting.

"The important thing to tell them," said Captain McAllister when the farmers had finished, "is that they must start their farms again. We're not here to change their way of life. We want them to live and be well. But there's a war going on and we just won't be able to feed everyone who comes in here. So they have to start planting now. Otherwise a lot of people will starve. And we don't want that."

"We shall be ready before dawn," the farmers chorused.

"Okay," the captain said. "Let's read the minutes."

City Clerk Gushumi wet his lips and read softly. Those hanchos who had taken notes compared the minutes with their jottings, and once there was a rapid-fire argument about the disposition of a particular issue. When Gushumi finished, Mayor Yi asked for question. There was none. Captain McAllister got up from his cramped seat. "Okay. We meet again tomorrow. And let's try to have everyone on time." He pointed at the police chief, who caught the meaning at once and bowed.

"Listen, mayor," the captain told Yi. "Let's have the hanchos get on the ball and stay on it."

Mayor Yi placed the tips of his index fingers to his forehead, his gesture when he is perplexed or cannot think of the proper English word. "On the ball?" he repeated. "This I can no' un'estan'. What mean?"

"Oh, see that everybody does as he's told to—as the hanchos tell them. That way we'll all be happy and we won't have so many headaches."

"Oh, oh, oh, oh, 'es, 'es," Mayor Yi chuckled. "Be happy, ev'body happy." He danced along at the side of the captain, the top of his Panama hat even with the officer's chest. Chief Futumai skipped behind them. Downstairs, Mayor Yi and the chief of police solemnly bade each hancho farewell and repeated the captain's advice about following orders. Then they strode toward the compound to detail men for work in the fields.

Along the way, Marines grinned and shouted, "Hi, Mister Mayor! How's it goin'?"

"Okay, very okay," laughed Mayor Yi. "See, ev'body say to me, 'Hi!' Feel like goddam king!" He slapped his knee as he bent double with laughter.

Yi and the chief walked off like a pair of cocky bantams. "Well," said one of the Marine MPs, "there they go. I bet those boys'll have a dozen new wards lined up for their ticket by morning. What a sweet pair of precinct captains they'd make in Jersey!"

Technical Sergeant Herman Kogan

That Old White Magic

My friend Juan is a native of the Marshall Islands who is learning to be an American. I met him almost two years ago, just after our invasion of the Kwajalein Atoll. He had been to a mission school and spoke a little English. Recently in going back through the Marshall Islands, I tried to find him. Another native told me that he had gone off to one of the smaller islets with a government-issued fishing rod. "But he will come back," the man said in crude English. "He like Spam."

A liking for American food is not the only thing Juan acquired from our occupation. Like thousands of his "brothers" all over the Pacific, he wears a pair of discarded GI dungarees, a straw hat, aviators' goggles, a colored sash into which he stuffs packs of American cigarettes, and—for the first time in his life—shoes.

Juan lives near an airbase. A culture of Coca-Cola, juke boxes, heavy machinery, crap games, and 10-cent-store jewelery has been casually deposited over his primitive civilization. He sleeps under white sheets and a Navy blanket—thanks to a little shrewd trading with the Seabees—and is likely to pull out a harmonica and break into the strains of "Chattanooga Choo Choo."

The first wages Juan earned from Uncle Sam were for burying dead Japanese soldiers. Later he was employed to build roads and help on the airfield. He looked wonderingly at bulldozers, and learned to drive a truck. While our fleet bobbed in the lagoon, he came down to the beach each morning and counted the ships. His first step in Americanization was not the trinkets we gave him but the discovery that we had machines to do the work that he had had to do by hand, and many more ships than he imagined existed in the world.

The second step was the discovery that we American GIs were friendly. Juan is brown, rather than black-skinned, and the term "bamboo American" grew up to describe him. It also describes our feelings about him, as though we regarded him as a "hyphen American" working his way into some kind of citizenship. We taught him baseball, and slang, made mascots of his children, and put him to work at the highest wages he had earned in his life.

Juan's sisters in the Pacific have not lagged far behind in adapting themselves to our customs. The girls on Funafuti, Samoa, and Guam especially have gone in for American "glamour." A Marine enlisted men's club on Samoa regularly invites Samoan girls to its dances. Three years ago, when we first came, it was necessary to add a line at the bottom of the invitation which read: "Only women wearing shoes will be admitted." Today, these maidens not only wear shoes, but have given up sarongs for American dresses. They use lipstick and smoke cigarettes. And when it comes to jitterbugging they are, as the GIs say, terrific.

On some of the islands the natives watch American movies in special sections reserved for them. At first, because of the old taboos, they turned their eyes from the screen in giggling embarrassment when lovers kissed; now, they sit through the clinches in something close to the ecstasy of a bobby-sox audience watching Bogart make love to Lauren Bacall. "See 'um and hear 'um in movies" is frequently the answer to the serviceman's query about how a native caught on to American ways.

Not all the habits Juan picked up from his association with the GIs are as amusing and as innocent. He has, for example, learned the value of driving a hard bargain, and trading inflation in the Pacific is rampant. In Honolulu one can buy a grass skirt for fifty cents. But on many Southwest Pacific islands the price is twenty dollars. This is true of most native souvenirs. Hardwood canes, inlaid with mother-of-pearl, which native craftsmen formerly spent days working on, are now turned out in a day at five times the old price, but with none of the old craftsmanship. Also thousands of natives, in working for the Yankee dollar, have put a value on their labor which will never again be what it was before we came. But in raising their wages we have also raised their self-esteem, which is another old American custom.

Another way in which Juan has become American is in the extent to which he has become dependent on us. We have built roads and bridges across his islands that only our bulldozers can keep in operation. In the Marianas we are teaching him scientific farming to make him self-sufficient, although at this stage it is the sufficiency of U.S. equipment, feed, and advice that is supporting him in the style in which he has become accustomed.

There is no doubt about it, Juan would rather swing a shovel than a fishing rod. Who can blame him? Civil affairs are providing self-government, sanitation, medical care, a good diet, and jobs. Malaria control and proper food are ridding him of century-old diseases. Our military government has begun to break up the old system of land control by the "kings" which netted them a good slice of both the natives' produce and wages, even those paid by Uncle Sam. In liberating Juan from the enemy, we have also liberated him from the past.

Quietly but hopefully we have extended to Juan and his people a Pacific Charter. Very recently, the Marshall Islanders petitioned the United States to retain jurisdiction of their islands when the war ends. These people don't want to be "natives" again in the old sense. They are happy as bamboo Americans who, in a few short years, have achieved not only freedom from want and fear but the freedom to see American movies, sing our songs, and get in a poker game with the ground crew. This is the old white magic that is winning them over.

Master Technical Sergeant David Dempsey

At Home Abroad

Marines Against the Jungle

What generations of city life have taken from Americans, the war in the Pacific, in an underhand way, has returned with interest. Here, on rain-spattered islands, under smoldering suns, American servicemen by necessity have returned to "outdoor life." That the American fighting man here has had to master a field of battle before he could even meet the enemy has been only lightly revealed in the language of communiques: "Our troops advanced through heavy jungle. . . ."

The men out here are not just so many battalions and regiments of intrepid Frank Bucks, but somewhere between the sweat and the strain they have done a pretty good job of living on barest essentials when the occasion demanded, surviving climatic conditions generally reserved for "mad dogs and Englishmen" and fighting in terrain you would not regard suitable for a crocodile.

Situations will rarely arise similar to those on Guadalcanal where Marines on one behind-the-lines raid lived off the jungle and a few captured supplies for thirty days, but in the swamp-pocked bush of the Pacific every serviceman learns that to survive he must "go native" to some extent in matters of moving, eating, sleeping and fighting. The men, it would seem, have capitalized on every means of converting themselves to a tattered-looking band of revolutionists. In battle areas, faces go unshaved, which also aids camouflage; clothes and equipment are daubed with splotches of paint to blend with the foliage, and uniforms look like soggy masses of wet wash with pant legs ripped off at the calf for comfort.

If you ever have made a camping trip into some virgin woodland carrying your supplies on your back, inspired by that stirring idea of sleeping under the stars and braving nature, you have a dim idea of what it is like. This woodland, however, is the kind you would try to avoid. It is too thick for free movement, too humid for comfort, and the swamps and marshes are what you would skirt rather than plow through.

In many places, a compass is useless. The jungle is so dense that landmarks on which to take a bearing are often impossible to find. Even after you locate an identifiable position and orient it on a map you will have a hard time reaching it, for a trail may start out heading west, then turn north or south or double back on itself. Following a compass course is generally out of the question unless you are prepared to hack a path through the foliage.

Perhaps you are familiar with many types of insect pests, but here are gathered all the varieties you have ever slapped or pulled off your skin—and many others. Mosquitoes, red ants and ticks, voracious flies, spiders, scorpions, centipedes, and scores that you cannot identify.

You wear a steel helmet with fiber lining; green dungarees or a camouflage suit; a cartridge belt carrying several clips of ammunition, a strong sheath knife, two canteens (one set into a canteen cup), a first-aid packet containing a battle dressing, and perhaps an extra packet containing sulfa tablets and powder; on your back is a rifle, and a pack containing several pairs of socks, an extra pair of shoes, extra pair of pants, soap, a hand towel (some men carry shaving gear), emergency rations, a spoon, cigarettes, matches, extra ammunition, rifle rod and rifle-cleaning gear, etc. Around the pack is a blanket roll with a poncho, shelter-half and maybe a blanket or half a blanket; in your pockets are more cigarettes, matches, a bottle of water-purification tablets, a pocketknife and several grenades.

Just how long and how far you can carry this amount of gear depends on your physical condition, how well you have the equipment packed about you, and primarily, the terrain. You are moving along a trail about two feet wide through heavy brush. This is a trail only in the strictest literal interpretation. It is crossed by vines, roots and fallen trees; sometimes it is blocked by boulders or travels along the bed of a stream; now it may lope over a ridge or cling doubtfully to the side of a hill. You step over the vines and roots (if you are lucky), crawl or roll over the larger fallen trees, and wade through the shallower waterways. "Wait-a-minute" vines tear your clothing and hands, and if there is mud, by the time the couple of hundred men in front of you go through it you will be wading rather than walking.

Most swamps look the same—until you step into them. Then you discover, unscientifically, whether they are ankle, calf, or waist deep. In the deeper ones you leap from tree root to tree root until you inevitably fall in and need help to regain your footing. If you get mad enough, you "storm" the swamp by crashing blindly ahead, which only makes the going worse.

After some distance your body will itch as the perspiration rolls down your back and into your shoes. You will suck salt tablets and try not to reach for your canteen too often. The column will halt periodically for a "rest," the time between rests depending on the difficulty of the terrain and the urgency of the march. The first few times you will be careful to pick a flat, dry spot to sit down, with your helmet placed under the bottom of the pack to ease the weight; eventually you will just flop down on your back anywhere and try to decide whether you have enough strength to reach the cigarettes in your pocket. When the cry comes to "saddle up" and move on you will think, "My God! We just stopped!"

In a march of several days through the jungle where you are unable to wash properly or change clothing, fungus infection is likely to develop. This is a general term; it covers a variety of ringworm and similar infections and may lead to open, painful, skin ulcers. Immersion foot, which drains the color from your feet, makes them throb painfully, and causes deep wrinkles in the skin like an overdeveloped case of "washerwoman's hands," comes after too much swamp marching where the feet are under water.

Finally, an hour or more before dark, your feet running into each other, your body bowed under the weight of the pack, you reach the bivouac area selected for the night. At long last, a genuine stop, a real place to rest—but your troubles are only beginning. If you are exhausted enough, you will be quite willing to settle for just a place flat enough to lay that weary body and imagine you are somewhere else. That is the first mistake.

As any veteran can assure you, the chances are about ten million to one that it will rain in the jungle, provided you say, "I don't give a damn if it rains or not." If you have never been in a jungle rainstorm without shelter, you have something new to experience. You don't just get wet, you get saturated.

A conventional pup tent, built from your shelter-half and a neighbor's, is generally frowned upon. For one thing, it is too cramped, with not enough room for your gear. Besides, it will probably leak. Your veteran, if he is a handy man at such things, has several courses open to him. He can build a lean-to covered with leaves, ponchos, or shelter-half, make a hammock with a poncho slung under a leafed roof, or any modification of either. In swamps men sometimes build platforms in the trees. If there is time, a bed can be made of a shelter-half stretched over two poles and buttoned underneath. If there is danger of bombing or enemy attack, a similar bed can be built in a foxhole. If there is enemy ahead you won't want a roof to curtail your vision, so you can just roll up in a poncho.

Almost anywhere in the jungle, saplings, vines, and palm fronds or floppy banana leaves are obtainable. That is all you need to build a "house," plus skill. Jungle-seasoned troops can build a lean-to accommodating three or four men with about thirty minutes' effort. Supports for the shelters are tied with vines, and leaves spread over the top. Equipment in the jungle must be guarded continually against rust or mold, for an unoiled rifle can rust overnight and leather goods will mold in a few hours if exposed to the dampness. Cigarettes, pipe tobacco, and even pipes will mold over a longer period.

Despite all the inconvenience and weariness of marching and camping, you will still have a man-sized appetite—unless there is an enemy near, where the tension tightens your stomach and blacks out hunger. Troops on the move usually carry D-ration chocolate bars, supplemented by the K ration of potted meat, cheese, etc.; the C ration of canned meat and vegetable stew, hash, or beans, with canned biscuits, which also contains soluble coffee or lemon powder, as does the K; or the J ration, which has more variety, including even toilet paper, but is bulky to carry. The Five-in-One ration which feeds five men three meals for one day is already the favorite in the Pacific. Although this, too, is bulky, it contains such things as canned spaghetti and meat balls, canned bacon, tinned roast beef, and evaporated milk.

Preparing food in the jungle will test your ingenuity, if you want to eat other than cold rations. As a rule, water is not too far away, or if it is raining you can catch rain water with a poncho held open, the neck of the poncho over a container. (On coral atolls water is almost always scarce. The troops dig wells, depend on rain water or carry water-distillation units.) The all-purpose steel helmet, which has served as a wash basin, pillow, and even a bedpan in field aid stations when the fiber inner helmet is removed, also can double as a cooking utensil if a fire is permissible and will not reveal your position to the enemy. Occasionally you will see an extra-resourceful serviceman even frying pancakes or fritters in his helmet. Empty cans are the most prominent substitute for pots and you can make a serviceable mess gear from a quart can cut open lengthwise.

Building a fire is often a problem, for most wood in the jungle is damp. General camping rules apply here. Dry wood can be found inside dead trees or if you can get a small fire going, dry your own. Marines sometimes carry Heatabs, small white lozenges which are lighted by a match and burn seven minutes, long enough to heat a canteen cup or a can of rations. If gasoline is available, a can partly filled with sand, impregnated with gasoline, makes a good fire. Another fire-making substance is the waxed package containing a K ration, which will burn with a steady, hot flame for several minutes.

If you know the jungle, or are lucky enough to get a native to show you around, you can augment the canned diet. You may find pine-apples, bananas, oranges, or limes, although these are rare in the un-settled areas. Green coconuts, usually plentiful, provide a refreshing drink and the top of the nut is easily lopped off with a heavy knife. Once you get the knack of removing the husks of riper ones, you will find the meaty, fruit-store version. The tender tips of the palm are edible, as are bamboo shoots. Breadfruit is sometimes obtainable, also papaya, arrowroot, tapioca, and taro, which is similar to a potato and is an all-purpose native dish.

One other food source exists in the jungle—the enemy's supplies. This is the choicest food of all, for it is flavored with victory. No matter what the food may be, the first bite of captured rations, even though it is moldy biscuits or watery salmon, will taste like ambrosia. On more than one occasion the added impetus to bring battered, battle-weary troops, low on rations, to rush into an attack on will power alone has been the tempting thought of dining on enemy supplies.

You know of men fighting for a principle, a belief, a country, an ideal—but if you want to see a group of hungry Marines *really* go into action against an enemy position, just watch them move when the word is passed:

"*They*'ve got chow up there, plenty of it. What are *we* waiting for?"

Then, friend, stand aside for the thundering herd.

Master Technical Sergeant Murrey Marder

Boomtown

The city limits of Boomtown are the palm-fringed edges of an advanced fighter strip in the Russell Islands, deep in the South Pacific battle zone.

"Welcome to Boomtown—Drive Carefully" reads a sign just beyond the sleek runway where Marine fighter planes race in after a zooming scrap with a sky full of Zeros over New Georgia or Bougainville. Civic pride runs high in this amazing jungle encampment.

A few short months ago Boomtown was a Jap-held base. Then the Marines moved in. Today it is a model camp, and its fame is spreading fast. There is running water and a one-day steam laundry service in Boomtown, screened in, portable living huts, and solid-mahogany mess halls. And the Japs are but a few air minutes away.

Boomtown boasts every Marine's dream come true—a genuine hamburger stand open eighteen hours a day, with everything on the house. There's free beer on Sunday for every enlisted Marine on the island. And a jungle edition of the Good Humor man makes the rounds each weekday, dispensing free ice cream, doughnuts, and lemonade to all hands.

It isn't a mirage.

Ask two pilots who flew in the other day from a base a thousand miles away to pick up fifty hamburgers to take back to their unbelieving mates. Or the unidentified inhabitants of Guadalcanal who forwarded eighteen bundles of laundry aboard a Douglas transport with the message: "Don't send it back if it ain't true." They got it back—washed.

There is nothing like Boomtown this side of San Francisco. But it didn't just happen. Somebody planned it that way and Heaven filled the gaps. The idea that, with a little forethought, some of the comforts of home could be taken along to the wars belongs to Lieutenant Colonel Raymond E. Hopper, commanding officer of the Marine aviation units now operating off the Boomtown strip. The city planners of this combat Utopia were he and his energetic executive officer, the late Lieutenant Colonel Nathan S. Clifford, whose home was in Coronado, California, and who later lost his life in a night aerial mission from the Boomtown strip.

When Lieutenant Colonel Hopper was told a few months ago that his outfit was shoving off to the South Pacific combat zone, he began by procuring equipment that you won't find in any training manual. A veteran of seventeen years' Marine service in Cuba, Puerto Rico and Guam, he found that there was only one way to find out what requirements a military unit needed to exist under unusual conditions. He ordered his command to make camp in a swamp, and then left it there to make its own way. When the experiment was over, he and his officers had a pretty good idea of what they would want to take along to the South Pacific jungles.

When the outfit boarded its transports for the trip Down Under, there were some unusual items in the holds—a well digger, a portable laundry, a sawmill, ten thousand feet of water pipe and 1,650 cases of beer. It was a tough job getting the stuff through. Before arriving at the coconut-dotted isle that was to become Boomtown, the Marines loaded and unloaded their unique cargo no less than eleven times.

Lieutenant Colonel Hopper flew in ahead to pick the campsite, walk over the ground, and personally survey his model jungle city of the future. The Marines were forced to go down 125 feet through coral to hit water, but the well digger did the trick. The sawmill went right to work on the tropical forests of mahogany and teak. And after a hard day's work in the equatorial heat, the beer tasted mighty good.

The Japs helped out, too. A stick of bombs conveniently cleared out a troublesome grove of coconut trees. Another bomb leveled a brick warehouse on an abandoned plantation. Today those bricks are doing duty as a bakery oven which produces thousands of doughnuts daily. When, during the Munda offensive, another raid demolished a refrigeration storage unit, the freezing mechanism was rescued and put to work making ice cream.

The daily customers for Boomtown's free traveling snack bar are the pilots and mechanics who keep the Corsairs fighting over New Georgia and Bougainville, and the Marines who stand by Boomtown's ack-ack guns twenty-four hours a day.

Boomtown's "always open" hamburger stand is the contribution of the United States Navy Construction Battalion which works along the fighter strip. The hamburgers are the real McCoy, made from fresh ground beef. When the Marines arrived they found a herd of seven thousand cattle on the island. Nobody seems to know to whom they belonged in prewar days. They appeared to be a vicious breed of bovine. A good many were shot by Marines in self-defense. Others had a way of wandering into jeeps. Result—hamburgers.

Boomtown isn't just fudge and frosting. Its reason for existence is the grim business of shooting the Japanese out of the Pacific sky. The Marines here may be living in style, but they are fighting that way, too. The well-cared-for citizens of Boomtown have accounted for more than a hundred Jap planes that will fly no more.

Captain Penn T. Kimball

Air-raid Coffee

A new beverage has been introduced out here. It is called "air-raid coffee"—strong enough to lift one's scalp several inches per gulp.

Marine cooks frequently put their coffee on the fire when all is quiet. Then the air-alarm siren will sound. Some mornings the raids continue for an hour or more, and the coffee boils merrily away. One morning the "chow hounds" maintained the coffee was so thick they could eat it with their knives—"just like peas." This correspondent, however, merely found that it snapped back at the drinker.

Master Technical Sergeant Theodore C. Link

The Shrine of Tarawa

The story of the battle for Tarawa needs no retelling. This is the story of Tarawa revisited. The part of Tarawa that is Betio is changed greatly. The tangled morass of coconut logs and bomb-pitted sand has been leveled. Orderly rows of tents have risen to shelter the Marines, the sailors, the airmen and the Seabees who man this outpost.

On the beaches, commanded still by the rusting muzzles of captured Japanese guns, lie shattered amphibious tractors and landing craft. Japanese barbed wire still guards the coral sands along the tidal flats. The landing strip for which Marines fought so fiercely, with every weapon at their command, today is in operation—as the enemy well knows. This is where a bulldozer, digging into a pile of blackened earth, shattered timbers and twisted metal, rolls out the body of a Japanese soldier, recognizable only by the stained uniform. The smell of death still lingers in some sections of the island despite the ocean breezes that sweep its narrow width.

Here is the largest of the several Marine cemeteries on the atoll, not very imposing by standards of granite and turf, but Marines, and soldiers and sailors too, turn grim and proud when they pass. It is only a hundred or so feet long, and not very wide, measured from rough board fence to rough board fence on either side. The wooden crosses, two boards nailed together, are a weather-beaten gray.

There are names on a few of the crosses, but most of them are blank. On the rough rail nearest the stand from which the brief but heartfelt services were held are three plaques, placed there by comrades of the fallen Marines. One plaque is in memory of "the valiant dead and sixty-eight missing" of an "amphibious tractor battalion." Another commemorates the heroism of the officers and men of the Special Weapons Unit.

The third is a poem of requiem by an unknown Marine. It reads:

> To you, who lie within this coral sand,
> We, who remain, pay tribute of a pledge
> That dying, thou shalt surely not
> Have died in vain.
> That when again bright morning dyes the sky
> And waving fronds above shall touch the rain,
> We give you this—that in those times
> We will remember.
> We lived and fought together, thou and we,
> And sought to keep the flick ring torch aglow
> That all our loved ones might forever know
> The blessed warmth exceeding flame
> The everlasting scourge of bondsman's chains
> Liberty and light.
> When we with loving hands laid back the earth
> That was for moments short to couch thy form
> We did not bid a last and sad farewell
> But only, "Rest ye well."
> Then with this humble, heartfelt epitaph
> That pays thy many virtues sad acclaim
> We marked this spot, and, murm'ring requiem,
> Moved on to Westward.

Captain Ellis M. Trefethen

The De Lux

To the roster of the world's famed hotels add a new and distinguished name—the De Lux of Bougainville. The De Lux is the De Lux because there isn't room on the sign for an "e."

This unique establishment, which occupies a 12-by-12 dugout on the beach, with adjoining bomb shelters—caters in the course of a day to everyone from a general to privates. Rank carries no weight.

Proprietor, host and supervising chef is William Stewart, USN, of Seattle. Do you want midafternoon coffee? The De Lux will fix you up. Hungry? The De Lux will break out a can of beans or fry some sausages. Tired? The De Lux has four cots with mattresses, a Bougainville rarity. Conversation and rumors at all hours.

Doorman and greeter of the establishment is John H. Latham, Jr., USN, of Florence, Massachusetts. First chef is Arthur Aguirre, USN, of Douglas, Arizona. Barber and conversationalist extraordinary is Emmett Rogers, USCG, of Sanford, Florida. And the customers come in droves. Only excavating difficulties prevent the enlargement of the establishment and the installation of a ballroom. Also Rogers is compelled to cut hair in the dining room, but no one seems to mind. When the hotel business is dull the boys operate a boat pool for the Navy.

Technical Sergeant Frank Devine

Chow Call

A wolf-hungry detachment of Marines, slogging wearily out of the jungle somewhere in the Southwest Pacific, stopped dead at the smell of steaks cooking in a field galley. But the galley was fenced and under armed guard. All the Marines could do was smell and wish.

Then Corporal John J. Smolka, of Niles, Ohio, broke into a wild run toward the galley. In a voice trained by umpiring in Ohio and the East Texas League, he bellowed as he ran:

"Condition Red! Condition Red!"

He ran right through the galley, still yelling, and nobody tried to stop him. For "Condition Red" was the culminating signal of an air attack and guards and cooks were bolting with him to the foxholes.

When the galley crew realized it was a false alarm, Corporal Smolka was gone. So were the Marines. So were the steaks.

Technical Sergeant Asa C. Bordages

Souvenirs

First Marine Division veterans of Peleliu, Cape Gloucester, and Guadalcanal were ready and willing at the mere drop of a mortar shell to pooh-pooh any insinuations that they were souvenir collectors.

Nevertheless, they blushed when the order was posted to turn in —along with certain other "souvenirs"—all "40-millimeter antiaircraft guns" taken from the Japs. Such a weapon weighs approximately three thousand pounds.

Corporal James Galloway

Semper Fidelis

The Army fights for freedom
The Navy for their lives,
But damn the guys who only fight
For trinkets for their wives.

Private James Rogers

Otto the Octopus

The sun was strong and most of the Marines splashed around in the water. Others lay on the float or dangled their feet from the walk. A month ago at Peleliu, their faces were bearded, haggard. Today they looked like a bunch of kids on the boardwalk at Long Beach. They stared at the coral formations—rainbowed antlers stretching from the Pacific bed. Every color was there and, it seemed, a fish for each shade. They were little fish—all hues of green, yellow-and-brown, sky blue; striped, two-toned, multi-colored. When they were still, they looked like tiny coral chips.

One of the Marines who had been lying on his stomach suddenly scrambled to his knees and pointed.

"An octopus," he shouted.

The others milled around him and followed the finger. It was like looking at a Disney cartoon on the bottom of a drinking glass. The water was that clear. At first it was hard to see the octopus. It was the identical shade of the rock around which its tentacles clung. Only large, blinking eyes and steady breathing gave it away. Its body was perhaps ten inches in diameter, but its tentacles may have spanned seven feet.

"Let's get him," a Marine said. He was a huge lad, at least six-three, with a bull-like neck and cropped black hair. Arm and back muscles bulged from his tanned, naked body.

"Careful, Jim, he's liable to grab you," a buddy grinned, "and then you might as well stay here as go back to the States."

"Don't worry about me when I get back to the States," Jim answered. "Besides, the octopus ain't that big."

Jim eased himself to the ledge, cautiously made his way to the octopus.

"Stay right where you are now, Otto," he said, "and we'll see if your feet are long enough for a necklace."

The octopus scooted under a rock and Jim called for a stick.

"Hey, fellers, we've taken Metz!" a blond kid shouted from the shore, but no one paid attention. He started down the walk.

"Fellers, we've taken Metz," he repeated, "I just heard it over the radio."

The blond was perhaps eighteen, but looked even younger. Probably it was the white face and the pale-blue, eager eyes. The others were naked or clad in trunks, but he wore khaki trousers and a shirt with corporal stripes. The chevron looked new.

Someone tossed Jim a stick and the big fellow poked around the coral. A wiry, redheaded lad slid into the water and breast-stroked to the rock.

"That newsboy friend of yours is yelling to you," he said.

"Hi, kid," Jim shouted to the blond.

"We've taken Metz."

"Where 'n hell's Metz? Philippines?"

"No, it's in Europe," another Marine broke in. "France or Germany."

"Sounds German to me," Jim ventured. He switched the stick to his left hand and continued to prod under the rock.

"It's important, our taking Metz." The blond's voice was almost plaintive.

"Sure, everything's important when you first get out here," Jim said.

"You talk like I'm a boot," the blond cried. "I've been out here fifteen months. I was at Cape Gloucester and Peleliu. But even if I was here fifteen years I'd still want to know what's going on."

"Well, I'll be back in the States soon and I'll write you." Some of the Marines laughed with Jim.

"Hey, Jim. Otto's moving!"

Sure enough, the tentacles were writhing and the beady eyes were emerging from beneath the rock. Jim thrust the stick, then backed away with a surprised grunt. The water was a dark brown. When it cleared, the octopus was gone.

"Did you see that? He put up his own smoke screen!"

"I'll bet that's where we got the idea of smoke screens," the redhead said.

"That's bile," said a Marine on the fringe of the crowd. "I read where octopuses excrete bile when they're scared."

"No, I think it's when they're mad," another contradicted.

Jim came back to the walk and sat down. The blond already was trudging through the coral sand to his tent.

"That buddy of mine worries me," Jim said. "He hangs around the radio all day. You'd think there was something going on. Oh, I don't mean that nothing's happening, but the only important thing is that little furlough paper. I want to read about you boys—in Stateside papers."

"Here he comes again. Maybe we've taken Berlin, or something," the redhead said.

This time the blond was running. He had a book in his hand.

"It says in the dictionary," he panted, "that an octopus is timid and inoffensive."

"So what?" Jim growled.

The blond put the dictionary under his arm and looked at Jim defiantly.

"So I'm glad he got away," he said, and walked back to the radio.

Staff Sergeant Victor Kalman

Everybody Thinks

Regardless of what camp command decrees
For dress: depressing khaki or that bane
Of pride and vanity, dull dungarees,
No uniform's imposed upon the brain.
Thus, regiments of individual minds
Twirl on axes fixed at random set,
Each one thinking everything it finds
Another cause for egoistic fret;
Angry whirlwinds shakily astride
Nightmares run on oval carrousels,
Which, the match of self-conceit applied,
Burst out into microscopic hells.
All this furious motion night and day
Would seem enough to blow the tents away.

Guadalcanal, April 10, 1944

Major Raymond Henri

Meeting in Melbourne

The Marines were moving up to attack Talasea, riding through the night in landing barges, and Corporal George Mahan was telling about his girl Margaret and their meeting in Melbourne.

"When I think how near I came never to meeting her," he said, "I get scared all over. It never would have happened if I hadn't busted my hand on Guadalcanal."

Because of his injured hand, he was transferred from a rifle company when the Marines reached Australia to rest from the months of battle on Guadalcanal. Until his hand healed, he was detailed to drive officers' cars.

"One night," he said, looking out ahead into the dark, "I drove a couple of officers to a party at a big house in a snooty section of town. I was waiting in the car when an Australian came out and asked why I wasn't inside. I explained I was an enlisted man. He said he'd get me a snack, at least, and he took me in the back way. He left me in the kitchen with a glass of beer and some savories. I was sitting there, sipping my beer, when an officer and a girl came in from the party. She was the host's granddaughter and came to tell the servants something. She and the officer stood there a few minutes laughing and talking, and I didn't think she noticed me.

"But I noticed her. You'd have to be blind not to. She had on a white dress, satin or chiffon or whatever you call it. Her hair was blonde, what they call a page-boy bob. I thought her eyes ought to be blue, but I couldn't tell. I just sat there with my beer. I heard her tell the officer to go back to the party because she had to attend to something in the kitchen. The next thing I knew, she was standing right by my table. She was smiling, and her eyes were blue like I'd thought they ought to be."

Corporal Mahan has blue eyes too, and an Irish pan with a snub nose and hair that won't stay combed.

"She said, 'Why are you sitting out here by yourself? Why don't you come with me into the living room and join the rest of the party?'

"I said, 'I'm an enlisted man.'

"She said, 'Well, you can have another drink, anyway.' So she got me a beer and she took one of those tiny liqueurs and sat down with me. She asked me my name and I told her. I asked hers, and she said, 'Margaret.' I didn't ask her last name. What was the use? She was out of a corporal's class. This talking to me was just something a little different for a girl like her.

"Well, we talked awhile. Then I said I'd better get back to the car and I asked her if she'd come and talk out there, but she said she couldn't. So I said goodby and went back to the car.

"In about fifteen minutes, she came out. She said she'd been looking in all the cars for me. I guess I kind of stammered I was so surprised, but then we sat there and talked and talked. I tried to tell her what Boston was like. I couldn't help wondering why she was so interested in Boston.

"Finally, people started leaving the house and she said she'd better go in. So I took her to the back door and said goodby. I didn't ask her for a date or anything. I didn't think I'd ever see her again. She wasn't a girl you'd figure on taking out on a corporal's dough. But I couldn't get her out of my mind.

"Well, a week later one of the officers asked me if I remembered the party. I said, 'Yes, sir,' and he said, 'The young lady you met would like you to come to see her.' I took off right then. I was all the way out to her house and ringing the bell before I remembered I didn't know her last name. It turned out to be Margaret Dieudonne —that means 'god-given'—Vanderkelen. She was wearing a blue print dress with flowers on it. She said, 'I never did think I'd see you again.'

"I had about fifty bucks, so I took her to dinner and a movie. I don't remember what the movie was. I don't think I even saw it. I went out with her almost every night, and then I was broke, so I just stayed away. When payday came I figured I'd get some real money and take her all the places she was used to going. So I got in a poker game. But I went broke. I figured that was that, and I wouldn't see her again.

"About a week later I got a telegram from her asking me to come out. I wanted to see her so much I finally went. I pretended I wanted just to sit home and talk. We did that three nights and finally she asked me if I was broke.

"I said I had plenty of money, but she got my wallet and found all I had was a ticket back to camp. She said, 'Now don't be silly, we're going out.' And she took me to a movie. It was the first time I ever had a girl take me out. After that, she introduced me to a lot of her relatives and her friends, and we went riding and swimming, and all the time I was almost busting inside wanting to ask her to marry me.

"Well, one night, in a fooling way, 'I'm going to take you to Boston with me. Will you go?'

"She said, 'Yes, I'll go.'

"She was looking straight at me, and all of a sudden I wasn't fooling. I said, 'You know what it means?'

"She said, 'A fellow doesn't ask a girl to go eight thousand miles just to see Boston.'

"So we decided to get married. I told her after the war all I could do was go to Wellesley and get a job, but she thought that was wonderful. I couldn't understand it. Maybe a man never does understand it. Maybe a man never does understand women. I was scared when I asked her mother, but all her mother said was, 'What does Margaret say?' Margaret said, 'I love him.' I found out later Mrs. Vanderkelen already knew all about me from the colonel. He was a friend of the family. He came to the wedding too.

"The colonel gave me seven days for a honeymoon and we went to a resort hotel. It was—well, you forgot there was a war.

"We'd been married three weeks when my outfit shoved off. Margaret said she'd wait at the railroad station to tell me goodby. Then, when it was too late to let her know, the colonel said I had to drive him to the boat. I felt sunk as I started out. After a little, the colonel said, 'You'd better go by the station and see Margaret.' It was a couple of miles out of his way, but he knew she'd be there.

"She was on the platform. We only had a minute. I kissed her. Her eyes were awful bright, but she didn't cry. I said, 'Don't worry, Margie.'

"So we drove off, and she watched us go. She was just standing there and her hair was blowing a little. All she'd said was, 'You'll come back.'"

Technical Sergeant Asa C. Bordages

Love Letters

Lieutenant Thompson is, unfortunately, he says, censor for his Marine unit. And because he reads hundreds of love letters every day he can no longer write an appropriate letter to his wife.

This is bad, Thompson said, because he and his wife are expecting an heir and it's obligatory he consider civilian morale, particularly his wife's. "And I love her more than ever," he moaned.

"Every time I put down 'Sweetheart,' 'My darling' or 'Dearest,' I recall that hundreds of other Marines use these terms of endearment. And it seems as if every pretty phrase I think of has already been used by another man. From the start my letter sounds imitative."

Consequently he commences his letters with a mundane "Dear." Once he explained his rather factual letters to his wife with: "If you could see the drivel I must read daily, you'd understand how childish romantic endeavors are." For good measure he added, "I'm glad you're mature enough not to expect such nonsense."

His wife didn't complain but she answered: "If your men could only read your early letters to me, they'd discover themselves modest love letter writers."

Thompson, formerly a sporting goods salesman in Boston, then threw originality to the winds and borrowed heavily from the love letters he read that day. But that failed because the culled phrases didn't blend together. Next he sought inspiration and at night he sat down, pen and tablet in hand, beside a palm tree and stared at the golden, tropical moon which left a silvery path across the Pacific.

"Inspiration came but I was soon embarrassed when Marines stuck their heads out of bushes and called for other Marines to come and look at some dope trying to write a letter by moonlight," Thompson recalled. When he returned to his tent he couldn't finish the letter because "I had a headache from straining my eyes in the moonlight."

His wife, Lieutenant Thompson concluded, will have to be satisfied with a simple, "I love you." Which, he said, he means with all his heart.

Staff Sergeant Elvis C. Lane

Censor on the Beam

From a Fifth Amphibious Corps bulletin board came indications that at least one Marine has reason to bless the censor. A private who may have been doing some double-time daydreaming found this note from the censor:

"Private Blank: Letter at mail desk. Name on envelope Dorothy, name on letter Bettye. Check and if correct, mail."

Sergeant Claude R. Powell

Jive Appeal

Marines on Saipan have appealed to the Red Cross to send new records of popular songs to Tokyo Rose and the Zero Hour—two propaganda broadcasts from Japan directed at American fighting men in the Pacific.

The programs have become so popular with the men of the Fourth Division that loudspeakers have been set up in bivouac areas to permit as many as possible to hear. Allen W. Fincke, of Tenafly, New Jersey, field director for the American Red Cross, admits that the Tokyo broadcasts are "doing a wonderful job of keeping the morale of our troops up."

The only complaint, Fincke reports, is that there is "too much crooning and not enough jive." "Deep Purple," "Star Dust," "Sleepy Lagoon," "Easter Parade," and other songs of the crooning era, stir few memories in the hearts of Marines here, most of whom are too young to have enjoyed them when they were at the height of their popularity.

It was the desire for more Benny Goodman and Harry James that sent the men to Fincke for help. Fincke forwarded the hepcats' plea to the head of the Red Cross of the Central Pacific Area in a personal letter, which spoke of the "wonderful job of pinch hitting done by our old friend Tokyo Rose, and the suave gentleman of the Zero Hour. The next step is to see that they are supplied with the latest popular recordings."

If such an arrangement could be brought about, Fincke pointed out, it would be a definite boost to the morale of U.S. troops in this area, who can't get too excited about the songs their older brothers danced to ten or fifteen years ago.

"If, through some continued miracle making," Fincke's letter continued, "late releases could be shipped via Switzerland, Russia, or where you will, Marines of the Fourth Division would, to a man, vote the Red Cross their most popular organization."

Master Technical Sergeant David Dempsey

Christmas for Jean

The day after Christmas, 1943, two Marines and a soldier were strolling along the hot, sleepy streets of Noumea, when they chanced across a small boy standing in front of a store window. He was looking at the gay Christmas decorations and crying.

A little questioning brought out his story. His name was Jean, and he was eight years old. His father was dead and his French mother had a job that brought her only enough money to keep the two of them alive. From the Americans who swarmed about the island he had learned of Christmas in the United States—of the visit of Santa Claus with his wonderful array of toys and surprises. He had prayed that this Santa Claus might somehow hear of him and bring him some gifts, but yesterday morning, when he awoke, he found nothing. And now, today, seeing the Christmas decorations had made him very sad. The three servicemen exchanged glances that sealed a silent pledge.

"Maybe, Jean," said one of the Marines, "the trip to this part of the world is so long that Santa Claus has been delayed. Come out to camp with us and maybe he'll be along later."

At the Marine camp, the soldier was assigned to show Jean around while the two Marines went back to town to see what the stores had to offer. Most of the stores' scanty stock had been sold out before the holiday, but the shoppers managed to buy a half dozen toys. Then they bought huge quantities of candy and cookies and started back to camp.

But one leatherneck remained unsatisfied with the gifts he saw, and went on an expedition of his own. He was back an hour later with a boy's bicycle. Immediately a whole crew went to work on it—repairing, painting and polishing.

From a Christmas box someone unearthed a 6-inch Christmas tree, set in a little red bowl. Another Marine was dispatched to the Red Cross to borrow a Santa Claus suit.

There came a sound of jingling bells (they didn't sound too much like tire chains). Then before Jean's startled eyes, down the tent pole came a roly-poly figure dressed in red. Over his shoulder was a sack. From the bag came gifts almost beyond the French lad's imagination. There were toys, and books, and pounds of candy, and souvenirs from America and from all over the Pacific. And caps and clothes were there. (To a certain quartermaster this may answer a problem that bothered him for a long time.)

Hardly had Jean had a chance to examine these gifts when Santa stepped outside the tent. In a moment he was back, pushing a gleaming bicycle. The Marines lifted Jean onto the seat, and helped him wheel his way around the camp. After a big dinner, Jean was loaded into a jeep with his precious bicycle and his other gifts and driven home in state. He was the happiest boy in all of New Caledonia.

The American servicemen, strangers in a strange land, went back to their duties. But how they felt was probably expressed by one of the Marines.

"It was a pretty lousy Christmas yesterday," he said, "but just being able to see this kid beam over his presents made it really seem like Christmas. We thought we were giving Jean a big treat but instead it was he who was giving us a real Christmas."

Staff Sergeant Raymond Fitzpatrick

Breakfast in Bed

It was the dawn of Christmas morning. Hardened Marines of the First Division were stirring in their sacks, half awake and half asleep, subconsciously aware that reveille was not on the holiday schedule. Through the blur of sleepy eyes they pictured scenes of home—familiar faces, gaily decorated yule trees, mistletoe, snow.

Then someone was shouting. The voice that broke the spell was unfamiliar. But the words fit the dream.

"Don't get up, guys, we're serving breakfast in bed."

It wasn't a dream. Voices in dreams of home are soft, soothing and sweet. The voice that shattered the early Christmas stillness was loud, almost as rough as a drill sergeant's. Sleep-laden eyes blinked open and mouths gaped in wonder at the sight of two Marines struggling up the company street, weighted down by a huge bucket of steaming coffee, trays of doughnuts, sugar and cream.

"Merry Christmas to you," chorused Corporal Charles A. McClelland of Los Angeles and Private Robert A. Bailey of San Diego, as they entered the first tent.

"Sugar and cream?" asked Bailey, a combat photographer. They visited every tent in the company area, pausing only to return to the galley to replenish supplies.

"Anyone out of the sack won't be served," they warned. No one stirred, not even the salty old-timers who first had scoffed at the thought of having breakfast in bed. Everyone was smiling, including the cooks who knew that the breakfast call was being sabotaged.

The public address system was blaring Christmas carols as the last tent was served. The lusty voices of the Marines joined in the holiday songs. Those who had not temporarily forgotten their homesickness were hiding all signs of it.

"What a difference a year makes," said Sergeant P. L. Stott of Blackfoot, Idaho.

"You said a mouthful," replied Corporal Stanley J. Koziol of Bridgeport, Connecticut.

Last year Christmas had been D day minus one at Cape Gloucester. The First Division spent the day aboard ship and went ashore to attack Jap positions December 26.

"And today we're having breakfast in bed," mused Stott, munching another doughnut, taking a final gulp of coffee and settling back comfortably on his sack.

Technical Sergeant Joseph P. Donahue

Civilization

The weary Marines after a long day of marching and skirmishing against the Japs on Tinian huddled under their ponchos to escape the torrents of rain.

They knew there would be no chance to build tiny fires over which they generally heated their coffee. They knew, too, that there was a wet, miserable night ahead.

Disconsolately, they opened their field rations, all the while trying for the most part unsuccessfully to shield them from the rain. In the rations were tiny cubes of sugar wrapped in gay-colored paper carrying the ad:

"Eat at the Waldorf!"

Staff Sergeant Jack Vincent

The Rule of the Sea

There were times during the campaign for this dewy island when Marines wouldn't have been surprised to see a destroyer sailing through their bivouac areas. Seven days and nights of incessant rain had turned roads into sea lanes, ravines into swimming pools. In some places the water was twenty feet deep. Tents, cots and clothing were afloat. So were Okinawan ducks. And . . . food.

Chow hounds who liked to swim enjoyed a field day as waterproof boxes of rations floated away from food dumps. One expert swimmer snagged a box of prized "Ten-in-One," a container bulging with enough chow for three meals for ten men.

As he rose dripping from the water, a mess sergeant hollered: "Hey, that's my box!"

"I found it afloat and it's mine," the other replied. "That's a rule of the sea."

The swimmer kept the food.

Even a Marine sergeant can't stay mad when he's laughing.

Staff Sergeant Victor Kalman

Mascots

In all the far-flung combat zones of the Pacific, mascots made their way into the lives of Marines. To the fighting men they meant home, or a hint of home. They meant affection. They also meant headaches and heartbreak. Siwash, the swashbuckling, beer-drinking duck of Tarawa, was no exception. He was more than a duck to the reporter who brought him fame. He was an ogre, an ungrateful, ill-bred beast. The reporter, Combat Correspondent Keyes Beech, was driven to the point where, shortly before Iwo Jima, he snorted angrily into his typewriter:

"War holds many terrors, but none quite like mine. I am a fugitive from a duck."

Staff Sergeant Beech proceeded to detail the story of Siwash. How he had made the duck a newspaper sensation by reporting Siwash's feat in landing on shell-swept Tarawa with an artillery unit. How the duck spent thirty-six hours there, putting to flight a Japanese rooster and pig. How radio networks, picture magazines, and newsreels made a national hero of Siwash. But, Beech complained, "Poe has his raven; I have a duck." He became known as "the guy who wrote the duck story." Friends plagued him with the salutation, "Beech the Birdman." And, worst of all, the duck itself dealt Beech a crowning indignity.

"I made this feathered Frankenstein what he is today, and what thanks do I get for it? The other day I went to see him and he quacked at me. It wasn't a friendly quack either."

It was, to be explicit, a ducky Bronx cheer. Siwash wasn't the only pet to conquer Japanese animals. Major Joe accomplished that, and more. The Major, a black cocker spaniel, even chased Japanese soldiers. When the Second Division took Tarawa, Joe moved in with the Marines and won a paw-to-paw battle with a Jap dog on the beach. Later, he broke into a stockade containing a few of the Jap prisoners taken on the island. With Major Joe snapping at their heels for an uneasy five minutes, the Japanese proved that they knew the tactical advantage of retreat.

But on Saipan, Major Joe fell in action. He died as did many Marines —moving toward the enemy. Several days later a sergeant paid him his final tribute: "He was just a pooch, but we kinda loved him."

One leatherneck garrison at a South American lend-lease base had an eagle for which it claimed the title of "most ferocious mascot of any military unit in the world." Another outfit arrived at its South Pacific base with a lion cub purchased from a Los Angeles zoo. And Queenie, the swine empress of Guadalcanal, won world fame as the pet pig of a Marine group there.

The units which adopted them treated mascots as full-fledged Marines. Many pets were given rank (not all were promoted as speedily as Major Joe, however), service record books and uniforms and they were promoted or "busted" as their actions warranted. Like Major Joe, mascots frequently were killed in action or wounded, suffered shell shock, and were treated for their wounds.

Bugs Bunny, a rabbit mascot of several hundred Second Division Marines, was a real-life replica of the movie cartoon Bugs. During the Tinian battle, he was found sitting beside a shellhole, near a battle-scarred house, nibbling grass. The white rabbit learned to chew gum, sip beer and munch doughnuts. And on Sundays, Bugs attended church services.

Although Bugs was on good terms with pet dogs in the area, a stray crossed his trail one night. The next morning, Bugs was found dead. His Marine buddies insisted that he went down fighting.

Staff Sergeant William Ross

Another pig, named James Burkdell Gunpowder, achieved the distinction of a citation. It was read to his adopted shipmates, who found him abandoned by his sow in the woods and nursed him back to health with a nipple bottle. His name was an amalgam of his adopters' names except the "Gunpowder." That was sheer poetic inspiration. At two months, James B. Gunpowder received the following "official" citation, before a formal assemblage:

"For conspicuous gallantry and intrepidity. When his tent was threatened by ravenous, pork-eating dogs, Gunpowder boldly, and with complete disregard for his own safety, did quickly, viciously and bodaciously attack the intruders with such fury as to cause their immediate withdrawal, inflicting heavy casualties by his timely attack. In further action on succeeding days, Gunpowder acquitted himself admirably, at one time attacking two fully-armed members of the U.S. Marine Corps and causing their precipitate flight. His courageous conduct was in keeping with the highest traditions of the United States naval service."

Second Lieutenant Cyril P. Zurlinden

On Okinawa, a combat patrol, cleaning up caves, reached a coral cavern and came upon a tiny brown puppy, apparently orphaned. The squad leader, a rawboned farmer from Ohio, lifted the little ball of fur and tucked it under his dungaree jacket so that only the pup's head stuck out in front, where a button was unfastened. Then, as the Marines moved toward Naha, the puppy took a stronger hold on the

· 337 ·

attacking force, until he became battalion mascot. He toddled behind his master when the going was smooth, and rode in the pouch of a discarded gas mask when it was rough. One week after their meeting, the squad leader was sent on a dangerous mission. Giving the pup a goodby pat, "Ohio" left him in the foxhole they had shared. Ohio never came back. As he led his men through new territory, he stepped on a land mine.

Back at the command post, the pup was forgotten during the excitement of a busy day of combat. He waited quietly as the hours crept past. When darkness came, he didn't whimper. But at midnight, Japanese artillery got the range. Shells roared among the foxholes. Out of the wild din, almost lost in the explosions and the calls for corpsmen, came the whines of the abandoned dog. A Marine heard the whimpering, dashed to the foxhole, and comforted the pup for the rest of the night. Early the next morning, the dog returned to his old shelter, awaiting his dead master. When the camp broke up, and the Marines resumed their advance, the pup would not leave. Another Marine had to pick him up and carry him.

Technical Sergeant William Boniface

The landing on Iwo Jima was the third for George, the dice-loving dog from Sydney, Australia, and the fourth for his master, Platoon Sergeant James E. Yates of San Diego, California. Before Iwo, George had seen action at Vella Lavella and Bougainville. Yates also fought at Guadalcanal before he bought George in a Sydney bakery shop. George acquired a dubious fame from his penchant for attending dice games. He was not a welcome guest, however. At unpredictable moments, George would dart forward, clamp his teeth on the galloping dominoes, scamper out of sight and bury them.

Master Technical Sergeant Keyes Beech

A surprising number of little dogs hit the beach at Iwo. They were good for morale; all members of an outfit that included one of them were as fond and proud of him as his legal, or at least titular, master.

So each pooch was a little blessing in himself, though one of them, a fox terrier, was a mixed one at one time.

On D plus one, the fellows digging in around him were aware, without noticing very closely, that he was frisking about a good bit, playing with something. When they did notice closely, they found it was a hand grenade. He was tossing it into the air, letting it fall, pouncing on it, rolling it about. He brought it over to the edge of a foxhole and wagged his tail and danced about with it. They poured out of the foxhole and ran like hell. He frolicked after them. They tried to get him to put it down. He wouldn't. He ran away with a "Chase me!" air. The pin was in, but at any time his teeth, in tossing it, might have pulled the pin out.

Then they tried to get him to hold it and stay away; so he trotted up to the foxhole again, and put it down. But he watched it, hawklike, and when a hand reached toward it, he would pounce and pick it up again, and canter about the hole. Roguish, full of fun. They tried to lure him with chow. He wasn't hungry. They tried throwing sticks for him to chase. He wanted to play, but only with that grenade. When finally they had got him to put it down by a pretense of not noticing him for a period (no paltry histrionic achievement) and had the grenade safely in their own hands, it is perhaps needless to say that thenceforth their area was as free of loose grenades as any area anywhere ever was.

Sergeant Francis W. Cockrel

Marines took pride in the acceptance of their war dogs, and they never tired of telling stories about them. Such stories as that of Casanova Otto, the Doberman pinscher with an eye for the ladies. He was always at his best, during maneuvers, when female dogs were eying him. Then his ears would twitch, his proud head would lift and his roving eye would be on the *qui vive* for hours.

They also told of Andy, another Doberman, fondly referred to as "a real chow hound." Andy had a helmet all his own, with the chin strap buckled for convenient handling. At chow call, Andy would, without prompting, pick up his helmet and quietly fall in line with the Marines, keeping his place until he reached the steaming vats of food. Then the messmen would fill his helmet, Andy would walk to his trainer's foxhole, make himself comfortable and eat.

But, more quietly and more seriously, they would tell you the numberless sagas of heroism—and sacrifice—by their dogs in combat. There was Red, the big Doberman scout dog. He died because he didn't follow the training rules. But the men whose lives he saved said it wasn't a question of forgetting the rules. "Red knew what he was doing," they declared.

While on a night patrol on an island off Okinawa, Red and his human buddies were pinned down by a machine gun. Its first long burst wounded twelve men. With his master and a unit of sharp-shooters Red was sent to locate the gun and knock it out. They were on a wooden road, Red in the lead, when a shot rang out. Red froze as his master fell dead.

"Then he did what we taught him not to do," said Sergeant Alfred Allen of Pocatello, Idaho. "Instead of holding the freeze, he took one big bound over a hedge and landed right in the middle of the machine-gun nest." There was a mad scramble, with the Japanese screaming and grunting, and Red snarling and thrashing around like a tiger. Pistol shots cracked. The snarling stopped. The Marine patrol dashed forward. One burst from an automatic rifle put an end to four Japanese.

The Marines gently removed Red from the machine-gun nest. But they found it hard to extract one Japanese hand from between Red's clenched teeth.

Technical Sergeant Murray Lewis

Iwo Transport

The Marines aboard this transport bound for Iwo Jima are old hands at transport life. Most of them have been in the Pacific more than two years. They have ridden transports in and out of action from the Solomons to the Marianas. Every few months they leave their camps ashore, hike to the beach and embark for another island nearer Japan. Nevertheless, there is a difference between this trip and all the others that preceded it. This one has taken us out of the tropics for the first time since we left the States, and it is cold. The holds, which are usually stifling hot without it, are steam heated. The fresh-water showers, a cooling luxury on trips farther south, are ignored. Instead, the men sit around in newly issued, lined combat jackets, huddling in the companionways or seeking warmth in sheltered corners on deck. At night no one sleeps topside. It is a shock to realize that the temperature is actually only in the sixties. It is not cold at all, but our blood has got thin after months in the jungle. It leads to a lot of unpleasant jokes by the southern boys about how the Northerners will be unable to stand it back home in New England and Chicago and the Northwest.

In any climate, transport life to the enlisted men can be miserable. This transport is more comfortable than many others. Unlike the converted passenger or cargo vessels, some thought seems to have been given to the comfort of the men. The holds are whitewashed, and the tiers of sacks have some room between them in which to move around. There is plenty of light and enough fresh air. The holds of the older ships were like sweltering Black Holes of Calcutta, so dark, crowded and oppressive that sleeping topside in a pouring rain was preferable to remaining below. The sacks, which are in roomy tiers of five on the new ships, are the same as always—oblong pieces of canvas, laced to pipe frames. Every so often one comes out of its moorings, and the unfortunate owner, together with his pack, blanket roll, helmet and whatever else he is lying on, crashes down on the men below him. Long, circling, whitewashed tubes carry cool air, blown down from the top deck. In warmer climates men sleeping beside the tubes punctured them so that some of the refreshing air would blow directly out on their faces. Now, in this comparatively freezing zone, the men have frantically stuffed the holes with paper and pieces of cloth.

Most of the Marines fortunately have something to do during the trip to keep them from becoming bored, although it is doubtful if they appreciate the work handed them. Some have been assigned to the mess hall to serve on the chow line and clean up after meals.

Others are doing guard duty along the companionways and railings. They keep order and see that no man gets too near the railing. A favorite occupation is considering whether or not a transport in convoy would stop to pick you up if you fell overboard. I still don't know the answer. Other Marines were put in sweeping details, cleaning gangs, and "break-out" parties. The latter groups bring up the chow each day from the ship's storage compartments. In the tropics this is considered a good job because you work in the ship's refrigerator where it is cool. This far north it's not so good. Aside from these official and not always appreciated jobs, there are very few pleasant ways to pass time. There is a lot of reading of pocket-size books, pony editions of magazines and comics, but even this becomes painful and not worth the effort when you have to keep moving around to stay out of the way of men cleaning the decks, officers moving back and forth, and sailors carrying on the daily routine of running the ship. Playing cards, cleaning weapons, discussing the coming operation, and arguing remain as the chief opponents to boredom.

The arguments particularly are worth while, serving as entertainment as well as merely something to do. An argument begins perhaps with an innocent remark concerning the help that naval gunfire will give us on D day. Immediately from several quarters an authoritative burst of screaming and yelling commences, continuing in more and more colorful language until finally a brawl is under way over whether or not a man can support a wife and two children on forty dollars a week. Sometimes the fact that the Marines doing the loudest yelling know little or nothing concerning what they are shouting about only adds to the fascination. The average Marine aboard is probably about twenty, but you would never know it to hear the enthusiasm with which they tackle subjects which older men would approach with care and hesitation. Arguing, however, is one of the few rights left to the Marines, and they exercise it to the fullest. Their other right, of course, is griping, and they gripe from the moment they awake until well into the night.

Although there is nothing concerning the Marine Corps, past, present or future, that escapes criticism, it is all strictly a family affair.

Let a sailor interject a word of criticism about the Marines, and every man on deck will mysteriously overhear him and take offense, and nothing will do until the bewildered sailor apologizes.

The Marines and sailors generally get on well together. The Marines acknowledge that they are traveling as guests of the "swabbies," a somewhat peculiar relationship which is justified by the realization that sailors view the transport they man as their home. But the sailors go to chow first, they usually get the best places from which to watch the movies shown on deck or in the mess hall while the ship is still in port, and they keep their eyes on the Marines like house detectives. Sometimes they resent having to go to dawn general quarters gun watch while the Marines sleep on, but often they get even with their guests by turning hoses on those they find still sleeping on deck after GQ.

A never-settled argument between the sailors and Marines is who leads the rougher life. The Marines point out that the sailors lead clean lives aboard ships, with no mud or foxholes. They have mattresses, clean sheets, pillows, showers and fresh food. The sailors reply that they are more often in danger. They are always in combat waters and at any time could be sunk by submarines, mines or planes. A little coxswain aboard probably has the right answer. According to him neither life is soft.

Master Technical Sergeant Alvin M. Josephy, Jr.

At Sea

When Marines boarded this ship for the strike at Guam, they carried in their packs and helmets reading matter of all kinds to offset the inevitable monotony. For the most part, they took along magazines and paper-covered books. Cloth-bound books are too bulky and heavy to carry at such times. The favorites were escape literature, romances and adventure stories, as well as news and picture magazines. Several viciously armed Marines were seen reading *Vogue,* though how that magazine got aboard remained a mystery.

English teachers would have had their hearts warmed also, by the popularity of serious books. On this ship, classics like *War and Peace* and *Crime and Punishment* made the rounds. Books about current affairs also were in evidence. Max Werner's *The Battle for the World* and Herbert Agar's *A Time for Greatness* were traded and discussed.

On the eve of the invasion, final mail was distributed to Marines aboard this ship. When it was given out, the men moved away by themselves, opened the letters with tender care and read them slowly, again and again. They dwelt on each detail, whether serious or trivial, hoarding among their memories the precious words from home. Before H hour, they placed the letters in their packs or dungaree pockets, to carry into combat ashore as their most treasured possessions.

Here are some samples of this last mail from home:

A private first class was told by his mother that the First Baptist Church in his home town had hung a gold star in memory of his brother, killed recently over France.

Word came to a rifleman from his girl friend that he had been chosen "official pin-up boy" in his old neighborhood.

A communications man about to enter combat for the first time was notified of a job waiting for him after the war.

A machine gunner from Union City, New Jersey, was told that his girl had married someone else.

A buck sergeant learned that his younger brother's false mustache fell off during a school play.

Master Technical Sergeant Alvin M. Josephy, Jr.

The Battle of the Rocks

"Did you hear about Mac? He got the word that he was due to go back to the States and that his ship was on the way out here. So every day for a solid week he climbed up on top of the water tower and sat there trying to spot the ship coming in to take him home. He was sitting up there looking for it before the ship had even left Hawaii!" That's the story they tell about a Marine who was with an aviation outfit in the Central Pacific for nearly two years. One year of that time he had spent on the tiny sun-baked coral island of Midway. The last year was passed on even tinier and even more sun-baked Engebi Island in the Marshalls.

Mac's ship finally came in and he went home. The boys laughed about his daily watch on the water tower, but they didn't laugh hard. They knew that he had put in two years on the "rocks" and they figured he was entitled to his little display of eccentricity at a crucial time like that. It wasn't wounds or combat fatigue that made him more than ready to get back to the States. He had never been in combat. It was just an overdose of the "rocks."

The folks back home seem to have had two popular concepts of the war in the Pacific. Either they thought of their Marine or soldier as locked in a savage, hand-to-hand struggle with the Jap on some dark jungle path; or they pictured him taking it easy on a lush, moonlit tropical isle with a couple of exotic, grass-skirted native girls dancing a hula in the background. The less said about the latter version the better. Island scenes like that exist only in the minds of Dorothy Lamour's scenario writers, and if the girls at home are uneasy about competition from Micronesian belles—well, they should see one sometime.

The other picture is something else again. The fierce, bloody fighting, whether in dank jungle or in bomb-shattered atoll, or in the air, took the lives or limbs of thousands. In most cases, however, the fighting was as short as it was terrible. A single hellish week at Tarawa is written in fame forever, and then Tarawa is classified as history. But it isn't history to the sailors and Marines who were stationed on its treeless sands for more than a year. It was a day-by-day life and a day-by-day job to them. They lived and worked in the backwash of the war. They're the men who were "sweating it out" and there were a lot of them.

This was the forgotten Pacific war. For these little islands, almost microscopic in the incredible vastness of the Pacific, were pawns in the great problem of supply—what the military men call logistics. First, they were way stations. They were stopovers for the long, gray convoys heading westward—toward the Philippines, perhaps, and eventually toward Japan itself. Secondly, they were sentinel posts, guarding the supply lines. Many of them were little more than fixed aircraft carriers and they provided the bases from which our planes bombed and neutralized by-passed enemy territory. From the rocks a relatively small number of airmen were able to stalemate thousands of Jap troops still left in the Marshalls, Carolines and Palaus—the neutralization technique which made possible the big jumps across the Pacific in so short a time. These, plus the simple chore of garrisoning a captured territory, were the reasons for the war of the rocks.

Each of these far-flung bases has its own characteristics. Some are a little better, some are a little worse. One has some convenience that another lacks. One has better chow, the other has shower water that doesn't smell like something had crawled into the water tank and died. Some got fresh meats and vegetables every once in a while; at others you subsisted chiefly on Vienna sausage, Spam, and corned beef. At some, the men lived in tents; at others, they lived in tents with wooden floors and screened-in sides; at still others, they lived in Quonset huts or wooden shacks. Some have trees, some don't. Over them all the same scorching sun beats down, the same blue waters break in a white froth over the barrier reefs, and the same endless procession of identical days parades past.

There's Johnston. That's the first one you'll hit flying out from Pearl Harbor, one we didn't have to fight for. It's about half a mile long. When you first see it from the air, your immediate reaction is to wonder whether that crazy pilot up front is going to try and land the plane on that sand bar down below. There isn't a plant or a tree to mar the pure, clean whiteness of the sand, nothing but some garish yellow buildings, barracks and mess halls. The glare of the sun on sand and water is almost a tangible, stifling thing. Men live and work on it, day after day.

There's Engebi. Engebi is a tiny triangle of land at the far end of Eniwetok atoll in the western Marshalls. It's bigger than Johnston—a mile long instead of half a mile. There are a few palm trees left on the island, too, but they are torn or splintered by the savage pre-invasion shelling that ravaged the place a year ago. The fronds, if there are any left, are brownish in color, and they don't rustle in the wind—they crackle. That's where Mac spent his final year.

There's Peleliu. Secured at the cost of some of the bloodiest and most drawn-out fighting yet, Peleliu was our strangle hold on the Palau group on the western rim of the Carolines. It's maybe twice as big as Engebi, and it isn't all flat either. It has an abrupt spine of jagged ridges and cliffs—jutting dragon-tooth crags, bare and black where Marine infantrymen fought maniacal Japs holed up in impossible caves. In the moonlight, they loom up like a demon backdrop behind the clusters of green tents.

Then there is Guam and its sister islands of Saipan and Tinian. They're something different. There are rolling hills, plenty of trees and underbrush. The Navy is building "for keeps" at Guam—a paved, four-lane highway, a modern transport terminal, acres of warehouses, several airfields. Underneath the bustle and the trimmings, though, the pattern is much the same: aviation ground forces over the Orote Field—antiaircraft gunners watching the Japless skies . . . Seabees sweating over their construction projects. Guam is a big and verdant rock. But it's still only a rock. Guam and Saipan, however, have an asset that personnel stuck in the lonely Marshalls and Gilberts and Palaus considered almost legendary. They have civilians and they have cities, or what used to be cities before the war hit. It's hard objectively to consider them as that any more. Agaña, the prewar capital of Guam, was smashed into a formless heap of concrete rubble and shattered beams by our naval barrage and the progress of battle. It's hardly more than a ghost town. Yet one Marine, walking into its narrow streets for the first time, stopped to stare about him in happy amazement.

"Gee," he breathed, "a real town."

The sight of a scarlet Coca-Cola dispenser, twisted among the wreckage of what had once been a store, was the kind of sight he had dreamed of seeing again. It was a reminder of civilization.

Compared to life on a battle line, life on the rocks is a comfortable one. The difference is that a battle or a campaign ends, while the rocks go on and on. In the beginning, of course, in the days immediately after invasion, there were the dead and the smell of death, the filth and the blow flies, the dysentery and the dengue. Sometimes, as at Majuro and Ulithi where there were no battles, this period was omitted. At any event, within a few months conditions improved and the pattern set in.

You went about your work—that was the main thing. You went to the movies every night, regardless of what the film was, even if it was a three-year-old B picture that you had seen twice before. You read anything you could get your hands on. Three times a day you walked to the mess hall. The staples of your daily diet were C-ration hash, Spam, Vienna sausage, corned beef, dehydrated potatoes, canned corn, cheese, and dehydrated eggs. These items were alternated with fresh food according to the location of your base, the length of time it was secured, the shipping demands of the moment and the trading ability of your mess sergeant.

Then you went back to your tent, held long irrational conversations and arguments with your tentmates, went to the movies, came back and hit the sack. To make the hours pass, maybe you started making watch bracelets and picture frames from scrap metal, or jewelry out of shells. At some bases, you found other things too. Many outfits had a beer ration, ranging from two cans a night to two or three cans a week. There were softball leagues, equipment for such sports as touch football, volleyball, horseshoe pitching, fishing, swimming was usually available, though it was frequently limited and sometimes prohibited by razor-sharp coral bottoms, fungus, tides and undertow.

You had a cot and mattress to sleep on and almost always an electric light in your quarters. You washed and shaved out of your helmet. If you were lucky enough to own a radio, or your camp had a central loudspeaker hookup, you could listen in to local Pacific Network radio stations that were dotted everywhere on the islands, broadcasting news, records and decommercialized transcriptions of Stateside programs.

It wasn't a tough life itself. The veteran of the rocks won't claim that it was. But he will point out that it went on, just the same—day after day, for twelve months, eighteen months, two years.

He came home, in nine cases out of ten, without ever having fired a shot in anger. He didn't come home and tell you about the big battles you read about in the paper because he never saw a battle. Sure, he was on Makin and Kwajalein, but he was fixing airplane engines, not fighting Japs. Except for a few bombings and leftover snipers, his life wasn't dangerous. It was monotonous and enervating.

Does the relative security compensate for the lack of excitement? For an answer, we recall the time the Guam invasion convoy put in at a Marshall Islands port. A couple of dozen aviation Marines sneaked aboard the troop transports and went on to fight the battle for Guam with the infantrymen. One was killed, several were wounded—but that's the way they felt about it. Their deed can't be condoned, but anyone who has put in some time out here will understand their human reactions.

It is for the companions of these boys, for Mac who climbed the water tower every day, for all the thousands of veterans of the rocks—Army, Navy and Marine—that this is written. It's not a gripe. It's written to tell about a phase of this global war that was never in the communiques or the headlines and will never be in the history books. Yet it is a phase which comprised the bulk of the war experience of many men in uniform.

Don't sell those boys short. Maybe they didn't fly fifty missions over Germany or hit the beach with an assault wave at Saipan. But neither did they get a weekend pass to London, or rest camp in Honolulu or Auckland. They just sat out on a forlorn little island and did their jobs and acquired a permanent squint from the sun glare and maybe fell into a curious apathetic, vague, lightheaded condition known as being "rock-happy." They don't give battle stars for sweating out the battle of the rocks. But, brother, it wasn't easy.

Technical Sergeant Gerald D. Gordon
and Technical Sergeant Robert W. Harvey

Somewhere in the Pacific

Somewhere in the Pacific, where the sun is like a curse,
And each day is followed by a night that's slightly worse,
Where the coral dust blows thicker than the shifting desert sands,
And the white man dreams and wishes for the greener, fairer lands.

Somewhere in the Pacific, where a girl is never seen,
Where the sky is never cloudy and the grass is always green,
Where the Japs' nocturnal prowling robs a man of blessed sleep,
Where there isn't any whisky and the beer is never cheap.

Somewhere in the Pacific, where the nights are made for love,
Where the moon is like a searchlight, and the Southern Cross above
Sparkles like a blazing diamond in the balmy tropic night,
It's a shameless waste of beauty with not a girl in sight.

Somewhere in the Pacific, where the mail is always late,
And a Christmas card in April is considered up to date,
Where we never have a payday, we never get a cent,
But we never miss the money, 'cause we'd never get it spent.

Somewhere in the Pacific, where the ants and lizards play,
And a hundred fresh mosquitoes replace each one you slay . . .
Oh, take me back to Alabam' where everything is swell,
For this God-forsaken country is a substitute for Hell.

Anonymous

You Can't Win

A group of officers attached to a Second Marine Air Wing unit on Okinawa have decided that you can't win in dealing with the weather here. They found the site of their tent was a bad one—water draining down from the rocky hills poured through the shelter no matter how carefully they ditched it. So they spent the morning moving the tent and all their belongings to dry ground a couple hundred yards away. That afternoon a freak twister of wind came roaring across the island, veered around the old tentsite, picked up the newly pitched tent and tossed it over a near-by cliff into the ocean.

Technical Sergeant Robert W. Harvey

Delegate at Large

For the United Nations Conference, San Francisco,
April 25, 1945

Mr. Speaker . . . Distinguished gentlemen of many lands . . .
I shall be direct, even blunt:

I speak for men who already know a lasting peace,
My credentials scattered on a thousand battlefields
   (a name scratched on a shell casing, at Dunkerque;
   a dog tag nailed to a cross, on Wake Island;
   a crude headstone deep in the rubble of Sevastopol).
I am the nameless Soldier, Sailor, Marine,
Plural, on a global scale, not yet entombed,
Having failed to return from a mission over enemy territory,
Having gone down with a warship no longer at war,
Having been blown to bits on an alien beach.
I am the Purple Heart, posthumously given,
Kin of the next of kin, Man of the Hour.

I have come to speak of malice.
I say you must bury malice, as it buried me
   (on the road to Athens, and again at Alamein;
   at the gates of Warsaw, and again at Narvik;
   in the jungles of Guadalcanal, and Guam).
Truly there is much malice already buried

Where my friends and I are at peace. So to speak,
We have been at pains to begin the job. But, were we able,
Any one of us would gladly step from his grave . . .

Having finished the grave, place on it the usual cross.
Pay attention only to the spirit of the thing
   (slats of a ration crate, like one I know on Tarawa;
   propeller blades, twisted, earthbound now, somewhere in France;
   a bayonet, stuck up against a wall in Manila),
Not to formalities, such as the transfer of earthly remains
To a landscaped cemetery. Get the cross into the ground
Where the body fell, so long as you embrace it!
I would be happy to contribute my own cross . . .

And now with the grave dug, and the cross planted,
There is one more thing: Pause briefly, if you will
   (in prayer, as was done when plasma, for once, failed a
   Marine dying at Iwo Jima;
   in silence, as when we buried a bosun's mate at sea
   on the Murmansk run;
   with an anguished cry, as when we watched a bomber plunge
   some thirty thousand feet into a Burma jungle),
Then turn away. Seek no occasion to decorate the mound,
Proclaim the patriot false who would avenge us.
Rather, fix your venture on the far horizon, and set forth,
Keen to the multitude of sorrows that await you,
As awaited us, but keener still to the hope now liberated
In a billion souls—the living who serve in your command.
Would that I and my company might rise again to this . . .

For this, eminent sirs, is the ultimate battle, the Holy Task
To which I now enjoin you.

Captain Patrick O'Sheel

Frank Acosta
Edward Adolphe
William B. Allen
Joseph L. Alli
Norris A. Anderson
Paul Arlt
Harold Azine
Dana N. Babcock
Gilbert Bailey
M. Daniel Bailey
Burt B. Balaban
Bernard Barol
Francis H. Barr
Leo T. Batt
Roy J. Battersby
Keyes Beech
Joseph E. Bell
Daniel W. Bender
Norman Berg
Howard E. Biggerstaff
Francis F. Birnbaumer
Jack A. Bishirjian
John W. Black
Harold T. Boian
Harry S. Bolser
William Boniface
Asa C. Bordages
Jean P. Boxell
Donald W. Braman
John H. Breiel
Harold A. Breard
William C. Brennan
Walter L. Briggs
Walter Y. Brooks
William Brunk
Mason C. Brunson, Jr.
James R. Bucknam
Edward J. Burman
William H. Burnett
Robert H. Burrill
Winthrop R. Cady
Charles J. Callanan

Everett C. Callow
Charles J. Calvin
William M. Camp
Daniel A. Campbell, Jr.
James F. Campbell
John B. T. Campbell, Jr.
Claude R. Canup
James Carol
Donald N. Carpenter
Lynn Carrick
James N. Carroll
Thomas P. Carson
John W. Chapman
Henry F. Childress
Albert M. Chop
Robert J. Clark
Walter C. Cochrane
Remsen J. Cole
Leodel Coleman
David R. Compton
Walter F. Conway
Eugene Cook
Robert Cook
Franklin O. Cooke
Charles V. Corkran
William T. Crouch
Eric J. Cudd
Charles B. Cunningham
Tennis A. Darling
John O. Davies, Jr.
Robert T. Davis
Frederick K. Dashiell
Robert L. Debo
John A. DeChant
David Dempsey
Frank Devine
Donald Dickson
Joseph H. Donahue
Victor P. Donahue
Robert J. Donovan
Paul Dorsey
Alvin D. Doyle

James H. Driscoll
Joseph Dube
James S. Dugan
David D. Duncan
Maxfield H. Dunlap
Crozet J. Duplantier
Wilbur J. Dvorak
George A. Edson
Wilbur Eickelberg
Paul R. Ellsworth
Arthur A. Engel
Sidney Epstein
Charles P. Evans
John Fabion
Odom O. Fanning
Frederick Feldkamp
Byrd F. Ferneybough
James Finan
Stanley Fink
Raymond Fitzpatrick
Harold E. Foreman
William S. Frank
Lowell P. Freeland
Meigs Frost
James Galloway
Maurice E. Garber
George Gass
Peter B. Germano
John F. Gerrity
Neil H. Gillespie
Henry Giniger
Benjamin J. Goldberg
James B. Golden
Walter Golub
William F. Goodrich
Harold L. Goodwin
Charles R. Gordon
Gerald D. Gordon
Gordon Grietzer
Odell Griffith
Gordon A. Growden
Edward R. Hagenah
James E. Hague
Donald A. Hallman
Gregoire D. Hamilton
William R. Hannah
James O. Hardin
George N. Harding
William T. Harrell, Jr.
Frank Harrington
William C. Harris
Robert W. Harvey
Norman Hatch

Arthur D. Hawkins
Loyal B. Hays
James E. Healey
Joseph F. Heiberger
Roy E. Heinecke
William L. Hengen
Raymond Henri
Keene Hepburn
Robert E. Hilburn, Jr.
Paul T. Himes
William K. Holt
Paul B. Hoolihan
Frank O. Hough
John D. Howell
Wesley B. Howland
Ward W. Hubbard
Robert A. Hunter
James W. Hurlbut
Hyman Hurwitz
Harry A. Jackson
Garth P. James
Roland G. James
Welden S. James
Clarence L. Jay
Rolfe Jenkins
Charles W. Jensen
Philip N. Joachim
Hans R. Johansen
Earle W. Johnson
James D. Johnson
Pendleton T. Johnson
Robert E. V. Johnson
Franklin R. Jones
Robert L. Jones
Alvin M. Josephy, Jr.
Victor Kalman
Millard Kaufman
James A. Kelly
Penn T. Kimball
Arthur C. S. King
John T. Kirby
Robert W. Kirby
Robert H. Kirkpatrick
S. Martin Kivel
Harold Klessig
Andrew B. Knight
Francis J. Knorp
James H. Knox
Herman Kogan
Charles P. Kopp
Fred A. Kraus
Irvin H. Kreisman
Herbert H. Laidman

Elvis C. Lane
Burns W. Lee
William H. Leininger, Jr.
Chester F. Lentz
Stanley R. Leppard
Dan Levin
Alfred E. Lewis
Murray Lewis
George Liapes
Theodore C. Link
Basil R. Littin
Paul G. Long
George E. Lord
Jim G. Lucas
William P. McCahill
Arthur C. McCarroll
Milburn McCarty
John McDermott
Frank J. McDevitt
Robert E. McKay
Douglas F. McKean
Wallace R. McLain
George E. McMillan
James H. McNamara
Robert V. McMenimen
Charles E. McVarish
Wallace J. MacKay
Walter F. Mackie
Murrey Marder
Peter Margolies
Gordon D. Marston
Murray W. Martin
Charles L. A. Mathieu
Allen R. Matthews
George H. Mattie
George Mattson
Richard E. Mawson
Heber Maxwell
Edward F. Meagher
Henry P. Meisinger
Herbert L. Merillat
Arthur E. Mielke
Norman A. Miller
Bernard J. Milligan
Joseph W. Mintzer
Thomas Moore
Maurice E. Moran
Joseph Morang
George E. Morgenstern
James F. Moser
Alan Mott
Thomas V. Mullahy
Leonard J. Murphy

Scott E. Myers-Summers
Clifton B. Naughton
Franklin F. Neill
Oscar O. Nelson
Obie Newcomb
David E. Nopper
Cyril O'Brien
Daniel T. O'Brien
Francis X. O'Donnell
David Ohman
Henry Olczak
Jeremiah A. O'Leary
Louis M. Olszyk
Stanford Opotowsky
Willis C. O'Rourke
Patrick O'Sheel
Chester D. Palmer
Harold Palmer
James S. Parsons
Peter Pavone
Charles R. Payne
Ralph A. Peck
John S. Pepper
C. Brooks Peters
Paul S. Peters
Donald R. Petit
Glenn W. Pfeil
Charles M. Platt
Douglas W. Polivka
John N. Popham
Claude R. Powell
Harold O. Powell
Edward J. Prendergast
Bem Price
Robert A. Price
Frederick B. Putman
John T. Randazzo
Alexander G. Raymond
Bernard Redmont
John F. Reilly
Nelson S. Reppert
Jonathan C. Rice
Theron J. Rice
Robert E. Rivenbark
Nolle T. Roberts
Roger L. Roberts
James B. Rogers
Benjamin Roscoe
Jay Rosenberg
Donald T. Ross
William Ross
Ross L. Rowe
Edward F. Ruder

John V. Sandberg
Tim J. Sanders
Jeremiah Sarno
Irving Schlossenberg
Albert F. W. Schulenburg
Samuel Shaffer
Norman Sheppard
Ellsworth A. Shiebler
Walter J. Shipman
Herbert L. Shore
Herbert Schultz
Frank A. Sisk
John F. Slocum
Chester H. Smith
Edward P. Smith
Jack C. Smith
Tony Smith
William Smolkin
Allen A. Sommers
Arthur M. Spalding
Russell L. Spera
Milton Sperling
Saul W. Spiegel
Woodrow H. Sporn
Ernest Stanley
Samuel E. Stavisky
David C. Stephenson
David Stick
Maynard W. Stitt
Edward E. Stodel
Charles R. Stokes
Philip H. Storch
Cecil S. Stowe
Paul G. Sturges
Edward B. Talty
Richard A. Tennelly
Robert S. Terrell
Pat Terry
William K. Terry
George R. Theeringer
Edward C. Thomas

John W. Thomason
Norman L. Thurston
Frank X. Tolbert
William K. Topping
George Torrie
Fred R. Travis
Ellis M. Trefethen
Tallant Tubbs
Harold W. Twitty
Charles R. Vandergrift
George T. Van der Hoef
Diggory Venn
Peter Viertel
Jack Vincent
George R. Voigt
Edward L. Volk
Benjamin Wahrman
Gerald A. Waindel
Doyle R. Walker
Ward Walker
John F. Walsh
Gene Ward
Earl G. Waters
Henry A. Weaver
Elmer Wexler
Douglas Q. White
Ned White
Norman H. White
Robert White
Joseph H. Whritenour
David M. Wilburn
Harvey F. Williams
Earl J. Wilson
Arthur C. Wimer
Walter H. Wood
John Worth
Richard T. Wright
Charles W. Yeager
Wayne F. Young
David Zeitlin
Edmund M. Zschau

Cyril P. Zurlinden, Jr.

Public Information Personnel Killed in Action

Captain Eugene M. Key
Technical Sergeant Richard J. Murphy
Staff Sergeant William T. Vessey

Staff Sergeant Solomon I. Bleckman
Sergeant Robert W. S. Stinson
Sergeant James J. McElroy

Sergeant John Barberio

Index

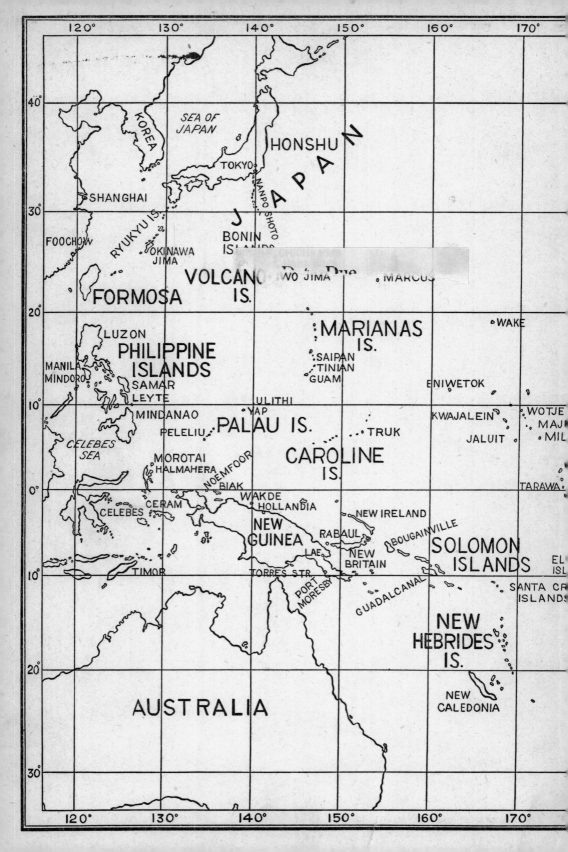